THE CAMBRIDGE COMPANION TO
# FRANCIS OF ASSISI

Francis of Assisi (1181/82–1226) was one of the most vibrant and colourful personalities in the Middle Ages. The life of this remarkable reformer of the medieval Church was celebrated in art, drama, poetry, music, the new vernacular literature and architecture. His ideal was to enter into a restorative and enriching relationship with Jesus Christ, whom he wished to imitate in the most perfect manner, a direct and immediate goal which captured the contemporary imagination. This *Companion* explores the life of Francis of Assisi and his enduring legacy throughout the centuries. The first part concentrates on his life and works, whilst the second explores the way in which his heritage influenced the apostolic activities of his followers in the century after his death. This book is a must-read for students and scholars of Church history, as well as medieval social and intellectual history.

Michael J. P. Robson is Dean of Chapel, Fellow, Praelector and Director of Studies in Divinity at St Edmund's College, Cambridge. He is the author of *Saint Francis of Assisi: The Legend and the Life* (1997), *The Franciscans in the Medieval Custody of York* (1997) and *The Franciscans in the Middle Ages* (2006).

CAMBRIDGE COMPANIONS TO RELIGION
A series of companions to major topics and key figures in theology and religious
studies. Each volume contains specially commissioned chapters by
international scholars which provide an accessible and stimulating
introduction to the subject for new readers and non-specialists.

*Other titles in the series*

THE CAMBRIDGE COMPANION TO CHRISTIAN DOCTRINE
edited by Colin Gunton (1997)
ISBN 0 521 47118 4 hardback     ISBN 0 521 47695 x paperback

THE CAMBRIDGE COMPANION TO BIBLICAL INTERPRETATION
edited by John Barton (1998)
ISBN 0 521 48144 9 hardback     ISBN 0 521 48593 2 paperback

THE CAMBRIDGE COMPANION TO DIETRICH BONHOEFFER
edited by John de Gruchy (1999)
ISBN 0 521 58258 x hardback     ISBN 0 521 58781 6 paperback

THE CAMBRIDGE COMPANION TO KARL BARTH
edited by John Webster (2000)
ISBN 0 521 58476 0 hardback     ISBN 0 521 58560 0 paperback

THE CAMBRIDGE COMPANION TO CHRISTIAN ETHICS
edited by Robin Gill (2001)
ISBN 0 521 77070 x hardback     ISBN 0 521 77918 9 paperback

THE CAMBRIDGE COMPANION TO JESUS
edited by Markus Bockmuehl (2001)
ISBN 0 521 79261 4 hardback     ISBN 0 521 79678 4 paperback

THE CAMBRIDGE COMPANION TO FEMINIST THEOLOGY
edited by Susan Frank Parsons (2002)
ISBN 0 521 66327 x hardback     ISBN 0 521 66380 6 paperback

THE CAMBRIDGE COMPANION TO MARTIN LUTHER
edited by Donald K. McKim (2003)
ISBN 0 521 81648 3 hardback     ISBN 0 521 01673 8 paperback

THE CAMBRIDGE COMPANION TO ST PAUL
edited by James D. G. Dunn (2003)
ISBN 0 521 78155 8 hardback     ISBN 0 521 78694 0 paperback

THE CAMBRIDGE COMPANION TO POSTMODERN THEOLOGY
edited by Kevin J. Vanhoozer (2003)
ISBN 0 521 79062 x hardback     ISBN 0 521 79395 5 paperback

THE CAMBRIDGE COMPANION TO JOHN CALVIN
edited by Donald K. McKim (2004)
ISBN 0 521 81647 5 hardback     ISBN 0 521 01672 x paperback

THE CAMBRIDGE COMPANION TO HANS URS VON BALTHASAR
edited by Edward T. Oakes, SJ and David Moss (2004)
ISBN 0 521 81467 7 hardback     ISBN 0 521 89147 7 paperback

*Continued at the back of the book*

THE CAMBRIDGE COMPANION TO
# FRANCIS OF ASSISI

Edited by Michael J. P. Robson

*St Edmund's College, Cambridge*

CAMBRIDGE
UNIVERSITY PRESS

CAMBRIDGE UNIVERSITY PRESS
Cambridge, New York, Melbourne, Madrid, Cape Town,
Singapore, São Paulo, Delhi, Mexico City

Cambridge University Press
The Edinburgh Building, Cambridge CB2 8RU, UK

Published in the United States of America by Cambridge University Press, New York

www.cambridge.org
Information on this title: www.cambridge.org/9780521757829

First published 2012
Reprinted 2013

A catalogue record for this publication is available from the British Library

Library of Congress Cataloging-in-Publication Data
The Cambridge companion to Francis of Assisi / edited by Michael J.P. Robson.
    p.   cm. – (Cambridge companions to religion)
    ISBN 978-0-521-76043-0 (Hardback) – ISBN 978-0-521-75782-9 (Paperback)
    1. Francis, of Assisi, Saint, 1182–1226.   I. Robson, Michael J. P., 1946–
BX4700.F6C323 2012
271′.302–dc22
2011001817

ISBN 978-0-521-76043-0 Hardback
ISBN 978-0-521-75782-9 Paperback

# Contents

# Contributors

**Michael W. Blastic,** OFM is an associate professor and the Chair of Franciscan Theology and Spirituality Studies at the Washington Theological Union, Washington DC. He is co-editor of a series of volumes of studies on the early Franciscan sources to be published by the Franciscan Institute, St Bonaventure University, New York.

**Michael F. Cusato,** OFM is Director of the Franciscan Institute, St Bonaventure University, New York, co-editor of *That Others May Know and Love: Essays in Honor of Zachary Hayes, OFM* (1997) and *Defenders and Critics of Franciscan Life: Essays in Honor of John V.Fleming*, The Medieval Franciscans 6 (2009), and the author of *The Early Franciscan Movement (1205–1239): History, Sources and Hermeneutics* (2009).

**E. Randolph Daniel** is Professor Emeritus of Medieval History of the University of Kentucky, Lexington. He is the author of *The Franciscan Concept of Mission in the High Middle Ages* (1975) and produced a critical edition of the first four books of Joachim of Fiore's *Liber de Concordia* (1983). David Burr and he translated *Angelo Clareno, A Chronicle or History of the Seven Tribulations of the Order of Brothers Minor* (2005).

**Petà Dunstan** is a Fellow of St Edmund's College and librarian of the Faculty of Divinity, University of Cambridge. She is the author of *This Poor Sort: A History of the European Province of the Society of St Francis* (1997) and *The Labour of Obedience: A History of the Benedictines of Pershore, Nashdom, Elmore* (2009).

**Sean L. Field** is an associate professor of history at the University of Vermont and the author of *The Writings of Agnes of Harcourt: The Life of Isabelle of France and the Letter on Louis IX* (2003) and *Isabelle of France: Capetian Sanctity and Franciscan Identity in the Thirteenth Century* (2006).

**Jean François Godet-Calogeras** is Professor of Franciscan Studies at St Bonaventure University, New York, and the editor of *Franciscan Studies*. He is internationally well known for his publications on the early Franciscan documents, in particular the writings of Francis and Clare of Assisi, for his lectures and workshops on early Franciscan history, and for his participation in the elaboration of the new *Rule* of the Third Order Regular of St Francis.

**Peter Jackson** is Professor of Medieval History at Keele University. His research interests cover the Crusades and the Latin East, the Mongol empire and its relations with Europe, and the eastern Islamic world in the Middle Ages. His publications include *The Mongols and the West, 1221–1410* (2005) and *The Seventh Crusade, 1244–1254: Sources and Documents* (2007).

**Timothy J. Johnson** is Professor of Religion and Chairperson of the Humanities Department at Flagler College in St Augustine, Florida. A German–American Fulbright Scholar, he holds a Doctorate in Sacred Theology from the Pontifical Gregorian University. Dr Johnson has taught in North America, Europe and Africa, authored or edited several books, and published in numerous North American and European journals. He is senior theology co-editor for *Franciscan Studies* and a member of the Bonaventure Texts in Translation Editorial Board of the Franciscan Institute.

**Annette Kehnel** is Professor of Medieval History at Mannheim University. She is the author of *Clonmacnois: The Church and Lands of St Ciarán* (1997), and co-editor of *Generations in the Cloister* (2008) and *Institution und Charisma* (together with F. Felten and S. Weinfurter, 2009).

**Steven J. McMichael**, OFM Conv. is Associate Professor in the Theology Department at the University of Saint Thomas (Saint Paul, Minnesota). He has published in the area of medieval Jewish–Christian relations, particularly on the writings of Alonso de Espina (d. 1464). He is currently researching and writing on the topic of the resurrection of Jesus (in medieval theology, preaching and interreligious polemical literature) and theological issues between Christians and Muslims in the fifteenth century.

**Patrick Nold** is Associate Professor in the Social Sciences in the Department of History at The University at Albany (SUNY). He is the author of *Pope John XXII and His Franciscan Cardinal: Bertrand de la Tour and the Apostolic Poverty Controversy* (2003) and *Marriage Advice for a Pope: John XXII and the Power to Dissolve* (2009).

**Ingrid Peterson**, OSF was awarded by the Franciscan Institute the Franciscan Medal in 2001 for outstanding scholarship in Franciscan studies. She is the author of *Clare of Assisi: A Biographical Study* (1993) and the co-author of *Praying with Clare of Assisi* (with Ramona Miller, 1996) and *The Franciscan Tradition: Spirituality in History* (with Regis J. Armstrong and others, 2010).

**Michael J.P. Robson**, OFM Conv. is Director of Studies in Divinity at St Edmund's College, Cambridge, and the author of *Saint Francis of Assisi: The Legend and the Life* (1997), *The Franciscans in the Medieval Custody of York* (1997) and *The Franciscans in the Middle Ages* (2006). With Jens Röhrkasten he co-edited the first volume of *Canterbury Studies in Franciscan History* (2008) and *Franciscan Organisation in the Mendicant Context: Formal and Informal Structures of the Friars' Lives and Ministry in the Middle Ages* (2010).

**Bert Roest**  is Professor of History at the University of Groningen, the Netherlands. He is the author of *A History of Franciscan Education (c. 1210–1517)* (2000) and *Franciscan Literature of Religious Instruction before the Council of Trent* (2004). With Stephen Gers he co-edited *Medieval and Renaissance Humanism* (2003).

**Jens Röhrkasten,**   formerly the editor of *Midland History*, is a lecturer in Medieval History at the University of Birmingham, author of *Die englischen Kronzeugen, 1130–1330* (1990) and *The Mendicant Houses of Medieval London 1221–1539* (2004), and editor of *The Worcester Eyre of 1275*, Worcestershire Historical Society, new series, 22, 2008. With Michael J. P. Robson he co-edited the first volume of *Canterbury Studies in Franciscan History* (2008) and *Franciscan Organisation in the Mendicant Context: Formal and Informal Structures of the Friars' Lives and Ministry in the Middle Ages* (2010).

**Neslihan Şenocak**   is Assistant Professor of Medieval History, Columbia University, Department of History. She has published articles in *Frate Francesco, Archivum Franciscanum Historicum, Scriptorium* and *The Journal of Religious History*, and is completing her monograph entitled *The Rise of Learning in the Franciscan Order 1210–1310*.

**William J. Short**,  OFM is Professor of Christian Spirituality at the Franciscan School of Theology, Berkeley. He was one of the three editors of *Francis of Assisi: Early Documents* (1999–2002), and the author of *The Franciscans* and *Poverty and Joy: The Franciscan Tradition* (1999). He is also editor of the Academy of American Franciscan History series, *United States Documents in the Propaganda Fide Archives: A Calendar*.

# Acknowledgements

Dr Kate Brett, Cambridge University Press's commissioning editor in theology, first broached the prospect of my editing this volume. With her customary professionalism and perseverance she presided over the early stages of the project. Ms Laura Morris succeeded her half-way through the completion of the book, and I am indebted to her sound advice, encouragement, flexibility and patience in bringing the book to completion. Mr Christopher Jackson was a highly efficient copy-editor, whose professionalism and vigilance have enhanced this volume.

# Notes on editions and translations

The writings of Francis of Assisi have been edited in four major editions since 1904. First, the *Sancti Patris Francisci Assisiensis sec. Codices mss. emendata et denuo edita a PP. Collegii S. Bonaventurae*, Bibliotheca Franciscana Ascetica Medii Aevi, 1 (Quaracchi, 1904, 1941, 1949). Secondly, K. Esser (ed.), *Opuscula Sancti Patris Francisci Assisiensis denuo edidit iuxta codices mss.*, Bibliotheca Franciscana Ascetica Medii Aevi, 12 (Grottaferrata, 1978). Thirdly, Esser and E. Grau (eds.), *Die Opuscula des hl. Franziskus von Assisi, Neue textkritische Edition*, Spicilegium Bonaventurianum 13 (Grottaferrata, 1989). Fourthly, C. Paolazzi (ed.), *Francesco d'Assisi Scritti*, Spicilegium Bonaventurianum, 36 (Grottaferrata, 2009). The Latin texts of these writings and the early biographies of Francis are published in *Fontes Francescani*, E. Menestò, S. Brufani *et al.* (eds.), Medioevo Francescano, collana diretta da Enrico Menestò, *Testi*, 2 (Assisi, 1995).

For an English translation of the writings of Francis see R. J. Armstrong and I. C. Brady (eds.), *Francis and Clare: The Complete Works*, translated by The Classics of Western Spirituality (Ramsey, N.J., 1982). The saint's writings and the early biographies are translated in M. Habig (ed.), *St Francis of Assisi, Writings and Early Biographies* (Chicago, 1973). More recent scholarship is represented by R. J. Armstrong, J. A. W. Hellmann and W. J. Short (eds.), *Francis of Assisi: Early Documents*, 4 vols. (New York, 1999–2002), where a historical introduction and commentary precede each text.

# Chronology

| | |
|---|---|
| 1181/2: | birth of Francis, son of Pietro and Pica Bernardone, in Assisi. |
| 1193/4: | birth of Clare, daughter of Favarone di Offreduccio and Ortulana. |
| 1199–1200: | civil war in Assisi. |
| 1202, November: | battle of Collestrada, between Assisi and Perugia. |
| 1202–3: | Francis is held as a prisoner of war in Perugia. |
| 1206: | Francis's conversion through a series of events outside Assisi. |
| 1208, April: | the conversion of Bernard of Quintavalle. He and Francis consult the text of the Gospel in the church of San Nicolò. |
| 1209: | initial approval of Francis's form of life and his fraternity by Innocent III. |
| c.1212: | Clare makes her penitential profession at the Porziuncula, below Assisi. |
| 1215, November: | the fourth Lateran Council is held in Rome. |
| 1216, 16 July: | Francis is present at the death-bed of Innocent III. |
| 1219–20: | Francis reaches the Holy Land during the fifth Crusade, when he preaches to the sultan, al-Malik-al-Kâmil. |
| 1220, January: | the martyrdom of five friars in Morocco. |
| c.1220: | Hugolino dei Conti di Segni, cardinal bishop of Ostia, who had already intervened in the life of the fledgeling order, becomes its protector, representing its interests at the papal court. |
| 1221: | the Earlier *Rule* (*Regula non bullata*). |
| 1222, 15 August: | Francis's sermon in the piazza of Bologna. |
| 1223, 29 November: | formal approval of Francis's *Rule* by Honorius III. |
| 1223, 24–5 December: | Francis celebrates Christmas at Greccio and re-enacts the crib. |

| | |
|---|---|
| 1223–4: | Francis commissions Anthony of Padua to teach the friars theology, provided that this does not extinguish the spirit of prayer. |
| 1224, September: | on his retreat at La Verna Francis receives the stigmata, the five wounds which marked the body of the Crucified Christ. |
| 1225: | Francis is nursed at San Damiano and composes praises and exhortations in the vernacular. |
| 1226, 3 October: | the death of Francis at the Porziuncula. |
| 1226, 4 October: | Francis's body is carried to Assisi for burial in the church of San Giorgio, where he had attended school. |
| 1227, 19 March: | Cardinal Hugolino is elected pope as Gregory IX. |
| 1228, 16 July: | Francis is canonised by Gregory IX in the piazza di San Giorgio. |
| 1228–9: | Thomas of Celano compiles his first biography of Francis at the command of Gregory IX. |
| 1230, 30 May: | the solemn translation of Francis's body to the basilica di San Francesco. |
| 1230, 28 September: | *Quo elongati*, the first papal exposition of the *Rule* of Francis. |

# Abbreviations

| | |
|---|---|
| *AFH* | = *Archivum Franciscanum Historicum.* |
| AP | = *The Beginning or Founding of the Order and the Deeds of Those Lesser Brothers Who Were the First Companions of Blessed Francis in Religion* (The Anonymous of Perugia) by John of Perugia (1240–1), in *FAED*, vol. II, pp. 34–58. |
| CA | = *The Assisi Compilation*, in *FAED*, vol. II, pp. 118–230. |
| *FAED* | = R. J. Armstrong, J. A. W. Hellmann and W. J. Short (eds.), *Francis of Assisi: Early Documents*, 4 vols. (New York, 1999–2002). |
| *FS* | = *Franciscan Studies*, new series. |
| Jordan of Giano | = *The Chronicle of Brother Jordan of Giano*, in *XIIIth Century Chronicles: Jordan of Giano, Thomas of Eccleston and Salimbene degli Adami*, pp. 1–77. (See below.) |
| *LM* | = *The Major Life* (*Legenda Maior*) *of Saint Francis* (1260–1263) by Bonaventure, in *FAED*, vol. II, pp. 525–683. |
| *LSCA* | = *The Legend of St Clare*, in R. J. Armstrong (ed. and trans.), *Clare of Asssi: Early Documents Revised and Expanded* (New York, 1993), pp. 259–308. |
| MP | = *A Mirror of the Perfection, Rule, Profession, Life, and True Calling* (The Lemmens edition, 1901) and *A Mirror of the Perfection of the Status of a Lesser Brother* (1318) (The Sabatier edition, 1928), in *FAED*, vol. III, pp. 214–372. |
| OMT | = Oxford Medieval Texts. |
| RB | = the *Rule* of Francis which was formally approved by Honorius III on 29 November 1223, in *FAED*, vol. I, pp. 99–106. |

| | |
|---|---|
| RNB | = Francis's *Rule* of 1221, which was not formally approved by the pope, in *FAED*, vol. I, pp. 63–86. |
| Salimbene | = *The Chronicle of Salimbene de Adam*, eds. and trans. J. L. Baird, G. Baglivi and J. R. Kane, Medieval and Renaissance Texts and Studies, 40 (Binghamton, NY, 1986). |
| SC | = *The Sacred Exchange between Saint Francis and Lady Poverty*, in *FAED*, vol. I, pp. 529–54. |
| Thomas of Eccleston | = *The Chronicle of Thomas of Eccleston*, in *XIIIth Century Chronicles: Jordan of Giano, Thomas of Eccleston and Salimbene degli Adami*, pp. 79–191. (See below.) |
| 1 Cel. | = *The Life of Saint Francis* by Thomas of Celano (1228–9), in *FAED*, vol. I, pp. 180–308. |
| 2 Cel. | = *The Remembrance of the Desire of a Soul (The Second Life of Saint Francis* by Thomas of Celano (1245–7), in *FAED*, vol. II, pp. 239–393. |
| 3 Cel. | = *The Treatise on the Miracles of Saint Francis* by Thomas of Celano (1250–2), in *FAED*, vol. II, pp. 399–468. |
| 3 Soc. | = *The Legend of the Three Companions* (1241–7), in *FAED*, vol. II, pp. 66–110. |
| *XIIIth Century Chronicles*: | *Jordan of Giano, Thomas of Eccleston and Salimbene degli Adami*, trans. from the Latin by P. Hermann, with intro. and notes by M.-T. Laureilhe (Chicago, 1961), pp. 91–191. |

# Introduction

MICHAEL J. P. ROBSON

The young Francis of Assisi, son of a prosperous merchant, dreamed of earning fame as an intrepid and chivalrous knight, whose deeds would be praised and celebrated at home and beyond the confines of his native Umbria, spreading to the neighbouring provinces. This aspiration survived his spell as a prisoner of war in Perugia after the battle of Collestrada in November 1202 when he may have witnessed horrific deeds. On his release, his interests, manner and spirit were noticeably different. The new restlessness and growing detachment could not be explained solely by a period of incarceration as a prisoner of war. Despite this enduring sense of disorientation, the hope of becoming a bold and fearless knight persisted and led Francis to join a nobleman of Assisi who was making preparations to depart for Apulia in southern Italy, where Walter of Brienne was leading the papal militia against Markwald of Anweiler, the seneschal of the German emperor. About 1204/5 Francis set out from home and travelled as far as the neighbouring city of Spoleto, where a dream about arms and their use caused him to discard his military ambitions and return home. On his journey back to Assisi he undoubtedly pondered the ruins of his military ambitions with his ardent desire to win renown and honour. The next stage in his life was far from clear. Notwithstanding the feelings of disappointment and frustration, the seeds of another vocation were being sown imperceptibly with a form of life which would bring him celebrity and universal acclaim, albeit of an unexpected kind.

Uncertainty about the new direction of Francis's life lingered for an uncomfortably long time, spanning at least two years. During this period he spent an increasing amount of time in prayer and reflection with a growing asceticism. His restless search for a clue to his future life led him to make more regular visits to churches and chapels, where he prayed with a new earnestness and eagerly awaited a sign about his future. Although the chronology is unclear, it is during this period that he encountered the leper, heard the voice from the crucifix at

San Damiano instructing him to repair the ancient church and sold his father's cloth at the market square adjoining the cathedral of San Feliciano at Foligno. This sequence of events, particularly the last one, snapped the patience of his puzzled father, Pietro Bernardone, who was deeply perplexed by the increasingly unpredictable and eccentric behaviour of his older son. The ruptured relations were cemented during the hearing in the court of Guido I, bishop of Assisi, who would play a significant role in the development of Francis's new vocation and the evolution of a new type of religious fraternity. The fifth fresco of Francis's life in the upper basilica in Assisi depicts him returning his clothes to his father and renouncing his family inheritance, while his nudity is concealed by the cloak of this bishop, a prelate whose earlier conduct made him an unlikely ally and protector. Francis is seen to be responding to the hand at the top of the fresco, slightly left of centre, slowly discerning the direction of his new vocation which sounded the death-knell to life as a merchant.

Francis's new form of life gradually crystallised after a period when he lived as a hermit outside Assisi, and he spent his time in the restoration of dilapidated rural churches. In this period he strove to correct his earlier mistakes by grounding his life in the Scriptures, which he started to interpret in a literal fashion; this disposition would remain a feature of the awe which he attached to the Word of God; on occasion, he was happy to consult the sacred text at random. The command to restore the church of San Damiano prompted him to gather stones for its repair, bringing himself ridicule from his former companions among the youth of Assisi; his old friends deemed him to be in the grip of some form of madness and callously derided him. His changed demeanour was attributed to being in love (1 Cel., 7). He was determined that his earlier folly had to be corrected by a greater attentiveness to the teachings of the Bible. The celebration of Mass at Santa Maria degli Angeli, one of the three churches which he had repaired with his own hands, gave a broader perspective to his mandate to restore the church of San Damiano; now he thought of renewing the Church by perpetuating the apostles' ministry of calling people to penance. The proclamation of the Gospel challenged him to revitalise the Church by embracing a penitential life and living in accordance with the teaching of his divine master. That process would begin in the city of his birth rather than in some distant and remote missionary territory. Forthwith he returned to Assisi to announce the Gospel and to exhort the citizens to do penance for their indiscretions and failings. His new vision was conveyed through his sermons and exhortations.

The clarification of Francis's vocation was accompanied by a grow-ing spiritual focus and maturity. He was resolved to live in the style of the apostles. Like them he was to be unencumbered and ready to take his master's message to the people of Assisi and then Umbria. There-after the impetus passed from an imitation of the apostles to the literal following of their divine teacher. Francis wished to walk in the foot-steps of Jesus Christ, who had called people to reject their earlier errors (*metánoia*). This reflection on the virtue of poverty was also nurtured by the Psalms and the Old Testament. The spirit of renewal was fed by his frequent meditations on the crib and the cross, the two pivotal moments in the drama of the redemption, which paved the way for the resurrection. His biographers dwell on devotion to these two decisive moments in the salvation of the human race. His prayerful reflection on the circumstances of the Incarnation led him to concen-trate on the poverty of the life and death of the Son of God. This aspect of the life of Jesus Christ challenged Francis to renounce not only his possessions, but also his very self. Francis, too, would empty himself and surrender himself to the divine influence and endeavour to follow God's will in all things. This self-emptying was symbolised by the nakedness of the crib and the cross, a gesture which signified his fuller identification with the will of God the Father; it became a motif favoured by Francis and his biographers.[1]

Lengthy meditation on the life of Jesus and the mode of human redemption enabled Francis to enter into this sacred mystery, moving him to tears at the recollection of the passion and the crucifixion. Jesus's self-giving was encapsulated in the voluntary poverty which he embraced. Evangelical poverty became a central virtue for Francis, a vow to take its place alongside the obedience, chastity and stability of the religious life. It was not fully explained by the renunciation implicit in the monastic conversion of conduct; it was not merely confined to the rejection of possessions, as the fourteenth Admonition attests. It was a broader and much richer concept: evangelical poverty was a redemptive and ennobling force, which inspired Francis to strip himself interiorly in imitation of Jesus; this selfless process is described in St Paul's letter to the Philippians (2: 6–11). The abandonment of all material possessions was to be matched by an internal act of renunciation which finds expression in the term that the friars should live without anything of their own (*sine proprio*). The poverty of the Incarnation enriched a penitent humanity, as Francis explains in his *Letter to the Faithful*. Voluntary poverty brought with it a sense of liberation and freedom to invest in the pursuit of spiritual development. Francis's vow created the conditions for an interior development and enrichment, offering a fertile ground for the blossoming of the Christian virtues. His espousal of evangelical poverty permitted him to flourish in the most dramatic manner.

A radically new dimension was brought to the history of religious life in the western Church by Francis's renunciation of all forms of ownership and his rejection of the customary forms of economic support for a community of friars. He and his followers lived in both individual and corporate poverty, a significant departure by a religious community. This freshness is reflected in the chroniclers' comments about the penury in which the friars lived. While it was claimed that Francis had injected a new theme into the discourse of religious life, evangelical poverty and its benefits had deep roots in the history of the Church; it appeared in some patristic texts and was beginning to emerge with greater frequency in the writings and teachings of monastic reformers of the eleventh century, such as St William of Volpiano (962–1031), who revitalised numerous monastic communities, seeking poverty and holiness.[2] Twelfth-century reformers sought a return to a simpler and more authentic form of religious life and commented on the poverty of the Son of God. Penitents such as Ranieri (1118–61), patron saint of Pisa, anticipated features of Francis's discipline, asceticism and voluntary poverty, and Cistercian hagiography talked unselfconsciously about the poverty of the monks' living conditions.[3]

Like earlier reformers, Francis initially regarded the life of the apostles as the apex of Christian observance, although the focus moved from the idyllic community gathered in Jerusalem (Acts 2: 42–7) to the itinerant preaching of the Gospel. This image was undergoing development in the course of the twelfth century, when new ideas about religious perfection were surfacing. Francis was the heir to these reflections, and his decision to 'flee the world' was conditioned by a commitment to spread the Gospel.[4] His ideals, which serve as the culmination of this movement of renewal, were derived primarily from the Scriptures, and he expanded these, making them the foundation of his new vocation. His teaching was regarded as ground-breaking, and contemporaries saw his witness to evangelical poverty as something of a novelty, the return to a long-neglected virtue (2 Cel., 55).

Francis was acutely conscious of the pervasive divine presence, making the whole world a theatre for the praise of the Creator. No longer was the parish church deemed to be the only place where the things of God were aired. The biographies of *il poverello* show how the Gospel migrated to the piazza and other places where people were accustomed to gather. Francis found the divine footprints everywhere and wished to bring his neighbours to a greater recognition of their Creator. Harmony was restored to the created order. Thus, the early hagiographical tradition of the saint reflects the laity's new thirst for the principles of spirituality, which had previously been seen as the preserve of a cloistered elite. The monastic rhetoric regarding the excellence and supremacy of the religious life was ceding ground to newer models of lay piety. This prevalence of what Professor Lawrence called a *fugitive piety*, embracing the monastic habit in the face of death, was under challenge.[5] New assumptions and patterns were manifest in Innocent III's canonisation of Homobonus in 1199, an act which signalled the growing self-confidence of the laity in the realm of spirituality. These fresh currents of asceticism and piety found expression in the proliferation of penitential groups and individuals in the first decades of the thirteenth century.

While Francis's teaching was addressed to the friars, his message was not limited to the cloister. His salutary advice was especially apposite and timely in a society which bristled with new economic opportunities for the accumulation of material possessions and wealth. It was a message tailored to the lives of the residents of the newly expanding commercial centres, the mercantile community, figures like Giovanni Boccaccio's disreputable Ciappelletto of Prato.[6] Such merchants were inclined to invest an inordinate amount of time and energy in seeking their salvation through material goods, the false gods. The hagiographical literature, supported by material from the probate registers, dwelled upon the perils which lurked in the urban centres, where honesty and probity of life ensnared many and avarice and usury menaced others. For example, Ugolino Cavaze testified on 29 March 1237 that his father, a citizen of Bologna, had accumulated many things illicitly and dishonestly as much through usury as any other way.[7] The friars' voluntary poverty, humility and preaching were seen as a divinely inspired remedy for the vice of avarice. Within fifty years Francis would be presented as the patron saint of merchants.[8]

Echoing the monastic concept of the pilgrim, the sixth chapter of Francis's *Rule* exhorted his disciples to live with a spirit of detachment; they should be like visitors and strangers in a world of change (1 Peter 2: 11). The same salutary advice is applicable to all Christians, whose consciousness of the transitoriness of life should shape their values and decisions. Christians were exhorted to work for the values that endure to eternal life (John 6: 27). Evangelical poverty was, moreover, clothed in an eschatological dimension, and this confirms the fact that material possessions are to be used in a responsible, balanced and detached manner. From the early 1230s preachers such as Robert Grosseteste, then the master of theology at the friars' school in Oxford, saw this vow as a foretaste of the celestial harmony in which everything would be shared. It is unclear whether Francis was aware of a patristic tradition connecting the Fall with the institution of private property. Ironically, this patristic debate was revived in the discussions regarding the order and its observance of the vow of poverty.

Francis's genius was to recognise the sheer power and persuasiveness of the acquisitive instinct, the itch to amass possessions and wealth in the illusory search for absolute security this side of the grave. As a young man from a wealthy and privileged background, he was keenly aware of the connection between wealth, influence, power and violence, the very antithesis of the Son of God who voluntarily lived in poverty to fill humanity with spiritual gifts in abundance. Keenly aware of the divisiveness of money, Francis taught that material possessions should not become the cause of dispute and division between people. His intense desire to immerse himself as completely as possible with the Son of God accounts for his unbending refusal to compromise by accepting coins for his work or the charity dispensed by the friars; this explains his insistence that friars should on no account touch money, as the *Rule* ordains. Furthermore, he pointed out that ownership and wealth alone were incapable of providing happiness. In some situations, they constituted an impediment to safety, harmony, charity and love. That limitation is articulated by Iris Origo, who prepared for the German occupation of her Tuscan home at the Val d'Orcia. Her diary for 11 October 1943 reads:

> Our 'thirty-two boxes, carefully packed, with the name printed clearly on each' are now ready, stored and walled up. As the last brick was set in position, we began to remember the things we had omitted to put away, as well as to regret those which we have packed, but will probably need. It is, however, quite impossible to attach importance to any material possessions now. All that one clings to is a few vital affections.[9]

Ownership is coterminous with life, and its propensity for imperilling the quest for eternal life is conveyed by Francis's evocation of the scene of the death-bed, where material concerns blight the celestial prospects of the dying man, who may have been a merchant. An attachment to material things, regardless of how great or small their value, is capable of polluting human relations, violating friendships and destroying families. The inclination to raise a protective wall of possessions around our lives calls for corrective remedies. Francis's teaching has a timeless freshness which makes it just as incisively pertinent today as it was 800 years ago. His insights run counter to the temptation to obtain an ever greater number of material goods and to measure life by ownership, possessions, valuables and money. The maldistribution of the planet's finite material and financial resources endangers the harmony and peaceful co-existence of the nations. The transient nature of ownership is demonstrated by the request of the dying Francis, *il poverello*, to be placed on the naked earth as he awaited Sister Death at Santa Maria degli Angeli on 3 October 1226 (2 Cel., 214). This gesture associated him with an earlier ecclesiastical tradition whereby clerics and prelates went nakedly to their deaths, like the exemplary Ralph Luffa, bishop of Chichester (1091–1123). As he lay dying he gave all his possessions to the poor, even his bedclothes and mattress.[10]

*The Cambridge Companion to Francis of Assisi* offers a series of studies of one of the most fascinating and most lovable figures in the life of the medieval and modern Church. A volume of this size has the limited objective of introducing Francis and explaining some of the key aspects of his life and thought. It is neither a biography of the saint nor a history of the order which he founded. Its focus is twofold. The first is the magnetic appeal of the founder, and this is treated in the first eight studies, which explore features of his life, from his conversion to his death and canonisation. The second part of the volume, chapters 9 to 17, is devoted to his influence on the friars and his legacy. It deals primarily with the abiding impact of the saint on the friars' vocation and their wide-ranging contribution to the life of the Church. The century following the death of *il poverello* is the historical framework for these essays. The last study is the chronological exception, and it reflects the ecumenical dimension of Francis's appeal to Christians of diverse traditions.

Francis was buried at the church of San Giorgio, where he had first attended school and later preached his first sermon (1 Cel., 23); the church was subsequently absorbed by the basilica di Santa Chiara. Within a short time of Francis's death miracles were attributed to him, and these reports attracted pilgrims to his tomb in search of healing. The troubled and sick came from all parts of Umbria and from further afield. The miracles were sufficiently numerous for Gregory IX, formerly Cardinal Hugolino, to examine them and to canonise Francis within a comparatively short time, that is, on 16 July 1228 (1 Cel., 124). The inseparable bond between the life of the saint and the genesis of his fraternity is explored by Michael F. Cusato in the volume's opening study. The circumstances of Francis's dramatic conversion, triggered by a series of events in which God spoke to him with increasing clarity, are narrated by the *Testament*. Francis's unexpected encounter with the leper re-orientated his life completely, leading him among the sick and the marginalised people in the neighbourhood. His comparatively small collection of writings and exhortations forms the basis of the second chapter, which maps out the new direction of Francis's life. Pride of place among those writings went to the *Rule*, whose evolution and content are described by William J. Short. The saint's new vision and his originality shine forth in the *Rule*, the first to be approved between the *Rule* of St Benedict (*c.*480–*c.*550) and the constitutions of St Ignatius of Loyola in the middle of the sixteenth century.[11] The *Rule* was regarded as a significant addition to the older codes of religious life, and it was copied verbatim by Matthew Paris, the monastic chronicler of St Albans.

The writings of Francis were quoted and summarised by the early hagiographical tradition of the new order. Quotations from the *Testament* and other writings invested the work of Thomas of Celano with a new authority. The first biographer wrote at the request of Gregory IX in connection with the ceremony of canonisation and completed his task within six months. Celano displays his familiarity with the standard works of hagiography, the lives of St Antony the hermit, St Martin of Tours, the dialogues of St Gregory the Great and the *Confessions* of St Augustine. The complexity of Franciscan hagiography during the first half of the thirteenth century is explored by Michael W. Blastic, who introduces the seminal texts which left an indelible mark upon the subsequent tradition. The twenty years following the death of *il poverello* witnessed the production of a series of texts which incorporate various accounts of his life and teaching. These portraits reflect the diverse perceptions and the growing ideological differences among the friars; they mirror the formation of parties or groups containing the seeds of the division of the order which became increasingly visible from the end of the thirteenth century, paving the way for the Observant reformers from the later fourteenth century.

An example of how the biographical tradition reflects discussion among the friars is the treatment of the saint's attitude towards breviaries and manuscripts, which were costly items in the Middle Ages. Debates concerning the acquisition of the textbooks required for study and preaching entered the hagiographical tradition of the first century, as Neslihan Şenocak demonstrates. The biographies of the saint are supplemented by a rich tradition in the composition of chronicles, a subject treated by Annette Kehnel, who sifts the evidence provided by the order's three principal chroniclers, Jordan of Giano, Thomas of Eccleston and Salimbene de Adam, who record an immense amount of detail on the missions to Germany and England and the friars' varied contribution to the life of the Italian communes and provinces. Salimbene adds that Francis spent twenty years in the service of God. Nonetheless, he could not refrain from boasting about his knowledge of the famous and the influential friars. He portrayed Bernard of Quintavalle as his close friend, adding that they were members of the community at Siena for a winter. The first friar to be received into the order told Salimbene many things about the founder which may have escaped the hagiographical net.[12]

The striking message of renewal preached by Francis attracted a wide spectrum of Umbrian society. One of those touched by his fiery and incisive sermons was the aristocratic young woman, Clare di Favarone di Offreduccio, who heard him preach in the cathedral church of San Rufino. It is one of the ironies of Franciscan history that this noblewoman of Assisi should become the staunch and heroic defender of the ideal of evangelical poverty from 3 October 1226 until her death twenty-seven years later. Her unshakeable firmness of purpose was a reproach to the friars, some of whom were prepared to accept an accommodation, if not compromise, with their ideal of evangelical poverty. The unfolding of her vocation as his first female follower and first abbess of San Damiano is analysed by Jean François Godet-Calogeras. Jesus's mission to effect the reconciliation of the human race inspired Francis, the former prisoner of war, to extend the greeting of peace to all whom he encountered; friars were regarded as the only religious who gave this exhortation to all whom they met, presaging their crucial ministry of restoring peace to the cities of Italy. The concept of universal respect and charity was a further enrichment of Francis's spiritual development, and it knew no exceptions. It is perhaps best illustrated by his remarkably enlightened and courteous dealings with the sultan of Egypt, al-Malik-al-Kâmil, during the fifth Crusade, a dramatic gesture which recommended him as a model of wider ecumenical dialogue. This encounter forms the basis of Steven J. McMichael's study. The same openness to all life informs the colourful accounts of Francis's easy rapport with the world of animals, recalling the earlier Celtic tradition. His exhortation to the birds at Bevagna is narrated by Thomas of Celano, and it features prominently in the earliest iconography of the order from the panel by Bonaventure

Berlinghieri at San Francesco, Pescia, in 1235. This respectful disposition towards all the works of the Creator is reviewed by Timothy
J. Johnson. Parisian scholastics, such as Bonaventure of Bagnoregio,
would provide a theological framework for the saint's meditation, the
source of life, beauty and harmony.

Historians treat the appearance of the friars as a providential
response to the defects besetting the medieval Church. At a time when
many of the parochial clergy were ill-equipped and unsuited to expound
the teaching of the New Testament to their parishioners, the friars
accomplished this ministry in a persuasive, cogent and attractive form.
Their personal example and words of exhortation drew their hearers to
a deeper love of God and neighbour. The priests who had been admitted
to the fraternity were authorised to preach and hear confessions. The
orthodoxy, fervour and power of their sermons played a central role in
many provinces of the Church from the thirteenth century. The friars'
effectiveness is summarised by the first biographer of Anthony of Padua
(1195–1231), an outstandingly popular preacher who applied the principles of the Gospel to the practices and customs of the market place.
As a result of his sermons in Padua the estranged were brought to
peace; prisoners were liberated; restitution was arranged for whatever
was taken through usury or violence; and many who had mortgaged
houses and fields made satisfaction for what they had illicitly gained
through extortion or bribery.[13] The friars' impact on the cities and
towns of western Europe is considered by Jens Röhrkasten, who focuses
on the urban nature of the order's ministry and their ties with the local
community. While the friars sowed the Word of God in the churches of
a city, their ministry was not confined by parochial or urban boundaries. They ministered to those who escaped the parochial net; Simone da
Collazzone, for example, preached to the lepers.[14] One of the reasons
for the sheer effectiveness of the friars' programme of pastoral renewal
was their solid theological and moral preparation. Their qualities recommended them for specialised apostolates, such as the campaign
against heresy in northern Italy and southern France; they were required
to give an account of what they believed (1 Peter 3: 15), a quotation cited
at the beginning of St Anselm's treatise on the Incarnation, *Why God
became Man*. The emergence of theological studies in the order was
viewed by some friars with caution and misgiving; before the end of the
thirteenth century it was attracting some eloquent critics. Bert Roest
charts the genesis of theological studies in the order from the 1220s and
highlights the earlier appearance of schools, beginning with Anthony of
Padua, who is regarded as the first lector of the new order.

The penitents who evolved into the Third Order are described by Ingrid Peterson, who recounts the history of this movement, which attracted innumerable men and women. Their devotional activities intrude from time to time in the order's hagiography and chronicles. The catalogue of the saints of the Franciscan family includes several members of the Third Order, some of whom were interred in the order's churches. Men and women of outstanding holiness were drawn to this lay movement, including St Lucchesio of Poggibonsi (†1251), an avaricious man prior to his meeting with St Francis who passed through the Tuscan town in 1221. Friars preached sermons on the feasts of the canonised members of the Third Order, such as St Peter Pettinaio (†1289), who was renowned for his care of the needy and the infirm in Siena. This movement was embellished by the lives of some exceptional women who have already attracted a great deal of scholarly interest in recent decades, Ss Elizabeth of Hungary (d. 1231), Rose of Viterbo (d. 1251), Margaret of Cortona (d. 1297) and Angela of Foligno (d. 1309).[15]

Just as Francis's ideal appealed to a wide variety of people from varied backgrounds, so his followers were seemingly ubiquituous and took their message of penitence and renewal throughout the parishes of the western Church and into its missionary territory. From the outset they forged strong bonds with the royal families of western Europe, with the notable exception of Frederick II (d. 1250), the emperor, who was at loggerheads with Gregory IX and then Innocent IV. Thomas of Celano noted the devotion of the French royal family towards the new saint, whose pillow they venerated (1 Cel., 120). The order's links with the royal families of western Europe are illustrated by Sean L. Field with particular reference to the court of Louis IX and his immediate successors. For example, Louis's younger cousin across the English channel, Edward I, dispensed alms to the poor on the feast of St Francis in 1300.[16] In view of the founder's close links with Innocent III, Honorius III and curial figures such as Leo Brancaleo, cardinal priest of Santa Croce in Gerusalemme, the friars were engaged in the papal court as chaplains, confessors, penitentiaries and masters of theology throughout the thirteenth century. One of them, Arnulph, a papal penitentiary, played a crucial role in the deposition of Elias of Cortona at the general chapter of Rome in 1239. The order's links with the curia facilitated their appointment as papal messengers, envoys and emissaries from the middle of the century. Innocent IV sent John of Piano Carpini to the Mongol empire in 1245; within a decade Louis IX of France dispatched William of Rubruck as a messenger and missionary. Peter Jackson shows how the friars were drawn into the service of Innocent IV and

Louis IX. While Francis was committed to the re-evangelisation of the people of Italy, he also nurtured the desire to contribute to the Church's missionary endeavour, which was exemplified by his visit to Damietta in 1219. One of the distinctive features of his *Rule* was its provision for friars to undertake missionary activity. From the inception of the order friars were dispatched throughout western Europe and then into the missionary fields in the Holy Land and in Morocco. This dynamic drive is surveyed by E. Randolph Daniel.

Francis's *Rule* was recognised as the binding force in the new movement. When the general chapter of 1230 at Assisi was unable to resolve doubts about the appropriate interpretation of the friars' charter, they turned to Gregory IX for a binding decision, creating a new source of authority. Papal interpretations of the *Rule* from the 1230s onwards wrestled with the practical implications of the order's renunciation of the traditional means of support for religious orders, and these documents spawned a new wave of glosses and commentaries by friars. The solution of investing the order's goods in the hands of the papacy led to situations not envisaged by Innocent IV. The polemical exchanges in the middle of the thirteenth century posed searching questions about the theological and canonical basis of the friars' vocation. Nicholas III's bull (*Exiit qui seminat*) on 14 August 1279 provided a definitive solution to the problems of the previous forty years. Despite the good intentions of Nicholas III, the disputes continued unabated and were intensified in succeeding decades, exposing the friars to much controversy and ridicule. These situations were exacerbated by the friars' own rhetoric of excellence and a disturbing propensity to invoke the law rather than seek a solution. While John XXII was initially drawn into disputes concerning the growing number of friars who wished to live by the *Rule* in all its simplicity, he was later compelled to face the order's rationale for evangelical poverty. The complexity of these exchanges and the series of rulings which he gave is narrated by Patrick Nold.

The previous sixteen studies in this volume concentrate upon the founder and the first century of the life and apostolate of his far-flung disciples. The last chapter belongs to the modern age and the world of ecumenism in which Francis is such an attractive figure. Petà Dunstan recounts the historical movements of recent centuries and dwells on the English love and enthusiasm for Francis of Assisi. The renewal of interest in the historical figure of the saint owes much to the scholarship of Paul Sabatier (†1928), the Swiss Protestant pastor whose *Vie de S. François d'Assise* re-ignited the search for the authentic portrait of *il poverello* from 1894 onwards. His baton passed to a succession of exceptional scholars in England, notably Dr Andrew George Little, Bishop John Moorman and Dr Rosalind Brooke. Their erudition has illuminated the person of Francis and the movement which he inspired during the second and third decades of the thirteenth century. The immense contribution made by these distinguished scholars reflects the breadth of the saint's appeal to Christians of all traditions and communities. The ecumenical gestures inspired by Francis led to a series of initiatives in Assisi, where the ancient chapel of San Gregorio was placed at the disposal of Anglican pilgrims. One of these was the establishment of the Centro Nordico, which flourished in the 1970s, and another was the formation of a community of friars from the Anglican Society of St Francis in the city. The pioneering work of Fr Maximilian Mizzi, OFM Conv. (†2008) in this field of ecumenism was recognised by the Anglican Church. An illustration of the depth of Francis's influence and his appeal is reflected in the circumstances of the death of Bishop Moorman on 13 January 1989. This eminent scholar and prelate welcomed Sister Death while the vicar of St Oswald's in Durham read the *Canticle of the Creatures* in Italian at his death-bed.[17]

## Notes

1 Cf. L. S. Cunningham, 'Francis Naked and Clothed: A Theological Meditation', in J. M. Hammond (ed.), *Francis of Assisi: History, Hagiography and Hermeneutics in the Early Documents* (New York, 2002), pp. 164–78.

2 *Rodulfus Glaber Opera*, J. France, N. Bulst and P. Reynolds (eds.), OMT (Oxford, 1989) pp. 268–9: *pauperiem ... vel extremitatem*.

3 *The Life of Ailred of Rievaulx by Walter Daniel*, F. M. Powicke (ed.), Nelson Medieval Texts (London, 1950), p. 11.

4 C. H. Lawrence, *The Friars: The Impact of the Early Mendicant Movement on Western Society* (London, 1994), pp. 15–19.

5 E.g., *Chronicles of the Reigns of Stephen, Henry I and Richard I*, R. Howlett (ed.), 4 vols., Rolls Series, 82 (London, 1884–9), vol. III, p. 140.

6 *Giovanni Boccaccio, Decameron, Filocolo, Ameto, Fiametta*, E. Bianchi, C. Salinari and N. Sapegno (eds.), La Letteratura Italiana: Storia e Testi, 8 (Milan, 1952), vol. I, 1, pp. 25–38.

7 *Acta Franciscana e Tabulariis Bononiensibus deprompta*, B. Giordani (ed.), Analecta Franciscana (Quaracchi, 1927), vol. IX, nos. 1165, 1668, pp. 592, 593.

8 *Les Sermons et la visite pastorale de Federico Visconti archevêque de Pise (1253–1277)*, N. Bériou (ed.), Sources et documents d'histoire du Moyen Âge publiés par le École française de Rome, 3 (Rome, 2001), no. 12, pp. 778–9.

9   I. Origo, *War in Val d'Orcia: An Italian War Diary, 1943–1944*, with an introduction by D. Mack-Smith (London, 1947, 1984), pp. 93–4.

10  *William of Malmesbury, Gesta Pontificum Anglorum, The History of the English Bishops*, M. Winterbottom, with the assistance of R.M. Thomson (eds.), 2 vols., OMT (Oxford, 2007), vol. 1, book 2, c. 96, pp. 322–3. Cf. R. Newhauser, *The Early History of Greed: The Sin of Avarice in Early Medieval Thought and Literature*, Cambridge Studies in Medieval Literature, 41 (Cambridge, 2000).

11  D. Knowles, *From Pachomius to Ignatius: A Study of the Constitutional History of the Religious Orders* (Oxford, 1966), p. 46.

12  *The Chronicle of Salimbene de Adam*, ed. and trans. Joseph L.Baird, G. Baglivi and John R. Kane, Medieval and Renaissance Texts and Studies, 40 (Binghamton, NY, 1986), pp. 9–10, 13.

13  *Life of St Anthony 'Assidua' by a Contemporary Franciscan*, trans. B. Przewozny (Padua, 1984), c. 13, nos. 11–12, pp. 18–19.

14  E. Menestò, *Simone da Collazzone Francescano e il suo processo per la sua canonizzazione (1252)* (Spoleto, 2007), c. 43, p. 53.

15  E.g., O. Gecser, 'The Lives of St Elizabeth: Their Rewritings and Diffusion in the Thirteenth Century', *Analecta Bollandiana*, 127 (2009), 49–107; J. Cannon and A. Vauchez, *Margherita of Cortona and the Lorenzetti: Sienese Art and the Cult of a Holy Woman in Medieval Tuscany* (Pennsylvania, 1999); and *Angela of Foligno: Complete Works*, trans. and intro. Paul Lachance, pref. Romana Guarnieri, Classics of Western Spirituality (New York, 1993).

16  British Library, MS.Add.35291, f.22r.

17  M. Manktelow, *John Moorman* (Norwich, 1999), p. 139.

**Part I**

*Francis of Assisi*

# 1 Francis and the Franciscan movement (1181/2–1226)

MICHAEL F. CUSATO

## HISTORIOGRAPHY AND HERMENEUTICS

Francis of Assisi is one of the most popular and attractive saints of Christian history. And yet therein lies the challenge for those attempting to authentically understand him and the movement which gathered around him. In popular and scholarly treatments Francis and his spiritual achievement are often understood in isolation from the historical conditions and realities which gave rise to the man and the movement he inspired. Such works concentrate instead either on his heroic and saintly virtues of simplicity, humility and poverty or on his fate as an isolated victim of manipulative clerics intent on using his movement to advance their own ecclesial agenda. In either case concentration is fixed upon the man to the exclusion of the multi-faceted movement.

The reason for this is not simply our genuine fascination with *il poverello*. It is also closely tied to the fact that our understanding of him has either been drawn largely from the hagiographical sources of the thirteenth and early fourteenth centuries, which viewed him through the lens of his canonisation as a saint in 1228; or, alternatively, from the personal reminiscences of his companions which reflected the polemical struggles raging within the order over its identity and its fidelity to the intentions of the founder. In either case, when the reader becomes focused too exclusively on the person and holiness of Francis, then the movement which he founded is eclipsed as inconsequential to our understanding of the achievement of this remarkable man. But to understand Francis without his movement is to understand very little of the historical figure. For it is, ultimately and precisely, the interaction of Francis with his brothers and sisters in those early formative years that gave rise to the unique charism which constitutes the Franciscan phenomenon. The focus of this essay is to present Francis within the context of the movement which gathered around him and the historical circumstances which gave rise to both.

The validity of this broader, more integrative optic depends, more-over, upon the sources which one privileges as more appropriate for conveying the historical origins of Francis and his movement. Following the path blazed during the last decades of the twentieth century most notably by David Flood, it is our contention that any such survey needs to give priority to two sources in particular: the Early *Rule* (1208–1221), and the *Testament* of Francis, dictated a few days prior to his passing.[1] These sources frame the early Franciscan story, being the first and last documents encompassing the life and charism of Francis and his brothers. His other writings can then be reliably used to fill out the historical frame culled from these two fundamental sources. And the content of the vignettes and testimonies found within the hagiographical and polemical literature that emerges over the course of the next century can then be accepted and used as historical to the degree that it complements the historical picture already established by these privileged sources.

## THE ORIGINS OF FRANCIS AND HIS MOVEMENT (1198–1210)

Born in 1181/2 to Pietro di Bernardone, a fairly prosperous mer-chant, and Pica, a woman of uncertain provenance, Francis was a member of the middle class of merchants which was in the ascend-ancy in the small but ancient town of Assisi. His appearance on the scene of history occurred simultaneously with the tumultuous events which gave rise to the birth of the free commune of Assisi. Assisi and its powerful neighbour were located in the duchy of Spoleto and were swept up into the struggle over competing claims of sovereignty that was raging during the last quarter of the twelfth century.[2] In his bid to reassert its claim over the cities of the duchy, in 1173 Emperor Frederick I had named Christian of Mainz as duke of Spoleto and count of Assisi: his personal representative in the region. He was replaced the following year by Conrad of Urslingen, who built the Rocca Maggiore above Assisi. In 1198, taking advantage of a power vacuum created by the sudden death of the German Emperor, Henry VI, and the minority of his son, Frederick-Roger, the middle class of Assisi rose up to overthrow both of their overlords, attacking the Rocca Maggiore, ejecting Conrad from the city and plundering the urban properties of the nobility, thus forcing them into exile. These merchants began to assert their authority out in the countryside over the lands of the nobility. In November 1202 one such raid onto lands near Collestrada owned by the Ghislieri clan was, however, ambushed by allies of this noble family, resulting in a crushing military defeat of the merchant class and the return of part of the nobility to the city. This turn of events is reflected in a Charter of Peace signed in the public square in November 1203 between representatives of both classes. In it, power in Assisi was now entrusted to an uneasy coalition of members of both classes. Hence, the movement towards the full independence of Assisi was temporarily blunted. By November 1210, however, the situation had once again shifted, for this date marks the signing of a new agreement between the two primary classes in Assisi, for the first time referred to as the *maiores* (the greater ones) and the *minores* (the lesser ones) of Assisi: each group pledged loyalty to and co-operation with each other for the sake of 'the glory and prosperity of Assisi'. This charter of independence created the free commune of Assisi and marked the end of internal strife within the town.[3] It was significant for two further reasons. First, members of the class of merchants could now definitively purchase their freedom from the *maiores* for a price. And secondly, citizenship was defined by the amount of wealth that one possessed. One was *maior* or *minor* depending on one's demonstrable wealth; and wealth became the distinguishing criterion for citizenship. Entirely missing from the charter was any mention of approximately three-quarters of the population: the peasant class of workers. Such individuals and their families were, by definition, non-citizens – one might even say non-persons – virtually invisible to the powers that governed Assisi: those whom Francis would soon identify as 'the poor, the weak, the sick, the lepers, those who sit and beg on the side of the road' (RNB, 9, 1–2).

It was into this tumultuous political and socio-economic upheaval that Francesco di Bernardone was born. At the time of the great revolt of 1198 he would have been 17 years of age: certainly conscious of – if not a participant in – those momentous events. He took part in the raid at Collestrada, resulting in his capture and imprisonment for perhaps as much as one year in Perugia (until he could be ransomed by his father). But the isolation and hardship of prison began to temper this impetuous and ambitious young man. Nevertheless, released from captivity he quickly hired himself out as a mercenary on a new military expedition, setting out for Apulia in the company of Walter of Brienne. A day's journey out, however, near Spoleto, something began to disturb his conscience. The official hagiographer of the order, Thomas of Celano, tells us that God appeared to Francis in a dream and asked him, 'Which was it better to serve: the master or the servant?' The next morning Francis abandoned his quest and returned home, much in disgrace but also inwardly in turmoil.

These and other events are the seeds of what can be called the conversion of Francis: the period of time when this young man began to turn his life in a radically different direction, with wholly different values and priorities. This complex and hidden process of inner transformation came to be distilled in his own mind into one key moment: his chance encounter with a leper. This was the moment that prompted a complete reversal of his manner of valuing what was important and righteous and what, by contrast, was either unimportant or sinful. His heart had already been prepared from the time of Collestrada; now this one event came to symbolise the moment when God put him on a completely different path.

The hagiographical accounts tell us that Francis encountered Christ within these lepers. And this is true. But it is also crucial to point out that Francis also encountered and *saw*, perhaps for the first time in his life, suffering human beings, cast aside by the city of his birth and left in such misery and isolation.[4] Through the workings of grace, Francis now came to discover the cardinal insight of his life: that all men and women are brothers and sisters, one to another, created equal in dignity and worth by the same Creator God. This is Francis's discovery of the universal fraternity of all creatures and, most importantly, the sacredness of the human person. Moreover, everything that ruptures the bonds of this sacred fraternity willed by God for human life is what Francis means by 'sin'. And to understand what he means by sin is to grasp what he means when he tells us that from that point forward, he began to 'do penance'. And this sheds light on the content of his penitential preaching in the world.[5]

Historians postulate that this famous encounter might possibly have occurred in the spring of 1206. His way of life began to take concrete shape as he found habitations in remote areas outside Assisi at ramshackle churches like San Damiano and Santa Maria degli Angeli. And yet it was only in early 1208 that Francis began to attract a few companions from his native town. These men – people like Bernard of Quintavalle, Peter Catania and Giles – were drawn to his way of life primarily from the upper and middle classes. Some certainly were intent on becoming downwardly mobile: consciously choosing to live among, as and for the poor and miserable of Assisi. Others, perhaps more simply, saw in this radical way of life a truly Christ-like manner of living. Such men became his followers as well as fellow travellers on the road of this renewed Christian life, taking their message of respect, peace and repentance to others. After some time and with experiences both positive and negative, they began to consciously think out and then put down in writing what God was calling them to be and to do in the world: the general outlines of their *forma vitae* (form of life).

The far-ranging scope of these preaching missions beyond the confines of Assisi and the Spoleto valley is probably what prompted these brothers in the spring of 1209 to seek approval for their way of life from Innocent III in Rome. This event signals a watershed in the history of the Franciscan movement. For not only was their *propositum vitae* (proposal of life) approved by the pope, who also authorised them to spread their message of penance in the form of moral preaching, but their oral approval – since, as itinerant hermits, Rome did not have a specific formulary to offer them – gave them official legitimacy and thereby opened the door for a sudden and more rapid influx of followers increasingly from beyond the Umbrian valley.

What had they taken to Rome for approval which now captivated people beyond Assisi with a more universal, Christian message of renewal so that they, too, would decide to radically alter their way of life and follow the vision of Francis and his brothers? That vision is contained in the Early *Rule* of the Friars Minor. Recent work on this important source suggests that the document is a text which began with a core vision or original statement of intention: the *propositum vitae* presented to Innocent III. Historians hypothesise that this core material was comprised of an introductory statement, much of chapter 1, part of chapter 7 and all of chapter 14. This material closely matches what Francis tells us in his *Testament*: namely, that he composed it 'simply and with few words', using 'words of the holy Gospel . . . and [inserting] a few other things necessary for a holy way of life' (1 Cel., 32).

These three passages present a positive statement of intention announcing the brothers' desire 'to follow the teaching and footprints of our Lord Jesus Christ'. But what, exactly, did this mean in the real world? As the brothers attempted to live out these high ideals, experiencing privation, want and hunger while receiving the mockery and scorn of their fellow citizens, they were forced to define more fully for themselves what this evangelical life actually meant in practice. As a result, the original core material began to grow, develop and expand over time. These amplifications, admonitions and warnings represent discrete layers of material in chapters 7 to 9 that can be detected by careful analysis within the text of the Early *Rule* as we have it today.

The charism of the Franciscan movement – that which uniquely characterises its *forma vitae* and distinguishes it from other groups of similar inspiration – is to be found not simply in its original *propositum* but especially in the second and third layers of the *Rule*. For herein lies the specificity of their particular form of the evangelical life.

The content of these first chapters and their expansions deals primarily with three issues: work, money and alms, and dwellings. For the early brothers who had left behind the security of their families and previous livelihood, finding work of some kind was absolutely essential. They worked first and foremost to sustain themselves. Initially, all work that could be done 'without danger to their souls' was permissible. Many of them often found employment in local *leprosaria* or hospices. And yet, as they soon discovered, not all forms of work were consonant with their new way of life. Any work that involved them once again in the use of money was proscribed (RNB, 7). Nor would they even allow themselves to receive money as remuneration for their work. For money, though an increasingly common means of exchange in the urban centres of Italy, was viewed by the friars as a pernicious instrument used by the rich and powerful to exploit the poor at the workplace as well as in the market place. To use it or receive it was to legitimate it as a proper means of exchange among human beings.[6]

Nor were the friars to even be 'in charge' in those places where they worked and sometimes lived. This prohibition can only be understood in the light of its opposite value. For, while many would gladly serve as administrators within the *leprosaria* or infirmaries, few would choose to place themselves on their knees to bathe and care for the lepers so as to be the face of the compassionate Christ to those cast aside as repugnant or useless. But this was the special calling of these friars.

Nor would they claim any place as their own or defend it against anyone. Rather, they would regard all things and use all things as coming forth from the hand of God, intended for the use of all creatures and to be used on the basis of honest human need. It was left to human beings to determine how best to realise this. This positive ethic of the proper use of creation is the original and essential meaning of poverty according to the early Franciscans.

These radical values were all premised on the lessons learned by Francis in his encounter with lepers. This experience then became the formative bedrock of the early fraternity. Vowing to live beside their unfortunate brothers and sisters, the friars were intent on creating a kind of alternative society, built upon the Christian principles of love, respect and mercy, where no creature of God was to be neglected, exploited or humiliated by the wilful attitudes or actions of others. These unfortunate ones were the true *minores* (the little ones) of their society. And the brothers pledged to live among them not only as fellow *minores*, but also as their brothers. They would, in short, be Friars Minor.

This radical posture then comes to be summarised in the opening lines of the ninth chapter of the Early *Rule*, which serves as a kind of encapsulation of minorite identity. Written to give encouragement to one another, perhaps in time of great difficulty and doubt about their vocation, they urge one another to persevere in the way of life God has called them to live:

> And let all the brothers strive to follow the humility and poverty of our Lord Jesus Christ; and let them remember that we should have nothing else in the whole world except, as the Apostle says, 'having food and sufficient clothing, with these we are content.' [1 Timothy 6: 8]. And let them rejoice when they find themselves among those of vile and despised condition, among the poor, the weak, the sick and lepers and those who beg by the wayside.
>
> (RNB, 9, 1–2)

Their encouragement comes from remembering that the life they have promised to live is the very life Jesus himself had lived. But we now can appreciate that this famous descriptor for the life of Christ is actually much more than nice-sounding spiritual virtues: rather, they are deeply spiritual social postures. For the humility of Jesus is a life lived among the *minores* of society; the poverty of Christ is a life devoted to using creation on the basis of need, according to the intentions of its Creator, while ensuring that others are provided with the necessities of life as well. This is what constitutes the minorite charism.

### THE GROWTH AND DEVELOPMENT OF THE MINORITE MOVEMENT (1210–19)

After the approval of the *propositum vitae* by Innocent III, the friars chose as their base of operations the restored church of Santa Maria degli Angeli. This tiny chapel would serve not only as a place of temporary residence in Assisi, but also as a point of sending forth and return from the preaching missions which the brothers embarked upon.

The legitimacy conferred upon this little group by the approval of their *propositum vitae* by Innocent III brought the minorite vision of Christian life to others who, for a variety of reasons, could not physically join the brothers in this new venture. For in this period one must include the dramatic story of a noblewoman from Assisi, Clare, from the powerful Offreduccio family, who fled her family to live out the *forma vitae* as a *minor*. The preaching of Francis and his friars touched certain people of means such as Giovanni di Vellita and Orlando, count of Chiusi, to use their wealth and possessions in a more just manner, offering La Verna and Greccio for the use of the friars as places of quiet and prayer. Lady Jacopa dei Settesoli of the great Frangipani family of Rome was similarly moved to drop long-standing litigation with the papacy. That their preaching also had profound effects upon the poor is likewise narrated by Thomas of Celano (1 Cel., 58–71).

It was at this time that the preaching of Francis took on a dramatic new focus. During the summer of 1212, shortly after the news of the resounding Christian victory over Muslim forces at Las Navas de Tolosa in southern Spain, Francis and several companions decided to make their way across the Mediterranean to 'preach the Christian faith and penance to the Saracens' in the Holy Land. The formulation by Celano is interesting: their desire was not only to bring the Christian message, but also to bring the message of penance, that is, the core vision of the minorite movement concerning the universal fraternity of all creatures. This desire was thwarted by a violent storm which shipwrecked them off the coast of Dalmatia, forcing them to return to Italy. The following year, Francis attempted again to engage with the Muslim world, this time going west to Spain in the hopes of meeting the miramolin of Morocco. But illness forced him, once again, to return home.

An important event in the life of the fledgeling fraternity occurred at the fourth Lateran Council, which opened on 11 November 1215. Convened by Innocent III, it had three primary aims: the launching of a new crusade to retake the Holy Places in Jerusalem; the eradication of heresy – notably that of the Cathars with their denial of the validity of the Catholic sacraments, especially the Eucharist; and the reform of the Church in its structures and practices and the holiness of its members. There are at least two important achievements of the council which were to have a direct bearing upon the Franciscan movement.

One of the most important decrees issued by the council was canon 13, which ended Innocent III's recent policy of recognising new religious movements by ordering those without approved *Rule* to adopt one or amalgamate to an already existing order. The Franciscan fraternity did not have an officially approved *Rule*; their *propositum* had been orally approved without having received the papal seal. And yet they not only continued to exist after the council, but also did not have to abandon their developing *Rule*. There is, however, little documentary evidence to help us understand how this might have occurred. One can conjecture that it was due in part to the intervention of friendly prelates, most probably Cardinal Hugolino dei Conti di Segni. But the only solid testimony is that the fraternity was approved 'in consistory', that is, outside the council's plenary sessions during one of the curial gatherings (3 soc. 52). Had this not happened, the minorite experiment would have been brought to an abrupt end.

Francis was influenced by some of its reform currents, especially regarding the centrality of the Eucharist and the respect and care that ought to be accorded to its sacramentals.[7] But what is unmistakable is that the third aim of the council had a dramatic impact upon him, for it confirmed the theme of conversion and penance. Indeed, Francis adopts as his own the very symbol used by Innocent to depict all three conciliar aims: the sign of the Tau. This image, drawn from the Book of Ezekiel (9: 4) in the shape of the Hebrew 'X', symbolises the passing-over by the avenging angel of those whose lives had remained faithful to the covenant and who bore the mark of the Tau on the lintels of their houses. In the Book of Revelation (14: 1), this same Hebrew letter 'X' becomes transformed in Greek into a 'T' which the elect bear upon on their foreheads. This evocative symbol now comes to be used by Francis virtually as his own signature, so deeply personal was the conviction that the authentic Christian must live a life renewed by the Gospel values of Jesus Christ, exemplified in his life-giving cross ('T'). However, it is also crucial to point out that Francis never once associated this Tau cross – as did the pope and his council – with the Crusade. Indeed, it was *the* sign of the fifth Crusade placed upon the crusaders whose physical passing-over was believed to be blessed by God. Francis's total silence on the matter is striking; he could not agree.[8]

After the conclusion of the Lateran Council, the early Franciscan fraternity attempted – in accordance with canon 12 – to initiate more formal gatherings for its members in the form of an annual chapter. But with the continued growth in the numbers of men coming from all parts of Italy and with the ever-deepening conviction of the universal importance of the minorite vision of penance and poverty, Francis and his brothers came to believe that the time had come to take that message beyond Italy. The chapter of 1217 thus marks a critical turning-point in the life of the early community. Missions were sent to France, Spain, Germany and the Holy Land, and they were, for the most part, ill-prepared. The friars who were sent to Germany, without benefit of the language and ignorant of conditions north of the Alps, found themselves harassed and brutalised as heretics, beating a quick retreat home.[9] Of Elias of Cortona's mission to the Levant, we know little. Francis himself set out 'for France' but was impeded in Florence by Cardinal Hugolino from going any further, lest his fraternity be left without a shepherd and needing guidance in times of development. The French mission may have resumed the following year under the direction of Brother Pacifico, who led the group to Saint-Denis, on the outskirts of Paris.

In addition to the extension of the Franciscan mission as a result of this chapter, a second critical transition took place. For the sending of missions to these far-flung places obliged the friars to ensure that someone serve as organiser of the mission and spiritual leader of the group. The chapter, for the first time, was forced to create organisational structures of authority within the fraternity. These structures took the form of delineating various zones of action for these missions called 'provinces' and of designating certain individuals to serve as leaders of these roving bands of friars. This momentous change is captured in three chapters which were hammered out and eventually added to the text of the Early *Rule*: chapters 4 to 6.[10]

These chapters say very little about what these new leaders were to actually do. Their roles were twofold: provide the friars with a place to stay and occasionally visit them to encourage them and watch over their spiritual lives. The content of this Franciscan reflection on authority is more concerned with how to exercise authority among the friars. This is reflected in the very title which Francis gave to these new figures of authority in the fraternity. Drawing on two words (Matthew 20: 26–7), these friars are to be 'the ministers and servants':

> Likewise, let all the brothers not have power or domination in this, especially among themselves. For just as the Lord says in the Gospel: 'The leaders of the people lord it over them and the great ones make their authority felt over them; it will not be thus among' the brothers. For whoever wishes to be the greater let him become their 'minister' and 'servant'. And let the one who is the greater among them become like the lesser.
>
> (RNB, 5)

Such a passage reflects the keen awareness which the friars had of the manner in which power was often used and the deleterious effects such exercise had especially upon the weakest and most vulnerable in society. That knowledge would be used to good effect within the fraternity now that they were being forced by circumstances to create their own structures of authority among themselves. The remedy for the tendency to dominate is to orientate the use of power towards service: the washing of feet, especially of those who have sinned or are having difficulty remaining faithful to the life they promised to live. Hence, each minister is a guardian whose special charge was to watch over and guard his brother from falling away. These passages represent some of the most eloquent passages in the early Franciscan corpus.

## THE FLOWERING AND FRACTURING OF THE FRANCISCAN VISION (1219–21)

Two years later, the friars gathered once again in chapter in Assisi. The chapter of 1219 had similar, if not even more ambitious, intentions, for the primary achievement of this gathering was not only the sending-out of new missions to Hungary and southern France, it also set in motion a three-pronged effort to engage the Muslim world. Five brothers were sent to Coimbra for a missionary push into Muslim Seville, an expedition that would eventually take them to Morocco. Brother Giles was sent to Tunisia. And Francis himself was determined to go to the Holy Land and Egypt.

Some historians theorise, moreover, that Francis may have attempted to explain to the friars his rationale for going since it could lead to his death among the Muslims in the East. The trace of such a statement of intention – what David Flood calls 'the *Testament* of 1219' – may be found today embedded in the RNB, in the first four verses of chapter 22. The message to the friars was this: those who the Church and world claim are our enemies are, in fact, Francis claims, our friends. But Francis is not speaking about the sentiment of friendship; rather, the one who is deemed the enemy is, in fact, a brother or sister. And Francis desired to go and live out this vision among the Muslims, even if this evangelical witness might cost him his life. And if it did, eternal life would be his, since he would have been utterly faithful. His dramatic encounter with Sultan al-Malik-al-Kâmil is analysed by Steven J. McMichael in Chapter 8 below.

Once Francis and Illuminato had returned to Acre, they were presented with alarming news about recent events in Italy.[11] The two vicars he had left in temporary charge of the fraternity, Gregory of Naples and Matthew of Narni, had taken it upon themselves to change the fasting practices of the friars to be more in line with 'real' religious. Philip the Tall, Francis's delegate to provide for the needs of the Clares, was forced to seek letters of protection from the papacy to prevent unspecified interference in their lives. John Capella was rumoured to be starting a separate order (or perhaps just a confraternity of penitents?) comprised of the lepers of Assisi. There was considerable concern about the indiscriminate acceptance of untested candidates into this fraternity of itinerant preachers. Francis returned home with his brothers to confront and resolve these new problems.

By mid September he had made his way from Venice down to Viterbo, where the curia was then staying. After what must have been serious consultations, Honorius III issued the bull *Cum secundum consilium*, mandating a year of probation for all future aspirants to the fraternity. For it was the opinion of a growing number of ecclesiastics that the extraordinary freedom accorded to this supra-diocesan order of penitential preachers required more careful scrutiny and discipline. Faced with such criticism, Francis relented. It may also have been at this time that Francis was asked to receive the diaconate to help bring greater legitimacy to his authority as leader of the growing and diversifying community.[12]

Whatever the original purpose of calling an emergency gathering of the friars in Assisi at a time which would normally have been reserved for a local provincial chapter, the result was that, by its conclusion, Francis had resigned his position as 'minister and servant', turning over the reins of functional leadership to Peter Catania. Why would Francis have resigned at such a critical moment in the order's history, when it needed his leadership most? The posthumous sources give two reasons. Celano claims that he resigned due to illness. He had indeed returned from the East with malaria and other related ailments which would progressively worsen and lead to his death in 1226 (2 Cel., 143). The Companions tradition (CA, 11) claims that, while using illness as the ostensible reason for stepping aside, Francis had become profoundly disenchanted with the 'deviations' introduced by those friars who, having only recently entered the community, were unfamiliar with the social dynamics of the foundational period and who were attempting to steer it in the direction of more traditional forms of religious life. This conflict of visions between the original *forma vitae* and a form of life more aligned with apostolically inclined monastic communities erupted at this chapter. The famous account (CA, 18) of the confrontation between Francis, Hugolino and the clerics probably occurred here. Indeed, Jordan of Giano tells us that Francis preached to the friars on the text of Psalm 143 [144], using its opening line as his theme: 'Blessed be the Lord, my God, who trains my hands for battle, my fingers for war.' The Psalm goes on to warn of those 'alien sons' who 'swear false promises'. Stunned by the clashing visions contending within the fraternity and overwhelmed by what he might have to do to bring the order back to its original way of life, Francis chose instead to resign as minister: perhaps the most bitter moment of his life and one which took him years to come to terms with (2 Cel., 158).

Francis still attempted to serve as a formative influence in the lives of the friars: offering himself as an exemplar of how to remain faithful to the *forma vitae* while beginning to write to the friars and others about the fundamentals of the minorite charism and its concrete ramifications for a renewed Christian life. His first effort was the *Letter to the Faithful* in its long version: a kind of *summa* of the call to penance sent to clergy, religious and laity, indeed 'everyone in the whole world'. A distilled version of this famous letter was crafted a little later and sent specifically to those penitents now coalescing into urban confraternities desiring to live the Christian life in accord with minorite values. For, similar to what he had done with the Clares in 1219, Hugolino had drawn up for them in 1221 a generic *Rule* of life which had no obvious connection to the Franciscan life. This short version of a growing Third Order was Francis's minorite word to the penitents.[13]

## THE LAST YEARS AND FINAL ACTIVITIES OF FRANCIS OF ASSISI (1221–6)

Peter Catania was dead within six months of taking office. The chapter of 1221 replaced him with Elias of Cortona and launched a vigorous new mission to Germany. Francis now turned his attention to another pressing matter. The dreadful experiences recounted by Jordan of the missions in Germany (1217) and Hungary (1219) were largely exacerbated by the fact that the friars had no officially approved *Rule* to show authorities proving their legitimacy and orthodoxy. The papal bulls issued on their behalf in 1219 and 1220, while helpful, were apparently insufficient. More important, from the perspective of the curia, this non-approved *Rule* had ballooned from a general statement of intention in 1209 to a rambling collection of admonitions, exhortations, legislative rulings, prayers and an overabundance of scriptural quotations by 1221. What was needed was a streamlined, more juridically precise *Rule* which would merit official papal approval. Francis spent the better part of two years working with Hugolino and other curial officials to distil the essence of the *forma vitae* into something more acceptable to Rome without violating the intentions of the Early *Rule*. The result was an entirely new *Rule* in the Roman Church.

With his exhausting – and perhaps frustrating – work on the *Rule* now complete and with its official promulgation in the bull, Francis began to increasingly withdraw into solitary places in the company of a few trusted companions in the Spoleto and Rieti valleys. These are the companions of later lore who cared for and prayed with him during his final painful years. One of the most famous episodes during this time was his memorable celebration of Christmas Eve at the hermitage in Greccio in which he attempted to bring to life, visually and palpably, the very concrete conditions of poverty and humility experienced by Jesus of Nazareth. Other than the experience among lepers, it represents the quintessential realisation of Francis's deeply incarnational spirituality and displays his unique genius for conveying the realities of faith to popular, uneducated audiences.

By the summer of 1224, storm clouds were gathering in Europe once again as a new military campaign was being organised against al-Malik-al-Kâmil in Egypt by Cardinal Pelagius with the support of Honorius III and now with the mighty forces of the Holy Roman Emperor, Frederick II. Scheduled to be launched the following April, the venture portended further bloodshed in the Holy Land. Deeply distressed at this prospect and dismayed over recent developments within the order, Francis, accompanied by a group of chosen companions, decided to make his way to La Verna to make a 'Lent of St Michael': a forty-day fast from the feast of the Assumption (15 August) until 29 September. 'On or around the feast of the Exaltation of the Cross' (14 September), Francis experienced a kind of mystical transport, the content and meaning of which can only be conjectured. At the conclusion of this profound mystical experience, he was bearing what has come to be called the stigmata: marks resembling the five wounds of Christ, in his hands, feet and side. Much has been written about this crucial moment in the life of Francis; numerous artists have attempted to depict the language used by his biographers to describe this ineffable experience. So profound was his meditation upon the mystery of the cross of Christ that he became the object of his prayer: Christ Crucified.[14]

In the immediate aftermath, he wrote on a small piece of parchment a prayer in thanksgiving to God for the pain and consolation which had been given to him in this revelatory experience. These are the *Praises of God*: a prayer which some authors believe can be likened to his own version of the *Ninety-Nine Beautiful Names of Allah*. He was praying in an Islamic mode. This prayer was written on the recto side of the famous *chartula*, later given to Brother Leo. According to this brother, Francis then turned the *chartula* over and, on its verso side, inscribed the Aaronic blessing from the Book of Numbers, a Tau cross, and a head with several oddly placed words under and through the shaft of the Tau. Recent scholarly opinion has grappled with the configuration and meaning of these elements. The key to the ensemble seems to be the enigmatic head. According to some, the head is actually a representation of the sultan, al-Malik-al-Kâmil, and the prayer of protection (Numbers 6: 24–7) is for the well-being of his beloved brother in Egypt. But more: Francis was also praying for the sultan's conversion, that he confess the cross, before it was too late and he would be lost in death for all eternity. Finally, Francis would have appended a clever little blessing for Leo himself who, after these events, had come to his father troubled in spirit. If accurate, the events on La Verna bring to its most profound intensification the minorite vision which had first been revealed to him and which he had lived out throughout the course of his life: namely, that all men and women are creatures of God, come from the same hand of a good and loving Creator, brothers and sisters one to another, and are on a journey back into the same God, and that each has a God-given responsibility to help the other along the way.[15]

The last days of Francis were difficult ones filled with physical pain and suffering. Despite this, he managed to compose one of his most exalted writings: the *Canticle of the Creatures*, a mystical hymn of praise written out of the depths of his own suffering to a gracious God who is praised through each creature living out its created purpose. The goal of all life was the praise of God in word and deed. Then, after first refusing but later accepting unsuccessful treatment for his eye ailment, he returned to Assisi and the Porziuncula, where his journey had first begun. He managed to compose several things for Clare and her sisters, including a *Last Will and Testament* in which he explicitly defined their pursuit of evangelical perfection as 'the most holy life and poverty of our Lord Jesus Christ'. And, after dictating a final testament and admonition to his brothers to remain steadfast to the *forma vitae* which God had revealed to him and which he had handed on to them from the earliest time – even when told differently by others both inside and outside the order – Francis surrendered his spirit back to God from whom he had come forth and to whom he now returned to praise for ever.

## CONCLUSION

The Gospel of Mark opens with the declamatory words: 'Here begins the Gospel of Jesus the Christ, son of God.' The formulation was meant to announce that the life and death of Jesus of Nazareth only represents the beginning of the good news of the revelation of God in Him. The Gospel continues in the life of His disciples striving to maintain fidelity to his words and teaching. Similarly, the charism of Francis and his brothers would continue in the life of the Franciscan family.[16] However, the understanding of that charism, at least since the chapter of 1220, was no longer uniform among the friars. Already by the general chapter of 1230, significant controversies were beginning to arise over the precise understanding of the wording used in the definitive *Rule* and the intention of Francis. Indeed, the seeds of the future controversies over the observance of evangelical poverty were already sown in this famous chapter. Franciscan history from this point forward will for ever be marked by the unease and co-existence of these two, quite different, forms of Franciscan life and work: each challenging the other to remain faithful to the founding charism or to be open to the needs of the Church at any given time. For both aspects were, in some way, already present in the person of Francis.

### Notes

1   D. Flood and T. Matura, *The Birth of a Movement: A Study of the First Rule of St Francis*, trans. P. Lachance and P. Schwartz (Chicago, 1975).
2   P. V. Riley, 'Francis' Assisi: Its Political and Social History, 1175–1225', *Franciscan Studies*, 34 (1974), 393–424.
3   L. A. Bartoli, 'La realtà sociale assisiana e il patto del 1210', *Assisi al tempo di san Francesco*, Società internazionale di studi francescani, 6 (Assisi, 1978), 271–336; Flood and Matura, *Birth of a Movement*.
4   R. Manselli, 'San Francesco dal dolore degli uomini al Cristo crocifisso', *Analecta T.O.R.*, 16 (1983), 191–210.
5   M. F. Cusato, 'To Do Penance/*Facere Penitentiam*', in Cusato, *The Early Franciscan Movement (1205–1239): History, Sources, and Hermeneutics*, Saggi, 14 (Spoleto, 2009) (orig. publ. in *The Cord*, 57.1 (2007), 3–24); G. Miccoli, 'The Christian Proposal of Francis of Assisi: A Problem of Interpretation', *Greyfriars Review*, 3.2 (1989), 127–72 (orig. publ. as 'La proposta cristiana di Francesco di Assisi', *Studi medievali*, 3rd series, 24 (1983), 17–83).
6   M. F. Cusato, 'The Early Franciscans and the Use of Money', in D. Mitchell (ed.), *Poverty and Prosperity: Franciscans and the Use of Money, Spirit and Life*, 14 (St Bonaventure, New York, forthcoming).

7   This is evident most particularly in the letters written by Francis after his return from the Holy Land (1220).

8   M. F. Cusato, 'The Tau', in Cusato, *Early Franciscan Movement*, pp. 69–80 (orig. publ, in *The Cord*, 57.3 (2007), 287–301).

9   On this mission see Jordan of Giano, c. 5. The chronology of the missions reported by Jordan in these chapters needs to be treated with great caution.

10  M. F. Cusato, 'Guardians and the Use of Power in the Early Franciscan Movement', in Cusato, *Early Franciscan Movement*, pp. 249–81.

11  The issues are enumerated in Jordan of Giano, cc. 11–13.

12  M. F. Cusato, 'Francis of Assisi, Deacon? An Examination of the Claims of the Earliest Franciscan Sources 1229–1235', in Cusato and G. Geltner (eds.), *Defenders and Critics of Franciscan Life: Essays in Honor of John V. Fleming*, The Medieval Franciscans, 6 (Leiden, 2009), pp. 9–39.

13  M. F. Cusato, 'The Letters to the Faithful', in Cusato, *Early Franciscan Movement*, pp. 153–207 (to be published in *Essays on the Early Franciscan Sources*, vol. 1, ed. M. Blastic, J. Hammond and W. Hellmann (St Bonaventure, forthcoming).

14  M. F. Cusato, 'Of Snakes and Angels: The Mystical Experience behind the Stigmatization Narrative of 1 Celano', in Cusato, *Early Franciscan Movement*, pp. 209–48 (orig. publ. in *The Stigmata of Francis of Assisi: New Studies, New Perspectives* (St Bonaventure, 2006), pp. 29–74).

15  Ibid.

16  Cf. 1 Cel. 37.

## 2 The writings of Francis

MICHAEL J. P. ROBSON

Francis of Assisi expounded the mysteries of the Gospel in an attractive and persuasive manner. A good description of him was given by Thomas, archdeacon of Split, who was present at a sermon which Francis preached in the piazza at Bologna on 15 August 1222. His clothing and personal appearance were contrasted with the vigour and power of his words, which restored harmony and peace to a troubled and divided city.[1] Dr Rosalind Brooke describes Francis as 'a subtle, self-conscious, imaginative teacher' who communicated the Gospel with a telling clarity.[2] Words, symbols and gestures were deftly used to convey the teaching of Jesus Christ. Thomas of Celano remarks that Francis made a tongue of his whole body in the service of Christianity (1 Cel., 97). Francis's collection of letters is minuscule in comparison with the voluminous correspondence of Anselm of Canterbury (c.1033–1109), Bernard at Clairvaux (1090–1153) and Peter the Venerable (1092–1156).[3] Apart from the *Rule*, his writings take the form of exhortations to observe the Gospel as fully as possible, while some letters deal with specific matters, such as the implementation of Honorius III's instruction *Sane cum olim* on 22 November 1219. There are two autographed texts: first, the letter to Brother Leo and secondly, the praises of God and a blessing upon the same friar.[4] Copies of Francis's writings were treasured and distributed with his blessing. They circulated during his lifetime and not long after his death,[5] forming the basis for the early manuscript tradition and the critical edition of his works.[6] Francis's biographers quote the canon of his writing and reproduce summaries of his teaching or comments. The following four themes – his decisive encounter with the leper, his new life according to the Gospel, the formation of a family of penitents within the Church and moves towards a universal fraternity – offer a sample of the richness of his thought.

## FRANCIS AND THE LEPER

The *Testament* pinpoints the pivotal moment of his conversion, narrating the circumstances of his fuller response to the Gospel. Francis was riding in the plain below Assisi when he unexpectedly encountered a leper, the symbol of horror and potential contagion. His customary instinct was to recoil in dread and take to his heels. At this telling moment his usual responses were dulled, and a new and mysterious energy was at work. He dismounted from his horse and kissed the leper, a spontaneous and generous gesture which showed that his earlier sense of revulsion was beginning to yield to a new spiritual sensitivity. For the first time he saw the leper as a fellow human being, wracked with pain and suffering. Looking beyond his fears, he saw a man for whom Jesus had laid down his life, a brother who had been denied the courtesy owed to him. This meeting probably occurred in the vicinity of the *lazaretto* of San Rufino dell'Arce. Francis's new self-mastery was demonstrated in his decision to work among the lepers. Now, guided by grace, he bathed and tended the wounds of these men and women who had been rejected and excluded from Assisi. Henceforth, lepers were addressed as Christians to remind Francis of their dignity and his earlier fallibility.

The encounter showed that Francis's values and assumptions were deeply flawed. It was a corrective and healing moment which exposed serious *lacunae* in his grasp of the teaching of Jesus. A mixture of fear and prejudice had distorted his perception of the world. Although he had been reared in a society deeply proud of its Christian identity and the heroism of its martyred bishops, it became painfully clear to him that the teaching of Jesus had not been applied to the whole of his life. His earlier experience was now regarded as a period in which his ear had not been finely attuned to the Scriptures. His conduct had to be changed at its deepest level and to be brought into closer conformity with the Gospel through penance. His defective dispositions reflected his tainted nature, which had blinded him to his responsibilities towards the suffering and socially disadvantaged. His conversion starts with the divine initiative; the first two sentences of the *Testament* begin with the word 'Lord'.

The change of perception is articulated in such phrases as 'when I was in sin' to distinguish events prior to Francis's conversion. There was a stark contrast between the two phases of his life: the bitterness of his earlier view of lepers and the resultant sweetness of mind and body wrought by grace. The first position is mapped out in the earlier recension of his *Letter to the Faithful*, where Francis states that people can be deceived into finding pleasure in sin and experiencing a corresponding bitterness in serving God.[7] Hitherto, Francis had shared the assumptions of his fellow citizens by ostracising lepers. Leprosy segregated its victims from their neighbours in the cities of western Europe and forced them to live on the fringes of society. By responding to grace and the teaching of the Scriptures, Francis acknowledged that the cares and worries of life were capable of distracting people from the letter and the spirit of the Gospel, as he makes clear in his *Letter to the Rectors*. Like Winston Smith in *Nineteen Eighty-Four*, Francis discovered that in moments of crisis people have to fight against their bodies rather than external enemies.[8] Francis describes the forces of disorder as a domestic enemy, and he states that fasting and prayer were allies in the purification of the mind, as he affirms at the beginning of chapter 3 of the earlier *Rule*.

The summary report of the moment of revelation for Francis was followed by a statement that afterwards he did not wait long before 'leaving the world'. This phrase denotes swapping secular society and its values for the security of the cloister, where he would be guided by his divine master. His decision, however, found a rather different focus from that of Matilda, daughter of Fulk of Anjou and wife of William, son of Henry I of England. She abandoned her former life and became a nun of Fontrevault on the advice of Geoffrey, bishop of Chartres, in 1122.[9] In an earlier age Francis may have abandoned Assisi and betaken himself to a distant cloister. Now he was inching his way towards a new vocation, one which owed much to the perennial principles of monasticism. New vistas were gradually being opened to him. The term 'leaving the world' does not denote Francis's root-and-branch rejection of Assisi, a city which he loved greatly and to which he returned throughout his life. A man who was so sensitive towards the goodness of the Creator could not spurn the bounty of creation. Instead, this customary phraseology heralded a new and broader meaning: he had no more turned his back on secular society than the ailing Samuel Pepys who, in a letter of 1697, commented that 'the world and I have been strangers a great while'.[10] The term 'flight from the world' was not to be understood solely as a physical retreat from society or to the desert or a separation from one's homeland. It indicated that the conventions of medieval society would henceforth be subordinated to the teaching of Jesus (Acts 5: 29). Bishop Moorman reflects that Francis was not called to flee society, 'but to give himself to the world'.[11] This was mirrored in his later return to Assisi as a penitential figure, who would challenge his former neighbours to live the Gospel in a more literal manner. Francis was now starting to respond to the call to penance (*metánoia*) issued by Jesus at the beginning of his public ministry (Mark 1: 15). His first task was to divest himself of his possessions and his social status. He would be identified with those on the margins of society. The *Letter to the Faithful* introduces the complementary notion of the religious having renounced the world.[12]

Francis's retreat from Assisi was accomplished by his emancipation from parental expectations and the rejection of his former career as a merchant. The obedience which he had hitherto owed to his father was transferred to the Word of God. Urban life was swapped for a rural retreat, where he reflected upon his life, its priorities and its uncertainties. His fine and expensive wardrobe was swapped for the garb of a penitent, and the young man who had led the revels in Assisi now gave himself to asceticism and prolonged prayer. Lepers bestowed a new focus and direction to his life and he was determined to distance himself from the values which had precipitated this crisis in his life. During this transitional phase he lived as an oblate or hermit at San Damiano, where he obeyed the instruction from the Crucified Christ to repair the dilapidated church. A keen awareness that his earlier instincts had misguided him fuelled the penitential life which Francis adopted; the former soldier knew that he had to live in a disciplined manner. Penance, with its process of self-emptying in imitation of Jesus, permitted him to combat the results of original and actual sins. This is made explicit in the tenth Admonition, where a blessing is pronounced upon the religious who subjugates the enemy which leads him into sin. G.K. Chesterton maintains that 'any Catholic society must have an atmosphere of penance'.[13] The call to undertake penance was to become a constant feature of the friars' preaching, on the insistence of Francis. The friars were perceived as men devoted to the life of penance and were described as penitents from Assisi (AP, 19c). The *Letter to the Faithful* contrasts those who reject the Gospel with those who embark upon a penitential lifestyle.[14] Francis's earlier life had been more in tune with the former, who were enslaved by secular society and the desires of their lower nature, subjecting themselves to the power of the devil, whose deeds they performed. The world, the flesh and the devil were identified as the deceitful enemies of humanity and the sources of temptation.

## A LIFE ACCORDING TO THE GOSPEL

Francis's retreat from Assisi was accompanied by a new commitment to the Gospel. A further clarification in the understanding of his vocation came when he attended Mass on the feast of an apostle in the church of Santa Maria degli Angeli. There he heard the account of the missionaries dispatched by Jesus (Matthew 10: 9–10). Although he had previously heard that passage, on this occasion he instantly recognised its application to his life. From that moment he was wedded to a literal observance of the Gospel, even down to the detail of discarding his shoes and dressing as an apostle. His biographer proclaims that Francis was a man who was not deaf to the Gospel (1 Cel., 22). From that moment Francis held the book of the Gospel in the greatest reverence. The words to the rich young man intent on perfection (Matthew 19: 16–22) have challenged generations of Christians for two *millennia*. One of the best-known responses is that of St Antony (251–356), the father of western monasticism, who immediately abandoned society and embraced the ascetical life.[15] Francis was no exception, because this was the first of the passages to be revealed to him and Bernard of Quintavalle when they went to San Nicolò in search of divine guidance for their future. The New Testament was opened thrice at random and the texts on which their eyes fell formed the foundation of their fraternity. Francis had already renounced his paternal inheritance in the presence of his father and the bishop of Assisi. Now Bernard divested himself of his possessions in the piazza di San Giorgio and in the process laid the seeds for the vocation of Sylvester, an elderly secular priest from the city. Shortly afterwards Giles, another man of Assisi, did the same, reviving images from the life of the apostolic community in Jerusalem (Acts 4: 32–7). The dramatic effect of these two scenes undoubtedly strengthened Francis's desire to re-enact the Gospel and to bring it to life by word and gesture.

Fidelity to the Gospel in everything prompted Francis to meditate upon the circumstances of Jesus's life. The statement that Jesus had nowhere to lay his head (Matthew 8: 20) was contrasted with the comfort, affluence and excess of Francis's early years. This factor undoubtedly weighed heavily with the men who followed him: they were encouraged to lay aside the wealth of the Umbrian cities and to live according to Jesus's teaching. The conviction that Jesus had accepted a life of penury for the salvation of the human race reinforced Francis's earlier act of renunciation. He told Clare di Favarone di Offreduccio that he wanted to imitate the poverty of Jesus until the end of his life. Accordingly, he eschewed any form of ownership, which he regarded as a compromise with his earlier renunciation. This explains the strength of his response when he heard friars talking in proprietary terms about Rivo Torto, a hovel outside Assisi, and Bologna.

Contemporaries were struck by Francis's imitation of the poor and naked Jesus and commented on the friars' hardship and voluntary poverty. The monastic chronicler of St Martin of Tours comments that the friars renounced everything and walked in the manner of the apostles, that is, in their bare feet.[16] Friars were instructed to be poor in profession and deed; their patched tunics mirrored their commitment to live in poverty, which was not to be tempered by the customary forms of support for religious through estates, endowments and rents. They chose to live in poverty for the kingdom of heaven. The prohibition on seeking privileges from the papal court suggests that Francis was keenly conscious of the disputes and causes of scandal besetting religious houses in the later twelfth century. As poor disciples of Jesus who died nakedly on the cross, they were to have no truck with privileges, which were primarily beneficial to the wealthy. Jacques de Vitry commented in July 1216 that the friars revived the life of the apostolic community.[17] Francis's concentration on the poverty experienced by Jesus was perceived as recovering a long-lost element in the Christian lexicon; he looked upon poverty as especially dear to Jesus. Although both the *Rule* of Columbanus (c.543–615)[18] and the sermons of Bernard of Clairvaux refer to voluntary poverty,[19] some artistic licence was enjoyed by Dante Alighieri in his observation that *il poverello* espoused Lady Poverty who had been bereft of her first husband, despised and obscure for 1,100 years and more.[20] The theme of the mystical marriage was beautifully depicted above the high altar in the basilica di San Francesco, Assisi, and described in detail by Giorgio Vasari.[21]

Frequent reflection on the life of Jesus and its implications nurtured Francis's piety. This went hand-in-hand with his spiritual development and his desire to imitate Jesus as closely as possible. Like St Paul, he came to see voluntary poverty as the means of self-emptying on Jesus's part for the redemption of humanity (Philippians 2: 6–11). What his divine master had accomplished became the norm for Francis, who not only imitated his poverty, but also entered into the mystery of the redemptive process. A joyful poverty disarmed the vices of cupidity and avarice, as the penultimate Admonition teaches. There are echoes of 2 Corinthians 8: 9 in the *Letter to the Faithful* where Francis explains that Jesus was rich beyond measure but chose to live in poverty with his mother. The centrality of this teaching is reflected in the *Rule*, whose opening words ordain that the friars should be poor in material terms. Friars were, however, instructed to pass beyond the letter of the dominical injunction to the surrender of their lives, holding nothing back for themselves. The term 'without anything of their own' also appears in the eleventh Admonition to denote a wider poverty and self-emptying, such as that explained in the fourteenth Admonition and based on Matthew 5: 3. Poverty of spirit enabled the friars to walk in the footsteps of their divine teacher and it addressed one of the vices operating within the heart, the instinct to acquire, to possess and to own in an illusory pursuit of security. Despite Francis's renunciation of his material goods, he counselled his friars not to despise those who dressed in fine clothes and enjoyed the best refreshments. The friars' critical faculties should be trained upon themselves rather than their neighbours. Francis maintained close contacts with a number of men and women who enjoyed wealth and prestige. His meal in the home of the knight of Celano has been immortalisd as the sixteenth scene in the cycle of frescoes in the basilica di San Francesco.

A former merchant, Francis came to share contemporary suspicions about the probity of his former profession.[22] Experience taught him that money and possessions were potentially divisive forces, erecting and perpetuating barriers between people and constructing artificial partitions within society. At an early stage in the life of the fraternity Guido I, bishop of Assisi, had urged Francis to moderate his absolute reliance upon divine providence and to accept some possessions as a form of security. Francis's masterly riposte that, if he had possessions, he would need arms to protect them (3 Soc., 35) illustrates his perspicacity in the matter of ownership. Francis was sufficiently familiar with the ways and conventions of the market place to conjure up an uncomfortable death-bed scene in the *Letter to the Faithful*, where the wife and children of the dying man implored him to put his affairs in order. When a priest was summoned to grant absolution, a dialogue ensued between the confessor and the would-be penitent. The dying man sought forgiveness, but the stumbling-block was the necessary reparation for his sins. When urged to make satisfaction, his reply was that it was too late because he had already bequeathed his property to his relations. Shortly afterwards he went to his death impenitent, surrendering his soul to the devil, while his relatives grumbled that they should have received more from him.[23] This sketch charts the profound change in Francis's outlook and his awareness that avarice was capable of reasserting itself during the last moments of life to condemn the dying man; this vice prevailed over the fear of divine judgement, even in the last moments of life. Elsewhere Francis laments the fate of those who die impenitent, who are the children of the devil (1 John 3: 10). The former merchant's life was increasingly shaped by Jesus's teaching, which made him a herald of penance.

## A FAMILY OF PENITENTS WITHIN THE CHURCH

Francis's new discipline of life and evangelical fervour attracted the attention of his neighbours. His *Testament* speaks of God giving him some brothers, and he lays down procedures for those divinely inspired to seek admission to the fraternity (RNB, 2). The lives of these penitents were shaped by an imitation of the poor and humble Jesus, and they became known as Friars Minor. While Francis and his first companions continued to live outside the walls of Assisi, deriving their inspiration from the teaching of Jesus, their mandate to communicate the Gospel by word and example took them back to the city. Their first communal base was at Rivo Torto; Francis's biographers celebrate the poverty and cramped conditions of the site. The structures of a religious community are not to be sought in the life of this fledgeling group; new members were accepted on condition that they renounced their possessions and gave the proceeds to the poor. The friars were not bound to the perpetual stability in a religious house. They had no homes, possessions or cloisters, they were exhorted to live as pilgrims. Francis was the teacher and animator of this small fraternity living in penitence and charity, although he had no initial blueprint for his followers, except the imperative of living according to the Gospel. He was forging a new path which differed markedly from the traditional forms of religious life.

This novel community was perceived as a family, as chapter 6 of the *Rule* explains. Friars were to live as members of one family, and the ministers were to be gentle and compassionate, bearing in mind the divine example of serving rather than being served (Matthew 20: 28). They were required to relate to the ministers as masters to a servant. Francis frequently signs himself as the servant of all. As the community grew, its leaders were styled ministers after Jesus's example rather than the monastic officials or superiors who administered vast estates and wielded authority for many years or, in some cases, for life. The minister's tenure of office was temporary and was not to be sought or coveted. Maternal imagery was invoked in the *Rule for Hermitages*. The three or four friars living there should be divided into mothers and sons, with the former following the example of Martha and the latter Mary. The *Testament* insists that Francis did not have any mentors to show him what to do; he was acting on what God had revealed to him. Francis's statement does not preclude his seeking advice from men more familiar with the constitution of a healthy religious community. He was already on good terms with some monks, who were well placed to proffer advice about the organisation of a community.

Intermittently he also enlisted the counsel of Bishop Guido I and worked with Cardinal Hugolino on the compilation of the *Rule* and other policies.

The friars were predominantly laymen who were authorised to summon people to penance. Borrowing the language from Cistercian literature, Thomas of Celano describes the first school of the friars who were groomed by Francis in accordance with his insights. His task was to shape the minds of men who shared his ideals. By turning towards the Gospel the new recruits would undergo a period of re-orientation; they had to be weaned from secular values. A primitive version of the *Admonitions* helped to inculcate the new outlook and took them to labour among those on the margins of society. Like many religious reformers of the Middle Ages, Francis engaged in manual work, taking food as payment, as he recalled in his *Testament*. The acceptance of coins was firmly proscribed and friars were strictly forbidden to touch money, even for an ostensibly good cause.

Francis kept his religious family within the structures of the Catholic Church and he co-operated fully with the pope, the local bishop and the parish priest. Despite the clerical failings with which he was so well acquainted, his ecclesiological conservatism distanced him from some of the twelfth-century reformers who found themselves at odds with the episcopate. His resolve to co-operate with the hierarchy is reflected in his eucharistic teaching which was conditioned by the reforming decrees of the fourth Lateran Council.[24] Professor David Knowles observes that the religious life from its inception never saw itself as independent of ecclesiastical authority, not even the monastic movement in Egypt and other comparable groups which withdrew from urban society.[25] When the number of friars had reached the biblical figure of twelve, Francis decided to seek papal blessing for his form of life, which consisted of a series of excerpts from the Gospel. Francis's early biographies cast Bishop Guido I in a peripheral role, reporting that he *chanced* to be in Rome at the same time as the friars. Francis would not have been received by Cardinal John of St Paul and Innocent III without the glowing endorsement of the local bishop. Guido's guarantee gained Francis and his companions a hearing inside the papal court and paved the way for approval by the pope, who authorised them to preach penance and instructed them to return when their numbers had increased.[26] Guido opened the pulpits of Assisi's churches to Francis, who preached there as a deacon, beginning in the small church of San Giorgio and then San Rufino, where the young Clare was starting to be fascinated by his stirring message of renewal.

The reverential attitude shown towards those who exercised spiritual authority was grounded in Francis's devotion towards the patron
saints of Assisi and Rome, whose tombs he frequented. The relationship between the patron saint of a diocese or an abbey is articulated in
St Anselm's prayer, where the patron saint emerges as the source of
spiritual authority, which is merely exercised in his name by his vicar,
the incumbent prelate.[27] Accordingly, the bishops of Assisi and Rome
signed themselves as the vicars of San Rufino and the prince of the
apostles. While invoking the authority of the prince of the apostles,
Innocent III preferred the loftier title, the vicar of Jesus.[28] Thus, dis-
obedience towards the vicar brought a slight upon the patron saint.
This is a key assumption in all of Francis's dealings with the bishops
of Assisi and Rome. A profound respect for the episcopal office was a
salient feature of his ecclesiology, and he regarded papal approval of his
fraternity as a mark of divine approbation; the *Testament* states that
the pope confirmed the short *Rule* of the fraternity. The *Rule* enjoins
friars to obey the pope and all his canonically elected successors, and
the office of cardinal protector bound the friars to the Roman curia. Leo,
Rufino and Angelo relate that one reason for Francis's respect for the
episcopal office was the conviction that God had spoken to him
through the bishop of Assisi during the process of his conversion.

Priests had played a positive role in Francis's conversion and in
the development of his vocation. The basis of this respect was the
office which they exercised in the confection of the Eucharist, and this
is exemplified by the twenty-sixth Admonition where a blessing is
pronounced upon the religious who have confidence in priests. Francis
laments the fate of those who despise priests ensnared in sin, and he
astutely reminds friars that judgement was reserved to God; it did not
behove them to be judgemental (cf. Romans 2: 1). The *Testament* attests
that God inspired Francis with great faith in priests whose lives were
shaped by the discipline of the Church. If he were as wise as Solomon and
met a poor priest, he would still refuse to preach in his parish against that
priest's will; this observance of the proper ecclesiastical jurisdiction is
also expressed in the *Rule*, which reflected Francis's teaching that the
friars should be submissive towards the bishop in the celebration of the
sacraments and the office of preaching. Unlike the early Dominicans
who were predominantly priests, Francis's first followers were laymen
whose company included only a small number of priests. This may have
prompted him to safeguard the friars' orthodoxy at a time when various
heretical groups were proliferating and damaging the Church. His *Rule*
ordains that the ministers should examine candidates for admission on

the Catholic faith and the sacraments. The letter to the whole order admonishes the friars to celebrate Mass with a reverential openness towards the divine presence on the altar, thereby making the sacrament a vehicle for personal association with the redemptive self-sacrifice of Jesus on the cross. The expansion of the fraternity throughout the western Church and into missionary territory reflected the breadth of Francis's vision.

## TOWARDS A UNIVERSAL COMMUNITY

The focus of Francis's apostolate differed sharply from earlier models of religious life. Monastic renewal had centred on a small and elite band which had proclaimed that the cloister was the most secure place in which people might seek salvation. While Peter of Celle, abbot of Saint-Remi, Reims (1162–81), contrasts the moral dangers in the Parisian schools with the cloister where Jesus teaches the heart with the word of virtue, some forty-two years later Francis's conversion took him back to Assisi, where he urged his former neighbours to seek their salvation within its ancient walls.[29] The earlier pessimism about the laity's prospects of salvation was steadily eroded, and the new mood is captured by the growing belief that 'the population of heaven had increased substantially' during the twelfth century, a view that was grounded in the emphasis on Jesus's humanity and the development of the doctrine of purgatory.[30] The riches of monastic spirituality with its discipline, asceticism and devotional methods were communicated to the laity by Francis, whose fervent sermons attracted recruits: a homily at Ascoli Piceno brought thirty men to the fraternity. His solicitude for the Poor Ladies of San Damiano is reflected in the recruits whom he entrusted to the guidance of Clare, the abbess of San Damiano. Sister Cecilia recalled a day on which Francis had sent five women to be received into the community. Those whose vocation remained in secular society found spiritual fulfilment in an association of penitents which came to be known as the Third Order, the subject of Chapter 12 below by Professor Ingrid Peterson. The three orders established by Francis were celebrated by one of Julian of Speyer's antiphons for Morning Prayer in the Divine Office. A hymn composed by Rainiero Capocci of Viterbo, the Cistercian cardinal deacon of Santa Maria in Cosmedin (1216–50), presents Francis as the father of the truly poor and prays for the inculcation of poverty of spirit.

Members of the laity were Francis's sisters and brothers to whom the call to holiness was addressed. His message sought the sanctification of each area of medieval society, and this is mirrored in his sermons, which were not confined to churches or cloisters. He was just as likely to expound the Scriptures arrestingly in the piazza or the countryside. His preaching brought him face to face with the religious aspirations of numerous people. His response was to assist them in the development of their devotional lives. The advice dispensed to penitents reflects the *Letter to the Faithful*, which encapsulates the new outlook and rehearses many of the themes that recur elsewhere in Francis's writings. One of the salient features is that the advice is common to all, although on occasion specific recommendations are made to judges and members of religious orders. The letter is addressed to all who embrace the penitential life and wish to live as Christians. Jesus becomes the brother of all for whom He lays down His life and makes intercession with the Father. The Father's will is that all should be saved through Jesus and they should receive the Eucharist with a pure heart and a chaste body. Purity of heart identifies one of the dispositions for a fruitful approach to the sacrament. Very few, Francis laments, are anxious to be saved and to receive the Eucharist. Christians should praise God and pray to him night and day. They should be insistent in their petitionary prayer, where a place of honour is awarded to the Lord's prayer. Their sins should be confessed to a priest, who would then nourish them at the Lord's table. Penitents are counselled against receiving the Body of Christ in a routine manner. Mindful of the Pauline injunction (1 Corinthians 11: 29), they should see with the eyes of faith and communicate with fitting dispositions.

This treatment of the appropriate reverence towards the Eucharist prefaces advice about loving one's neighbour as oneself. Francis was aware that some people might find the command to be charitable too taxing. Such people are counselled to be ministers of goodness rather than harm. Penitents should love their enemies and act benevolently towards all. Those charged with the administration of justice should conduct themselves in a merciful manner. The lives of the faithful should be regulated by the virtues of charity and humility, and they should give alms in expiation of their sins. While Christians leave everything behind them in this world, their deeds of charity and alms-giving secure them a reward at the judgement seat. Fasting was mandatory for the penitents, who were enjoined to avoid excesses in food and drink. They should visit churches often; they may have been expected to recite the prayer regarding the link between the cross and its sacramental re-enactment in churches; this prayer was inserted into the *Testament*. The penitential discipline is invoked to curb the lower nature of human beings, because it is the source of so much vice and sin (Matthew 15: 18–19). Penitents must renounce themselves and bring their lower nature into subjection under the yoke of obedience. Those who acknowledge their shortcomings provide a home for the divine spirit. Indeed, those who do the divine will are hailed as the brides, the brothers and the mothers of Jesus. The *Letter to the Rulers of the People* contains an injunction that God be held in great reverence among their subjects.

During the first decade of the thirteenth century Assisi was recovering from a civil war and the internecine struggles which scarred many cities and towns of Italy. This experience inspired Francis to announce peace to everyone, and this became a central ingredient of the friars' ministry. On entering a house, the friars' first words should offer a greeting of peace (Luke 10: 5). The fifteenth Admonition pronounces a blessing upon the peacemakers (Matthew 5: 9). When Francis was ill at San Damiano, he composed a hymn of thanksgiving, the *Canticle of the Creatures*, which was written in Italian and later translated into Latin (see discussion below). Reports of the escalating dispute between Bishop Guido II and Oportulo di Bernardo, podestà (chief magistrate) of Assisi, saddened the ailing Francis. This quarrel led to the sentence of excommunication imposed on the podestà, who retaliated by imposing a commercial boycott on the prelate. As a result of this bitter dispute Francis composed another verse to his canticle in praise of those who grant pardon for the love of God and foster peace. The two protagonists and their supporters were summoned to meet at the vescovado (bishop's palace), where two friars sang the vernacular version of the *Canticle of the Creatures*. This resulted in the reconciliation of the two men.

The global dimension of the *Rule* is reflected in the provision made for those who were divinely inspired to become missionaries. Francis's desire for martyrdom led him to set out for the Holy Land thrice. Thwarted twice, he succeeded in reaching the Holy Land during the fifth Crusade in 1219. Thomas of Celano attributes conventional motives to him, that is, the desire to preach the Gospel and to lay down his life in imitation of his divine master. Accompanied by Brother Illuminato, Francis walked into the Muslim camp and audaciously sought a meeting with the sultan of Egypt, al-Malik-al-Kâmil, a dramatic event which has been interpreted in various ways by biographers since 1219.[31] His respectful dialogue with the sultan has made him the precursor and prophetic hero of the wider ecumenical movement. It was fitting that over 200 leaders of the world's religions should meet in Assisi on 24 January 2002, at the invitation of John Paul II. Francis's

time in the Middle East and his awareness of Islamic devotional practices, especially the *salât*, the call to prayer issued five times a day, may
lie behind the plea to civil leaders that they create a climate in which
God is praised and that the hours of prayer may be announced by a
messenger.

Francis's respect and love for his neighbours embraced all the works
of the Creator and his respect for the entire order inspired his *Canticle
of the Creatures*, a hymn of thanksgiving for the bounty and beauty of
everything made by God. This canticle celebrates the unity, diversity
and richness of the universe. The elements of the sun, wind, moon,
stars, water, fire and death are addressed as brothers and sisters.
Creation became a ladder which Francis might climb to embrace his
Creator. His rapport with the animal world recovered an earlier strand
within the Celtic tradition where saints like Modwenna enjoyed close
relations with the animal kingdom, exercising her spiritual power over
wolves on two occasions.[32] Francis's sermon to the birds at Bevagna
was narrated by Thomas of Celano and captured by artists. It was one of
the six scenes painted in 1235 by Bonaventure Berlinghieri in an altar
panel at San Francesco in Pescia. Francis's exhortation to the birds is
painted by two artists by the middle of the thirteenth century: Matthew
Paris depicts the scene where the saint exhorts the five birds to give
thanks to their Creator, a scene reproduced on the dust jacket of this
volume (Corpus Christi College, MS.16), and the second, a Flemish
Psalter assigned to the middle of the thirteenth century (Chester Beatty
Library, MS.W61), shows the saint preaching to seven birds, one of
which is perched on his head. The remainder, which include a hawk
and an owl, are on a tree, except for a stork, which remains in the
foreground.

CONCLUSION

Francis's *Testament* offers a precious insight into his frame of mind
before his key meeting with the leper. This moment of grace showed
him the defects of his earlier conduct; social conventions and the fear
of contagion had subverted the norms of the New Testament and
blinded him to the plight of the suffering lepers. Thereafter obedience
to the Gospel became Francis's priority. A series of readings from the
Gospels provided him with a new orientation. Such texts laid the
foundation for his vocation as an urban evangelist and were central
to the evolution of his *Rule* of life. Francis wished to empty himself in
order that God might work in him. While earlier forms of the religious

life were centred on the cloister, Francis's vision embraced all peoples, and this is reflected in his concern for his neighbours. His fraternity of penitents brought a new form of religious life to the western Church, whose ecclesiastical reforms provided the impetus for their pastoral mission. He wished to collaborate closely with the bishops and clergy. He was inspired to look beyond the confines of western Christendom and to urge the entire universe to unite in praise of its Creator and Lord.

## Notes

1   Thomas, archdeacon of Split, *History of the Bishops of Salona and Split*, in *FAED*, vol. II, pp. 807–8.

2   *Scripta Leonis, Rufini et Angeli Sociorum S. Francisci. The Writings of Leo, Rufino and Angelo, Companions of St Francis*, R. B. Brooke (ed.), OMT (Oxford, 1970, corrected reprint, 1990), p. 22.

3   *S. Anselmi Cantuariensis archiepiscopi opera omnia*, F. S. Schmitt (ed.), 6 vols. (Rome and Edinburgh, 1938–68), vol. III, pp. 93 – vol. V, p. 423; *Sancti Bernardi Opera*, J. Leclercq, C. H. Talbot and H. M. Rochais (eds.), 8 vols. (Rome, 1957–77), vols. VII and VIII; and *The Letters of Peter the Venerable*, ed. with an intro. and notes by Giles Constable, 2 vols. (Cambridge, Mass., 1967).

4   A. B. Langeli, *Gli autografi di frate Francesco e di frate Leone*, Corpus Christianorum Autographa Medii Aevi, 4 (Turnhout, 2000).

5   Cf. P. Zutshi and M. J. P. Robson, 'An Early Manuscript of the *Admonitions* of St Francis of Assisi', *Journal of Ecclesiastical History*, 62 (2011), 217–54.

6   C. Paolazzi, 'Nascita degli "Scritti" e costituzione del canone', in A. Cacciotti (ed.), *Verba Domini Mei: Gli Opuscula di Francesco d'Assisi a 25 anni dalla edizione di Kajetan Esser, OFM*, in Medioevo, 6 (Rome 2003), pp. 55–87.

7   *FAED*, vol. I, pp. 41–4.

8   G. Orwell, *Nineteen Eighty-Four* (London, 1949, 1989), p. 106.

9   E.g., *The Ecclesiastical History of Orderic Vitalis*, M. Chibnall (ed.), 6 vols., OMT (Oxford, 1972–80), vol. VI, pp. 330–1.

10  C. Tomalin, *Samuel Pepys: The Unequalled Self* (London, 2002), p. 365.

11  J. R. H. Moorman, *Saint Francis of Assisi*, 2nd edn (London, 1950, 1979), p. x.

12  *FAED*, vol. I, pp. 45–51.

13  G. K. Chesterton, *St Francis of Assisi* (London, 1923, 1996), p. 27.

14  *FAED*, vol. I, pp. 41–4.

15  *Sancti Augustini Confessionum libri XIII*, Corpus Christianorum Series Latina, 27 (Turnhout, 1981), vol. VIII, 12, no. 29, p. 131.

16  'Ex chronico S. Martini Turonensis', O. Holder-Egger (ed.), in *Monumenta Germaniae Historica, Scriptorum*, vol. XXVI (Hanover, 1882), pp. 458–76, 464.

17 *Lettres de Jacques de Vitry (1160/1170–1240) évêque de Saint Jean-d'Acre, Edition critique*, R. B. C. Huygens (ed.) (Leiden, 1960), pp. 75–6.

18 *Sancti Columbani opera*, G.S.M. Walker (ed.), Scriptores Latini Hiberniae, 11 (Dublin, 1970), vol. IV, pp. 126–7.

19 E.g., *Sancti Bernardi Opera*, vol. IV, pp. 182–7.

20 *Dante Alighieri, La Divina Commedia, Paradiso*, N. Sapegno (ed.), La Letteratura Italiana: Storia e Testi, IV (Milan, 1957), XI, vv.64–6, p. 924.

21 *Giorgio Vasari, Le vite de' più eccellenti pittori scultori e architettori nelle redazioni del 1550 e 1568*, vol. II, *Testo*, R. Bettarini and P. Barocchi (eds.) (Florence, 1966), p. 101.

22 E.g., *Giovanni Boccaccio, Decameron*, I, 1. pp. 26–38. The dubious reputation of the merchant informs the story about the cunning and duplicity of Ser Ciappelletto of Prato.

23 *FAED*, vol. I, pp. 45–51.

24 R. J. Armstrong, *St Francis of Assisi: Writings for a Gospel Life* (New York, 1994), pp. 43–9.

25 D. Knowles, *From Pachomius to Ignatius: A Study in the Constitutional History of the Religious Orders* (Oxford, 1966), p. 38.

26 N. D'Acunto, 'Il vescovo di Assisi Guido I presso la curia Romana', in A. Cacciotti and M. Melli (eds.), *Francesco a Roma dal signor Papa*, Atti del VI convegno storico di Greccio, Greccio, 9–10 maggio 2008 in occasione dell' VIII centenario dell'approvazione della prima regola (Milan, 2008), pp. 41–60.

27 *The Prayers and Meditations of Saint Anselm*, B. Ward (trans.) (Harmondsworth, 1973), pp. 207–11.

28 E.g., C. R. Cheney and W. H. Semple (eds.), *Selected Letters of Pope Innocent III concerning England (1198–1216)*, Nelson Medieval Texts (London, 1953), pp. 177–9.

29 *The Letters of Peter of Celle*, J. Haseldine (ed.), OMT (Oxford, 2001), pp. 656–9.

30 R. B. and C. N. L. Brooke, *Popular Religion in the Middle Ages: Western Europe 1000–1300* (London, 1984), pp. 59–60.

31 Cf. J. Tolan, *Saint Francis and the Sultan: The Curious History of a Christian–Muslim Encounter* (Oxford, 2009).

32 *Geoffrey of Burton: Life and Miracles of St Modwenna*, R. Bartlett (ed.), OMT (Oxford, 2002), cc. 7, 16, pp. 18–21, 68–71. *Malachy Kinnerney read an advanced draft of this paper and made many helpful comments about the style and contents and raised a number of wider issues. Any errors of interpretation are my responsibility.*

# 3 The *Rule* and life of the Friars Minor
## WILLIAM J. SHORT

The *Rule* and life of the Friars Minor is this: to observe the Holy Gospel of Our Lord Jesus Christ by living in obedience, without anything of one's own, and in chastity.

(RB, 1)

These opening lines of their *Rule* have guided the followers of Francis of Assisi for some 800 years. To 'observe' the Gospel can mean both looking at it carefully, as in 'observing' the stars, and carrying out what it asks, as in 'observing' a law or a principle. The Franciscan *Rule* thus requires those who profess it to pattern their lives according to the Gospel of Christ, putting its teachings into practice as members of a religious order of the Catholic Church.

The earliest draft of this *Rule* followed by Francis of Assisi and his brothers received its first approval in 1209. Since that time it has inspired many to become saints, just as it has spawned bitter controversies over its application in changing circumstances of Church and society.[1] Bearing in its train this complex heritage, it continues to guide the lives of a multitude of the followers of Francis to this day. A thorough history and analysis of the Franciscan *Rule* and its influence through the centuries would require a long study indeed, and one that is highly desirable. Our purposes here are more modest, and of an introductory nature: to examine critical moments in the development of that *Rule* and its interpretation, from 'a few words written down simply' in 1209, through its several redactions, its formal approval in 1223, and its early interpretation by the brothers themselves and the papacy in the years immediately after the death of Francis.

## THE EARLIER 'RULE' AND THE LATER 'RULE'

Two redactions of a Rule composed by Francis of Assisi and his brothers have come down to us. One is called the Earlier *Rule*, First *Rule*,

*Rule of* 1221 or *Regula non bullata;* and the other is known as the Later *Rule, Rule* of 1223 or *Regula bullata.* In addition we have several sets of Fragments of an Earlier *Rule,* which are not identical to the redactions of 1221 and 1223.

The 'original' manuscript of the Earlier *Rule,* if such a term is correct, has not come down to us. Instead, we have a rich and complex tradition transmitting the text of the Earlier *Rule,* with some twenty-two manuscripts from the fourteenth and fifteenth centuries. Its earliest printed edition was prepared by the Irish Franciscan scholar Luke Wadding in his *Opuscula beati Francisci,* published at Antwerp in 1623.[2] Modern critical editions of its text, with inevitable variations, have been published by David Flood, Kajetan Esser and Carlo Paolazzi.[3]

For the Later *Rule* matters are more straightforward: we have the original papal bull containing the text of the *Rule* as it was approved in 1223, as well as an authentic copy in the Vatican Registers of the pontificate of Honorius III.[4] Oddly enough, there are slight discrepancies even between these two texts. The standard Latin edition is that of Kajetan Esser.[5]

Several texts offer citations from a version of the *Rule* that is neither that of the Earlier *Rule* nor the Later *Rule.* These Fragments can be found in three independent collections: a fourteenth-century manuscript of the Worcester Cathedral Library (cod. Q 27); in the work of the French friar and author Hugh of Digne, *Exposition of the* Rule *of the Friars Minor* (1245–55); and in the *Remembrance of the Desire of a Soul* by Thomas of Celano (1247). The full text of this version of the *Rule,* one perhaps developed between the 1221 and 1223 redactions, has not come down to us in any manuscript.

## THE EARLIEST FORM OF THE 'RULE'

A famous fresco in the basilica di San Francesco in Assisi shows Brother Francis and his first companions as they are received in Rome by Innocent III at St John Lateran in 1209. The setting, as rendered by the artist, was meant to impress, and it did, foreign dignitaries and visiting bishops, kings and ordinary pilgrims. Within that great complex of the Lateran Basilica and the papal court, the small group from the north-central town of Assisi was probably notable only for being poorly clad and unshod. But groups of reformers, both orthodox and dubious, inspired by the words and deeds of Jesus in the Gospel, were no strangers to that grand house. Pope Innocent, astute and careful about any hint of heterodoxy, was capable of flexibility as he tried to

steer towards the mainstream of Church life lay and religious move-
ments that were expanding during his pontificate (for example, the
Humiliati of northern Italy, the Trinitarians, the Hospitallers of the
Holy Spirit).

After what the early documents describe tactfully as an initial
hesitation, it appears clear that Innocent granted an 'approval' of some
kind to this small band of sincere men from nearby Umbria, with
Brother 'Francesco' as their guide. No document from the papal chancery mentions this meeting or any approval of a 'proposal of life'
(a *propositum vitae*), the most basic text regulating the life and activities of a nascent community in the Church.

As he was approaching his death, the same Brother Francis, now
nearly blind, composed his *Testament*, in which he serves as the chief
witness to the events of 1209. 'The Most High himself revealed to me
that I should live according to the form of the Holy Gospel. And I had
this written down simply, in few words, and the Lord Pope confirmed
it for me.'[6]

The approval was most probably simply verbal, as can be gathered
from this early account of the meeting by Thomas of Celano, whose
*Life of St Francis* was written shortly after the saint's death:

> When he [Innocent III] recognised the wish of the men of God, he
> first considered the matter and then gave his assent to their request,
> something he completed by a subsequent action. Exhorting and then
> warning them about many things, he blessed St Francis and his
> brothers and said to them: 'Go with the Lord, brothers, and as the
> Lord will see fit to inspire you, preach penance to all. When the
> almighty Lord increases you in numbers and grace, come back to me
> with joy, and I will grant you more things than these and, with
> greater confidence, I will entrust you with greater things.'
>
> (1 Cel., 33)

### BEGINNING FROM THE GOSPEL

The earliest elements shaping the *Rule* must be sketched by using
biographical (hagiographical) sources, since we have no texts from
Francis about these early stages. At the beginning of his conversion
(1206–7) Francis apparently followed a way of life recognised within the
sphere of ecclesiastical jurisdiction, probably associated with the 'order
of penance', the life of devout laity ('penitents') who followed a sober

and prayerful way of living, whether as solitaries or in communal settings.[7] Bishop Guido of Assisi indicated that he considered the young Francis under Church jurisdiction by allowing a dispute between Francis and his father Pietro to be heard in his episcopal court (1 Cel., 15). The young Francis worked, we suppose with appropriate approval, on the repair of churches owned by the canons of San Rufino (the church of San Damiano) and by the Benedictine monks of the abbey of San Benedetto of Mount Subasio (the chapel of Santa Maria degli Angeli) (1 Cel., 21). Francis at some point had begun to dress in the clothing of a hermit and had worked among lepers, perhaps in the hospice of San Rufino dell'Arce, staffed by 'penitents' of Assisi (1 Cel., 17). We have no indication of a *'Rule* of life' that the young Francis was following, unless it was generally the life of these 'penitents'.

The next phase of development may be that described by Celano, when Francis hears the reading of the Gospel in the little church of Santa Maria degli Angeli:

> The restoration of that church took place in the third year of his conversion. At this time he wore a sort of hermit's habit with a leather belt. He carried a staff in his hand and wore shoes. One day the Gospel was being read in that church about how the Lord sent out his disciples to preach. The holy man of God, who was attending there, in order to understand better the words of the Gospel, humbly begged the priest after celebrating the solemnities of the Mass to explain the Gospel to him. The priest explained it all to him thoroughly line by line. When he heard that Christ's disciples should not *possess gold* or *silver* or *money*, or *carry on their journey a wallet or a sack, nor bread nor a staff,* nor *to have shoes* nor *two tunics,* but that they should preach *the kingdom of God* and *penance,* the holy man, Francis, immediately *exulted* in the *spirit of God.* 'This is what I want', he said, 'this is what I seek, this is what I desire with all my heart.'
>
> (1 Cel., 22)[8]

This amalgam of synoptic texts (Matthew 10: 9–10; Luke 9: 2; Mark 6: 12) would find its way into the brothers' Earlier *Rule* (chapter 14). Here we may have the memory of an initial inspiration from the Gospel as recalled by Francis and communicated to his brothers in later years. At the time, as the account makes clear, Francis was alone. This 'life' was to be lived by a single, enthusiastic young man: only with the arrival of the earliest companions would this 'life' become the heart of an order's *Rule.*

## THE FIRST BROTHERS CONSULT THE GOSPEL

In his *Testament*, Francis affirms, 'And after the Lord gave me some brothers, no one showed me what I had to do, but the Most High Himself revealed to me that I should live according to the pattern of the Holy Gospel.'[9] We know the names of some of the earliest brothers of Francis. The first to arrive was Brother Bernard (of Quintavalle), followed shortly afterwards by a Brother Peter (perhaps Peter Catania) (1 Cel., 24). The question of a 'form of life' was thus posed in a new way, not for Francis alone, but for a small group of men. When referring to the 'revelation' of how to live according to the Gospel, the memories of Francis's companions describe the event of consulting a Gospel book (AP, 11 and 3 Soc., 29). After sincere prayer for divine guidance on their 'way of life', they opened the book three times and found the following three texts in answer to their prayer:

> If you wish to be perfect, go, sell everything you have and give it to the poor and you will have treasure in heaven; and come, follow me.
>
> (Matthew 19: 21; 'everything' from Luke 18: 22)

> If anyone wishes to come after me, let him deny himself, and take up his cross and follow me.
>
> (Matthew 16: 24)

> If anyone wishes to come to me and does not hate father and mother and wife and children and brothers and sisters, and even his own life, he cannot be my disciple.
>
> (Luke 14: 26)

Those texts are probably among the earliest elements of the brief document presented by Francis and his brothers in their meeting with Innocent III in 1209. Over the next decade and more, they were retained in the very opening chapter of the brothers' Earlier *Rule*.[10]

## THE EARLIER 'RULE' (1221)

During the next twelve years the 'form of life' followed by these brothers gradually expanded into the document known as the Earlier *Rule* or *Regula non bullata*. By the time of its final revisions at the brothers' Chapter at Pentecost of 1221, the content of the *Rule* had increased greatly from those 'few words' originally presented to Innocent III. A brief summary of the content of the Earlier *Rule* will illustrate this, dividing the text into thematic sections.

### The life of these brothers (Prologue–chapter 3)

Overall, the focus in this section is on the basic commitment required by the life of the brothers: this life is approved by the Church (Prologue); is based on the Gospel (1); and identifies norms for joining (2.1–3), along with specific practices of prayer and fasting (3).

### Brothers and ministers (chapters 4–6)

The superiors or prelates are to be called 'ministers', and their service to the brothers is described (4.1–6), as well as the correction of the ministers and the other brothers (5.1–17), recourse to the minister in time of difficulty, and the avoidance of other titles (e.g., 'prior') (6.1–4).

### Daily life of the brothers (chapters 7–9)

The work of the brothers is outlined in a general way (7.1–16), as is the prohibition of money as payment for their work (8.1–12). The brothers' work is supplemented by seeking alms, and all should care for the needs of their brothers (9.1–16).

### Brothers who are lesser (chapters 10–13)

Caring for the sick is an important task (10: see 7.15). The use of harsh words is forbidden (11: see 7.13–16). Relationships with women are regulated, especially for clerics (12: see 7 in general). Sexual misconduct is severely punished (13: follows from 12).

### Living in the world as evangelical men (chapters 14–17)

The brothers' behaviour in the world is formed by the Gospel's demands (14). The brothers' use of animals is strictly limited (15). The brothers' behaviour among Muslims and others should be humble (16). The brothers' external behaviour and internal attitudes in ministry should reflect humility (17).

### Issues of Catholic identity (chapters 18–21)

Chapters 18 and 19 may answer questions faced by ministers in the provinces and contain no scriptural references. These may reflect the concerns and the vocabulary of the ministers themselves, lacking the characteristic marks of Francis's way of writing. These can also be read as brief formulas to implement decrees of the fourth Lateran Council, added to the *Rule* presumably in 1216, at the first chapter of the brothers after the council. Chapter 20 also harks back to the fourth Lateran Council, specifically on norms for confession of sins and reception of Holy Communion, followed by a model text for preaching (21).

### Assorted topics (chapters 22–4)

An account of salvation history, or perhaps an early *Testament* of Francis, is included (22). It is followed by an invitation to praise and an exhortation (23). As a conclusion, there is a 'cover letter' to accompany the text once it had received the anticipated confirmation of the pope (24).

### CARDINAL HUGOLINO, AND THE QUESTION OF ADOPTING ANOTHER 'RULE'

An important figure in the development of the *Rule* is Hugolino, cardinal bishop of Ostia, designated by Honorius III as cardinal protector of the growing fraternity of Friars Minor (or, *fratres minores*). The circumstances of this designation are given by Thomas of Celano in these terms:

> At that time St Francis approached the lord Pope Honorius, who was then at the head of the Roman Church, humbly asking him to appoint the lord Hugolino, bishop of Ostia, as father and lord for him and his brothers. The lord Pope bowed to the holy man's request and, kindly agreeing, entrusted to the bishop his authority over the order of the brothers.
>
> (1 Cel., 100)

Cardinal Hugolino served as legate, a diplomatic representative of the papacy, with special responsibility for bringing order to the highly varied world of new religious communities in central and northern Italy. He was actively involved in advising Francis during the time the *Rule* was being developed. As cardinal and later as pope, he also drafted legislation for the community of Clare and her sisters at San Damiano, and used this legislation as the basis for an 'order of San Damiano' which he founded (though Clare did not join it).

The early 'form of life' of Francis and his brothers was 'confirmed' by Innocent III six years before restrictive legislation on religious *Rules* was enacted at the fourth Lateran Council in 1215. Its canon 13, 'On the prohibition against new religious orders' (*Ne nimis religionum prohibitis*), forbade the approval of any new religious *Rules*, so it was important for Francis and his brothers to demonstrate papal approval previous to the council, as Francis explicitly recalls in his *Testament*. Because the years following the council still saw no definitive, written approval of the *Rule* of the Friars Minor, some brothers with wide knowledge of religious *Rules*, apparently with the support of Hugolino, tried to convince Francis to accept an already approved *Rule* and to abandon the project of a new *Rule* based on Gospel texts that had been 'in process' for more than a decade and was still unfinished at the time of the famous chapter of Mats (dated by many to 1221).

> When blessed Francis was at the general chapter called the chapter of Mats, held at Santa Maria degli angeli, there were five thousand brothers present. Many wise and learned brothers told the Lord Cardinal, who later became Pope Gregory, who was present at the chapter, that he should persuade blessed Francis to follow the advice of those same wise brothers and allow himself to be guided by them for the time being. They cited the *Rule* of blessed Benedict, of blessed Augustine, and of blessed Bernard, which teach how to live in such order in such a way.
>
> Then blessed Francis, on hearing the cardinal's advice about this, took him by the hand and led him to the brothers assembled in chapter, and spoke to the brothers in this way: 'My brothers! My brothers! God has called me by the way of simplicity and showed me the way of simplicity. I do not want you to mention to me any *Rule*, whether of St Augustine, or of St Bernard, or of St Benedict. And the Lord told me what He wanted: He wanted me to be a new fool in the world. God did not wish to lead us by any way other than this knowledge, but God will confound you by your knowledge and wisdom. But I trust in the Lord's police that through them He will punish you, and you will return to your state, to your blame, like it or not.'
>
> The cardinal was shocked, and said nothing, and all the brothers were afraid.
>
> (CA, 18)

The story, as recalled by Francis's companions some years after the event, certainly points to awareness among the brothers of other 'approved' *Rules*, and Francis's clear rejection of these. What did the *Rules* of these three saints, Benedict, Bernard and Augustine, signify in the lifetime of Francis?

Francis knew the Benedictine monks, with their abbey of San Benedetto above the walls of Assisi, on the slopes of Mount Subasio. Their monastic life presented the figure of a community of monks gathered around its abbot, bound by obedience and stability of place. Their community was affiliated with the Cluniac abbey of Farfa, an influential and prosperous monastery to the south. When Clare came to join Francis and his brothers at Santa Maria degli Angeli on the evening of Palm Sunday in 1212, they accompanied her first to a monastery of Benedictine nuns where she stayed for a short while, San Paolo delle Badesse, in nearby Bastia. The monks of San Benedetto granted the use of the little church of the Porziuncula to Francis's early fraternity, after he had worked on its restoration early in his conversion. There is thus no hostility between the Friars Minor and the followers of St Benedict – quite the contrary! Yet Francis did not wish to accept the *Rule* for monks that guided Benedictine monasticism in his day.

Bernard of Clairvaux and Cistercian monks followed the *Rule* of St Benedict, so the reference to a '*Rule* of St Bernard' probably refers to the basic Cistercian legislation outlined in St Stephen Harding's early twelfth-century *Carta Caritatis*. The Cistercians represented a highly esteemed form of Benedictine life in the thirteenth century within the circle of Cardinal Hugolino (two Cistercians served as his advisors), and these 'white monks' were considered a model for religious life in the pontificates of Innocent III and Honorius III. Their legislation, with provision for regular international chapter meetings, became the norm for religious orders after the fourth Lateran Council. The Cistercian reform's insistence on architectural simplicity, personal poverty and manual labour had gained the admiration of many in the Church of Rome and beyond. Yet Francis does not wish to adopt the '*Rule* of St Bernard'.

Various communities of Clerics Regular followed the *Rule* of St Augustine. These were groups of priests sharing a common life modelled on the Acts of the Apostles (hence, 'apostolic life'), holding property in common, praying together and frequently dedicated to a ministry of preaching. Such twelfth-century communities as the Canons of Prémontré under Norbert of Xanten followed a form of this 'apostolic life'. Dominic Guzman similarly chose the *Rule* of St Augustine at the time of the official recognition of the order of Preachers or Dominicans by Honorius III in 1216. But this *Rule*, intended for communities of clerics, was not chosen by Francis and his brothers.

While not accepting any of these already tested *Rule* for himself and his brothers, Francis incorporated elements that would have seemed familiar to members of other orders: common liturgical prayer; the importance of work; obedience towards a superior; and regular gatherings for decision-making. But there are also significant differences. For monks, though travel was allowed, it was hardly the norm, as the ordinary daily occupations of prayer and work presumed a settled, orderly and cloistered life. Francis presumed movement as part of his brothers' way of life. Preaching at this time frequently included disputation, public argument between opposing sides, especially against heresy, as was the case of Cistercian preachers in the south of France, and that of Dominic and the Friars Preacher, in the context of the Albigensian or Cathar heresy. Francis forbids preaching of this kind, emphasising instead the importance of an example of meekness and an attitude of submission towards others, whether friend of foe. And while he emphasises the importance of obedience, the one to be obeyed is called 'minister and servant' of the brothers, and the obedience owed to him is limited by such criteria as discernment and the demands of conscience.

Most basically, the difference that Francis and (some) brothers insisted on was the inspiration of texts taken directly from the Gospel as the organising principle of their 'life and *Rule*'. They insisted that the 'form' or 'pattern of the Holy Gospel' (not the description of the 'Apostolic Church' in the Book of Acts) was to be their guide in shaping their life together. To use the Gospel as the basis for this '*Rule* and life' was not unprecedented among the new religious movements of the time, but it was the privilege of Francis and his brothers to see their version of a Gospel-based life (*vita evangelica*) officially approved. For Francis, as his *Testament* indicates, this commitment to an 'evangelical life' was a matter of divine inspiration and required of him firm resistance to pressures (whether from Hugolino or the brothers) to accept a previously approved *Rule* for his fraternity.

## HONORIUS III CONFIRMS THE 'RULE' ('SOLET ANNUERE' 1223)

Late in 1223, 'Brother Francis' finally received the official approval of the '*Rule* and life' of the order of Friars Minor, addressed to him on 29 November. Fourteen years had passed since he had presented to Innocent III those 'few words' that expressed his understanding of a life 'according to the pattern of the Holy Gospel', as he explains in his *Testament*. The original papal bull, *Solet annuere*, approving the *Rule* of the Friars Minor, is kept at the basilica di San Francesco in Assisi, enshrining, between its salutation and conclusion, the text which still serves as the *Rule* of the order.

When read with a knowledge of the Earlier *Rule* of 1221, several of its characteristics are immediately apparent. It is much briefer than the earlier text (less than half its size). Rather than the twenty-four chapters into which the Earlier *Rule* is customarily divided, the Later *Rule* has twelve. Nearly all the citations of the Gospel and other scriptural passages have been removed. There is some technical language from canon law and a more orderly structure, eliminating some of the repetitions and lengthy exhortations of the 1221 document.

When considering the authorship of the *Rule* in its various forms, a word must be said about the presence of Cardinal Hugolino, a protector of the order in its early years. Several years after the death of Francis, when Hugolino had become pope as Gregory IX, he issued an important document that interpreted the meaning of the Later *Rule*. In *Quo elongati* (28 September 1230) he describes his role in the composition of the *Rule* in these terms: 'as a result of the long-standing friendship between the holy confessor and ourselves, we know his mind more fully. Furthermore, while we held a lesser rank, we stood by him both as he composed the aforesaid *Rule* and obtained its confirmation from the Apostolic See.'[11] This role of 'standing by' Francis during the *Rule*'s composition could imply that Hugolino–Gregory had a role in shaping its content, though it is not possible to determine from the text of the *Rule* itself what that role might have been.

### THE CONTENT OF THE LATER 'RULE'

In recent decades scholars have proposed a division of the text into thematic units, rather than using the artificial division of twelve chapters (most probably chosen for purposes of public reading). The text can be summarised under the following headings for each theme:

#### *'To observe the Gospel of Jesus Christ'* (Prologue–1.1)
The basis of the brothers' life is the Gospel (1.1); and it is lived in the Church (1.2–3).

#### *'To receive this life'* (2.1–3.9)
The basic demands of conversion include renunciation of possessions, correct Catholic belief and commitment to chastity (2.1–6). Those joining the brothers must be free in giving their goods to the poor (2.7–8). During the year of probation they are clothed in poor clothing (2.9–10). 'To be received to obedience' at profession of this *Rule* has life-long consequences (2.11–13); the clothing of the brothers is simple, and those who dress differently are not to be judged (2.14–17). The common prayer of the brothers is the Divine Office (3.1–4); and they undertake bodily fasting like the other faithful (3.5–9).

### Lesser ones in the world (3.10–14)

The brothers are to be peaceful among others, humble, walking from place to place, greeting others with 'Peace', relying on the hospitality of others.

### Work and providing for the brothers (4.1–5.4)

Provision must be made for the needs of the brothers, but without use of money (4.1–3). Brothers should 'work faithfully and devotedly' for their daily support (5.1–4).

### 'Heirs and kings of the kingdom of heaven' (6.1–7.3)

Renunciation and itinerancy are hallmarks of this life (6.1–6); and brothers should show they are members of the same family, brothers in the Spirit (6.7–9). Penance for the brothers' sins is accompanied by mercy (7.1–3).

### The ministers and the brothers (8.1–10.6)

The minister general is elected at a chapter (8.1–5). The preaching of the brothers is regulated by the minister (9.1–4); and authority and obedience in the fraternity are to be governed by this *Rule* and the needs of the soul (10.1–6).

### The brothers' attitudes and behaviour in ministry (10.7–12)

The brothers must be on guard against pride, desiring the 'Spirit of the Lord' and avoiding worldly norms for success.

### The brothers' relationships with people they meet (11.1–12.2)

The brothers among believers (lay, religious, men, women) must behave in an upright way, avoiding occasions of scandal (11.1–3); the brothers are to be 'submissive and subject' when among Saracens and non-believers (12.1–2).

### Assuring fidelity (12.3–4)

The brothers must have a cardinal protector, appointed by the pope, helping to assure their constancy in Catholic identity.

## A FIXED 'RULE' AND A CHANGING CONTEXT

Early Franciscan texts record tensions among the brothers in the period immediately preceding the final approval of the *Rule*. There are several accounts, some embellished with dramatic details, illustrating a particular tension between Francis and a group of ministers from various provinces or regions. The Thomas of Celano himself gives one example, in his second account of the life and virtues of Francis, *The Remembrance of the Desire of a Soul*:

> there are some among the prelates who draw [the brothers] in a different direction, placing before them the examples of the ancients and paying little attention to my warnings ... Who are these people? They have snatched out of my hands my religion and that of the brothers. If I go to the general chapter, then I'll show them what my will is!

> (2 Cel., 188)

The changing demographics of the order saw better-educated clerics, including those from higher ranks of medieval society, joining the brothers in large numbers. The number of 5,000 brothers given for the chapter of Mats, dated to 1221, may be an overstatement, but there was a significant growth in numbers. Those 'senior brothers' and 'prelates' who are pictured as allies of Cardinal Hugolino at that chapter represent forces that were not always favourable towards Francis and his ideas. The so-called *Dictate on True and Perfect Joy*, generally considered an authentic *logion* of Francis, pictures Francis as one who is rejected at the central meeting-place of the order, Santa Maria degli Angeli, because he is 'simple and stupid', one who does not fit the profile of the brothers' new membership.[12]

These tensions between certain leaders within the fraternity and Francis as chief author of the *Rule* may help to explain the vehemence with which he will write his wishes about the observance of the *Rule* shortly before his death.

## THE 'TESTAMENT' AND THE DEATH OF FRANCIS (1226)

The most lasting and authoritative interpretation of the brothers' 'life and *Rule*' was issued by Francis in his *Testament* composed shortly before his death (3 October 1226). In it he explains, among other things, the approach the friars are to take in interpreting the *Rule*. Its words are to be understood *simpliciter*, a term that can be rendered as 'simply', or 'plainly' or 'sincerely' (all three nuances of meaning can be found in the *usus scribendi* of Brother Francis). The way its words are *not* to be understood is also indicated: 'without gloss' (*sine glossa*), that is, without the official interpretation given by an *auctoritas* in the margin of the document. Francis intends to bind his brothers to interpret the *Rule* through the lens of his *Testament*, ordering that whenever the *Rule* is copied or read, the *Testament* must accompany it. Yet, he insists, 'the brothers may not say: "This is another *Rule*." Because this is a remembrance, admonition, exhortation, and my testament.' The reason for its composition is also given: 'that we might observe the *Rule* we have promised in a more Catholic way'. So, while not being a *Rule*, it is a guide to living according to the *Rule*. The ministers may not add or take away from its words; they are always to keep this text together with the text of the *Rule*.

The great care shown by Francis in trying to protect the *Rule* and his own *Testament* from the work of *glossatores* reveals a real preoccupation. We sense from his words that some brothers (or others) had the legal acumen to reinterpret both texts in a way that changed their original meaning. The *Testament* is meant to prohibit treating these documents in the way that experts in canon law or theology interpreted texts by means of authoritative commentaries (*auctoritates*). By linking the public reading of the *Testament* to the reading of the *Rule*, Francis is trying to assure that such an approach will never be allowed.

Of particular concern seems to be preserving certain basic values, based on the Gospel itself. Francis mentions the requirement of poverty in buildings and churches used by the brothers, the importance of manual labour among them, and the obedience of the ministers and all the brothers to the *Rule*'s prescriptions. From the emphatic tone of the *Testament* one is tempted to detect in Francis a certain fear about future developments in the order and its observance of the *Rule* after the founder's death. In fact, it would not be long after his death that questions about both the *Rule* and the *Testament* would need to be answered at the highest levels.

## THE 'RULE' AFTER THE DEATH OF THE FOUNDER: 'QUO ELONGATI', GREGORY IX, 1230

Hugolino was the man who, as cardinal protector, had served as intermediary between Francis's followers and the Roman Church. Following the death of Honorius III, in 1227, he (Hugolino) was elected pope on 19 March 1227 with the name of Gregory IX. Within a short time he canonised Francis; he commissioned the *Life* of the new saint composed by Thomas of Celano; and he began preparations for the building of the great basilica di San Francesco in Assisi, laying the foundation stone on 17 July 1228.

In 1230, two years after his election, Gregory already had a serious question to answer about the authority of Francis, one posed by a delegation of brothers sent by the general chapter of the order. Its members included the respected preacher Anthony of Lisbon (later of Padua); the future minister general, Haymo of Faversham; and Leo of Perego, a future archbishop of Milan. They had come in order to ask Gregory to clarify certain doubtful points regarding the *Rule*. Specifically, the brothers wished him to decide how the rapidly expanding order could legitimately make use of property, buildings and materials (books, for example) while remaining faithful to the text of their *Rule*, which forbade appropriating anything to themselves. And, to make things more difficult, they had to interpret those provisions of the *Rule*, it seemed, according to the meaning that Francis had given in his *Testament*.

Their questions received close attention from a pope whose career had been built on the elaboration and interpretation of *Rules* for newly founded or reformed religious communities. His response, in the bull *Quo elongati* on 28 September 1230, was the beginning of a long series of papal interpretations of various points of the *Rule*, one that concluded only with the pontificate of Paul VI after the second Vatican Council (1962–5).[13]

The first difficulty to be addressed was the binding force of the *Testament* of Francis, with its prohibition of 'glosses' and explanations of the *Rule*. If that prohibition could not be overcome, no further reflection on the *Rule* and its interpretation would be possible.

Gregory addresses it as a problem of uncertainty: 'Since you are doubtful in regard to your obligation to observe this *Testament*, you have asked us to remove the uncertainty from your conscience and that of your brothers.'[14] He resolved the question by using the principle that 'equal cannot bind equal', i.e., that Francis could not bind others who were to follow him in the future as ministers general of the order.

Furthermore, the *Testament*, unlike the *Rule*, lacked the official approval of any competent authority, that is, the general chapter of the order or the Holy See: 'For without the consent of the brothers, and especially of the ministers, Francis could not make obligatory a matter that touches everyone.'[15] It was a heartfelt appeal of Francis, venerated as the founder of the order, but it was no more than that. With this authoritative statement, Gregory opened the way for successive interpretations of the *Rule* by the order itself and by the Holy See for the next eight centuries.

The general problem of what was demanded by making profession of a *Rule* identified with observing the 'Holy Gospel of Our Lord

Jesus Christ' was also faced and resolved rather simply: 'You are not bound by the *Rule* to observe the counsels of the Gospel, other than those explicitly contained in the *Rule* to which you have committed yourselves.'[16]

Having resolved that question, Gregory then moved to the more specific problems presented to him, with special attention to the material support of the friars and their work, which could now be answered after the matter of the *Testament* and its authority had been resolved. He clarified that the property used by the friars is not theirs by ownership (*dominium*) but is rather the property of those who gave it, the donors. Friars have the use of these things (books, buildings, furnishings) without being their proprietors.[17] This reply allowed the friars, in good conscience, to assent to large building projects to house the increasing numbers of brothers, including many well-educated men, and to solidify their presence in the world of higher learning in the growing universities of Europe.[18]

While the text of the *Rule* remained unchanged, as it does to the present day, the institutional framework in which the *Rule* would be lived had changed substantially by the time Gregory drafted these responses. Over the course of some twenty years, from the early approval of the 'form of life' by Innocent III in 1209 to the promulgation of *Quo elongati*, what had first been a constantly changing response to an early fraternity's experience became a solemnly approved juridical text, with accompanying legal commentary, to be observed within a large and increasingly stable international religious order.

## THE 'SACRUM COMMERCIUM' AS COMMENTARY

An extended allegory called the *Sacrum commercium* may serve as a commentary on Gregory's *Quo elongati*. The work of an unnamed author, but one who is well-informed about the early days of the order, *The Sacred Exchange between St Francis and Lady Poverty* presents the personification of poverty as the Beloved whom Francis seeks.[19] This exaltation of poverty, with rich imagery based on the biblical figure of Wisdom, could represent an elaborate critique of the interpretation of the *Rule* offered by Gregory. We are told, 'poverty is the only thing that everyone condemns so that it cannot be discovered in the land of those living comfortably'.[20] Later in the text Lady Poverty asks Francis and his brothers, 'First show me your oratory, chapter room, enclosure, refectory, kitchen, dormitory and stable; your beautiful chairs, polished tables and large houses.'[21] She is amazed to find they have none of these things, and that they can provide neither a dish of cooked food nor a knife to cut bread; and no pillow for her head except a stone.[22] When they finally comply with her wish to see their enclosure, 'taking her to a certain hill, they showed her all the world they could see and said: "This, Lady, is our enclosure."'[23]

The praise of a life with only the barest necessities, the notion of a world-wide enclosure, and the critique of those with 'kitchen, dormitory and stable' mark *The Sacred Exchange* as a call to return to an earlier understanding of the brothers' life and, just as clearly, an earlier way of understanding the *Rule*. The seeds of division and disagreement over the way the *Rule* should be lived are already evident in this carefully crafted allegory of Francis and his Lady.

## CONCLUSION

Eight centuries ago, the *Rule* of the Friars Minor took its earliest form, as Francis of Assisi, according to his *Testament*, had it written down 'simply and in a few words'. Over a span of more than a decade, that early text developed and changed, leaving the record of its growth to 1221, like the rings of a tree, in the rich and complex text of the Earlier *Rule*. With its final confirmation by Honorius III late in 1223, The *Rule* and Life of the Friars Minor assumed the definitive form it has kept until the present. Based on the pattern of the 'Holy Gospel of Our Lord Jesus Christ', it was, according to Francis, 'revealed' to him by the Most High. Early accounts by his companions about their opening the book of the Gospel provide concrete descriptions of the way in which that revelation occurred. Following Francis's death, the issue of interpreting the *Rule* fostered both reform and division among his followers. Its text unchanged, though often reinterpreted over the intervening centuries, that *Rule* remains the fundamental legislation for the Friars Minor in their various branches (order of Friars Minor, order of Friars Minor Capuchin, order of Friars Minor Conventual) throughout the world to the present day.

### Notes

1  Cf. D. Nimmo, *Reform and Division in the Franciscan Order (1226–1538): From Saint Francis to the Foundation of the Capuchins*, Bibliotheca Seraphico-Capuccina cura instituti historici ord. Fr. Min. Capuccionorum, 33 (Rome, 1987).

2  B. P. *Francisci Assisiatis Opuscula Nunc Primum Collecta, Notis et Commentariis Asceticis Illustrata* (Antwerp, 1623), pp. 170–7.

3  D. Flood, *Die Regula non bullata der Minderbrüder*, Franziskanische Forschungen, 19 (Werl im Westfalen, 1967); K. Esser (ed.), *Opuscula Sancti Patris Francisci Assisiensis denuo edidit iuxta codices mss. Caletanus Esser, O.F.M.*, Bibliotheca Franciscana Ascetica Medii Aevi, 12 (Grottaferrata, 1978); C. Paolazzi, 'La "Regula non bullata" dei Frati Minori (1221), dallo "stemma codicum" al testo critico', *AFH* 100 (2007), 5–148.

4  Archivio Segreto Vaticano, *Registra Vaticana* 12, beginning on fol. 155r.

5  Esser, *Opuscula*, pp. 225–38.

6  *Test.*, 15 *FAED*, vol. 1, p. 125.

7  See the full description of the life of penitents in the Middle Ages in G.G. Meersseman, *Dossier de l'ordre de la pénitence au XIIIe siècle* (Fribourg, 1961).

8  These events were recalled by his companions, with some variation, in the AP, 8–9; 3 Soc., 25; and *LM*, 3:1.

9  *Test.*, 14, *FAED*, vol. 1, p. 125.

10  RB, I. Another text (Matthew 19: 29, Mark 10: 29 and Luke 18: 30) was added to these at an early date: *Everyone who has left father or mother, brother or sisters, wife or children, houses or lands because of me, will receive a hundredfold and will possess eternal life.*

11  *Quo elongati* 3, in *FAED*, vol. 1, p. 571.

12  *FAED*, vol. 1, p. 166.

13  *Quo elongati*, in ibid., 570–5.

14  Ibid., 571.

15  Ibid.

16  Ibid., 572.

17  Ibid., 573.

18  The developments of 1230 would find their culmination at the beginning of the next decade, when the experience of the preceding years was codified in the 'Exposition on the *Rule* of the Friars Minor' by the 'Four Masters' (1241): Eudes Rigaud, Alexander of Hales, John of La Rochelle and Robert de la Bassée. A reverent but legal-minded reading of the *Rule*, it would serve generations to come as a guide to the interpretation of that text. *Expositio quatuor magistrorum super regulam fratrum minorum (1241–1242)*, L. Oliger (ed.), Storia e Letteratura Raccolta di Studi e Testi, 30 (Rome, 1950).

19  *FAED*, vol. 1, pp. 529–54.

20  Ibid., 532.

21  Ibid., 551.

22  Ibid., 552.

23  Ibid.

## 4 Francis and his hagiographical tradition

MICHAEL W. BLASTIC

### INTRODUCTION

Within two years of his death, Francis of Assisi was celebrated as the 'form of minors' in a liturgical antiphon composed by Cardinal Rainiero Capocci. This role given to Francis would give rise to a significant number of hagiographical accounts in the thirteenth and fourteenth centuries, texts that continued to re-propose a model of Francis to be imitated. Each of these accounts reflects a particular historical context which determined the way the story of Francis would be told. Thus, no two hagiographical accounts of Francis are the same, even those that used the same sources. This fact is often referred to as the 'Franciscan Question', whose origin goes back to Paul Sabatier, who challenged the accepted image of Francis, at that time largely determined by Bonaventure's *Major Legend*, claiming that it was a manipulation of the real Francis, who was represented more accurately in the accounts of his companions, and especially that of Brother Leo.

As long-forgotten Franciscan legends came to light in the early twentieth century they were approached first from a philological perspective and investigated with a literary methodology. More recently, historical criticism has been employed to unravel the relationship of these many texts, and today scholars are able to identify the sources, the historical contexts and the authors for almost every hagiographical account of Francis's life. This paper will provide an introduction and brief overview of the major hagiographical texts of Francis composed up until 1253. Each text will be placed in its historical context, information about the author will be provided, its sources will be discussed and a brief description of the author's approach to Francis will be supplied. With this background, the reader will have the necessary information to investigate each text in more detail.

## THE CANONISATION OF FRANCIS

Francis of Assisi died at Santa Maria degli Angeli on the evening of 3 October 1226. He was buried the next day in the church of San Giorgio within the walls of Assisi, the church where he learned how to read and write as a youth. His vicar, Brother Elias of Cortona, sent a letter to the brothers informing them of the death of Francis and to announce as well the new miracle that 'our brother and father appeared crucified, *bearing in his body* [Galatians 6: 17] the five wounds which are truly *the marks of Christ* [John 20: 25]' (*FAED*, vol. II, p. 490).[1] Within a year and a half of Francis's death, Cardinal Hugolino, elected Pope Gregory IX on 19 March 1227, began to plan for the canonisation of Francis by purchasing land for a new burial church. The canonisation itself took place in Assisi, on 16 July 1228, when Gregory IX presided and preached a sermon on the text of Sirach 50: 6–7 (*FAED*, vol. I, p. 295). Gregory issued the bull of canonisation *Mira circa nos* (*FAED*, vol. I, pp. 565–9) on 19 July 1228, in which he celebrated Francis as the renovator of the Church, sent by God at the eleventh hour. According to Gregory, Francis accomplished this through his 'preaching in simple words', just as Samson destroyed the Philistines with the jawbone of an ass (*FAED*, vol. I, p. 567). While Gregory provided an allegorical narrative of Francis's mission in the Church, there is scarcely a trace of the historical Francis in the papal bull, and no mention at all of the brotherhood he established.

A second, somewhat shorter bull, *Sicut phialae aureae*, was issued by Gregory IX on 12 September 1228, addressed to the clergy of northern Italy, and was sent throughout the world on 21 February 1229.[2] While *Mira circa nos* presented a well-constructed image of Francis as a preacher saint who fought against heretics, *Sicut phialae aureae* presented him as the 'founder and rector of the order of Friars Minor', whose great number now invigorates the Church with lives that call all to penance, but without any mention of Francis's preaching mission. There is no evidence that *Mira circa nos* was ever promulgated, and it was the simple image of Francis as founder in *Sicut phialae aureae* that became popular.

## THOMAS OF CELANO, 'LIFE OF ST FRANCIS'

Around the time of the canonisation of Francis, Gregory IX commissioned Thomas of Celano to produce a hagiographical legend to promote the new saint's cult. Prior to this time there exists very little information about Celano himself. He was from the town of Celano in the Abruzzo region of Italy and joined Francis and his early brothers as an educated cleric around 1215, an event which he himself describes in his *Life of St Francis* (1 Cel., 56–7).[3] In 1221 he was a part of a missionary expedition to Germany, where he remained until the canonisation, perhaps being summoned to Assisi specifically for that event. His hagiographical corpus reflects his knowledge of the Latin classics and the tradition of ecclesiastical hagiography which he alludes to quite frequently. One of the nineteen extant manuscripts of the *Life of St Francis* carries the note that Gregory IX himself approved the text in February 1229, in Perugia. Thus, it took Celano about seven months to complete the legend.

Celano divides his text into three books. The first narrates the conversion of Francis, his discovery of the Gospel in the church of San Nicolò in Assisi, the arrival of his first companions, the approval of the *propositum vitae* of the brotherhood by Innocent III in 1209, Francis's visit to the sultan, al-Malik-al-Kâmil, in Acre, miracles worked during his life, his love of creatures and his ability to see Christ in the poor and all creation, concluding with a description of the celebration of Christmas at Greccio in December 1223. Book 2 opens with a recapitulation of the life of the saint through the lens of Francis as a new evangelist, then describes his increasing illness, the event of the stigmata at La Verna in September 1224, how he continued to preach even with declining health, his final sickness and death, his funeral and the translation of his body to the church of San Giorgio. Book 3 describes the consistory which pronounced on his holiness and an eyewitness account of the celebration of the canonisation of Francis in the church of San Giorgio with Gregory IX presiding. The text concludes with a listing of the miracles of Francis read out at his canonisation.

Given the short period of time that Thomas of Celano had access to Francis, that is, between 1215 and 1221, he needed to rely on eyewitnesses for most of the details concerning Francis's conversion and the foundation and early growth of the brotherhood. And, because Celano was absent from Italy from 1221 until 1228, he was not present for the significant events that took place with regard to the redaction of the *Rule* between 1221 and its confirmation on 29 November 1223 by Honorius III, which is not even mentioned in the text, or for the stigmata and death of Francis. For Francis's conversion and the life of the early brothers Celano followed the description given by the saint's *Testament*, with other information taken from the *Rules* of 1221 and 1223. But, even after having consulted witnesses, as he claims in the prologue, he was still unable to fill in the gaps of his knowledge with the standard historical information. To fill this vacuum Celano turned to the hagiographical tradition, employing classical texts such as Anthanasius's *Life of Antony*, Sulpicius Severus's *Life of Martin of Tours* and Gregory the Great's *Life of Benedict*, as well as Augustine's *Confessions*.[4]

Celano presented Francis as a new kind of saint, bridging in himself different expressions of religious life in the Church. On the one hand, Francis was a simple preacher through word and example, 'following the life and *footsteps* [1 Peter 2: 21] of the Apostles' (1 Cel., 88), and a faithful and obedient servant of the Church of Rome enjoying the special favour of Cardinal Hugolino. On the other hand, Francis lived the life of a monk in his prayer and asceticism, yet he was not confined to a cloister but took the Gospel out into the world. He achieved what the traditional forms of religious life could not, that is, effective witness and preaching of the Gospel in the midst of the people.

Celano underlines that Francis's life was focused principally on 'the humility of the incarnation and the charity of the passion' of Christ (1 Cel., 84). In fact, book 1 concludes with a description of the celebration of Christmas at Greccio in 1223, which Francis wanted to celebrate so that people could see with their own eyes 'the discomfort of his infant needs' (1 Cel., 84). Book 2 focuses on the passion of Christ with the events surrounding the stigmata on La Verna where Francis was marked with 'the marks of the passion and cross as if he had hung on the cross with the Son of God' (1 Cel., 90).

For the stigmata Thomas relied on the *Encyclical Letter of Elias* for a description of the wounds of Francis. Because Elias offered no historical information as to when, where or how this event occurred, Thomas had to describe what to this point had remained unspoken. He placed the event around the time of the feast of the exaltation of the cross, using Luke's account of Jesus's agony in the garden as his model, where Jesus's struggle was so intense that his sweat became like blood and God sent an angel to comfort him (Luke 22: 39–44). At this point in his life Francis suffered physically in addition to his own spiritual and emotional distress with regard to the order. Seeking to know God's will, Francis opened the book of the Gospel thrice and each time it opened to a prediction of the Lord's passion, understanding from this that his life would be marked with suffering.

Celano described the stigmata as the result of a vision that Francis had, a vision of 'a man like a seraph, standing above him, arms extended and feet joined, affixed to a cross' (1 Cel., 94). After trying to understand it, and after the vision had left him, the marks of the nails appeared in his hands, feet and side, just as he saw them on the man in the vision. Now marked with these wounds, Francis travelled down from La Verna to begin again his life of preaching and penance. His sickness continued to grow more intense, and eventually he returned to Santa Maria degli Angeli and died there.

Book 3 celebrates Francis as a new light, 'gladdening the whole world with the gift of new joy' (1 Cel., 119). Gregory IX is the central character who 'rejoiced and exulted, dancing with joy, for in his own day he was seeing the Church of God being renewed with new mysteries that were ancient wonders' (1 Cel., 121). Chased out of Rome by the allies of Frederick II, Gregory travelled to Assisi to visit the tomb of Francis, and from there he went to Perugia to hold the consistory for the canonisation. The new saint, Francis of Assisi, was thus presented by Celano to the world as both an evangelical man and a new evangelist!

### TEXTS DEPENDENT ON CELANO'S 'LIFE OF ST FRANCIS'

Celano's legend would remain the point of reference for information about Francis until 1241, and it was used as the basis for a number of hagiographical and liturgical works. The *Legend for Use in Choir*, attributed to Thomas of Celano, was written between 1230 and 1232. This choir legend was arranged in nine short readings for insertion into the office of Matins for the feast of St Francis. It is a radical reduction of the *Life of St Francis*, with some new material, largely a collection of posthumous miracles and the announcement of the new church which was being built to receive Francis's remains. The text places a heavy accent on miracles worked both during Francis's life, among which Celano counts the stigmata, and those worked after his death. Four of the total nine paragraphs are devoted to miracles presenting Francis as not only the converted founder of the order of Friars Minor and an effective preacher (even to the sultan), but above all as a miracle worker and intercessor!

Around the time of Francis's canonisation, liturgical texts such as hymns, responsories, antiphons and sequences were composed by Gregory IX, Thomas of Capua and Rainiero Capocci. These texts were included by Julian of Speyer in his *Divine Office of St Francis*, completed before 1235. He was the 'master of chant' at the convent of the Friars Minor in Paris who were studying at the university there. Julian himself was an accomplished musician, trained at Paris and part of the royal chapel choir until he entered the order around 1224. He was a member of the mission to Germany sent from the general chapter of 1227, and Jordan of Giano in his *Chronicle* identifies him as the the one who wrote the office of Francis and Anthony in a 'noble style'.[5] Julian was in Paris by 1232, where he composed the office, as well as his *Life of St Francis*. Julian's *Office* is referred to as a *historia*, a historical narrative of Francis's life set to music. Inserting the pre-existing liturgical pieces into his own composition, Julian tells the story of Francis from his birth through to his death, arranged from Matins to Vespers, with antiphons, responsories and hymns. The major source for the *Office* is Thomas of Celano's *Life*, but Julian brings his own perspective to bear on Francis, who is celebrated primarily as 'the valiant Catholic and perfectly apostolic' poor man and founder of three orders (*FAED*, vol. I, pp. 327, 338).[6] While the order of Friars Minor is certainly present in the text, the focus is almost completely on Francis and his apostolic holiness.

Julian of Speyer also composed a *Life of St Francis* in Paris between 1232 and 1234. His position as *magister cantus* and *corrector mensae* at the convent of Paris included the responsibility of instructing the student brothers in chant and public reading, and it is assumed that he wrote his *Life* for table reading at the convent. His primary source is Thomas of Celano's *Life*, which he shortened, mainly by eliminating the hagiographer's commentary and moralisations, thus focusing more directly on Francis. Julian also borrows from the *Legend for Use in the Choir* and the *Encyclical Letter of Brother Elias* for his description of the stigmata. The new information Julian includes is minor, amounting to an account of the translation of Francis's body to the new basilica on 25 May 1230, noting that both the order and the Poor Ladies were spread beyond Italy, and mentioning in passing that Honorius III confirmed the *Rule* for Francis, a detail omitted by Thomas of Celano.

Julian rearranged the material by gathering information into thematic chapters. Thus, the first four chapters deal with Francis's conversion, the establishment of the order, the approval of the *Rule* and the formation of the brothers. Chapters 5 to 11 abandon the narrative chronology and open thematic reflections, such as on Francis's poverty, his desire for martyrdom, love for creatures, his preaching and miracles, and his prayer which concludes with a description of the stigmata. Chapters 12 and 13 return to the chronology of Francis's final sickness and death, his miracles, the canonisation and the translation of his body. The effect of these structural changes places the focus entirely on Francis as the model of virtue for the brothers, and the story of the brotherhood is somewhat disconnected from the life of Francis. This leads to an emphasis on asceticism, as for example when Francis encounters the leper: Julian notes that Francis had to do violence to himself and conquer himself in order to kiss the leper.[7] Julian comments that, 'Blessed Francis himself served the order of Friars Minor in the perfection of every virtue by going beyond what was asked.'[8] This focus on the person of Francis also increased attention on the miraculous element in the ordinary actions of Francis; what was a heroic act on the part of Francis for Thomas of Celano becomes a miracle for Julian. Francis's eloquence in preaching is described as 'miraculous' by Julian whereas Celano had described it as 'great'.[9]

Julian's prologue celebrated the radical change in Francis's life from his initial state as a person in need of conversion to the final manner of his life worthy of imitation. This emphasis placed on the example of Francis's conversion makes him the model for the brothers in the convent of Paris, who had to assimilate Franciscan life without experiencing the lifestyle of the early brothers. No longer itinerant or simple workers, the brothers in Paris were engaged in study, and thus what Francis and the early brothers experienced as they travelled around Italy as working heralds of the Gospel Julian translated into acts of asceticism and mortification for the individual brother living in a convent.[10]

Thomas of Celano was at work again in the last years of the 1230s to write a short text known as the *Umbrian Legend*.[11] This work opens with Francis at La Verna and the vision of the seraph, followed by the imprinting of the wounds of the Crucified Christ, then moves directly to his final sickness and death, his burial and canonisation, and ends with the translation of Francis's body to the new basilica di San Francesco. Part II contains a small collection of miracle stories beginning with a description of Francis the 'standard bearer' of the great king, through which Thomas of Celano links the miracles directly to the stigmata, emphasising the holiness of Francis by underlining his unique role in the development of the order, and suggesting that Francis's role within the order is God-given and therefore cannot be set aside.

One of the striking characteristics of this short narrative is Thomas of Celano's attention to the role of Brother Elias as Francis's chosen successor. Elias is mentioned five times and always in a positive light. In this text Thomas of Celano also names the companions whom he referred to in his *Life of St Francis* as his 'four pillars' (1 Cel., 102), namely, Elias, Rufino, Angelo and Leo. Clare too is named in the context of her lament over the body of Francis as it was being taken up into the city for burial. This emphasis on Francis's special role in the order, together with the focus on the four companions of Francis with Clare, suggests a defensive tone on the part of the author. Elias, the minister general (1232–9), was deposed by Gregory IX in 1239, bringing to a conclusion a process that had begun earlier in Elias's term of office based on complaints against him and the insistence of the ministers from northern Europe, and focused in Paris, that Elias needed to be removed so that the order of Lesser Brothers could progress. It seems likely that this text was written by Celano, perhaps with the approval of Elias himself, as a statement of support for Elias, but even more with the insistence that the intentions of Francis with regard to the direction of the Friars Minor must be respected. The most likely hypothesis is, then, that this short narrative was written between 1237 and 1239.

## THE BEGINNING OR THE FOUNDING OF THE ORDER OF FRIARS MINOR

The deposition of Elias at the general chapter of 1239 in Rome marked a significant turning-point in the development of the order. Albert of Pisa, a priest, was elected as Elias's successor, marking the end of lay leadership within the order. This same chapter enacted a series of constitutions which set the order on the path towards clericalisation and invested the general chapter with full authority. Henceforth, the minister general was required to implement the policies determined by the chapter, and the chapter elected leadership at the general and provincial levels.[12]

The text of the *Anonymous of Perugia*, or, as the *incipit* indicates, *The Beginning or Founding of the Order*, narrates the history of the order from the perspective of the events of 1239. In twelve chapters, the author who today is identified as Brother John the disciple of Brother Giles of Perugia narrates the growth of the Friars Minor from a fraternity to a *religio* (Penitents from Assisi) to a clerical order, arguing that this change in institutional status was Francis's intention from the beginning. The order is thus the primary focus of the text, while Francis remains in the shadows after the arrival of the first brothers, and the order takes on a life independent of him and his intentions. The author's intention to marginalise Francis from the story of the Friars Minor can be seen reflected in his description of their trip to Rome in 1209, where Bernard was elected leader of the expedition (AP, 31). What is emphasised throughout is how the Friars Minor reflected the pattern of the 'primitive church of the apostles' (AP, 27). When they were few in number, Francis told them not to worry because soon 'many learned, prudent and noble men will be with us' (AP, 18), a prophecy that was fulfilled at the time of Francis's death (cf. AP, 47). The *Anonymous of Perugia* thus reflects the perspective of the clerical brothers at the time of its writing, with indications of adjustments in lifestyle, such as building 'their own dwellings in the cities and towns' (AP, 41), stating that the 'ministers were elected' (AP, 44), that letters of protection were being sent by the cardinal protector wherever the brothers encountered problems (AP, 45), and including a detailed description of how a chapter is to be celebrated and the business to be conducted (AP, 36–40). Francis's stigmata and death are mentioned only in passing in the final chapter, and no mention is made of any of his miracles. These details, which describe the reality of the order after 1239, suggest that this text was written to provide a revised history of the development of the order that would fit with the changed circumstances of life by 1241. Francis, in a real sense, was 'used' to validate the changes and to assure that the clerical direction of the order was his intention from the beginning.

## THE 'LEGEND OF THE THREE COMPANIONS'

Mindful of the passing of so many friars who had known the founder, at the general chapter of 1244 in Genoa the newly elected minister general, Crescentius of Iesi, invited friars to forward to him whatever they might know factually about Francis's life and miracles. Thomas of Celano was commissioned to receive this material and to incorporate it into his revised and expanded *Life of St Francis*.[13] This request indicated that the brothers were no longer satisfied with Thomas of Celano's *Life*, especially in the light of the recent hagiographical production surrounding the events of 1239. Given that the bull *Ordinem vestrum* was issued by Innocent IV on 14 November 1245, it seems likely too that the chapter of 1244 requested another papal interpretation of the *Rule* based on further questions that arose concerning the brothers' experience.[14]

Brothers Leo, Rufino and Angelo responded to this request in a letter that remains attached to the text of the *Legend of the Three Companions* in the manuscript tradition. The letter, dated 11 August 1246 and sent from Greccio, indicated that the general chapter requested 'signs and wonders' of Francis, but the authors state that they will not focus on this but instead on 'some striking aspects of his holy manner of life and the intention of his pious desires'; nor did they intend to write a legend but rather to pick 'from a field of flowers those that were the most beautiful'; finally, they would not follow a chronological order (3 Soc.). Claiming their own experience with Francis as their source, they also list Brothers Philip, Illuminato, Masseo and John, the companion of Giles, as their sources.

The text attached to the *Letter* in the manuscript tradition is indeed a *Legend*, providing a narrative of Francis's life from his birth to the translation of his body to the new basilica in Assisi. The ideological perspective of the *Legend of the Three Companions* is close to that of the *Anonymous of Perugia*, but the author has restored Francis to a central position in the narrative. The author made good use of the lives already compiled by Thomas of Celano and Julian of Speyer, the first two biographers of the saint of Assisi.

The author of the *Legend* knew the customs and procedures of the commune of Assisi well, and he presented a new account of Francis's youth and conversion which focused on his ambition to become a knight (3 Soc., 4–6) which was achieved when he became 'a new knight of Christ' (3 Soc., 17). Additional details of Francis's conversion included the description of the prayer in the church of San Damiano where the voice from the cross lamented 'Don't you see that my house is being destroyed? Go, then, and rebuild it for me' (3 Soc., 13). The *Legend* also underlines the strong links with the bishop of Assisi, the pope and the Roman curia, focusing on the approval of the *Rule* with attention to the change in the saint's status from penitent, to hermit, to his tonsure in Rome when the *Rule* was approved, thus underlining the canonical transition from fraternity to order (3 Soc., 37). The author also included the story of the dream of Innocent III, who saw a small man holding up the Lateran Basilica a few days before Francis and the brothers' arrival in 1209, which convinced him that this would be 'that holy and religious man through whom the Church of God will be sustained and supported' (3 Soc., 51). Francis is clearly indicated to be the founder of three orders: that of the brothers, the sisters and the penitents.

The brothers' life of poverty was modelled on that of the apostolic Church, as the author stated: 'they did not appropriate anything as their own, but used books or other items in common according to the pattern handed down and observed by the apostles' (3 Soc., 43). The final two chapters of the *Legend of the Three Companions* return to Francis with a description of the stigmata and their significance in his life, death and canonisation. The basilica di San Francesco, in which the body of Francis found final rest, was described by the author as 'the head and mother of the whole order of Friars Minor' (3 Soc., 72), declared such by Gregory IX and all the cardinals.

While the *Letter* is always attached to the *Legend* in the manuscript tradition, the fact that the authors state they were not going to write a legend in the strict sense raises the question of what else might have been attached to the letter from Greccio.[15] An answer was found by examining the works which Thomas of Celano composed using this material from 1246, namely *The Remembrance of the Desire of a Soul* (also referred to as Celano's *Second Life*),[16] whose first redaction was completed by the time of the general chapter in 1247, and *The Treatise on the Miracles of St Francis* (attached to the second redaction of *The Remembrance*) in 1253.[17] These works of Celano contain a significant amount of material hitherto unpublished, and one can thus assume that the source of this new information was the material sent with the letter from Greccio. Thus, in addition to the *Legend of the Three Companions*, there was a collection of stories (not a narrative) about Francis referred to in the *Letter* as a 'collection of flowers', often referred to as the *Florilegium* by scholars, which Celano used primarily for book 2 of *The Remembrance*, plus a large collection of miracle stories which served as the basis for the 198 paragraphs of his *Treatise on the Miracles*. Somehow in the transmission of this material, the *Florilegium* and the collection of miracles were disconnected from the *Letter* and the *Legend*.

### THE 'FLORILEGIUM' OF 1246 – THE 'ASSISI COMPILATION'

While the text of the *Florilegium* of 1246 is not extant, it is the position of most scholars that the text of the *Assisi Compilation* contains a primitive version of much of this material, but preserved in a manuscript dating from 1311.[18] In addition to material from 1246, this manuscript includes pericopes from Celano's *Remembrance* as well as other texts of Leo that circulated independently of the *Florilegium* ('The words of St Francis', CA, 15–20; 'The intention of St Francis on the *Rule*', CA, 101–6). Jacques Dalarun argued that the compiler of the manuscript was Ubertino da Casale who did so to supplement Bonaventure's *Major Life* in preparation for the discussions taking place in Avignon between the Community and the Spirituals (the two tendencies or parties within the Friars Minor) in preparation for the council of Vienne, and the material was compiled at Ubertino's direction from manucripts containing Leo's texts, the *Florilegium* and Celano's *Remembrance*.[19]

The pericopes of the *Assisi Compilation* concern primarily Francis in the last years of his life, after the confirmation of the *Regula bullata* in 1223. Francis is presented as the 'form and example' for the brothers, even after his resignation as minister upon his return from Egypt in late summer 1220 (CA, 11). He is depicted as being very disheartened over changes in the order which had led it away from its original perfection. He is often upset by the laxity and laziness of the brothers, wanting all the brothers to work (CA, 48), beg for alms (CA, 51) and serve lepers. While on the one hand Francis praises the *Rule* approved by Honorius III (CA, 46), on the other hand he had wanted to add some things which were excluded, sometimes because the ministers did not approve, other times because the pope was not in agreement (CA, 108). Santa Maria degli Angeli is presented as the heart of the brotherhood, and Francis wanted it to be a 'model and example' for all the brothers in terms of buildings and lifestyle (CA, 56). Francis was extremely generous to the poor, giving away his tunic to anyone poorer than himself, and he paid attention to the smallest of things, even a cricket (CA, 110). At the same time, Francis was mistreated and disrespected by some of the brothers causing him to turn to prayer so that he could bear this in peace (CA, 11). There is almost no mention of miracles, and the stigmata are mentioned only in passing, as the focus is placed on the human Francis who is proposed as a model that all brothers might follow. Thus, the Francis of the pericopes of the *Assisi Compilation* is a complex and tormented man, committed to the principles on which the fraternity was based, but dissatisfied with the direction the order had taken.

## CELANO'S 'REMEMBRANCE OF THE DESIRE OF A SOUL'

Celano's *Remembrance of the Desire of a Soul* is composed of a prologue and two books. The prologue dedicates the work to Crescentius of Iesi, indicating that the first redaction of the text was completed prior to the general chapter of 1247. Celano states that in the first book (2 Cel., 3–35) he will include some details of Francis's conversion that were not contained in previous legends, information that he received from the *Legend of the Three Companions*, while book 2 (2 Cel., 26–223) will treat of the 'good, pleasing and perfect will of our most holy father' (2 Cel., 3), based on material taken from the *Florilegium*. In addition Thomas took some material from his and Julian's *Life of St Francis*. However, even with these known sources there remains some material in *The Remembrance* for which extant sources have not been found.

The first book of Celano's *Remembrance* accents the prophetic quality of Francis. Emphasising the divine confirmation of Francis's *Rule*, Celano remarked that the pope 'recognised without any doubt that Jesus Christ had spoken in this man' (2 Cel., 17). Celano high-lighted the role of Santa Maria degli Angeli, which Francis wanted to be 'like a mirror for the order', but anachronistically Celano stated that he 'kept its ownership in the hands of others, keeping for himself and his brothers only the use of it' (2 Cel., 18). Celano closed the first book with Francis entrusting the order to the Roman Church.

Given the vast amount of material in the *Florilegium*, and since it did not contain consistent geographical or chronological indications, in book 2 Celano presented Francis as 'the holiest mirror of the holiness of the Lord, the image of his perfection' (2 Cel., 26) by organising the pericopes into thematic units, beginning with prophecy and then poverty, the longest sections in the book. Stories are included about Francis and women (2 Cel., 112–14) that reflect monastic misogynistic attitudes and that are also applied to Francis's relationship with the sisters at San Damiano (2 Cel., 204–7). There are stories that describe Francis's preaching, his strict asceticism, his struggle with temptations and demons, his observance of the *Rule*, his relationship with creation, his desire for martyrdom and his visit to the sultan, al-Malik-al-Kâmil, as well as his final sickness and death. It is one of the last paragraphs that best summarises the perspective of Celano here: after his death, Francis appeared to a 'brother of praiseworthy life' clothed in a purple dalmatic and followed by a large crowd of people who could not distinguish between Francis and Christ, who seemed to be one and the same person (2 Cel., 219). Celano set out to present Francis as a mirror of the holiness of the Lord, and that is what Francis was seen to be by this brother at the end of his life.

## 'THE TREATISE ON THE MIRACLES'

Celano completed the task given him by the chapter of 1244 with his *Treatise on the Miracles*. As mentioned above, this was completed in 1253 at the insistent urging of the minister general, John of Parma. Celano used miracles from his *Life of St Francis*, the *Legend for Use in the Choir* and the *Umbrian Legend*, together with miracle stories from the collection of 1246 to complete the work. The treatise is composed of nineteen chapters without a prologue. Celano ordered the miracles from the most significant to the least significant.

Chapter 1 describes the foundation of the Friars Minor, who revived the 'footprints of the apostles' and the 'perfection of the primitive church', as the miracle by which 'the world was warned, by which it was roused, and by which it was frightened' (3 Cel., 1), emphasising the order's role in salvation history and its function within the Church. The second chapter presents the stigmata of Francis, which were already stamped on his heart when he heard the crucifix speak to him in San Damiano telling him to repair God's house (3 Cel., 2), thus suggesting that the life of Francis sealed by the cross of Christ is at the same time God's seal on the existence and mission of the order. The truth of the stigmata, still doubted by some, is demonstrated by the witnesses who saw them on his body, as well as the miracles worked through their intercession. Chapter 7, which begins the post-mortem miracles, includes a series of stories in which Francis raised the dead to life. The remaining chapters report miracles commonly recorded in miracle collections of the Middle Ages.

In the epilogue (3 Cel., 198) Celano expressed his frustration at the task he was given: 'The insistence of our brothers' requests extorted it, the authority of our prelates ordered it', protesting at the difficulty he experienced. In a sense, Celano's words describe what had been happening since 1239 to the image of the founder in the order's hagiographical tradition: 'We cannot forge something new every day, nor square circles, nor bring to agreement the innumerable variety of times and wishes that we received in a single block.' Given all the material he received in 1246, it was impossible to create a seamless narrative of Francis's life. But in addition, Celano seems to be suggesting that, in not being able to 'square circles' or 'create something new every day', one cannot honestly create an image of Francis to justify the designs and needs of the brothers and the order at different moments of their history.

CONCLUSION

Thomas of Celano's lament proved to be prophetic, and his synthesis in his second biography of the saint and *The Treatise on the Miracles* were soon found to be unsatisfactory by the brothers. In 1263 the minister general, Bonaventure, produced his own *Major Legend of St Francis*, and three years later the general chapter decreed that all preceding hagiographical texts concerning Francis should be destroyed. Despite this, in the later thirteenth and throughout the fourteenth centuries, new hagiographical texts about Francis would continue to appear. Jacques Dalarun has commented that 'Francis is the first author of the Franciscan Question. The Franciscan Question is not just an enjoyable little game played by scholars, like a curtain placed in front of the *poverello*'s face. In itself it teaches something fundamental about Francis, namely, that his experience and his message could not be reduced to a single voice.'[20] The complexity of Francis himself is reflected in the complex history of the movement he founded, as well as in the complex hagiographical tradition which attempts to represent him. But, in order to retrieve Francis from these different witnesses, it is necessary to approach these texts critically and with a historical methodology that serves to help unlock the meaning encoded within them. Perhaps one can understand the reason for the enduring popularity of Francis through the ages in terms of Dalarun's insight: Francis's 'experience and his message could not be reduced to a single voice'. The hagiographical texts give us access to Francis, but only if one reads them in the context of what has come before them, and each in their own historical context. Each of the authors or compilers of these texts would agree that simplicity was a primary trait of Francis. But today it is not a simple exercise to understand him and his intentions as these are recorded in his complex hagiographical tradition.

### Notes

1   While the edition of the letter appeared first in William Spoelberch, *Speculum vitae beati Francisci et sociorum eius* (Antwerp, 1620), and there are redundancies in the letter itself, the first part of the letter (paragraphs 1–7) is held by scholars to be authentic.

2   R. Armstrong, '*Mira circa nos*: Gregory IX's View of the Saint, Francis of Assisi', *Greyfriars Review*, 4 (1990), 75–100.

3   A systematic analysis and exegesis of Thomas's *vita* can be found in R. Michetti, *Francesco d'Assisi e il paradosso della minoritas: La vita beati Francisci di Tommaso da Celano*, Nuovi Studi Storici, 66 (Rome, 2004).

4   The footnotes in the cricitical edition of the *Vita beati Francisci* give indications of the hagiographical texts that Thomas uses to present Francis as a saint.

5   *XIIIth Century Chronicles: Jordan of Giano, Thomas of Eccleston and Salimbene degli Adami*, trans. from the Latin by P. Hermann with intro. and notes by M.-Th. Laureilhe (Chicago, 1961), nos. 53, 59.

6   'The Divine Office of Saint Francis by Julian of Speyer and Others (1228–1232)', in *FAED*, vol. 1, pp. 327–45, 327, 328.

7   Ibid., 12; 1 Cel., 17.

8   The *Life of Saint Francis* by Julian of Speyer (1232–5), 24, in *FAED*, vol. 1, p. 385.

9   Ibid., p. 58; 1 Cel., 72.

10   Henri d'Avranches wrote a *Versified Legend of St Francis* for Gregory IX in the early 1230s using the information from Celano. He offers a heroic reading of Francis's life, comparing him to Roman and Greek heroes, and offers some of his own comments about medieval life along the way.

11   J. Dalarun, *Vers une résolution de la question franciscaine: La Légende ombrienne de Thomas de Celano* (Paris, 2007), provides a thorough analysis of the text and a critical Latin edition and French translation at pp. 250–311. Dalarun's recent critical edition of the text differs from that published in Analecta Franciscana, vol. x (Quaracchi, 1926–41), which is the basis for the text in English in *FAED*, vol. ii, pp. 473–82.

12   C. Cenci, 'De fratrum minorum constitutionibus praenarbonensibus', AFH, 83 (1990), 50–95.

13   Consult Dalarun, *Vers une résolution de la question franciscaine*, pp. 204–8.

14   *Ordinem vestrum*. English translation in *FAED*, vol. ii, pp. 775–9.

15   Cf. J. Dalarun, 'Introduction', in *François d'Assise vu par les Compagnons. Du commencement de l'Ordre, Légende des trois compagnons*, intro. and trans. Jacques Dalarun. Révision par François Delmas-Goyon (Paris, 2009), pp. 31–56.

16   *Vita secunda s. Francisci, Fontes*, pp. 443–642; English translation in *FAED*, vol. ii, pp. 239–393.

17   Felice Accrocca has demonstrated that the two manuscripts which serve as the basis for the edition of *The Remembrance* and *The Treatise on Miracles* represent different redactions. The Roman manuscript contains omissions and additions with respect to the Assisi manuscript.

18   Accrocca suggests that Celano first redacted *The Remembrance* in the form it has in the Assisi manuscript. Subsequently, and at the urging of Minister General John of Parma, he completed a second redaction, to which were added the miracles. See Accrocca, 'Due diverse redazioni del *Memoriale in Desiderio Animae* di Tommaso da Celano: una discussione da riprendere?' *Collectanea Francescana*, 74 (2004), 5–22, and 'Le due redazioni del *Memoriale nel desiderio dell'anima* di Tommaso da Celano', *Frate Francesco*, 72 (2006), 153–86.

19   The manuscript, Perugia MS. 1046, has been edited a number of times by different scholars, resulting in different ordering and numeration of the texts. For a description, analysis and study of the manucript, consult J. Dalarun, 'Plaidoyer pour l'histoire de textes. A propos de quelques sources Franciscaines', *Journal des Savants* (July–December 2007), 319–58.

20   J. Dalarun, *The Misadventure of Francis of Assisi: Towards a Historical Use of the Franciscan Legends*, trans. Edward Hagman (St Bonaventure, 2002), pp. 22–3.

## 5 Voluntary simplicity: the attitude of Francis towards learning in the early biographies

NESLIHAN ŞENOCAK

The historical question of whether or not Francis approved of the pursuit of learning by the clerical Franciscans is a tough one in view of the scarcity of the evidence, and Bert Roest in Chapter 10 here offers an answer to this question. A medieval Franciscan who asked the same question had much less material in his hands for an answer than we do now. In the Middle Ages, with the exception of the *Rule* and the *Testament*, the writings of Francis remained inaccessible to the great majority of the friars who joined the order in places remote from Italy and who never had the chance to meet Francis or any of his early companions. If a clerical friar's conscience was burdened by a suspicion that his enthusiasm for the pursuit of booklearning was in conflict with the saintly founder's intentions, he could find no help in the *Rule* or the *Testament*. Francis did not approve of a quest for learning by illiterate friars, but he remained silent about the pursuit of learning by clerical friars. He did, however, prohibit the appropriation of things (which included books, with the exception of a breviary), but this ban ceased to be an obstacle to studying after the papal permission given to friars in 1230 to use things, including books. Francis's *Testament* was not helpful on the subject of learning either. Therein he admonished friars to respect theologians, but this hardly meant that he wished to see his brothers become theologians. One can safely assume that until the publication of Thomas of Celano's *Second Life* in 1247, most friars knew little about whether Francis was predisposed to approve of the clerical friars' enthusiasm for study.

By 1247 the order was already vastly different from what it had been when Francis died in 1226. Perhaps the biggest transformation was in the sphere of learning and its integration into the order's vocation. This transformation initially started with the entry into the order of learned men, who were quickly promoted to ministerial positions. This came rather naturally because the ministerial positions necessitated some knowledge of theology.[1] Once the learned friars took the ministerial positions, they thought it a good idea to promote learning within the order by way of showing a conscious effort to recruit learned men and by trying to give an education to the friars. This effort manifested itself in the introduction of the office of lector, whose main responsibility was to train the friars in theology. The first lectors were appointed by 1228, and by the 1240s the order had in place the backbone of an educational organisation where the intellectually most gifted friars from every province were trained in theology at the Franciscan school in Paris in order to fulfil the office of lector.[2]

All ministers general of the order elected after 1240 were friars educated in the Parisian studium and often bachelors or doctors of theology. Ministers provincial and custodians also came to be selected increasingly from among the learned, as more learned men were available by the 1240s. This was at once indicative and supportive of an emerging culture within the order, which saw learning and education as the necessary features of an 'ideal' Franciscan and which undermined the position of the illiterate lay brothers, who were not represented at the administrative level any more.[3] Illiterate or poorly educated brothers were increasingly alienated and officially not wanted. The ambition of the administration to enrol educated men became explicit in a statute formulated around 1239–42, where the legislating chapter decreed that only men who taught in the universities or important towns and boroughs were to be recruited into the order.[4] The intake of laymen was limited to only those whose social status was exemplary. This marked a distinct change from the early days in the order's recruitment strategy.

Some friars saw the integration of learning into the Franciscan vocation by way of systematic education as dangerous. We become aware of this concern in the texts written on Francis, and there in particular in the representations of his attitude towards learning and books. In this study, I shall consider the major hagiographical texts written in the thirteenth and fourteenth centuries: Thomas of Celano's *Second Life*; the writings of Leo, Rufino and Angelo; Bonaventure's *Major Life*; the *Mirror of Perfection*; and the *Deeds of Blessed Francis of Assisi and his Companions*. The analysis of the way Francis's attitude towards learning and books was depicted in these texts reveals both the presence of different viewpoints in the order and also change over time, which was the consequence of the transformation that the order was experiencing.

## THOMAS OF CELANO'S 'SECOND LIFE'

Although in his *First Life* of Francis, written around 1228, Thomas of Celano had made no reference to Francis's ideas with regard to the keeping of books and the pursuit of theological studies, his *Second Life* did incorporate a few chapters on this subject. This is not surprising since, whereas in 1228 the educational enterprise was in its infancy, by 1247 the pursuit of learning had not only been substantially integrated into the clerical Franciscan vocation, but the administrative positions in the order were being filled almost exclusively by the learned friars. Learning was increasingly defining the kind of institution Franciscans were becoming.

The first section that bears on the subject of learning is entitled 'On the Saint's Understanding of the Sacred Scripture and the Virtue of his Words' (2 Cel., 102–6). In the first chapter of this section Thomas of Celano represents Francis as a man with a deep understanding of Scripture, although he had made no study to acquire such learning (2 Cel., 102). His knowledge and understanding of Scripture were gifts from God. Francis used to read the sacred texts and was keen on writing from memory what he learned by reading. But he held no high regard for scholastic learning where the reading went far beyond Scripture: 'He used to say that this was a fruitful way of learning and reading, and not to wander through a thousand treatises' (2 Cel., 102). It is worth noting that among the thirteenth- and fourteenth-century texts on Francis, the contents of this chapter in the *Second Life* are cited only by Bonaventure (*LM*, 11:1). Next, Thomas gives an account of how a Dominican doctor of theology asked Francis to expound to him a passage from the Bible.[5] Francis at first refuses, on the grounds that he is ignorant, but upon the Dominican's insistence he explains the passage. The doctor of theology is impressed by his answer and says to the saint's companions that the theology of Francis is sublime, whereas his own learning crawls on its belly. This depiction of Francis as a 'learned' man was to become a strong influence on Bonaventure and his understanding of the importance of the study of theology for the Franciscan vocation.[6]

The section in the *Second Life* where Thomas discusses Francis's views with regard to the place of learning in the Franciscan vocation is entitled 'Holy Simplicity' (2 Cel., 189–95). In the first chapter, we learn that simplicity is to be content with God alone and to despise everything else. It is not to know or speak evil. It is to choose to do rather than to learn or to teach. This last sentence gives the first clue as to Thomas's position on Francis's understanding of the friars' vocation: learning or teaching are activities inferior to setting an example by deeds. It is reminiscent of Francis's preference for preaching by example over preaching by words.

> The holy simplicity was what the most holy father demanded in both learned and lay brothers. He believed it not to be contrary to wisdom, but rather its true sister, although those who are poor in learning would have it more readily and put it into use more willingly.
>
> (2 Cel., 189)

Here, then, Thomas construes a direct link between a friar's state of learning and his tendency to simplicity. Those who are poor in learning are more likely to have holy simplicity. A question flashes in the reader's mind as to what solid basis there is for the idealisation of the uneducated lay brothers as those more likely to be content with God. As if to pre-empt the question, in the next chapter Thomas narrates the story of John the Simple.[7]

John, a most simple man, is a farmer. His profession and Thomas's expression '*simplicissimus*' leave little doubt that he is an uneducated, most probably an illiterate, man. He leaves his plough and asks Francis if he may join his brotherhood. Once John takes the habit, he starts imitating Francis quite literally in everything, almost to the degree of ridicule. He coughs when Francis coughs and spits when the saint spits. When Francis asks him why he behaves this way, his reply is simple but wise: 'Everything you do' he says, 'I promised to do. It is dangerous for me to omit anything' (2 Cel., 190). This simple reply is an allegory of the Franciscan vocation. If the friars were to imitate Christ, then a literal and wholesale imitation, where they did not deliberate about which aspects of Christ's life to imitate and how to imitate, was the only guarantee of success. Francis rejoices at this answer and, when John dies, Francis remembers him as St John. According to Rosalind Brooke's study, this tale was in the corpus of the Leonine text that was sent to Thomas of Celano. It is therefore quite likely that Thomas extracted the story from that source. What is interesting, however, is that Thomas adds a final conclusion to the story, which is not in the Leonine version:

> Note that it is typical of holy simplicity to live by the norms of the elder and always to rely on the example and teaching of the saints. Who will allow human wisdom to follow him now reigning in

heaven, with as much care as holy simplicity conformed herself to him on earth! What more can I say? She followed the saint in life and went before the saint to Life.

(2 Cel., 190)

Having thus made a point about the higher potential of the simple friars in achieving sanctity, Thomas then moves on to explain what a learned brother should do to achieve the same end. The answer is rather simple: the learned brothers must imitate the simple brothers. This is the idea in the section that follows:

He [Francis] once presented a moral parable, containing no little instruction. 'Imagine', he said, 'a general chapter of all the religious in the Church. Because the literate are present along with those who are unlettered, the learned, as well as those who, without learning, have learned how to please God, a sermon is assigned to one of the wise and another to one of the simple. The wise man, because he is wise, thinks to himself: 'This is not the place to show off my learning, since it is full of understanding scholars. And it would not be proper to make myself stand out for originality, making subtle points to men who are even more subtle. Speaking simply would be more fruitful.'

The appointed day dawns, the gathering of the saints gathers as one, thirsting to hear this sermon. The learned man comes forward dressed in sackcloth, with head sprinkled with ashes, and to the amazement of all, he spoke briefly, preaching more by his action. 'Great things have we promised', he said, 'greater things have been promised us; let us observe the former and yearn for the latter. Pleasure is short and punishment is eternal; suffering is slight and glory infinite. Many are called; few are chosen, all are repaid.' The hearts of the listeners were pierced, and they burst into tears, and revered this truly wise man as a saint.

(2 Cel., 191–2)

Here, then, are Francis's expectations of the learned brothers: they should embrace voluntary simplicity and imitate the simple brothers. It is not an arbitrary choice that the setting in which Thomas chooses to make his point is that of preaching. Preaching was used as the major justification for the necessity of the pursuit of learning in the order. Its first written articulation was after 1254, when the mendicant–secular conflicts started at Paris.[8] However, this argument must have been expressed within the order long before in the provincial and general chapters. We can safely assume that Thomas was aware of it. It seems that Thomas was not convinced by the argument that learning improved one's preaching, nor does he suggest that Francis would be pleased if the friars preached elaborate sermons. Rather, his tale is reminiscent of Francis's admonition in the *Rule* that sermons should be short and clear. The imagery of the Franciscan preacher in the tale is that of a penitent with sackcloth and ashes. It is first and foremost as a simple penitent and not as a subtle scholar that the learned friar preaches and impresses his audience.

The idea that the learned brothers should imitate the simple brothers in their life and preaching was not the only point that Thomas wished to convey with regard to Francis's intentions. He also warns that this is the only way to preserve unity and equality within the order, which drew friars from all classes of society. Moreover, there was absolutely no hierarchy set between these various classes of friar. To preserve this particular nature of the early brotherhood, it was necessary that the learned did not undermine the simple. However, this proved to be difficult. As mentioned before, the legislation made after the 1240s restricted the recruitment of uneducated men into the order, and the lay brothers were increasingly ousted from the selection process for the administrative offices. In the conclusion to the parable, Thomas is keen to remind his readers of the initial vision of Francis for the unity of the order:

> The man of God would then explain the moral parable he told: 'Our religion is a very large gathering, like a general council gathered together from every part of the world under a single form of life. In it the learned can draw from the simple to their own advantage when they see the unlettered seeking the things of heaven with fiery vigour and those not taught by men knowing *spiritual things by the Spirit*. In it even the simple turn to their advantage what belongs to the learned, when they see outstanding men, who could live with great *honour* anywhere *in the world,* humble themselves to the same level as themselves. Here', he said, 'is where the beauty of this blessed family shines; a diverse beauty that gives great pleasure to the father of the family.'
>
> (2 Cel., 191–2)

Perhaps the clearest expression of Francis's attitude towards learning is represented in the last chapter of the section on 'Holy Simplicity'. Here we learn that already in Francis's time some friars were too keen to seek learning instead of strengthening their virtues, and this upset Francis. By using prophecy as a narrative technique, Thomas places in Francis's mouth contemporary criticisms with regard to the order's contemporary state:

> 'For', he said, 'a tribulation is approaching, when books, useful for nothing, shall be thrown out of windows and into the closets' . . . Besides, he could smell in the air that a time was coming, and not too far away, when he knew learning would be an occasion of ruin, while dedication to spiritual things would serve as a support to the spirit.
>
> (2 Cel., 195)

Thomas feels the need to redeem the negative tone of the chapter by suggesting that the study of Scripture did not displease Francis; rather, the saint wished to divert the friars from a superfluous concern with learning. At the closing of the same chapter, the contemporary articulations within the order that linked the pursuit of learning to the preaching apostolate, and Thomas's disagreement with this, become clearer. Thomas narrates the story of a companion of Francis who was too much given to preaching. Francis appears to him in a vision, forbids him to do this and advises him to walk in simplicity.

Closely linked with the pursuit of learning in the order is the subject of the keeping of books. In this respect, Francis's attitude towards the presence of books in the order is also indicative of his attitude towards learning. At the time of Francis, there was no question of any friar keeping and collecting books except a breviary. *Quo elongati* of 1230 had revised that by allowing the friars the use of books. In the last chapter on 'Holy Simplicity' mentioned above, Thomas recounts the story of a lay brother who asks Francis permission to have a Psalter and is offered ashes instead, a reminder of the penitential aspect of the Franciscan vocation. In an earlier section of the *Second Life*, whose major theme is poverty, Thomas tells us that Francis allowed the brothers to keep a few books but to use them only for edification and not to seek value in them for themselves. He is, however, displeased when a minister asks him whether some expensive books can be kept, but he allows the minister to do as he likes [2 Cel., 62]. While the enthusiasm for learning threatens the order's unity, the presence of books threatens the evangelical creed of poverty.

## THE WRITINGS OF LEO AND OTHER COMPANIONS OF FRANCIS

The early companions of Francis presumably had the best information concerning Francis's intentions and the kind of brotherhood he wished to form. Three of these companions, Leo, Rufino and Angelo, sent their memoirs of Francis to Thomas of Celano sometime between 1244 and 1246, which Thomas used while composing his second official biography of the saint. The original manuscript of these memoirs is no longer extant and can only be reconstructed through an analysis of the texts surviving in a number of late thirteenth- and fourteenth-century manuscripts, and even then without any guarantee of re-creating the original work. These texts are primarily the *Legend of the Three Companions* and the *Assisi Compilation*. Rosalind Brooke, after a meticulous text-critical analysis, identified certain parts in these manuscripts as the original writings of Leo and the companions. She published these under the title of *Scripta Leonis*.[9] The parts of these Leonine writings where the problem of learning and books are addressed come primarily from a separate tract inside the *Assisi Compilation* known as the *Intention of the Rule*, whose date of composition is not clear; neither is it known whether it was written before or after the *Second Life*.[10]

The *Intention of the Rule* covers essentially the problem of books and the pursuit of study, and bears substantial similarities to the last two chapters of Thomas of Celano's 'Holy Simplicity'. However, the Leonine text recounts these stories in greater detail and makes explicit references to Francis's discontent with the friars' enthusiasm for studying theology. The story of the minister wishing to keep expensive books is there, and, just as in Celano, the moral of the story is that expensive books are a violation of the solemn oath to observe the Gospel.[11]

The lay brother who wishes to keep the Psalter becomes a novice in the Leonine version, and the companions essentially use this story to reflect on Francis's attitude towards study. Thereby, unlike Celano, who treats the subject of books in the section on poverty and that of learning under simplicity, the companions see the problem of books and learning as interlinked. This story is told in five chapters and has many details that are not in the *Second Life*.[12] The novice wants to procure Francis's permission 'particularly because he had heard that Francis did not want his brothers to be eager for learning and for books, but wanted, and preached to the friars, that they should strive to imitate the pure and holy simplicity, holy prayer and Lady Poverty, on which the early and saintly brothers had built'.[13] Here too, just as in Celano, the major idea is that the learned brothers and those brothers who seek to be learned should instead follow the example of the simple friars, and try to convert and edify people, not so much by preaching but by prayer, living a simple life in evangelical poverty. They acknowledge Francis's respect for theologians, but the study of theology is simply not in the Franciscan vocation. Friars Minor are supposed to save souls not through teaching or preaching based on study, but through simplicity and prayer. Once, when Francis was upset about the behaviour of some friars, he was consoled with these words from God:

> I did not choose you as an educated and eloquent man over my family, but I chose you as a simple man, that both you and others might know that I will watch over my flock. I put you as a sign to them, that the works which I work in you they ought to perceive in you, and do them.[14]

This story is actually in Celano's *Second Life*, where Francis is referred to only as a 'simple man'.[15] The particular emphasis on Francis's not being an educated and eloquent man implies that the companions set education and simplicity in clear contrast as opposites.

The Leonine text also includes the prophecy about the future tribulations of the order that are narrated by Celano, but again with more intensity. The companions exhibit a remarkable knowledge of the breadth of justifications given by the brothers for the pursuit of learning, including (but not limited to) preaching, and none of these justifications convince them:

> Many brothers on the grounds of edifying others would put aside their vocation, that is to say pure and holy simplicity, holy prayer and Lady Poverty, and it will happen with these friars that they will afterwards come to believe that they are more imbued with devotion and fired with the love of God through the understanding of Scripture, so that occasionally they will remain frozen within and as it were empty... He [Francis] used to say: 'There are many who put all their efforts and their care day and night into learning, casting aside their holy vocation and devout prayer, and when they preach to a group or to the people and then see that some are edified or turned to penitence, they are puffed up and congratulate themselves on the works and profit of another: for those whom they believe they have edified or converted to penitence by their words, God has edified and converted through the prayers of saintly brothers, though they do not know it themselves. It is God's will that they should not pay attention to it, lest they grow proud.[16]

In the remaining three chapters of this section, there is no substantial difference between Thomas of Celano's ideas about Francis's attitude towards books and those of the companions. Francis tells the novice that once he was tempted to have books as well, but God through the

Bible gave him the message that only a true follower of the Gospel can attain true knowledge. The companions also make the point that the acquisition of books and learning lead to the feeling of superiority and consequently to a hierarchy in the order. In this version, Francis says to the novice: '"After you have a Psalter, you will covet and demand a breviary; after you have a breviary, you will sit in a chair, like a great prelate telling your brother: 'Bring me my breviary.'"'[17] The story concludes with Francis refusing to give his permission to the novice, saying that the true vocation of a friar minor is not to have anything except a tunic, a cord and breeches.[18]

## BONAVENTURE'S 'MAJOR LIFE'

In 1263, Bonaventure of Bagnoregio, a doctor of theology trained and taught in Paris and the minister general of the order (1257–74), submitted a new legend of Francis to the general chapter of Pisa. His legend was based on the texts of Celano's *First* and *Second Life*, and on Julian of Speyer's *Life of Francis of Assisi*. Like Haymo of Faversham and John of Parma before him, Bonaventure too was an exemplary figure of the 'new Franciscan', a friar of erudition and high intellectual capacity, but genuinely devoted to the idea of the evangelical life. He did not hesitate to renounce the life of scholarship in order to take up the position of minister general, and most of his intellectual production during his ministry of the order was directed at defending the Franciscan life against the secular masters, and to inspire his brothers and other learned Christians to a mystical union with God.

It is not surprising that many of the negative sentiments present in the Celano and Leonine texts with regard to the compatibility of learning with the Franciscan vocation are absent from the *Major Life*. Bonaventure does not seem to be at all convinced that the study of theology is not part of the Franciscan vocation. On the contrary, he believes that studying would improve a friar's life and deeds, provided that it was carried out with virtue, and for virtue. He therefore does not shy away from treating Francis's attitude towards learning in his legend, probably to settle once and for all the rumours circulating in the order about study as something in conflict with the Franciscan vocation. We find this discussion at the beginning of the eleventh chapter, entitled 'Francis's Understanding of Sacred Scripture and His Spirit of Prophecy'.

He starts the chapter by quoting verbatim from Celano's *Second Life* the section on Francis's profound understanding of Scripture and how he read the sacred texts.[19] However, he carefully leaves out the advice of Francis about not wandering through a thousand texts, which was included in the *Second Life*. What follows this description of Francis is an explicit treatment of the saint's position on the friars' pursuit of theological studies:

> Once, when the brothers asked him whether he was pleased that the literate men, who, by that time, had been received into the order, were aiming to study the Sacred Scripture, he replied: 'I am indeed pleased, as long as, after the example of Christ, of whom we read that he prayed more than he read, they do not neglect zeal for prayer, and as long as they study not to know what they should say but to practise what they have heard and, once they have put it into practice, propose it to others. I want my brothers', he said, 'to be Gospel disciples and so progress in knowledge of the truth that they increase in pure simplicity without separating the simplicity of the dove from the wisdom of the serpent.'
>
> (*LM*, 11:1)

The approach of Bonaventure to the issue of study is, then, decidedly different from the previous texts considered, and in fact this passage is not to be found in any other medieval work on Francis. Judging by the account given in the *Second Life* or the Leonine texts, it is difficult to imagine Francis as being pleased upon hearing that his brothers intended to study theology, even though the brothers had promised him to keep their zeal for prayer. Celano's and Leo's Francis would essentially be suspicious of the desire to pursue learning, since the perfect way to follow the evangelical life is to live the life of simple brothers, which, if done with complete devotion, will lead to a wisdom much higher than that which can be achieved through books. It is highly probable that while writing these lines Bonaventure had the letter of Francis to St Anthony in mind, where he had said that he was 'pleased' that Anthony taught sacred theology as long as the spirit of prayer and devotion was not extinguished. Apart from the section considered above, there is no other reference to Francis's attitude towards study and books in the *Major Life*. Bonaventure omits all the passages in Celano connected to Francis's attitude towards books, and Francis's prophecies with regard to learning being an occasion for ruin.[20]

## THE 'MIRROR OF PERFECTION'

The next major text on Francis is the *Mirror of Perfection*, which scholarly consensus dates to the early fourteenth century. The anonymous author (or authors) of this text is quite critical of the state of the order at that time, and he seems to blame it partly on the integration of learning and study into the Franciscan vocation. Hence, all the passages originally in Celano that recount Francis's criticism with regard to learning and books reappear in the *Mirror of Perfection*.

The first part of the *Mirror of Perfection* is dedicated to poverty, and here we find the stories from the *Second Life* and the Leonine texts concerning the minister who wished to keep his expensive books and the novice who required a psalter. However, there are important differences in the way the author of the *Mirror of Perfection* tells these stories. To the minister who wishes to keep his expensive books Francis denies his permission, saying that this is against the order's creed of poverty (MP, 3). From here onwards, the author talks of a general conspiracy of all ministers against Francis's insistence on absolute poverty. We are told of the sinister plan of the ministers that has resulted in the removal from the *Rule* of the sentence 'take nothing for your journey', so that 'they were not obliged to observe the perfection of the Gospel' (MP, 3). The story of the novice asking for the psalter is essentially the same as the Leonine version. However, here the author feels the need to make the message clearer and interprets Francis's message 'As if he were saying: "One must not care about books and learning, but about virtuous deeds, because learning pumps up, but love edifies"' (MP, 4).

From the sixty-ninth chapter onwards, the author turns his attention more directly to Francis's attitude towards learning. The discussion starts with the citation of the prophecy in the *Second Life* and the *Intention of the Rule* about the future tribulations, when books will be thrown away and learning will be an occasion for ruin (MP, 69). This is followed by the section from the Leonine texts where Francis deems the learned brothers mistaken in assuming that they edify people through their preaching. However, the author of the *Mirror of Perfection* adds his own comment at the end of this episode:

> But those who did not care for anything except to know and to show the way of salvation to others, and have done nothing on their own behalf, will stand naked and empty-handed before the judgement seat of Christ, bearing only the sheaves of confusion, shame and sorrow. Then the truth of holy humility and simplicity, of holy prayer and poverty, which is our vocation, will be exalted, glorified and proclaimed. Those inflated with the wind of learning betrayed this truth by their lives and by the vain sermons of their wisdom, by

proclaiming this truth to be falsehood and, as blind people, by persecuting cruelly those who walked in the truth. Then the error and falsehood of their opinions according to which they walked, which they preached as truth, and by which they have thrust many people into the pit of blindness, will end in grief, confusion and shame. And they with their murky opinions will be cast into exterior darkness with the spirits of darkness. Frequently blessed Francis, therefore, used to say about this passage: "The barren one has given birth to many children and the mother of many languishes." The barren one is the good, simple, humble, poor and looked-down-upon, the miserable and contemptible religious who by holy prayers and virtues continually edifies others and brings them to birth with sorrowful groans. He used to say this passage very often to the ministers and the other brothers, especially in a general chapter.

(MP, 72)

This passage not only offers a criticism of the learned brothers as those who misunderstood the Franciscan vocation, but also accuses them of persecuting the simple friars, who are considered to be the true followers of Francis. Its tone is angry, accusatory and vengeful. This rage fits with the historical context. In the preparations for the Council of Vienne in 1310–11, the pope had asked a group of friars to present their complaints in written form. The result was the texts of *Responsio*, *Rotulus* and *Declaratio*, which are believed to have been penned by Ubertino da Casale, who headed this dissident party.[21] A good part of the complaints of Ubertino was about the corruption and abuses of the lectors, and the general ambition in the order to take positions of authority.[22]

The penultimate sentence of the passage cited above is, in my opinion, the key to understanding why some brothers in the order thought an effort to become learned incompatible with the Franciscan vocation. In their view, Francis wanted his brothers to be lowly, despicable and miserable, and to achieve their own salvation and those of others by embracing joyfully this lowly life of penitence and prayer. Learning, however, inspires respect and enhances social value in the eyes of others, no matter how humble its pursuer tries to be. Francis himself in fact called on his brothers to respect theologians. It is precisely this respect and prestige that make learning incompatible with the friars' vocation. In fact, a common idea in the stories told so far, with the exception of Bonaventure's, is that many friars pursued learning precisely for the sake of that respect and prestige.

## THE 'DEEDS' OF BLESSED FRANCIS AND HIS COMPANIONS

The *Deeds* is believed to have been written between 1328 and 1337 by Ugolino Boniscambi of Montegiorgio. It includes two stories that are relevant to our subject. First is the story of the two students from noble families who take the Franciscan habit after listening to the preaching of Francis in Bologna.[23] Francis tells them to embrace humility. Following Francis's advice, one of them, Brother Pellegrino, refuses to become a cleric and remains a lay brother, despite being an expert in canon law. In the story of Brother Pellegrino, we find a perfect example of the idea of voluntary simplicity. Having chosen this path, the ex-scholar achieves great sanctity, and in the words of Brother Bernard of Quintavalle he was 'one of the most perfect brothers of this world' [Deeds, 30].

In Sabatier's edition of the *Deeds of Blessed Francis and His Companions* chapter 61 is the most explicit about Francis's attitude towards studying among all the stories considered here. It is entitled 'That Study did not Please Francis'.[24] The minister provincial of Bologna, John of Stacia, orders the foundation of a school in the convent of Bologna without the permission of Francis. Francis learns of this from a messenger, comes to Bologna in a fury and scolds the minister, accusing him of attempting to destroy his order. A similar version of the story is also found in the *History of the Seven Tribulations of the Order of Friars Minor* by Angelo Clareno. Modern scholarship has rejected the authenticity of this passage, which is found only in some manuscripts.[25] However, insofar as this passage was produced by the medieval friars, if not the actual author of the *Deeds*, it still serves the discussion of this chapter.


### CONCLUSION

All medieval texts on Francis, with the notable exception of Bonaventure's *Major Life*, seem to agree on the principle point that Francis did not approve of the 'desire to become learned'. The Franciscan vocation as it was understood by these authors involves a principle of voluntary simplicity that operates much like that of voluntary poverty. If voluntary poverty is the desire to be and to remain poor, voluntary simplicity is the desire to be and to remain simple. The meaning of simplicity here, materialized in the person of John the Simple, involves an unmistakable element of the absence of intellectual or scholarly activity. A 'simple life' in the Franciscan context is therefore a rigorous life of penitence and prayer, but systematic and regular study has no place in it. The simple should want to remain simple and not desire to become learned, and the literate or the learned should not try to advance their learning by further study, and should live as if they were simple brothers, like the canon lawyer, Brother Pellegrino. Particularly significant is the idea that the simple life, not study, is the best way to acquire true knowledge of the Gospels. Bonaventure's legend of Francis stands in contrast to this tradition. He writes explicitly that the intention of the friars to pursue theological study pleased Francis. He does use the word simplicity, but in his case simplicity seems to have the meaning of 'humility'. It is clear that Bonaventure as a minister general would not have wished to promote the idea of a completely ignorant brother like John the Simple as the exemplary, saintly brother.

It is not possible to know how close this theory of voluntary simplicity, as distinct from humility and marked by an absence of a desire to study, corresponds to the actual will of Francis, but it is supported by the clause in the *Rule* that the illiterate brothers should not bother to learn letters. The letter of Francis to Anthony of Padua, the first unofficial lector in the order, is not an obstacle, since it does not mention the desire of brothers to learn from Anthony, but only the wish of Anthony to teach the friars. In any case, the inclusion of the passages concerning Francis's attitudes to books and learning in these biographies from 1240s onwards, and the increasingly argumentative tone with which the idea of voluntary simplicity is defended, are proof that the consequences of the integration of learning into the Franciscan vocation had some undesirable and perhaps unforeseen consequences. Among them the creation of a hierarchy and devaluation of the lay brothers seem to be the most unwelcome to some friars. As the historical text is at once a product and a fabricator of its own historical context, the presence of the passages discussed above tells us more about the contemporary state of the order and the discontents of its authors with that state than about the actual attitudes of Francis towards learning.

### Notes

1   RB, chapters 2 and 9. The ministers were to examine preachers and the new recruits.
2   See C. Cenci, 'De Fratrum Minorum Constitutionibus Praenarbonensibus', *AFH*, 83 (1990), 93. Also B. Roest, *A History of Franciscan Education (c. 1210–1517)* (Leiden, 2000), pp. 8–9.
3   I discuss the emergence of a culture of learning in the order and its consequences in my forthcoming monograph tentatively entitled *The Rise of Learning in the Franciscan Order* (Ithaca, 2012).

4      Item, nullus recipiatur in ordine nostro nisi talis qui rexerit in artibus, vel qui [illeg.]... aut rexerit in medicina, in decretis aut legibus, aut sit sollempnizatus responsor in theologia, seu valde famosus predicator, seu multus celebris et approbatus advocatus, vel qui in famosis civitatibus vel castellis laudabiliter in gramatica rexerit, vel sit talis clericus vel laycus, de cuius ingressu esset valde celebris et famosa edificatio in populo et clero.

      C. Cenci, 'Fragmenta Priscarum Constitutionum Praenarbonensium', *AFH*, 96 (2003), 298.

5   2 Cel., 103.

6   Bonaventure used this image of 'Francis the Wise' precisely to argue why the friars should not try to imitate Francis in his learning but instead seek knowledge through teachers. E. Doyle, *The Disciple and the Master: St Bonaventure's Sermons on St Francis of Assisi* (Chicago, 1984), p. 64.

7   2 Cel., 190.

8   F. Delorme, 'Textes franciscaines (Lettre de S. Bonaventure Innominato Magistro)', *Archivio Italiano per la Storia della Pietà*, 1 (1951), 214; Anonymous, *Determinationes Quaestionum Circa Regulam Fratrum Minorum*, in *S. Bonaventurae Opera Omnia* (Quaracchi, 1898), vol. VIII, pp. 337–74, at 339.

9   R.B. Brooke (ed.), *Scripta Leonis, Rufini et Angeli Sociorum S. Francisci. The Writings of Leo, Rufino and Angelo, Companions of St Francis*, OMT (Oxford, 1970, corrected reprint, 1990).

10  On the textual history of the *Intention of the Rule*, see Brooke, *Scripta Leonis*, pp. 51–3.

11  CA, 102; R.B. Brooke (ed.), *Scripta Leonis*, c. 69, pp. 207–9.

12  CA, 103–5; R.B. Brooke (ed.), *Scripta Leonis*, cc. 70–4, pp. 208–17. See a discussion of these stories concerning the friar requesting the psalter in R.B. Brooke (ed.), *The Image of St Francis: Responses to Sainthood in the Thirteenth Century* (Cambridge, 2006), pp. 122–3. They are repeated also in Sabatier's edition of *Speculum Perfectionis: seu S. Franciscani Assisiensis legenda antiquissima auctore fratre Leone* (Paris, 1898), sections 150a–152.

13  CA, 103; R.B. Brooke (ed.), *Scripta Leonis*, c. 70, pp. 210–11.

14  CA, 112; R.B. Brooke (ed.), *Scripta Leonis*, c. 86, pp. 238–9 (Brooke's translation).

15  2 Cel., 158.

16  R.B. Brooke (ed.), *Scripta Leonis*, c. 70–1, pp. 211–13 (Brooke's translation with my slight modifications). A similar argument about knowledge making proud is in c. 72.

17  CA, 104; R.B. Brooke (ed.), *Scripta Leonis*, c. 73, pp. 214–17.

18  R.B. Brooke (ed.), *Scripta Leonis*, c. 74, pp. 216–17.

19  *LM*, 11:1.

20  In his *Arbor Vitae Crucifixae Jesu*, written in 1305, Ubertino da Casale wrote that Bonaventure purposely omitted such stories since 'he did not wish to disgrace the brothers prematurely before those outside the Order'. R.B. Brooke (ed.), *Scripta Leonis*, p. 54.

21  Ubertino da Casale, *Responsio*, in 'Zur Vorgeschichte des Konzils von Vienne no. 4 Vorarbeiten zur Constitution Exivi de Paradiso vom 6. Mai 1312', ed. F. Ehrle, *Archiv für Litteratur- und Kirchengeschichte des Mittelalters*, 3 (1887), 51–89; *Rotulus*, 93–137; *Declaratio*, 162–95.
22  See for example, *Responsio*, 73–6 and *Rotulus*, 118, ibid.
23  *The Deeds of Blessed Francis and His Companions* by Ugolino Boniscambi of Montegiorgio (1328–77), c. 30, in *FAED*, vol. III, pp. 500–1.
24  P. Sabatier, *Actus beati Francisci et sociorum ejus* (Paris, 1902), cap. 61, p. 183.
25  See the introduction by Menestò in E. Menestò, S. Brufani, G. Cremascoli, E. Paoli, L. Pellegrini and S. da Campagnolo (eds.), *Fontes Franciscani*, Medioevo Francescano, 2 (Assisi, 1995), pp. 2066, 2073.

# 6 Francis and the historiographical tradition in the order

ANNETTE KEHNEL

Some people have the misfortune to be remembered primarily through the writings of their critics. Others, such as Francis, who are mainly remembered in the writings of their admirers, are not necessarily better off. Uncritical adulation and hero worship can be worse than honest criticism. In this sense hagiography has long had a poor reputation among historians. They have never trusted the hagiographer (and still do not) and have rebuked him for being biased and uncritical, preoccupied with miracles and supernatural powers. Whereas the supposedly impartial historian is interested in reality and hard facts, the hagiographer simply tells us stories. However, in the foregoing chapters we have seen that Franciscan hagiography presents us with a surprisingly human saint: in fact, we find a remarkable concentration on the saint's humanity, on his needs, on his body, on his afflictions, his sufferings and weaknesses.

It is also clear that for thirteenth-century writers the difference between hagiography and history was far less significant than for scholars trained in the academic traditions developed in the nineteenth century. Finally, the modern historian's preoccupation with 'real facts' rather than 'stories' has been rudely shaken by the discovery that historical science, even in its most methodological, quantifying and analytical aspects, cannot exist independently of narrative constructions. In other words, history (whether an art or a science) is, and always will be, bound up with story-telling.

## ST FRANCIS AND THE FRANCISCANS' NEED FOR HISTORY

We have evidence that Francis set store on the preservation of a written tradition. We have but two pieces of parchment preserving the handwriting of St Francis. One is the so-called *Cartula fratris Leoni data* with a prayer in praise of God on the front page and a blessing for Brother Leo on the back. There is also a letter to Brother Leo written in Francis's own hand. Thomas of Eccleston suggests that Francis wrote poorly when he mentions his crude Latin (*falsum latinum*). Judging by the above-mentioned autographs, the indictment would be confirmed, for it contains mistakes in both spelling and grammar. Nevertheless, the record suggests that Francis had great respect for the written word. Thomas of Celano tells us that whenever Francis found anything written about God along the way, or in a house, or on the floor, he would pick it up with the greatest reverence and put it in a sacred place (1 Cel., 82). He wanted his own writings to be preserved. In two of his letters he addresses all the ministers of the order, present and future, and admonishes them to keep his writings with them, to put them into practice and to eagerly preserve them.

The Franciscan need for history can be rooted here. It agrees with what may be taken to be a universal human need for history, founded in the knowledge (or rather fear) that works not remembered are like works undone. This need to write things down, so that 'things done by man may not be forgotten in time' (Herodotus) found a remarkably fresh expression in the historical writings of all the new orders of friars founded in the thirteenth century. Mendicant historians were very aware of being part of a great movement and witnessing something special. Thomas of Celano, in his third *Life* of Francis, speaks of the great miracle of the beginning of the order: the infertile made fertile, St Francis – the new man who leapt upon the earth and who caused a new army to appear (3 Cel., 1). The members of the order were actively involved in this novelty; they took part in it and promoted it throughout Europe. Moreover, the friars lived as members of a transnational community with a strong feeling that community not only needs a common *Rule*, shared values and a personal founder, but also a unifying founding story.

This need for a unifying founding story grew stronger with the ever-growing spread of the order that accompanied its successful expansion throughout medieval Europe and into missionary territory. We can describe this distance both in spatial and temporal terms. Every Franciscan house founded in Spain, Ireland, Sweden or Poland meant an increase in geographical distance within the order. At the same time the days of the generation of friars who had met and got to know Francis were becoming part of a more and more remote past. The writing of history within the order has been interpreted as an attempt to come to terms with these growing distances.

First, the provincial chronicles are read by modern scholars as the expression of a growing self-confidence. The friars in the provinces – so it is assumed – discovered a need for their own history and identity. Secondly, the beginnings of Franciscan historiography have been read as a way of coping with the generational crisis, unavoidable in the early development of every institution, when the founder's generation dies out. How to see that the values and the spirit of the founder still speak in the future? How to pass on knowledge about the founder to the second and third generations? These questions clearly occupied the minds of those present at the general chapter in Genoa in the year 1244. Under the direction of the new minister general, Crescentius of Iesi, it was decreed that for future use not only documents and information about the life and work of the founder should be collected, but also 'other edifying deeds worth remembering' (*aliquod factum edificatorium dignum memoria*). To begin with, this decree inspired hagiographical writing. Thomas of Celano wrote his second biography at the instigation of Crescentius. It also inspired the compilation of exemplary stories and finally – if only indirectly – the writing of historical works, such as the early chronicles to be discussed in the following pages.

## THOMAS OF ECCLESTON, JORDAN OF GIANO AND SALIMBENE DE ADAM

Let us start with the earliest so-called provincial chronicle written in the Franciscan order, known under the title *The Coming to England of the Friars Minor*. Of its author next to nothing is known. He calls himself Brother Thomas. Even the 'de Eccleston' was added in one of the four surviving manuscripts of the text no earlier than the seventeenth century. His report is dedicated to a certain Brother Simon de Esseby, and we also learn from the dedicatory epistle that Thomas had been collecting materials for his chronicles over twenty-six years. From internal evidence we can deduce that Thomas finished his work before 1257–8. He is extremely well informed about internal affairs in the order. Thus we learn incidentally that the English friars had a seal stamped with a lamb bearing a cross, when Thomas reports on arrangements to succeed the first minister provincial, Agnellus of Pisa, who died on 13 March 1236. He also gives detailed information on the various officials in the order, papal legates, the officials of the province and other organisational issues. We might call him a patriot. He was convinced that standards in the English province were remarkable. He shows a sympathetic bias towards his own province and its members, and identifies entirely with his community. He writes: 'How I wish this province were placed in the middle of the world that it might be an example to all.' [1]

Although Thomas is honest, well-informed and accurate, his qualities as a historian have often been doubted. The arrangement of his material is chaotic, his sense of proportion appears deficient. There is but one single date mentioned in the whole chronicle: namely 10 September 1224, when the friars arrived at Dover. His work is not an account of the history of the early English friars remembered by one of them, but rather a text that assembles the collective memory of the group. It seems to document the friars' evening conversations as described by Thomas himself when he tells us how the friars in Canterbury in the evenings assembled in their emergency accommodation in the school house 'where they sat and built a fire for themselves; and they sat next to it and sometimes, when they had to have their collation, they put on the fire a little pot containing the dregs of beer, and they dipped a cup into the pot and each drank in turn and spoke some word of edification'.[2] Thomas gives written testimony of these cheerful meetings in the evenings, when the friars shared their experiences with each other. As the years passed by his stories were sometimes read aloud. And we can well imagine how they inspired other brothers to add their own experiences, and thus to continue the story once begun in Assisi by Francis and kept alive by the friars in Oxford, Northampton, Hereford and elsewhere. In fact the textual shape of the manuscripts preserves traces of an ongoing process of writing, reading, adding, copying and rewriting the shared memories of a local community.

Jordan of Giano, the chronicler of the German province, was an Italian who had spent most of his life in Germany. His account differs fundamentally from that by Thomas of Eccleston in that it reflects entirely the individual memory of one brother. Jordan must have been a brilliant story-teller, and he recounts anecdotes which he had told over and over again before his brethren begged him to write them down at the provincial chapter in Halberstadt in the year 1262. Agreeing to their request, he dictated his memoires to Brother Balduin of Brandenburg. In contrast to Thomas of Eccleston's compilation, his text reveals a strong individuality and a deep historical sense. We also find within the text a number of details regarding his own person: he introduces himself as a fragile older person (*iam senex et debilis*) and tells us that he was a deacon from the valley of Spoleto, that is from the same region as Assisi.[3] His estimated date of birth is 1195. He must have entered the order before 1219, because he regrets not having taken the opportunity to speak to the friars sent out to Spain in that year. In 1221 he left Italy on the mission to Germany together with Caesar of Speyer and his group.[4] In 1223 he was ordained priest, worked as guardian of Speyer, later of Mainz, was then custos of Thuringia and established the friaries in Eisenach, Gotha, Nordhausen and Mühlhausen. Twice, namely in 1230–1 and in 1238, he travelled to Rome and Assisi. It is also very likely that he is the author of three letters written around 1241, reporting on the cruelties committed in the fights between Mongol soldiers and Polish and Hungarian knights.[5]

His chronicle is most dense for the years between 1219 and 1239. It reflects the natural functioning of an individual memory: the more remote an event, the more present it is, so the earliest events are the most vivid. With noticeable amusement he calls to mind the human sides of his confrères, as well as the human sides of St Francis, whom Jordan knew in person. With a roguish smile he notes that his own career in the German provinces was the unintended consequence of intentional action. During the Pentecostal chapter of Assisi in 1221 his intention of shaking hands with the potential martyrs before their departure to Germany led to a dramatic change in his life. More or less against his will, young Brother Jordan was obliged to join the group by the gleeful Brother Palmerius, who simply told him, 'You too are one of us, and shall go with us.'[6] That at least is the version of the story told by the old Brother Jordan, who was – no doubt – a professional story-teller. On the burdensome journey to Germany it was he who caused local Austrian farmers to bring them bread, eggs and milk just by smiling at people and making them laugh.[7] He also remembers individual friars: Brother Hartmut, the German, who was renamed Andrea by the Italians because they could not pronounce his name.[8] He reports on the pious friars in Mühlhausen (in Thuringia) who were so eager in their prayers that they forgot to finish the roof on the house given to them by the duke of Velsekke-Gleichen.[9] Or there was the extremely humble Brother Nicholas, whose humility was so irritating that Jordan intentionally avoided coming near him.[10] One of the most remarkable stories in Jordan's account is the visit of a Franciscan delegation to Rome, when the friars appealed to the pope against the minister general, Elias of Cortona. Jordan himself was a member of the party and remembers how Gregory IX at first refused to talk to the friars. However, when they eventually got access, they were admitted right into his bedroom and found the pope lying in bed. Jordan himself – thus he tells us – stepped forth to the papal bed, took the pope's feet and kissed them, calling out to his confrères, 'Behold, we do not have such relics in Saxony.'[11]

These few examples might suffice to demonstrate the extraordinarily intimate insight offered by Jordan. With a deep sense of humour he describes early Franciscan life with a wry, often comical note. Jordan is a rational and precise observer, he tells us anecdotes instead of *exempla*, he favours common sense instead of visions, and he portrays human beings instead of saints.

Brother Salimbene de Adam was from Parma. Whereas Thomas of Eccleston tells us next to nothing about himself or his family background, Salimbene makes himself one of his main topics. While Jordan of Giano wrote on the urgent request of his confrères, Salimbene de Adam wrote – according to his own witness – for his niece Agnes in the convent of St Clare in Parma. Although Thomas of Eccleston and Jordan of Giano are mainly read by those interested in the history of medieval religious life, Salimbene has a reputation as one of the richest historiographical texts of the Middle Ages and one of the most important witnesses of the thirteenth century.

His work is extraordinary in its size. Although only preserved as a fragment, it covers 951 pages in the edition of the Latin original. The edition of Thomas's *Tractatus* covers 104 pages and Jordan of Giano 80 pages. It is the only work preserved by this author, although we know that he wrote many others. Salimbene was 62 years old when he started writing the chronicle in the year 1283, in the Franciscan convent at Reggio.

To get a solid impression of his work, one might best read the opening chapters starting with general European affairs, continuing with detailed information on Salimbene's childhood and his first years in the order. Born on 9 October 1221 in the city of Parma, he was baptised near Parma. As his godfather he claims an ostensibly famous Lord Balian of Sidon, a great baron of France and a crusader on his way back from the Holy Land. His mode of recording is very personal: when he was 14 months old, at Christmas 1222, there was a great earthquake in the city of Reggio to be felt throughout Lombardy and Tuscany and also in Parma. His mother later used to tell him that he was then lying in his cot and that she grabbed his two sisters, one under each arm (they were very small), and ran to her family's home. The little boy was left behind in the cradle. According to his mother the sisters were easier to carry. 'And because of this, I could never afterward love her as much as before, because she ought to have been more careful of me, the male of the family, than of the daughters.'[12] Such detailed information about the individual memories of a medieval mind has led to the chronicle's being called the most remarkable autobiography of the Middle Ages.

In similar detail the reader is informed about Salimbene's reception and first years in the order: in 1238, on 4 February on the evening of the vigil of St Agatha, in the city of Parma, by Brother Elias, the minister general. After one year in the order under his worldly name Ognibene, he met a holy friar who lived as a hermit near Città di Castello, who renamed him Salimbene. This man was, according to Salimbene's witness, the last brother whom St Francis himself had received into the order. Shortly afterwards he also got to know Bernard of Quintavalle, the first man whom St Francis received as a disciple. Salimbene announces that he spent an entire winter in the convent at Siena with Bernard and obtained precious information on the founder. 'He was my very close friend, and he told me and the other young men many great things about St Francis, and I heard and learned from him much that was good.'[13]

In great detail Salimbene reports the great lengths to which his father went in order to detach him from the order. This account of the exchange between father and son is valuable. Salimbene has high qualities as an inside informer and is sometimes rather critical. Thus he complains about the liturgy: 'For it contains much that is superfluous, which causes boredom rather than devotion, both to the congregation and to the celebrants.'[14] He has a very worldly side and loves to describe himself in the company of the great and famous, such as Innocent IV, Louis IX of France, Emperor Frederick II, King Henry III of England, and celebrated friars such as John of Piano Carpini, the friar who travelled to the Mongols as an envoy of Innocent IV. He also likes to eat and drink at their tables and is most famous for his expertise in wines. 'Take note too that there are three regions in France that produce an abundance of wine: La Rochelle, Beaune and Auxerre. It is noteworthy also that in Auxerre red wines have the lowest reputation, for they are not as good as the red wines of Italy.'[15] Salimbene is much appreciated for his power of painting lifelike portraits in a few words, for his rollicking humour and amazing egoism. His work has been neatly characterised by his modern translator, Joseph L. Baird, as a most remarkable record of an age, filtered through the consciousness of a thirteenth-century friar who was at the same time, somehow, an intensely aware, worldly man of the world.

A final remark about the distribution of these texts in the Middle Ages: these early Franciscan chronicles were certainly no bestsellers, unlike, for example, the *Legenda aurea*, also compiled in the mid thirteenth century and preserved today in over a thousand manuscripts. The *Tractatus* of Eccleston survived in only four manuscripts; Jordan's

chronicle comes down to us in three manuscripts, plus some continu-
ations dating from the sixteenth century; Salimbene's chronicle survived
in one single copy, handwritten by its author. We might deduce that they
did not meet the taste of their times; at least, later generations saw no
great need to preserve them for the future. It is, however, exactly this
feature that increases their value for us today, since they allow insights
into contemporary life, into medieval minds and into a culture otherwise often covered under the heavy burden of mainstream writers.

The order of St Francis produced some remarkable historians
already in the century of its foundation. These early Franciscan chronicles share an origin in the provinces rather than at the centre of the
order. They testify to the need to put into writing the Franciscan
experience. They testify to a genuine historical sense, alive in the order
especially in the second and third generation of friars. However, there is
yet another dimension: the chronicles testify to the friars' conviction
that they are part of something new and special, something worth
remembering in the future. At the same time all three were very aware
of the shortcomings of their own present, and they share a distinct
sense of humour.

Caroline W. Bynum, one of the great historians of religious history
today, once argued that the writing of history must come to terms
gracefully with the incomplete, that it must be a conversation open to
new voices and that its essential mode is comic. The Franciscan historians in the thirteenth century seem to have shared this understanding.

## THE IMAGE OF ST FRANCIS IN THE EARLY FRANCISCAN CHRONICLES

Finally we come to the question of how the early historians portrayed St Francis in their works. This time we start with Salimbene.
There is no denying it: Francis does not figure very prominently here.
In the whole of Salimbene's chronicle – 951 pages in the Latin edition –
the name of St Francis appears 58 times (cf. Emperor Frederick II, who
appears with 81 entries in the index of the English translation). Many of
the entries are, of course, indirect references that serve to specify other
persons or dates. However, Salimbene makes it quite clear that it is not
his intention to write a chronicle of the post-mortem deeds and miracles of the saint. Thus, in the record of the translation of the remains
of St Francis in 1230 he mentions the many miracles that accompanied
the event, only to refer the reader – for further information – to the life
and legend of St Francis.[16]

Francis does, however, appear as the founder and teacher. Salimbene quotes the founder as a moral exemplar in ambiguous situations, for example in a dispute about whether it is dishonourable for a preacher to be accompanied by women. Here the authority of Francis is quoted with an otherwise unrecorded piece of advice that some things should simply not be done, to avoid the possibility of public misinterpretation.[17] The same quotation reappears in the discussion about the behaviour of Lupus, archbishop of Siena, who was severely criticised by his whole court for his excessive love of his predecessor's daughter. Salimbene seems not too critical of the archbishop's sincere assertion that he loved the girl in purity of spirit, but he recommends to the reader: 'With regard to this matter it is good to do what St Francis teaches. For he says: it is good to put aside many things, lest opinion be harmed.'[18] We might agree that St Francis in Salimbene's chronicle seems rather to supply the background rather than be the central motif in this thirteenth-century portrait.

Like Salimbene, Jordan makes it quite clear in the beginning that his chronicle is not a life of St Francis and that 'because enough has been said in the *Legenda* about how his conversion took place, we will pass over it here'.[19] However, he begins with a neat biographical sketch. In contrast to Salimbene, who was born only in 1221, Jordan offers a number of valuable insights into the order's early history seen through the eyes of an insider who is sceptical rather than enthusiastic and generally prefers a 'rationalist' perspective.

His accounts of Francis's decision to travel to the Holy Land certainly do not reveal great piety. The decision to travel to the Holy Land is portrayed as an emergency solution after the saint had realised, towards the end of the general chapter meeting in 1219, that he did not want to stay behind when all the others climbed the ladder of perfection on their missions to foreign countries.[20] Jordan is both fascinated and irritated by the saint's humility. Admiration shines through when Francis acts in accordance with sound common sense. Thus, we are told that, when Francis was in the Holy Land, the two vicars who replaced him at home had decreed stricter fasting regulations. One of the lay brothers in the order, who was very worried about this development, set out to meet Francis in the Holy Land to present the new regulations to Francis and to hear his judgement. Francis read the new *Rules* and then asked Peter Catania, his companion, what was to be done. On the table before them a nice dish had just been served. Promptly they agreed: 'Let us then eat, according to the Gospel, what has been placed before us.'[21] In fact we owe our knowledge about the difficulties in the order during Francis's journey to the sultan of Egypt, al-Malik-al-Kâmil, almost entirely to Brother Jordan. The same respectful undertone seems to sound through when writing on the developments after Francis's return. Jordan seems to appreciate Francis's decision, instead of arguing with the group of friars opposed to his teaching, to travel straight to Rome to ask Honorius III for a procurator of the order.[22] On the Pentecost chapter, however, Francis's performance is once again very weak. According to Jordan, it appeared to Francis all of a sudden that the order was not yet established in Germany. Since he was ill at the time, Elias said whatever he had to say to the chapter. Francis, sitting at the feet of Elias, tugged at his tunic (*traxit eum per tunicam*). Elias bowed down to him and listened to what he wished to say, and then rose to speak.[23] Such behaviour seems more becoming to a shy child than the leader of a great movement. Jordan depicts the situation with a mixture of amusement and irritation.

There is one more story that might supply a key to Jordan's (let's say) rational approach to the founder. The event falls in the time after 1230. Jordan, on his way back to Germany from Assisi, met Thomas of Celano, who handed over to him some precious relics of St Francis (according to Nicolas Glassberger, the person who continued Jordan's chronicle); these were some hair and parts of St Francis's habit. Jordan then continued his journey, forgetting about the relics. However, when he reached Eisenach, he was received by the friars in a most reverential manner. They made him walk to the main door of the church and received him with crucifixes, incense, palm leaves and candles in a ceremonial procession. Jordan himself was thunderstruck at this new way of welcoming a brother and requested the brethren to stop. Only then did he realise that the brethren were celebrating the holy relics he had with him. 'And from then on', the elderly chronicler remembers, 'Brother Jordan began to hold in greater reverence and honour Blessed Francis, whom he had seen in life and for this reason something of whose humanity had struck him (*quem in presenti vita viderat et ob hoc quiddam ei humanitatis acciderat)*'.[24] Jordan here reflects in great honesty about his failure to recognise St Francis the saint (according to the principle that a prophet has no honour in his own country). In this confession we can almost see Brother Jordan still wondering and watching, critically shaking his head over the little man from Assisi – but ever more fascinated, and overwhelmed by the enduring power of Francis's weakness.

Though Brother Thomas of Eccleston wrote the earliest provincial chronicle of the Franciscan order he was in many ways the most removed of the three authors discussed here. Like Salimbene, he had never met Francis, and when he joined the order in 1232 St Francis was already six years dead. Unlike Salimbene, who, by styling himself a disciple of Bernard of Quintavalle, constructs a direct link to the oldest Franciscan community, Thomas never claims acquaintance with the early companions of Francis or other celebrated friars.

We might call him the historian at the greatest distance from Franciscan origins. Paradoxically, however, his text documents the most intimate acquaintance with the founder saint. Francis seems most present among his disciples in the English province, constantly acting, helping out and giving advice whenever needed. First of all he is present in visions. Such a thing was unheard of in the German province – at least according to the records of Brother Jordan of Giano. In England, however, St Francis regularly appeared to his friars. A story recounted by Haymo of Faversham states that the saint cured a young novice from constant thirst in a nocturnal vision.[25] Francis gave nightly advice each night to Brother John Bannister. He was troubled, since it had been decreed by a general-chapter decision that in every province certain brothers were to be chosen to write down what seemed problematic in the *Rule* to them. In this context Francis appeared to him at night, showing him a deep well. John told him about the intention of the order to interpret the *Rule* and begged him to interpret it himself. Francis answered: 'Son, go to the lay brothers and let them explain the *Rule* for you.' In the end the English friars wrote down a few points and sent them to the minister general in an unsealed parchment beseeching him not to allow the *Rule* to be changed but to let it have exactly the shape given by Francis at the instigation of the Holy Spirit.[26]

Quite obviously Francis here acts as a guarantor of true Franciscanism. The vision expresses a deep anxiety about being faithful to the founder's vision. The English friars were eager to realise the Franciscan way of life as close to Franciscan origins as possible.

The same concern finds expression in the following interventions by St Francis once it came to the building of new houses for the ever-increasing number of friars. According to a story narrated by Brother Robert of Slapton, Francis once appeared to a guardian. He was led round by the friars and was very pleased with the simple construction of the walls all about: walls made of wattle, smeared with mud and mire. Thereafter the guardian washed Francis's feet and kissed his stigmata.[27] Francis's joy in wattle and mud as the building-materials of Franciscan houses confirms the friars' intention to follow the *Rule* as closely as possible. A more radical interference of the founder saint occurred in Paris, where the brand-new Franciscan house in Valvert, near the Jardin du Luxembourg, simply collapsed some time around 1228. It had been a very large and tall building, far too large for a Franciscan house and entirely against the statute of poverty. According to Brother Henry of Burford, it was Francis himself who caused the house to fall down, in response to the prayer of some friars who had prayed to him to interfere.[28] The radical attitude of Francis against large houses was also confirmed by Brother Martin of Barton, who told his English brethren how he had been present himself when Francis gave the order to destroy the house that had been built especially for the chapter meeting in Assisi, probably in 1222 or 1223.[29] Quite obviously the authority of Francis is often quoted in this discussion about how to build houses in accordance with the statute of poverty.

The image of Francis is also kept alive by friars who had known him in person. Thus, the same Brother Martin of Barton once witnessed Francis writing a letter, standing in the open air in the rain, without the letter getting wet, and tells us how, on another occasion, Francis rescued a friar who had fallen into a well.[30] Brother Albert of Pisa recorded from his very own experience how Francis once admonished him, when he was in hospital, to eat twice as much as usual. Brother Albert in turn, in a similar situation, forced Brother Eustachius of Merc to eat fish.[31]

No doubt, Francis figures most prominently in the talks among the English friars. He is present as the ultimate authority, he helps the friars out and he binds the community together. There is one further aspect to be added here: the English friars' fascination with the stigmata and the saint's special relation to Christ. Thus, we are told how Brother Bonitius witnessed the stigmata of Francis at the general chapter in Genoa, and did so on the orders of John of Parma. Also Brother Warin of Sedenfeld is quoted, who wrote down from the mouth of Brother Leo how Brother Rufinus witnessed the Seraph, an angelic form, threaten St Francis and treat him severely. The Seraph told St Francis that his order would last to the end of the world, that no man of bad will would stay long in the order, that no one hating the order would live long, and that no one who loved the order would come to a bad end. St Francis bade Brother Rufinus to wash and anoint the stone on which the Seraph had stood.[32]

A final and most remarkable story, not related elsewhere, also circulated in English friaries. As always, Eccleston adds the exact reference for its origin. This story was narrated publicly in the friary at London by Brother Augustine, the brother of the provincial William of Nottingham. He in turn had heard it in a sermon by Pope Gregory IX on the feast of St Francis in Assisi. It is an anecdote about two heretics who, after their conversion in Venice, had the following vision: they saw Christ as judge with the apostles and all the other religious orders in the world. Unfortunately, they could not find the order of the Friars Minor, nor St Francis, who, according to the sermon of a papal legate, was exalted even above St John the Evangelist by the impression of the stigmata. So the converted heretics came to think that the papal legate had blasphemed. Jesus, reclining in the bosom of John, and John in his, 'opened the wound in His side with His hands and St Francis appeared most clearly within His breast; and the sweet Jesus closed the wound and enclosed him completely within it'.[33] Clearly, this extraordinary vision of St Francis in the wound of Christ is a piece of hagiography rather than history. It conveys an image of Francis as the saint most intimate with Christ – outdoing even St John the Evangelist. And here we come back to the introductory question about the difference between hagiography and historiography. The historian Thomas of Eccleston is the only source to relate this story. It is unknown even to the contemporary compilers of *exempla* collections. Brother Thomas the historian, however, carefully embedded the account in an historical context: the conversion of two heretics in Venice, authorised by Gregory IX in a sermon preached in Assisi, publicly related by a close relative of the English minister provincial in the friary in London. He thus works towards a 'historical' foundation of the image of St Francis as the most eminent saint in the Christian universe – the saint Christ-like by virtue of his wounds. And in fact it was this image of the wounded saint that proved most powerful in the future course of history.

## Notes

1   Thomas of Eccleston, c. 15, p. 185.
2   Ibid., c. 1, 97–8.
3   Jordan of Giano, no. 30, p. 45.
4   Ibid., no. 18, pp. 34–6.
5   Ibid., appendix, letter, pp. 73–7.
6   Ibid., no. 18, pp. 34–5.
7   Ibid., no. 27, pp. 42–4.
8   Ibid., nos. 25, 28, pp. 41, 44.
9   Ibid., no. 45, pp. 52–3.
10  Ibid., no. 47, pp. 53–4.
11  Ibid., no. 63, p. 65.
12  Salimbene, pp. 3–17.
13  Ibid., p. 13.

14  Ibid., p. 5.
15  Ibid., p. 209.
16  Ibid., p. 45.
17  Ibid., p. 60.
18  Ibid., p. 139.
19  Jordan of Giano, no. 1, p. 20.
20  Ibid., no. 10, pp. 25–6.
21  Ibid., no. 12, p. 28.
22  Ibid., no. 14, p. 29–30.
23  Ibid., no. 17, p. 33.
24  Ibid., no. 59, p. 63.
25  Thomas of Eccleston, c. 6, p. 123.
26  Ibid., c. 13, p. 158.
27  Ibid., c. 10, pp. 139–40.
28  Ibid., c. 10, p. 141.
29  Ibid., c. 6, p. 125–6.
30  Ibid., c. 6, p. 126.
31  Ibid., c. 14, pp. 171–2.
32  Ibid., c. 13, pp. 161–2.
33  Ibid., c. 15, pp. 177–8.

# 7 Francis and Clare and the emergence of the Second Order

JEAN FRANÇOIS GODET-CALOGERAS

## FRANCIS AND CLARE, THE MERCHANT AND THE LADY

Francis seemed to be surprised when other men asked to join him. But he welcomed those who came, and soon an evangelical fraternity was born. In 1209, when, according to the hagiographers, they had reached the symbolic number of twelve, Francis and his brothers went to Rome to seek papal confirmation of their form of living. Eventually they returned to Assisi, having been blessed by Innocent III. Did Francis consider the possibility of women joining his group? There is clearly no mention of a female presence on the journey to Rome. In the context of the time, it would certainly have created problems for unmarried men and women, especially from different social classes, to travel on the road together. It is quite unlikely that such a group would have been viewed positively in Rome, much less that it would have received the blessing of the pope. And yet some sources – including the *Testament* of Clare of Assisi herself – mention that before Francis had any brothers, while he was working on the restoration of the little church of San Damiano outside Assisi, he used to call out to people in French, talking about the coming of holy women to that holy place:

> While labouring with others in that work, he used to clamour to people living as well as passing by the church in a loud voice, filled with joy of the spirit, telling them in French: 'Come and help me in the work of the church of San Damiano which, in the future, will be a monastery of ladies through whose fame and life our heavenly Father will be glorified throughout the church.'[1]

The use of the word *lady* puts the story in the medieval context of chivalry and nobility, the social class that Francis, wealthy but only a merchant, had been longing to become part of.

Assisi was and remains a small world. By 1210 Francis had been making enough noise. Among those who had joined his fraternity was a young man from one of the noble families of Assisi, Rufino di Scipione di Offreduccio. Rufino had a first cousin named Clare, daughter of his uncle Favarone di Offreduccio. Brother Rufino was to be the one who enabled the encounter between Francis and Clare.

Coming from a noble and powerful family of knights, Clare was a lady by rank. But she was also respected for her personal qualities. According to men and women who had known her during her youth, she was good, kind and gracious. She was also beautiful, and several men would have liked to marry her. But it seems that, already at a young age, Clare had other ideas. In her desire to please God, she would often tend to the needs of the poor and share her food with them. And she always enjoyed talking about the things of God.

Clare most probably received a deep religious education from her mother, Lady Ortulana, who was also a religious and charitable person. Before Clare's birth, she went on pilgrimage to the Holy Land, to Rome and to Sant'Angelo del Monte Gargano, the shrine of St Michael the archangel. She would frequently visit the poor. As far as the sources let us know, Clare also had two younger sisters: Catherine, better known as Agnes after Francis renamed her, and Beatrice. Later, mother and daughters were to be reunited in the new community of San Damiano.

Brother Rufino must have talked of Francis to his cousin Clare, and of Clare to Francis. Clare was intrigued by this son of a wealthy merchant of the city; she knew how he had publicly and dramatically left his family, the city of Assisi and everything to follow Christ. But it seems that it is Francis who took the initiative and made a move. Having heard of the qualities of that young lady (she was about twelve years younger than he), a member of a powerful noble family and cousin to one member of his fraternity, Francis managed to meet Clare. It must have been around the year 1211. They went on to have several encounters. Clare and her friend Bona, the daughter of another nobleman of Assisi, would meet Francis, who was also accompanied by a companion, in secret to avoid the reaction of Clare's parents. After all, Clare and Francis were from different social classes, and the nobility of upper Assisi would not in any way have considered the merchants of lower Assisi as equals, hence not worth marrying into. During their encounters, Francis would talk of conversion, of penance, of leaving everything to follow Christ to live in humility and poverty according to the Gospel. The desire to join Francis's fraternity and penitential life grew in Clare. At some point, the bishop of Assisi, Guido, was informed of the situation. Guido was sympathetic, trusting and supportive of Francis's endeavour. Hence, he helped to make a seemingly impossible project become reality.

## FRANCIS AND CLARE'S CONVERSION

According to the author of the *Legend of St Clare*, Clare went to see Francis shortly before the feast of Palm Sunday, 1212.[2] She asked him how and when she should carry out her decision to join the fraternity. Francis told her to go with the people to the Palm Sunday liturgy, to receive a palm and to leave the city the following night. On 18 March 1212, Bishop Guido celebrated the Palm Sunday liturgy in his cathedral, dedicated to San Rufino, the first bishop of Assisi (d. 238). Clare, whose family house was adjacent to the cathedral, attended the liturgy, during which the bishop himself dramatically came over to her and gave her a palm. There must have been a plan well prepared by Francis and the bishop, and instructions must have been passed to Clare. As a matter of fact, the following night she walked secretly out of her home and left the city. At night time the gates of the city were locked and guarded, but one of those gates – the Porta Moiano – was conveniently under the custody of the bishop, hence it was no bar to Clare's escape.

A few miles down in the plain below Assisi, at the little church of Santa Maria degli Angeli, Francis and his brothers awaited Clare. When she arrived, they welcomed her. Then, Francis, most probably with the bishop's blessing and permission, tonsured Clare as a sign of religious consecration. It would later become known that Clare had done what the men who joined Francis and his community had previously done: she had sold her inheritance and given the proceeds to the poor.[3]

Clare had now become poor like Francis and his brothers. That same night, after the ceremony had ended, they all went together to the church of San Paolo delle Abbadesse in Bastia, a monastery of Benedictine nuns not too far from the Porziuncola. That monastery had among others – that is, among other privileges – a privilege of sanctuary that Innocent III had officially recognised and confirmed in 1201. Thus, it was a place of refuge, a place of asylum with immunity from arrest under penalty of excommunication. One may wonder again how Clare was able to get into that monastery in the middle of the night. Once more, the monastery was conveniently under the protection of the bishop of Assisi.

Clare certainly needed that protection, because her family did not approve of her decision. Squandering her inheritance and being received into a monastery as a poor servant – not even as a nun, since she had no dowry to offer – was shameful and unworthy of her noble status. Clare's relatives quickly heard where she was and came to take her back by force. But Clare met them in the church, grabbed the altar cloths and, removing her veil, revealed her newly tonsured head, denoting her presence as a woman consecrated to God.[4] The relatives left the church and, after a while, were resigned and abandoned all pursuit. It seems that during those days Clare dealt with events on her own. There is certainly no trace in the documents of any assistance or support from Francis.

Clare did not stay long at the Benedictine monastery. After a few days, she left and went to the church of Sant'Angelo in Panzo, a place closer to Assisi, where she joined another group of religious women leading a penitential life. Shortly after she had come to Sant'Angelo, Clare was joined by her younger sister Catherine.[5] The next day, their uncle, Monaldo, came with a cohort of armed men to bring Catherine back home. Since she had not yet been tonsured, she was not officially consecrated to God, and consequently they were under no threat of excommunication if they did her violence. But, as the tale goes, by Clare's prayer Catherine became so heavy that she could not be carried away. The uncle was furious and ready to beat his niece to death, but Clare convinced him to leave them alone. After that event, Francis tonsured Catherine and renamed her Agnes. Then he took the two sisters to the church of San Damiano.[6]

San Damiano was an old church with a little hospice. It was a place of healing under the patronage of St Damian, who, with his twin brother Cosmas, practised the art of healing in Asia Minor. They were later tortured and executed under Diocletian in 287. By the thirteenth century, that church belonged to the bishop of Assisi, who again helped Francis and Clare by giving them the use of San Damiano.[7]

This was the place where, a few years before, Francis had participated in the restoration of the church, prophesying the coming of holy women. The prophecy came true. As soon as Clare and Agnes settled in San Damiano, other women began to come: relatives and friends, often with their servants. The community of the Poor Ladies of San Damiano was born.

## THE DEVELOPMENT OF THE COMMUNITY
## OF SAN DAMIANO (1212–26)

Clare wanted to live like Francis and his brothers. Like them, she wanted to do penance (*facere penitentiam*).[8] She went through a lot of tribulations on that account. In San Damiano she was finally able to live truly as a member of Francis's fraternity, or *fraternitas*. Despite his admiration for Clare, Francis must have doubted that women could live the same life that he and his brothers lived and belong to the *fraternitas*. Clare proved him wrong. As she wrote in her *Form of Living*:

> When the blessed father realised we had no fear of poverty, hard work, trial, shame or contempt of the world, but, instead, regarded such things as great delights, moved by compassion he wrote for us a form of living.[9]

And, insisting that she promised obedience to Francis, Clare reproduced then the text of that form of living he had written for her and her sisters:

> Because by divine inspiration you have made yourselves daughters and servants of the Most High King, the heavenly Father, and have taken the Holy Spirit as your spouse, choosing to live according to the perfection of the holy Gospel, I want and promise, for myself and for my brothers, to always have, for you as I have for them, the same loving care and solicitude.[10]

The *forma vivendi*, succinct as it is, contains fundamental elements. Clare and her sisters were inspired by God to live the Gospel to perfection, seeking, that is, certainly nothing less than Francis and his brothers: poverty and humility. Therefore, Francis called them spouses of the Holy Spirit; but also, since Clare along with her sisters had promised obedience to Francis, as had the brothers, a bond was created that Francis acknowledged, and he promised in return to have the same care of the sisters as he had of the brothers. In other words, they all belonged to the same *fraternitas*.

The community of San Damiano kept developing, as Francis and his brothers continued sending them women.[11] Both Clare and Francis were also establishing ties with other religious communities of women, like San Severino in the Marches of Ancona, Monticelli near Florence and Monteluce in Perugia. Around 1215, Francis convinced Clare to accept the governance of the San Damiano community with the title of abbess.[12] Certainly, the growth of the community required a form of government, and it is plausible that, following the directives of the fourth Lateran Council held in Rome not long before by Innocent III, Francis and Bishop Guido of Assisi brought that to Clare's attention.

We can get an idea of the daily life of Clare and her sisters from a letter that Jacques de Vitry wrote in October 1216:

> I nevertheless found one consolation in those parts: many people of both genders, rich and wordly, after renouncing everything for

Christ, fled the world. They are called Friars Minor (*fratres minores*) and Lesser Sisters (*sorores minores*). They are held in great respect by the Lord Pope and the cardinals ... The women live together near cities in various hospices [that is, poor houses, shelters]. They accept nothing, but live from the work of their hands. In fact, they are exceedingly chagrined and disturbed because they are honoured by the clergy and the laity more than they would want.[13]

One of those cardinals, Hugolino dei Conti di Segni, bishop of Ostia, was to have a great influence on the new communities of religious women in northern and central Italy. In 1217, Pope Honorius III named him papal legate for Lombardy and Tuscany. A canonist educated in Paris and Bologna, Hugolino had also been influenced by Cistercian spirituality. Once in Tuscany, he rapidly became interested in the care of the female religious foundations that had recently been established. The community of San Damiano was one such.

Around 1218, building on the Benedictine *Rule*, Hugolino composed a 'Form and Manner of Living' (*forma et modus vivendi*) that he began to introduce into the female penitential communities. For Hugolino, religious women had to be nuns (*moniales*) living in enclosed monasteries (*inclusae*) in continuous fasting and contemplation. From 1219 on, Honorius III began officially to have Hugolino's Form and Manner of Living adopted in several monasteries – Monticelli, Siena, Lucca, Perugia – integrating them into what he called the order of the Ladies of St Damian of Assisi.[14]

Although Hugolino had encountered Francis in Florence in 1217, he did not approach Clare until Easter 1220, interestingly enough at a time when Francis was actually away in the Middle East. Hugolino tried to introduce his regulations into San Damiano. Clare refused to pass under the jurisdiction of the cardinal: she and her sisters belonged to Francis's *fraternitas*. Hugolino then gave Brother Philip the Long – to whom Francis had entrusted the care of the community of San Damiano – the care of the nuns (*cura monialium*) in his monasteries. But when Francis came back to Italy later that year, he promptly relieved Philip of that charge.

It seems that after his return from the Middle East Francis stayed closer to San Damiano, particularly during the times when he was seriously ill. Such was the case in the spring of 1225, when, staying there in a little cell made of mats, in the midst of much suffering, he composed his beautiful and famous *Canticle of the Creatures* (CA, 83–4). At that time he also composed a canticle of exhortation for the Poor Ladies, *Listen, Little Poor Ones* (*Audite, poverelle*) (CA, 85). In that little canticle, Francis expressed his concern and solicitude for Clare and her sisters. He was aware of their difficulties, so he told them to continue to live in true obedience and in the Spirit. He also beseeched them, out of love, to continue to use their own good judgement in deciding what to do with whatever might be given to them. He knew that illness and infirmities take a toll on both the sick and the care-giver, so he encouraged them to live in peace. One may see in that short canticle of exhortation an anticipation of the problems Clare and her sisters would face in the future, after Francis's death, with Cardinal Hugolino and the papacy, and also with the evolution of the order of Friars Minor. Francis's concern and solicitude for the community of San Damiano were to be expressed one more time, shortly before his death, as Clare herself reported in the heart of her *Form of Living*:

> I, little brother Francis, want to follow the life and poverty of our most high Lord Jesus Christ and of his most holy Mother, and to persevere in this until the end; and I ask you, my ladies, and counsel you to live always in this most holy life and poverty. And guard yourself well, lest by the teaching or counsel of anyone you ever in any way depart from it.[15]

In this last written message from Francis to Clare and her sisters the content is clear. First of all, Francis acknowledges that he and the sisters share the same way of life: to follow the life and poverty of Jesus Christ and his mother; and he beseeches the sisters again always to live that life. He could not have been more explicit in warning them to guard themselves against anybody who might try to take them away from that life and poverty. That kind of warning was not expressed without reason.

## AFTER FRANCIS'S DEATH, CLARE'S STRUGGLE TO DEFEND THEIR EVANGELICAL WAY OF LIFE (1226–52)

Francis died at Santa Maria degli Angeli on the evening of 3 October 1226. The funeral cortège bringing his body back to Assisi stopped by San Damiano, acknowledging clearly the relationship between Francis and Clare and her sisters. The following year, Cardinal Hugolino was elected pope, on 19 March 1227, and took the name of Gregory IX. Soon afterwards, on 28 July, he gave the care of the nuns (*cura monialium*) to Brother Pacifico, indicating his intention to charge the Friars Minor with the care of the monasteries he had founded.[16] Finally, later that same year, on 14 December, Gregory IX entrusted the recently elected minister general of the Friars Minor, John Parenti, with the care of the Poor Enclosed nuns (*pauperes moniales inclusae*), without any reference to a Franciscan origin.[17]

On 29 April 1228, Gregory IX sent out a letter to request donations for a basilica to be built in honour of Francis, even though he had not yet been canonised! The proclamation of Francis as a saint took place on 16 July that same year in the square of St George, the church in which he lay buried for four years.[18] In the meantime, Gregory IX had sent a letter to 'the abbess and the community of enclosed nuns of San Damiano in Assisi.'[19] And while in Assisi for Francis's canonisation, Gregory IX and his nephew, Cardinal Rainaldo – the future Pope Alexander IV – visited Clare at San Damiano. The purpose was to convince her to adopt the same form and manner of living as the other monasteries of the order of the Poor Enclosed nuns. Now that Francis was dead, Clare had to accept the inevitable and complied. And so, in a letter Cardinal Rainaldo sent on 18 August 1228 to all the monasteries of the order of St Damian, the name of San Damiano of Assisi appeared first in a list of twenty-four monasteries. In that letter, Rainaldo announced that Gregory IX had entrusted him with the care of the nuns, and that Brother Philip was replacing Brother Pacifico as visitator.

The autonomy of the community of San Damiano was now over. However, if the incorporation into the order of St Damian was a *fait accompli*, there was another area on which Clare remained uncompromising: the absolute poverty in which she had promised to live. When Gregory IX, because of the dangers and the precariousness of a life led in absolute poverty, especially for women, tried to convince Clare to accept at least some possessions that he himself actually offered, she refused categorically, saying that she did not wish 'to be in any way absolved from the following of Christ'.[20] Instead, standing her ground, Clare obtained from Gregory IX a document granting her and the community of San Damiano control of what they received:

> Therefore, as you requested, we confirm with our apostolic authority
> your proposal of most high poverty, granting you by the authority
> of the present letter that no one may compel you to receive
> possessions.[21]

This document is commonly known as the *Privilege of Poverty*, and is dated 17 September 1228.[22]

From then on and until her death, Clare struggled to make clear that the community of San Damiano had a Franciscan identity and belonged to the Franciscan order. In all her writings she insisted on the authority of *Saint* Francis and kept referring to him as the father, the founder, the pillar of San Damiano; she recalled that she, Clare, was Francis's little plant (*plantula*), which, in medieval Latin usage, means, far from any romantic connotation, Francis's foundation; she repeatedly proclaimed her obedience to the minister general of the Friars Minor, Brother Elias, and strongly advised Agnes, the Bohemian princess who, following the model of San Damiano, had founded a hospice and monastery in Prague, to do the same.[23]

## CLARE'S FORM OF LIVING OF THE ORDER OF POOR SISTERS (1253)

Gregory IX died on 22 August 1241. His successor, Innocent IV, held a similar attitude towards religious women in general and towards San Damiano in particular. With the bull *Cum omnis vera religio* of 9 August 1247 he even promulgated an updated version of Hugolino's form of living. The form of living (*forma vivendi*) of Innocent IV did, indeed, connect the order of St Damian to the observance of 'the *Rule* of the blessed Francis', but only 'as for the three counsels, namely obedience, renunciation of property in particular, and perpetual chastity'. And it maintained the order of St Damian under the jurisdiction of the ministers of the order of Friars Minor. But the contents of Innocent IV's form of living had everything to do with the constitutions of Hugolino and nothing to do with the *Rule* and life of the Friars Minor.

For Clare, that was unacceptable. So, knowing that death was approaching, she did something no religious woman had done before: she wrote her own form of living. Taking as her basis the *Rule* and life of the Friars Minor officially approved by Honorius III on 29 November 1223, and integrating – often with subtle little changes – parts of Hugolino's form and manner of living (1218) and Innocent IV's form of living (1247), Clare composed the form of life (*forma vitæ*) of the order of Poor Sisters (*ordo pauperum sororum*).[24] To make things definitely clear, Clare inserted at the centre of that form of living the memory of the beginnings of San Damiano, relating how instrumental Francis had been in her conversion and the foundation of the community. She insisted on writing that she and her sisters had promised obedience to Francis, and that Francis had promised to take care of them as he did of his brothers. To add additional strength and authority to her words, she always referred to Francis as 'saint' or 'blessed'.

Clare's form of living did indeed receive confirmation, first from the cardinal protector of the order, Rainaldo, on 16 September 1252, and, the following year, from Pope Innocent IV, on 9 August 1253.[25] Clare died two days later, on 11 August 1253.

### AFTER CLARE'S DEATH (1253)

Soon after Clare's death, Innocent IV began the process for her canonisation.[26] Even though the process ended on 29 November 1253 with the interview of the twentieth and last witness, it was not until 15 August 1255 that Alexander IV, formerly Cardinal Rainaldo, canonised Clare.[27] Clare had been buried inside the walls of Assisi, in the church of San Giorgio, where Francis had first been interred in 1226. There, a basilica and a new monastery were immediately built. The sisters left San Damiano and were solemnly transferred to that new settlement in 1260.

Clare had written her form of living for what she called the order of Poor Sisters, an appellation parallel to the order of Friars Minor. But that order of Poor Sisters was never recognised by the papacy. The approbation of Clare's form of living in 1253 made that very clear, since it was approved for San Damiano only. Clare had always claimed that she and her community were sisters – and not nuns – living in absolute poverty and were members of the Franciscan order. That again had never been understood or accepted by the papacy, and by the end of Clare's life it had become incompatible with the evolution of the order of Friars Minor.

In 1263, ten years after Clare's death – by which time Bonaventure of Bagnoregio was minister general of the order of Friars Minor – Urban IV promulgated a new *Rule* for the 'Poor Enclosed (*pauperes inclusae*) of the order of St Damian'.[28] With the promulgation of that new *Rule*, Urban IV had two goals. The first was to respond to the wish of the Friars Minor and to free them from any obligation towards the sisters. The second was to negate all previous legislation and constitute a new legislative unity while redefining the identity of the Franciscan women. They were the Poor Ladies no longer, nor the Poor Sisters, nor the Sisters Minor. From then on, following Urban IV's *Rule*, they were the order of St Clare. Urban IV's *Rule* had nothing to do with the form of living of the Poor Sisters, much less with the *Rule* and life of the Friars Minor. Francis and Clare were merely mentioned in the formula of profession and added to the holidays to celebrate. On 26 May 1288, the protomonastery (as it was now called) of St Clare in Assisi adopted the *Rule* of Urban IV and with it the right to own property.[29]

CONCLUSION

The relationship between Francis and Clare can only be understood correctly in the context of the original *fraternitas*, that is, prior to the institutionalisation into religious orders canonically recognised by the Church. Francis and Clare are the masculine and the feminine faces of an identical passion: to live radically according to the Gospel. Clare stated in her own words that it was because of Francis's example that she began to do penance, to embrace, as he was wont to say, the humility and the poverty of Jesus Christ. She and the women who followed her were received by Francis and his brothers into the circle of their *fraternitas*. Their mutual commitment influenced Francis, who was impressed by the way Clare and her sisters followed the perfection of the Gospel. In times of distress it was at San Damiano that Francis found comfort and healing. Right until he died he cared for his ladies, as he called them. And after Francis's death, it was Clare who remained a beacon for the early companions. To the end of her days, she carried on the life according to the Gospel initiated by Francis, tirelessly proclaiming the unity of the *fraternitas*.

### Notes

1   3 Soc., 24. See also Clare's *Testament*, 12–14, in R. J. Armstrong (ed. and trans.), *Clare of Assisi: Early Documents, Revised and Expanded* (New York, 2006), pp. 60–1.
2   *LSCA*, c.4.
3   Cf. Francis's *Testament*, c. 16, in *FAED*, vol. II, pp. 124–7; *Earlier* Rule 1:2 and 2:4, in R. J. Armstrong, J. A. W. Hellmann and W. J. Short (eds.), *Francis of Assisi: Early Documents*, 4 vols. (New York, 1999–2002), vol. I, pp. 63, 64. See also Luke 18:22 and Matthew 19:21.
4   *Process of Canonization*, 12:4, 18:3, 20:6, in Armstrong (ed. and trans.), *Clare of Assis*, pp. 183, 194, 196.
5   Cf. A. Brunacci, 'Agnese di Assisi', in *Bibliotheca sanctorum* (Rome, 1961), vol. I, cols. 369–70.
6   *LSCA*, cc. 5 and 15.
7   L. Bracaloni, *Storia di San Damiano in Assisi* (Todi, 1926); M. Bigaroni, *San Damiano, Assisi: la chiesa prima di san Francesco* (Assisi, 1983); L. Pani Ermini et al., *Indagini archeologiche nella chiesa di San Damiano in Assisi* (Assisi, 2005).
8   Clare's *Form of Life*, 6:1, in Armstrong (ed. and trans.), *Clare of Assisi*, p. 117; Clare's *Testament*, 24, in Armstrong (ed. and trans.), *Clare of Assisi*, p. 61.
9   Clare's *Form of Life*, 6:2, in Armstrong (ed. and trans.), *Clare of Assisi*, pp. 117–18.
10  Ibid., p. 118.

11　*Process of Canonization*, 6:15, in Armstrong (ed. and trans.), *Clare of Assisi*, p. 170.

12　Ibid., p. 146.

13　R. B. C. Huygens (ed.), *Lettres de Jacques de Vitry* (Turnhout, 1960), pp. 75–6.

14　*Ordo Dominarum de Sancto Damiano de Assisio*. Cf., e.g., Bull *Sacrosancta romana ecclesia* of 9 December 1219, in *Bullarium Franciscanum* (Rome, 1759), vol. I, pp. 3–5; English translation in Armstrong (ed. and trans.), *Clare of Assisi*, pp. 336–9.

15　Clare's *Form of Life*, 6:7–9, in Armstrong (ed. and trans.), *Clare of Assisi*, p. 118.

16　Bull *Magna sicut dicitur* of 12 August 1227, in Armstrong (ed. and trans.), *Clare of Assisi*, pp. 345–6.

17　Bull *Quoties cordis* of 14 November 1227, in *Sacrosancta romana ecclesia* of 9 December 1219, in *Bullarium Franciscanum*, vol. I, pp. 36–7.

18　Bull *Mira circa nos* of 19 July 1228, in *FAED*, vol. I, pp. 565–9.

19　Bull *Deus Pater cui vos*, January–July 1228, in L. Wadding (ed.), *Annales Minorum* (Quaracchi, 1931), vol. III, an. 1251, n. 17.

20　*LSCA*, c.9.

21　*Privilege of Poverty*, 7, in Armstrong (ed. and trans.), *Clare of Assisi*, p. 87.

22　According to some sources, Clare had previously obtained a similar document from Innocent III back in 1216. Even though it is not totally impossible, scholars tend to agree that there is little evidence of the authenticity of such a document.

23　*Second Letter of Clare to Agnes of Prague*, pp. 15–17, in Armstrong (ed. and trans.), *Clare of Assisi*, pp. 48–9.

24　Bull *Solet annuere* of 29 November 1223, in Armstrong et al. (eds.), *Francis of Assisi*, vol. I, pp. 99–106.

25　Bull *Solet annuere* of 9 August 1253, in Armstrong (ed. and trans.), *Clare of Assisi*, pp. 108–26.

26　Bull *Gloriosus Deus* of 18 October 1253, in *Bullarium Franciscanum*, vol. I, p. 684.

27　Bull *Clara claris præclara* of 26 September 1255, in Z. Lazzeri, 'Il processo di canonizzazione di S. Chiara d'Assisi', *Archivum Franciscanum Historicum*, 12 (1920), pp. 499–507; English translation in Armstrong (ed. and trans.), *Clare of Assisi*, pp. 263–71.

28　Bull *Beata Clara* of 18 October 1263, in *Bullarium Franciscanum* (Rome, 1761), vol. II, pp. 509–21.

29　Bull *Devotionis vestræ* of 26 March 1288, in *Bullarium Franciscanum* (Rome, 1768), vol. IV, p. 26.

## 8   Francis and the encounter with the sultan (1219)

STEVEN J. McMICHAEL

On 27 October 1986 in the basilica di Santa Maria degli Angeli John Paul II spoke to an audience gathered for the historic World Day of Prayer for Peace:

> I have chosen this town of Assisi as the place for our Day of Prayer for peace because of the particular significance of the holy man venerated here – St Francis – known and revered by so many throughout the world as a symbol of peace, reconciliation, and brotherhood. Inspired by his example, his meekness and humility let us dispose our hearts for prayer in true internal silence. Let us make this Day an anticipation of a peaceful world.[1]

Was the pope correct in choosing Francis as the model of peace, reconciliation and fraternity? Have many contemporary devotees of Francis been right about him and the values celebrated in 'the peace prayer' attributed to him? Was Francis a forerunner of modern-day ecumenical and inter-faith dialogue? Was his primary intent to be martyred – an objective left unfulfilled in his encounter with the sultan? Did he approve of the Crusades at the time of his visit to the sultan? The answers to these important questions have serious consequences for our understanding of Francis. If the last question is answered in the affirmative, for example, how does this affect our image of Francis as peaceful and compassionate? Is this a case of revisionist history and anachronistic thinking? The earliest report of this encounter comes from the writings of Jacques de Vitry in 1220:

> The head of these brothers, who also founded the order, came into our camp [at Damietta, in Egypt]. He was so inflamed with zeal for the faith that he did not fear to cross the lines to the army of our enemy. For several days he preached the Word of God to the Saracens and made a little progress. The sultan, the ruler of Egypt, privately asked him to pray to the Lord for him, so that he might be inspired by God to adhere to that religion which most pleased God.[2]

What is clear is that Francis crossed the line between the Muslim forces and the crusaders in the autumn of 1219. Aspiring to convert the Muslims, he was able to preach, at least for a few days, to Sultan al-Malik-al-Kâmal, and he returned to the crusader camp safe and unharmed. There are controversies about this encounter. Why did Francis go to Egypt? What actually happened in the sultan's court? What were the later effects of this meeting on Francis's life and writings? Did he support or disapprove of the fifth Crusade that was taking place in 1219?

The main question of historians, especially Crusade historians, is this last one: did Francis approve or disapprove of the Crusades?[3] It cannot be proved definitively either way. Francis never states explicitly what he believed about the Crusades, nor does a definitive answer to this question appear in the early hagiographical sources. All we can say with confidence is that he was present at the fifth Crusade and took advantage of it to preach to the sultan. The position I shall present in this chapter is that Francis most probably disapproved of the Crusades but used the occasion to present his case for Christian truth before Sultan al-Kâmal at Damietta.

I shall attempt to answer some of the questions concerned with Francis's encounter with the sultan, focusing on three primary considerations. First, I shall put this incident into the context of Francis's overall life and highlight events that may have shaped his approach to the encounter with the sultan. The writings of Francis are extremely important and must be taken into consideration in order to understand what happened at Damietta. RNB, 16–17 is of particular importance.[4] Then, I shall also look at the events that took place at Greccio (1223) and La Verna (1224) and see how they shed light on the Damietta experience.

## THE ENCOUNTER WITH THE SULTAN IN THE CONTEXT OF FRANCIS'S EARLY LIFE

One of the most important omissions of historians in regard to the question of Francis's encounter with the sultan is their failure to take into consideration the context of his entire life experience. They tend to focus on the years 1212–19, situating the event within Francis's missionary activity and desire for martyrdom. However, other major events of his life, both earlier and later, may well shed light on this encounter. Contemporary scholarship on the history of Assisi, the social and economic situation of central Italy in the twelfth and thirteenth centuries, and the history of religious life in the Middle Ages help us to see Francis within the world of his own day. Using this background, along with his writings and the hagiographical material, helps us understand in a fuller way his embrace of the Gospel way of life and what that meant spiritually and culturally for the society of his day.

A major influence in Francis's earlier life was his war experience. We know from contemporary scholarship that, during the battle of Collestrada between Assisi and Perugia, Francis lost significant friends, was imprisoned and became seriously ill.[5] He was ransomed by his father and, after a period of convalescence, set out for Apulia to join Walter of Brienne in his Crusade in southern Italy. He was prevented from fighting in another war. God appeared to him in a vision at Spoleto and asked him the famous question of whether he wanted to follow the Master or the servant. Francis chose the Lord and was told to return to Assisi where God's will would be revealed to him. The dream of being a glorious knight on a Crusade was replaced by a higher purpose. That purpose, as Thomas of Celano describes it, was to be the unstained bride of God, a servant of the Kingdom of God and a minister of the Gospel (1 Cel., 7–8). The knight of Christ was not to engage in war but was to devote himself totally to Lady Poverty. This major sign of early Franciscan spirituality symbolises the self-giving Christ who lived in poverty and simplicity in this world and was the source of salvation for those seeking forgiveness and reconciliation.

This early phase of his life is important. Francis had an experience of war brought about by the allure of power, money and prestige. His subsequent rejection of his father before the bishop of Assisi can be seen not only as his rejection of these three worldly values, but also as his renunciation of violence in order to gain them. Since the early biographical sources do not tell us much about these events, caution should be applied in their use. But the incident with the sultan makes more sense if one keeps the incident at Spoleto in mind. After Spoleto there is no known incident of Francis ever again condoning violence. In fact, it was quite the opposite. He subsequently sought out reconciliation not only with individual human beings, human communities and cities, but also with all of creation. It may very well be at Spoleto that God revealed to Francis the greeting he reports in his *Testament*: 'May the Lord give you peace.'

Sometime after Spoleto Francis had the encounter with the leper that he speaks about in such a dramatic way in his *Testament*. Certain contemporary scholars focus on this because they see it intimately connected with the later experience at Damietta.[6] In 1219, Francis extended his experience of reconciliation beyond the Christian world to the Muslim world.[7] Just as he went among lepers, he later went among Muslims; and in both cases he went among them in a spirit of peace and compassion.

In 1208, Francis heard the Gospel of Matthew describing the life of the apostles. He came to realise that he was being called to Gospel life and to the ministry of preaching. He and his earliest companions understood that to mean living in poverty, humility and simplicity. They needed to reject possessions and money, seeing them as obstacles to just and peaceful relationships. They aimed to live in harmony outside the confines of the city of Assisi and to share all things in common. They left the city because it was structured on principles of inequality, injustice and social disharmony, which, in turn, were caused by the pursuit of power, money and prestige. For Francis, the Gospel way of life meant the kind of harmonious living that comes only to those seeking social justice, the just sharing of goods and the renunciation of violence. All these elements were codified in the *Rule* of 1221.

After Innocent III approved their new way of life, Francis spent the next ten years preaching missions, serving the poor, outcasts and lepers, and working with his hands to supply daily needs. On at least two occasions during this time he tried to go among non-believers in Morocco and Syria. On another occasion he attempted to travel to southern France to preach to the Cathar heretics. During these years he learned what it was to be a 'servant' of God and later wrote about this powerfully in his *Admonitions*. Wherever he went, he was a messenger of peace and reconciliation, whether in Italy, Spain or Egypt. Francis, the servant, was a real apostle of Christ, who was subject to all creatures, as he would write in his *Rule* of 1221 (RNB, 16), and in the *Later Admonition and Exhortation to the Brothers and Sisters of Penance*. He also directed that enemies be treated as friends (RNB, 22).[8] An examination of Francis's christology reveals that he not only envisioned Jesus as the supreme Lord but also

> through his contact with the Gospel and the liturgy...discovered in Christ the servant who had washed the feet of the apostles, the beggar and pilgrim who had lived on alms, the suffering servant who had exposed Himself to the insults of His enemies, the worm, the lamb, and the Good Shepherd who gave His life by dying on the cross.[9]

## THE WRITINGS OF FRANCIS AND THE EARLY SOURCES

One of the major issues seriously affecting how one approaches Francis's experience at Damietta is the question of sources. Because they do not start with the writings of Francis himself, some scholars outside the Franciscan world who are not familiar with how the Franciscan Question has developed for well over a hundred years fall into certain errors concerning Francis and the Franciscan movement. Crusade historian Benjamin Kedar speaks of Francis's 'scanty writings'. Yet these twenty-eight texts need to be the starting-point for any discussions about Francis, including the issue of his encounter with the sultan. After studying these writings, one should examine the other sources (*legendae*, chronicles, choral offices, etc.), but with much caution.[10] Each source has its own perspective, and therefore each has an agenda that one should be aware of in any discussion of the life of Francis.[11]

Francis's writings are important because, except for much of the *Rule* of 1221 and possibly ten other writings, they originate from the period of his life after his encounter with the sultan. They reflect Francis's experience of living the Gospel way of life and his embrace of the role of servant, which had a very significant meaning for him (cf. the *Admonitions*). The later writings reflect the vision he intended to leave to those who followed him. These writings were influenced by his state of disillusionment and sickness from 1220 until his death. Looking at them in the context of the sultan event, we perceive that Francis saw the sultan and other non-believers as those who needed to convert to the truth of Christianity. He wanted to share the fullness of revelation with those who did not embrace the Christian faith. It embraced both high christology, which stresses the divinity of Christ, and low christology, which stresses the humanity of Christ.

Scholars agree that Francis had a number of occasions to preach to the sultan and his court. Whether or not this was a 'dialogue' is difficult to prove, but Francis was well received and listened to. Even though it is quite hypothetical to speculate about what Francis would have said to the sultan, it is tempting to imagine it for a moment. Based on the writings that give us the parameters of his thought and spirituality, I propose the following.

The most obvious thing in Francis's writings is his theology of the Trinity. He is so trinitarian that one can imagine how difficult it would have been for him to encounter Muslims who did not believe in the Trinity. They were considered 'non-believers' and not heretics. It seems quite sure that Francis would have spoken of the trinitarian nature of God in relation to the strict monotheism of his Muslim hosts.[12]

The second key element would have been the divine and human natures of Jesus. Francis would most probably have preached that the divine Word became flesh in the person of Christ, which Muslims explicitly deny. The doctrine of the Incarnation would, therefore, have been a central element of his preaching. Francis would have affirmed that the Word became flesh as an act of humility on God's part. This is not in the Muslim understanding of the supreme, omnipotent God. Francis believed that Jesus underwent passion and death, which most Muslims deny. Francis proclaimed that Christ was raised from the dead. Muslims deny this because they believe that Jesus did not die on the cross. Francis asserted that Christ ascended into heaven to be seated at the right hand of God as Lord of the universe. Muslims understand this as only an ascension to God and not as a resurrection. Francis taught that Christ would appear as judge of the world at the last judgement. Muslims believe that Allah will be judge at the universal judgement.

Francis would probably also have spoken about the Eucharist, since it is so prominent in his writings. It is in the Eucharistic event that God humbly appears among us on a daily basis on the altar (*Admonition 1*). The Eucharist sacramentally reflects the peace and reconciliation of the heavens and earth (*Letter to the Entire Order*). Because Francis held that 'whoever does not eat His flesh and drink His blood cannot enter the Kingdom of God' (John 6: 54, 57), he would have believed that Muslims were in grave danger in terms of their salvation.[13]

Francis would most probably have preached about the Holy Spirit, since this was such an important element of his theology. And since Mary was the bearer of the Word through the agency of the Holy Spirit, she would also have been a subject of his preaching to the sultan. (Muslims would understand her as the bearer of a prophet and not of the Word of God understood in a Christian way.)

## THE 'RULE' OF 1221

The importance of the *Rule* cannot be underestimated in understanding the central elements of Francis's approach to living the Gospel. Those engaged in discussions about the Damietta experience focus especially on chapter 16, which addresses the friars' mission to Muslims and other non-believers. This chapter, though, should be seen in the context of the entire *Rule*, especially the early chapters leading up to it and also chapter 17 on preaching.

The three scriptural texts (Matthew 19: 21, Matthew 16: 24 and Luke 14: 26) listed in the first chapter are the basis for the Franciscan embrace of the Gospel way of life. For Francis and the early friars this meant a commitment to live an itinerant poor life like Jesus and his disciples, to take up the cross of the Crucified Christ, and to preach by example and word. Chapters 2 to 12 speak of the inner life of the community and how the friars are to relate to one another, how they are to live in poverty and simplicity, and how they are to take care of each other, especially in sickness.

Portions of these earlier chapters are important in light of what chapter 16 indicates for the friars' relationships with non-friars. Chapter 11 asks the brothers 'not to slander or engage in disputes', emphasises silence and directs that the brothers do 'not quarrel among themselves or with others but strive humbly, saying: "I am a useless servant"' (Luke 17: 10). They are to love one another and express this by their deeds. They are not to revile anyone, grumble or detract from others. They are to be gracious to and not judge or condemn others.

Chapter 16 directs the friars to do as the apostles did in their preaching ministry, namely, to go about as poor persons and to eat what is placed before them. First they are to say, 'Peace to this house.' This greeting is important to Francis, who wrote in his *Testament* that the Lord himself revealed it to him: 'The Lord give you peace.' They were not to resist evil, as Francis understood Jesus's teaching in the Sermon on the Mount. In fact, much of the spirit of the Sermon on the Mount can be found in the writings of Francis. It is his interpretation that is significant in the early Franciscan approach to issues of going about the world in poverty and humility leading to peace. This is basic for those who say that Francis and the early Franciscans were persons of peace and reconciliation, and thus persons who rejected the use of violence.

The message of peace and reconciliation was to be lived by the brothers in community and in the world. Did Francis expect this of people at large? There is no way to determine this based on his writings. But it is significant that the Third Order *Rule* of 1221 had as a precept that the followers were not to take up arms against anyone. It extends a non-violent policy to others outside the First Order of friars.[14] It is also noteworthy that in chapter 23 Francis admonishes all the orders of church and society, including kings and princes, to persevere in the true faith and in penance, but he never mentions soldiers or crusaders.

The opening paragraphs of chapter 22 are especially significant. This chapter either was written just before Francis left for Damietta or is a synthesis of Franciscan discipleship written after this event. Francis states:

> All my brothers: Let us pay attention to what the Lord says: *Love your enemies* and *do good to those who hate you*, for our Lord Jesus Christ, Whose footprints we must follow, called His betrayer a friend and willingly offered Himself to His executioners. Our friends, therefore, are all those who unjustly inflict upon us distress and anguish, shame and injury, sorrow and punishment, martyrdom and death. We must love them greatly, for we shall possess eternal life because of what they bring us.

If Francis wrote this after visiting the sultan, he would have been referring to his Muslim hosts as his enemies-turned-friends. Some contemporary authors see this experience of an enemy-turned-friend as already having been experienced by Francis in his encounter with the leper.[15] If this was the case, it is questionable whether Francis could have condoned using violence on the enemies of the Christian faith. This would not conform to his vision of servant christology and his divinely given Gospel way of life. It would have gone against everything he believed about the identity and mission of Jesus as the servant of servants and his death on the cross as the self-sacrifice for all sinners.

Chapter 17 takes up the issue of preaching. What is significant here is that Francis directs the friars to preach the Gospel by their deeds, in humility, and to guard against the wisdom of the world and the flesh. There is no mention of preaching anything other than Christian truth. To preach in a derogatory tone to others is contrary to the wishes of Francis.

The central text for our consideration is chapter 16, which describes how the friars are to go among Saracens and other non-believers. This chapter is important, because it presents two different ways of missionising:

> As for the brothers who go, they can live spiritually among the Saracens and non-believers in two ways. One way is not to engage in arguments or disputes but to be subject *to every human creature for God's sake* [1 Peter 2: 13] and to acknowledge that they are Christians. The other way is to announce the Word of God, when they see that it pleases the Lord, in order that [non-believers] may

believe in the all-powerful God, Father, and Son, and Holy Spirit, the Creator of all, the Son the Redeemer and Saviour, and be baptised and become Christians because *no one can enter the Kingdom of God without being reborn of water and the Holy Spirit* [John 3: 5].

The first form of missionising, given in one sentence, is significant, because Francis directs the friars to live among non-believers as they would among themselves in community (chapter 11); and they are to do this in such a way that they are subject to all creatures. They are to witness by their lives and by their example, as Francis emphasised continually in his writings. The second form is to preach the Gospel, if it pleased the Lord, in order to bring non-believers to the fullness of truth and salvation. Just because the first form did not become the dominant one does not mean that it was not truly significant for Francis.[16]

A major portion of chapter 16, then, is devoted to preaching the Gospel and admonishing the friars about the attitude they should have when they go among non-believers. These are directives for any mission work, not just among Muslims (as Anthony of Padua and other friars experienced in southern France among the Cathars). The texts are all Gospel passages that remind the friars of the cost of discipleship, which includes the possibility of suffering and death.

## THE PROBLEM OF THE 'CHRONICLE OF THE TWENTY-FOUR GENERALS' AND TWO 'EXEMPLA' SERMONS OF FRANCIS

In his own writings, Francis never ridicules Muhammad and the Islamic faith. When we read what Francis wrote about preaching, he never tells his friars to do anything other than to preach the Gospel. Yet a text from the late fourteenth century, the *Chronicle of the Twenty-Four Generals* of Arnald of Sarrant, reports that Francis had instructed the five soon-to-be martyrs in Morocco with these words: 'My dear children, God has commanded me that I send you to the land of the Saracens to preach and to make known the faith of God and to assail the law of Muhammad.'[17] The key phrase is the last one. It appears that Francis was instructing his friars to attack or assail the law of Muhammad. Such instructions never appear in the *Rule* or in any of the other writings of Francis. This is a projection of the fourteenth-century polemical mentality towards Muslims rather than Francis's own mentality.

This same chronicle is a major source for those who wish to see a connection between the mentality of Francis and the early Moroccan martyrs. An often-quoted passage from this chronicle states that when Francis learned that the brothers who had been sent to Morocco had been martyred on 16 January 1220, he reacted spontaneously and exclaimed: 'Now I can truly say that I have five brothers!'[18] Even though certain historians have judged that 'there is no reason to doubt the veracity of the narrative', this passage is very problematic. First, it comes from a late fourteenth-century work that is filled with many errors concerning the order's history.[19] Secondly, there is a question as to whether Francis had actually heard the entire account of the friars' deaths and how they had attacked Muhammad and the Qur'an. It is possible that he simply heard that these friars had been martyred. Thirdly, there is an important question concerning Francis's own experience at Damietta. If the Moroccan martyrs provided Francis with a model for martyrdom, why did he not do likewise before the sultan? He certainly could have been martyred if that was what he truly intended. He knew there was danger of losing his life, but this does not seem to have been his primary motive. Rather, he desired to share his faith not only in the Trinity and in Jesus as Saviour, but also in the universal reconciliation of all humankind and creation based on the Gospel way of life. Fourthly, the account of the Moroccan martyrs makes martyrdom the primary aim of the preaching activity of these friars. Many of the early hagiographical sources tell us that one of Francis's main desires in life was martyrdom, and that this was what he intended to have happen in Egypt. This would not have been surprising, because the patron saint of Assisi was San Rufino, a martyr of the third century. Also, the little church in Assisi where Francis most probably prayed was devoted to St Stephen, the first follower of Jesus to be martyred (Acts, 7). But a close reading of chapter 16 of the *Rule* of 1221 reveals that living the Gospel by example and preaching is the central aim of the Franciscan movement. Martyrdom is simply a possible consequence.

A recent study by Christopher T. Maier on Franciscan preaching during the time of the Crusades presents two *exempla* attributed to Francis.[20] The first is about the sultan laying before Francis a cloth with crosses on it in an attempt to have Francis walk on them and thus degrade the cross. The other is about applying the Gospel verse 'If your eye causes you scandal, tear it out and throw it away', which was used as a justification for Christians to recover the Holy Land by means of war. The author concludes that Francis did support the Crusades as ordained by God. He asserts that Francis's overall objective was to liberate the Holy Places in Palestine from Muslim rule. What was different was his strategy. Francis went beyond the idea of simply expelling the Muslims from where they interfered with Christian life.[21]

Why is this conclusion problematic? First of all, Francis never mentioned anywhere that his objective in going to the sultan was to liberate the Holy Places. His manifest goal was to preach the Gospel of Christ and bring non-believers to the fullness of the Christian faith. Secondly, Francis never asserted that armed conflict is justified. His servant christology seems to contradict such a position. When we hear Francis speak about how true peace is established, he never allows that armed conflict is a means to peace. Thirdly, Maier never addresses the issue of authorship. Is this second *exemplum* Francis's own words or words placed in his mouth by subsequent friars justifying their own ministry of Crusade preaching? Since it in no way conforms to Francis's own words in his authentic writings, his christology or his approach to mission as outlined in the Earlier *Rule*, Maier's conclusion is problematic indeed.

## THE AFTERMATH OF THE DAMIETTA EXPERIENCE

Contemporary studies on the Damietta experience go in a number of directions. On the one hand, certain writers argue that it had a tremendously positive influence on Francis.[22] It helped him see the sultan as an enemy-turned-friend, and his subsequent writings express this new attitude. They also believe that Muslim spirituality impressed Francis – the call to prayer influenced him to have bells rung at certain hours honouring God. Francis's praises of God might have been influenced by the Islamic ninety-nine names of God.

Others argue that there was no positive influence on Francis and assert that this contemporary attempt to make Francis a model of modern-day interreligious dialogue is erroneous and fantastic.[23] One such author states:

> It is of crucial importance to emphasise that Francis visited the sultan for the purpose of converting him to the Christian religion, not to engage in a friendly dialogue in order to establish a non-belligerent tolerance of the two parties for each other's religion.[24]

What is true in this statement, based on Francis's own writings, is that he desired strongly the conversion of the sultan because he believed that Christianity was the true religion. This was a friendly conversation. All the earliest sources tell us that Francis spoke and the sultan listened. What is not true is that Francis used 'sharp and blunt statements that Islam was not the true religion'. Rather, he preached the Gospel. This is what he instructed his friars to do in the sixteenth chapter of the *Rule*.

## GRECCIO AND LA VERNA IN LIGHT OF 1219

In light of Francis's early life experiences of war, his rejection of violence and his encounter with the sultan, what he later experienced demonstrates the continuity of his approach to these issues. There is a theory that, when Francis went to Egypt, he also visited the Holy Places in Jerusalem.[25] However, the only mention he makes of the Holy Places is in his *Letter to the Entire Order*, where he speaks of how Christians venerate the tomb of Christ. If the primary sources are accurate, Francis loved drama. Therefore, both the Greccio and La Verna events can be seen as illustrations of Francis's appreciation for the Incarnation and passion of Christ. Actors in medieval plays implicitly demonstrated that one need not go to the Holy Land to experience it. If this was true for Francis, he might have felt no need for Crusades.

Greccio and La Verna also raise the issue of sacred space. Francis envisioned the true Gospel way of life as embraced by 'pilgrims and strangers' in the world who have no need of fixed dwellings. He saw the sacredness of all created reality as evidenced in his *Canticle of the Creatures*. He saw all churches as sacred because they housed the Eucharist and were reminders of the cross of Christ. Sacred space was, therefore, determined primarily by a spiritual attitude towards space and towards what it contained. A friary became a sacred space because this was where the brothers gathered in community. Above all, Francis saw the human person as the *locus* of the Spirit. From the moment of creation, this was the Holy Place of the encounter with God.

Greccio was sacred because this was where Francis gathered the friars and local community to celebrate the humility of the Incarnation of Christ. In a way quite common to medieval liturgical drama, Francis re-created in the Rieti valley a sacred scene that had originally taken place in the Holy Land. He wanted to see with his own eyes the event of Bethlehem. This echoes the experience of St Jerome's friend, Paula:

'I swear to you', she said to Jerome, kneeling beside her, 'that with the eye of faith I see the Divine Infant, wrapped in His swaddling clothes. I hear my Lord crying in His cradle. I see the Magi adoring the star shining from above; the Virgin Mother; the careful nursing father; the shepherds coming by night to see the Word was made Flesh; the slaughtered children; raging Herod; Joseph and Mary fleeing into Egypt.' And with mingled tears and joy, she said: 'Hail Bethlehem, House of Bread, where was born the true Bread, which came down from Heaven. Hail, Ephrata – the fertile – whose fruit is God.'[26]

Those who were present at Greccio in 1223 had such an experience. The fact that Francis's vision of the Christ child was in a Eucharistic context is an important connection with pilgrims such as Paula. The continual sacramental 'incarnation' of Christ happens, according to Francis, on the altar on a daily basis (*Admonition 1*). Francis is proclaiming implicitly that pilgrims do not need to go to the Holy Land for this experience. It can happen anywhere. Celano exclaims: 'Out of Greccio is made a new Bethlehem' (1 Cel., 85).

About nine months later Francis received the stigmata on La Verna. In subsequent Franciscan spirituality this place has been considered the Franciscan 'Calvary'. As Greccio was to Bethlehem, so was La Verna to Jerusalem. Pilgrims in Jerusalem retraced the steps of Christ on his way to the cross. Francis read the Gospel accounts of the passion of Christ and experienced a type of interior 'stations of the cross' or passion play. He imaginatively placed himself into the drama. Since the passion took place in Jerusalem, La Verna now became the New Jerusalem and Francis became 'the crucified servant of the crucified Lord' (1 Cel., 95). Just as Christ appeared to Francis as a child at Greccio, so did he appear to Francis in crucified form at La Verna. Here, however, the drama led to a unique outcome – the actor actually experienced the event and was marked with real wounds. What is also unique is that the space that became sacred was not just the mountain in Tuscany but the very body of Francis. The human person becomes the *locus* of the cross, which is the only thing, along with their infirmities, that human beings can glory in (*Admonition V*). The holy sepulchre, honoured by Christians as a reminder of Christ's passion, death and resurrection, loses importance when it is compared with the real place where these events are effective, namely, within the human being. Francis's writings testify to his belief that the human being is the bearer of the divine. Therefore, greater attention should be placed on the human person – body, soul and spirit – than on spatial things.

How can these two important experiences in Francis's life help us interpret his attitudes towards the Crusades? The Crusades were primarily about the recovery of land and the churches on that land. Francis proclaimed that the events of both Bethlehem and Calvary can be celebrated anywhere at any time. Since this is so, there is no need for fighting and killing over real estate. Based on his own experiences of fighting over power, property and prestige, Francis, later in life, rejected these motives. We can see how Francis's earlier experiences connect with and are consistent with the experiences of his later years.

### CONCLUSION

Even before Francis died, his own ideal of the Gospel way of life was being compromised by his followers. Without the ability to direct the order personally as he had in the 'golden age' and having lost the guiding power of the *Rule*, Francis's vision of universal reconciliation and peace was not passed on effectively to subsequent generations of friars. As the order became clericalised, conventualised, urbanised and strongly influenced by other religious groups around them, Francis's desire to observe the Gospel as a wandering group of mendicants living as pilgrims and strangers in the world was lost. His vision of missionising in both forms as outlined in the *Rule* was also lost to a significant number of friars. Many were setting themselves up for martyrdom by deriding Muhammad and the Qur'an, and they were becoming Crusade preachers. Francis took advantage of the fifth Crusade to preach to Sultan al-Kâmal. He accepted that this preaching mission might possibly end in martyrdom. Having gone with an attitude of peace and reconciliation, he left the sultan's court in peace. Judging from his own writings and their christology, we can safely conclude that John Paul II was correct in choosing Francis as a model of peace and reconciliation not only between Christianity and Islam, but also between Christianity and all other world religions.

### Notes

1   This speech and other speeches John Paul II gave during this event can be found on the Vatican City web page www.vatican.va/.
2   *FAED*, vol. I, p. 581.
3   See B. Z. Kedar, *Crusade and Mission: European Approaches toward the Muslims* (Princeton, 1984); and J. Powell, 'Francesco d'Assisi e la quinta crociata, una missione di pace', *Schede Medievali*, 4 (1983), 68–77 and 'St Francis of Assisi's Way of Peace', *Medieval Encounters*, 13 (2007), 271–80.
4   Cf. C. Paolazzi, 'La "Regula Non Bullata" dei Frati Minori (1221), dallo "stemma codicum" al testo critico', *AFH*, 100 (2007), 5–148.

5  A. Fortini, *Francis of Assisi*, trans. from the Italian, *Nova Vita di San Francesco*, by H. Moak (New York, 1981), pp. 119–65.
6  These scholars include J. Hoeberichts, M. Cusato and K. Warren.
7  Cf. J. Hoeberichts, *Francis and Islam* (Quincy, 1997); M. Cusato, 'Healing the Violence of the Contemporary World: A Franciscan Paradigm for Dialogue with Islam,' and 'From Damietta to La Verna: The Impact on Francis of his Experience in Egypt,' in 'Daring to Embrace the Other: Franciscans and Muslims in Dialogue', *Spirit and Life*, 12 (2008), 1–38 and 83–112; and K. A. Warren, *Daring to Cross the Threshold: Francis of Assisi Encounters Sultan Malek al-Kamil* (Rochester, 2008).
8  In this second source, Francis writes: 'We must never desire to be over others, but, instead, we must be subject *to every creature for God's sake.*'
9  N. Nguyên-Van-Khanh, *The Teacher of His Heart: Jesus Christ in the Thought and Writings of St Francis*, trans. E. Hagman (Saint Bonaventure, 1994), p. 56.
10  Cf. J. Tolan, *Saint Francis and the Sultan: The Curious History of a Christian–Muslim Encounter* (Oxford, 2009).
11  Thomas of Celano's focus on Francis's sanctity leads him to omit certain essential elements, such as the impact of the war of 1202.
12  Cf. L. Gallant, 'Francis of Assisi: Forerunner of Interreligious Dialogue: Chapter 16 of the Earlier *Rule* Revisited', *Franciscan Studies*, 64 (2006), 53–82.
13  See Francis's *Later Admonition and Exhortation to the Brothers and Sisters of Penance (Second Version of the Letter to the Faithful)* c.1220, in *FAED*, vol. I, pp. 45–51.
14  Cf. R. M. Stewart, '*De Illis Que Faciunt Penitentiam*,' *The Rule of the Secular Franciscan Order: Origins, Development, Interpretation*, Bibliotheca seraphico-Capuccina cura instituti historici ord. Fr. Min. Capuccinorum, 39 (Rome, 1991), p. 210.
15  Both Jan Hoeberichts and Michael Cusato make the case that the leper experience had a tremendous influence on Francis's approach to all other groups of people, including the Muslims.
16  This is my response to Bert Roest's 'Medieval Franciscan Mission: History and Concept', in Wout J. van Bekkum and P. M. Cobb (eds.), *Strategies of Medieval Communal Identity: Judaism, Christianity and Islam* (Leuven, 2004), p. 141. Even though there were a significant number of Franciscan martyrs in the Middle Ages, the vast number of friars who lived in Muslim lands, including the Holy Land, lived in relative peace with the Muslim inhabitants of those places. Therefore this first form of missionising did not disappear even though it was not included in the Later *Rule* of 1223.
17  The Latin text is found in *Chronica XXIV Generalium Ordinis Minorum* in *Analecta Franciscana* (Quaracchi, 1928), vol. III, p. 581.
18  The Latin text reads: 'Nunc possum veraciter dicere, quod habeo quinque fratres.' Ibid., p. 593.
19  Quoted from Tolan, *Saint Francis and the Sultan*, p. 7.

20  Cf. C. T. Maier, *Preaching the Crusades: Mendicant Friars and the Cross in the Thirteenth Century* (Cambridge, 1994). That the friars did become Crusade preachers is a historical fact. But there are others, like Roger Bacon, who criticised the Crusades. None of these early Franciscan writers refer to the vision of Francis in regard to their position on the Crusades. On Roger Bacon, see *The Opus Majus of Roger Bacon*, trans. Robert Belle Burke (Philadelphia, 1980), vol. 1, pp. 111–12.

21  Maier, *Preaching the Crusades*, pp. 16–17.

22  The writers include Jan Hoeberichts, M. F. Cusato and Kathleen Warren.

23  These writers include John Tolan and Frank Rega.

24  F. Rega, *St Francis of Assisi and the Conversion of the Muslims* (Rochford, 2007), p. 128.

25  The Crusades did change the importance of the Holy Places as objects of Christian pilgrimage. See C. Morris, *The Sepulchre of Christ and the Medieval West: From the Beginning to 1600* (Oxford, 2005).

26  St Jerome, *The Pilgrimage of Holy Paula*, ed. Edward Lewes Cutts, Fathers for English Readers (New York, 1897), pp. 125–6.

# 9 Francis and creation

TIMOTHY J. JOHNSON

What have they done to the earth?
What have they done to our fair sister?
Ravaged and plundered and ripped her and bit her
Stuck her with knives in the side of the dawn
And tied her with fences
And dragged her down.[1]

Long before contemporary musicians, scientists, theologians and polit-
icians lamented the toxic denigration of the environment, Francis of
Assisi displayed a profound empathy for the created world. Not surprisingly, the Roman Catholic Church confirmed the unique rapport of
Francis with creation by singling him out as the patron saint of ecology.
While the popular image of Francis in nature is often that of a painfully
pious, ornamental statue on a bird bath, an examination of his writings
and biographies reveals him as the embodiment of Paul's most fervent
hope for creation. He writes that all creation groans for the redemption
of the children of God, for the material world has been unwillingly
subjected to frustration, bondage and decay in the company of humanity. Nature will be set free only if and when humanity is freed in the
flesh through the death and resurrection of Christ (Romans 8: 18–27).
This chapter first and foremost considers Francis as a harbinger of this
eschatological hope, a man whose evangelical conversion draws him
into a compassionate, liberating relationship with animate and inanimate creatures alike. Indeed, Francis goes well beyond the Pauline
understanding of creation as companion to propose a gendered model
of familial equality and freedom in which men and women are joined
in prayerful ministry by other creatures, who are all brothers and
sisters under one Father in heaven. Following on Francis, we shall
then examine the insights of later Franciscans into the nature and
significance of creation, especially animals, in salvation history. The
writings of Thomas of Celano, Bonaventure of Bagnoregio, Roger

Bacon, Duns Scotus and Angela of Foligno provide a compelling witness to the variegated Franciscan appreciation of creation.

### FRANCIS OF ASSISI: CANTICLES OF CREATION AND DIVINE GOODNESS

Francis was neither by talent nor training a systematic theologian. A close reading of the *Canticle of the Creatures* is perhaps the most common, and certainly the most celebrated, entry point into his perspective on creation. Nevertheless, it is arguably his stance towards the Eucharist that illuminates his fundamental appreciation of material reality and grounds his familial praise of the elements. Francis states:

> I implore all my brothers to show all possible reverence and honour to the Most Holy Body and Blood of our Lord Jesus Christ in Whom that which is in heaven and earth has been brought to peace and reconciled to Almighty God.[2]

The simple rudiments of daily life, bread and wine, mediate the presence of him who is the hope of all creation. Indeed, the consecrated elements offer the only visible, corporal encounter possible in this world with the Redeemer.[3] To appreciate the presence of the Son of God in the sacramental bread and wine on the altar is to accept the humility of the Lord who deigned to dwell among the faithful in a corporal manner.[4] This affirmation flies in the face of those who would deny the goodness of creation and the willingness of the divine to enter into the materiality of the world. At this time the religious movement known as the Cathars explicitly denounced the redemptive potential of creation and sought to separate themselves, physically and spiritually, from what they perceived to be the corrupt influences of materiality. For the Cathars, matter only mattered inasmuch as it was an obstacle to, if not an outright betrayal of, the divine goodness found in spiritual realms when the imprisonment of the flesh was transcended. Francis, for his part, resolutely proclaims that God's original declaration regarding the goodness of creation found in Genesis 1: 31 has not been totally erased by the tragedy of sin.

What is perhaps most striking about the approach Francis takes towards the Eucharist is the link he identifies between the practice of reverential humility and the ability to discern the redeeming presence of God in the world. Just as the Lord descends from on high to dwell in lowly bread and wine, so too should the faithful humble themselves as they encounter Christ in the sacrament of the altar. Humility in the presence of the elements transformed by the spirit of the Lord fosters humility before all of God's creatures. Grounded in this humility, Francis is free to embrace the reality of the material world and enter into a relationship with creation on its own terms and praise the Creator. Liturgical worship, where Francis and his brothers encounter the humility of God in the Eucharist, becomes a privileged *locus* for celebrating the universal salvation offered in Christ. In his *Exhortation to the Praise of God*, written on a wooden panel in a hermitage chapel, reverent humility in this Eucharistic setting erupts in a call for all the creatures of the earth and heaven above to laud the Lord, for he is good, and worthy of praise and honour. As the Lamb of God, sacrificed for salvation, Christ is worthy of all glory.[5] Another liturgical setting, the Divine Office, evokes *The Praises to Be Said at All the Hours* in which Francis urges all creatures to praise and glorify the Lord God Almighty, together with the Lamb who was slain.[6] This divine offering makes salvation known to the entire world, and even the fields and all that dwells within them should take heart and be glad, for redemption is at hand.[7]

For Francis, the world around him revelled in the in-breaking of God's grace. He responded to this initiative by inviting his brothers in the *Canticle of the Creatures* to discern the intrinsic humility of creation, follow this example and praise the Creator. Quite rightly much has been said over the years about this unique Umbrian hymn, written not in Latin but in the regional dialect. Francis composed the initial part of the celebrated work in the midst of intense physical suffering. He wished "to write a new *Praise of the Lord* for his creatures, which we use every day, and without which we cannot live. Through them the human race greatly offends the Creator" (CA, 83). We are fortunate to possess this early witness, as it draws back the curtain surrounding the intentions of Francis and confirms his humility and longing to right the wrongs done to God's handiwork. Not only are human beings dependent on the elements throughout the day, but they are guilty of insulting the very source of life by taking advantage of the other creatures that populate their world. Instead of claiming the Pauline freedom of the children of God so as to free creation from the frustration, bondage and decay equated with sin, people further the original oppression by abusing the material world. This is not the path to reconciliation.

What Francis proposes in the *Canticle of the Creatures* is quite breathtaking. First of all, the creatures of the world surrounding the brothers are not objects but subjects in a wide-ranging network of relationships, marked by gendered equality and a shared, mutual source of vitality and life. The sun is a brother, so too are the wind and fire.

The moon and the stars, the water, the earth and even death are sisters to humanity. This sibling structure is not dominated by an overbearing, distant *pater familias* but is brought into existence and sustained by an all-powerful, good Lord who delights in creatures useful and desirable, beautiful and strong. Secondly, as siblings, creatures other than human beings have a certain agency that Francis intimates and imitates. While men and women have fallen desperately short of their vocation to lead creation to redemption, their creaturely brothers and sisters continue to heed the Creator and offer numerous examples of humble, salvific service. Through them and with them the Most High is praised, and humanity is reminded of what it means to be in a humble relationship of service with the divine. God created the sun to give light to the day, and this brother continues to do so, as Brother Fire for his part lights up the night. The moon and the stars, sisters one and all, filled the evening sky at God's pleasure and are still there to see in their clear and precious beauty. People cannot but trust Brother Wind, in the company of Sister Earth and Sister Water, to sustain life through the fruits of the field that are nurtured in all kinds of weather. Even death is welcomed as a sister, who has her natural place among siblings. Similar to his experience of the Eucharist, this encounter with his brothers and sisters in the midst of suffering moves Francis anew, and recalls the importance of redemptive service through their humble, manifold offerings to humanity. Not surprisingly, he concludes the *Canticle of the Creatures* on this note, "Praise and bless my Lord and give Him thanks and serve Him with great humility."[8]

### BIOGRAPHIES OF FRANCIS: IL 'POVERELLO' AND THE HOPE OF CREATION

Thomas of Celano (1185/90–1260) was the earliest writer to perceive the saint's sibling relationship with creatures as the embodiment of the Pauline hope for all creation:

"Fields and vineyards, rocks and woods, and all the beauties of the field, flowing springs and blooming gardens, earth and fire, air and wind: all these he urged to love of God and to willing service. Finally, he used to call all creatures by the name of 'brother' and 'sister' in a wonderful way, unknown to others; he would discern the secret of the hearts of creatures, like someone who has already passed into the freedom of the glory of the children of God."

(1 Cel., 81)

The delight Francis finds in the world around him stands in stark contrast to the earliest days of his conversion when he gazed unmoved at the beautiful fields and vineyards of the Umbrian landscape (1 Cel., 3). It would not be until he had renounced his patrimony before Bishop Guido and was thrown into a ditch filled with snow by thieves outside town that Francis would rejoice in nature and raise his voice in praise of the Creator of all (1 Cel., 16). Celano would later remind his brothers when they gathered for the Divine Office that the reason for their founder's change of heart was the new-found love he experienced for the source of life.[9]

What Francis would discover in the wake of his conversion was the incredible witness offered by creatures to those such as him who were seeking the will of God in their lives. He was initially ignorant of the salvific role of creatures but changed from what some might consider a simple, sentimental fondness for creatures to recognition of their agency when he was preaching to a flock of birds near Bevagna (1 Cel., 58). While travelling, Francis caught sight of many birds of various types and, moved with emotion, ran to speak with them. What happened next surprised even Francis, for when he greeted the birds with his accustomed salutation, "The Lord give you peace," he sensed they were listening, as they remained still instead of flying off. Conscious that the flock was, in fact, a willing congregation attentive to the Word of God, he reminded them of the incredible benevolence the Creator showered upon them. The birds responded to this sermon in a manner befitting their divinely apportioned nature, and Francis blessed them as he departed. After noting Francis's remorse at not preaching to the birds earlier, Celano writes that from this day forward Francis implored all animals, and even inanimate creatures, to praise and love their Creator. Indeed, in their obedient response, the poor preacher found a reminder of his need to invoke the name of the Saviour.

Other accounts of Francis among creatures highlight the salvific compassion of the saint. Emblematic of one who is already counted among the children of God, Francis displayed an ear for the suffering creatures he encountered as he wandered the world, preaching the Gospel; it is as if he could hear the groaning of those who were in bondage. This image comes into focus on a number of occasions when Francis is presented with animals who are held captive. Once, when offered a rabbit caught in a trap, he enquired as to why he, Brother Rabbit, allowed himself to be caught. Taking this small brother into a warm, motherly embrace, Francis caressed and then freed him. Such tenderness was clearly attractive, and the rabbit was quite rightly reluctant to leave. A fish offered to Francis at the lake of Rieti was also drawn by this tenderness. After admonishing this brother to avoid capture in the future, Francis released him back into the water, but the fish continued to frolic alongside the boat until sent on his way with a blessing (1 Cel., 60–1). Concern for the sufferings of his fellow creatures caused Francis to remove worms from the road lest they be trampled upon and place honey or fine wine out for bees so they would not die in the winter cold (1 Cel., 80). He was especially fond of sheep, since Jesus Christ is referred to as a lamb in the Scriptures. Celano says the saint once groaned aloud when he came across a lamb surrounded by goats. Calling to mind how Christ was once surrounded by the haughty, Francis delivered the animal to the care of the cloistered sisters of San Severino. Eventually the wool shorn from the rescued lamb became a welcome tunic for Francis (1 Cel., 77–8).

Celano's incredibly rich and compelling portrayal of *il poverello* as sibling to all creatures is furthered by Bonaventure (1221–74), whose biography notes that Francis was their humble companion in nature and grace (*LM*, 9:4). It was the ecstatic excess of Christ's love, brimming over into tenderness, which initially moved him to dismount from his high horse to kiss the leper and likewise later enlarged his heart to embrace all the creatures of the earth as his siblings. His willingness to bend to their needs called forth an equally humble response from creatures. On one occasion, he consented to undergo the fiery scourge of cauterisation to save his eyesight. To the amazement of the attending physician, he directly addressed the glowing-hot iron instrument used in the procedure and implored Brother Fire to be gracious and courteous. After the doctor burned a track from ear to eyebrow, Francis confessed that he felt neither the heat of the medical tool, nor any pain in his seared flesh. Mimicking perhaps St Lawrence, Francis exclaimed that the doctor could repeat the intervention if his flesh still required cooking. The story concludes with the note that the God of creation desired that creatures be subject to the will and command of Francis, who was in perfect harmony with God. Further instances of creation responding to the divine mandate by offering him wine from water when thirsty, music without instruments when he was sad and light in the midst of darkness when travelling led Bonaventure to ask his readers to appreciate the incredible ministry of creation:

> Consider that at his nod, that man of admirable purity and great virtue tempered the heat of fire, changed the taste of water, brought

comfort with angelic melody and was led by a divine light, so that, in this way, it might be proved that the entire fabric of the universe came to the service of the sanctified senses of the holy man.

(LM, 5:9)

Creation's ministry to Francis is nowhere more evident than in prayer. Chapter 9 of the *Major Life* begins with a sweeping paean of praise to the contemplative, uplifting power of creation. Creatures stoked the flames of the saint's love for God through their delightful witness to divine reason and purpose. Drawn to the beauties of the world around him, Francis beheld within them the beauty of his Beloved and ascended through the consideration of creatures upwards to the source of his desire. With a vocabulary dripping with sensuality, Bonaventure portrays a man who savoured the divine goodness flowing in every creature and, with a keen ear for the spiritual, heard within their power and activity what almost seemed to be a celestial choir. To take a proper part in this choir, Francis could count on the assistance of various siblings, such as Sister Cricket, who roused him from his cell at Santa Maria degli Angeli (*LM*, 8:9–10). For eight days, a liturgical octave, the cricket responded to the saint's invitation and appeared among the brothers, so that they might be moved to praise the Lord Creator with their sister. A flock of birds, and a raven in particular, welcomed the saint to La Verna and convinced him to stay awhile with the wonderful melody of their singing. A falcon formed such a bond of friendship with the newcomer that the bird could discern when to awaken his friend for the nightly Divine Office and when to let him sleep through to dawn, thereby allowing Francis the opportunity to regain his physical strength in the face of illness. While this falcon knew when and how to foster the celebration of the Divine Office, the same does not hold true for all his feathered siblings. In a story found in Bonaventure but not in Celano's various hagiographical accounts, Francis castigated a group of birds in the marshes of Venice. In a sense, these sisters were the victims of minorite clericalisation; they impeded their brothers who were trying to fulfil their clerical responsibilities by chanting the canonical hours (*LM*, 8:9). It was a different story when the friars had no books, were not obliged to pray the Divine Office and were taught by Francis 'to praise God in all and with all creatures' (*LM*, 4:3).

While Bonaventure takes pleasure in relating how creatures delighted in serving Francis and inspired prayer, he also echoes Celano's insight into Francis as the manifestation of the Pauline hope for cosmic reconciliation. Drawing on a story from the earlier biographer's *The Remembrance of the Desire of a Soul,* the Seraphic Doctor recounts the multiple misfortunes of the people of Greccio, who were completely subjected to the mercy of the elements (*LM,* 8:11). Hailstorms devastated their wheat fields and vineyards year after year, and, if that were not enough, wolves ranged over the countryside devouring animals and beasts alike. As a witness to this devastation in his hermitage in the environs of Greccio, Francis was moved to intercede. Laying the blame for the violence of the physical world squarely at the feet of the local populace, the saint called them to sincere repentance with the promise that they would once again experience the natural bounty and harmony of creation if they heeded his warning. The people responded with enthusiasm; they were then reconciled to the world around them to such a degree that the fields flourished anew, people and beasts were at peace, and the hailstorms punishing neighbouring fields either dissipated or changed direction at the Greccio boundaries. Bonaventure notes, "the beasts that had rebelled against fallen humankind" (*LM,* 8:11) were brought into a proper relationship with the divine that mirrored the rapport Francis shared with God.

## BONAVENTURE OF BAGNOREGIO: A THEOLOGY OF CREATURES AND THE COSMOS

Bonaventure's understanding of the unique relationship between Francis and animals emerges from his reflections as a young theologian in Paris. As was customary for aspiring masters of the thirteenth century, he was required to write a commentary on the ponderous collection of theological source material labelled the *Sentences* of Peter Lombard. One question posed by Peter Lombard regarded the obligation to love irrational creatures.[10] While his mendicant counterpart, Thomas Aquinas, spent precious little time on this issue and emphasised why these creatures are not to be loved, Bonaventure appealed to the experience of Francis in nature as the entry point into consideration of love and the nature of human interaction with animals.[11] With his customary flair for nuance and distinction, he resolves the opposing opinions by acknowledging that irrational beings cannot be loved in the same manner that human beings love each other and God, but that men and women are obliged to love irrational creatures since they are created to praise God and foster the salvation of humanity. It is natural affection and piety, best understood here as tenderness, which from the time of prelapsarian Eden moves a person to love animals and other creatures. Bonaventure turns to the image of Francis to underscore that this expression of love, which draws a similar response from the beloved creatures, is inextricably linked to conversion:

> To the degree that a person is reformed and returned to the state of innocence, he will find animals are peaceful in his presence and they will be moved by piety towards him. We read that St Francis experienced this kind of tender piety towards creatures because in a certain way he had recovered [the state of] innocence.[12]

What is striking here is the impact of human action on animals and, by way of comparison, on all creatures. If men and women respond to the Gospel and are reformed by grace, they will in kind foster the ultimate restoration of creation. The eschatological expectation of Romans 8: 18–27 comes into clear view now in Bonaventure's theological reflection. The desire for salvation is universal and proper to all created realities that God has brought into being, and divine assistance is at hand to bring their longing to fulfilment, "because every creature seeks to be saved, although it cannot do so by itself, and most of all that creature, which seeks to be beatified... And because the desire of nature is not in vain, where nature is deficient, God supplies a gratuitous influence."[13] Whereas rational creatures are ordered directly to God, the relationship between irrational creatures and God is mediated by men and women, who are responsible for ensuring that all other creatures remain faithful to our original, intended relationship to the Creator.[14] The burden of responsibility for creation's restoration falls squarely on the shoulders of sentient beings; they play a singular role in the salvation of other creatures, and, as Francis demonstrates, conversion is essential to this ministry of reconciliation. To the degree that sentient beings are reformed by the influence of grace, other creatures are restored to their original nature as witnesses to the Most High. There is a profound sense of mutuality in Bonaventure's reflections, since he posits that within the process of human restoration other creatures are released from the subjection they suffer due to no fault of their own, and are thus freed to render praise and to accompany the sons and daughters of God back to their mutual Creator.

Bonaventure's identification of Francis as something of a new Adam with the animals in Eden, which is rightly depicted in medieval frescoes and stained-glass windows of Francis preaching to the birds, is best appreciated by examining the Seraphic Doctor's insight into the status of animals before and after the fall from grace. In a fascinating, albeit rarely cited, segment of the *Commentary on the Sentences*,

Bonaventure delineates the original nature of animals and their relationship to humanity when responding to a query about the divine purpose behind the creation of creatures.[15] While God intended animals to be ordered to humanity, it is crucial to recognise that the present state of affairs is hardly what the Creator intended. The birds of the air, the fish in the sea and all the other creatures spread across the earth had a fourfold purpose in the original state of innocence. At one and the same time, in tandem with the trees, they confirmed human dignity through obedience, offered beauty to the terrestrial home of humanity, provoked wonder in the wisdom of the Creator through their diversity, and moved people to love God by acting according to the rectitude of their nature and likewise loving in accord with the Creator's commands. To those who disdain animals because of their cruel behaviour, Bonaventure states that the sin of humanity, pure and simple, corrupted creatures.

Now of course, things have changed, and the fourfold purpose of animals is interpreted in the light of human indigence. Animals are meant to provide us with food, clothing, service and solace. Whereas the previous focus was on companionship in Eden, the emphasis shifts to instrumentality and human need. Yet an echo of the original harmony is still perceptible to those who listen and contemplate the circle of life, which Bonaventure considers a cosmic poem, "As animals follow each other in succession, they adorn the universe like a most beautiful song, in which one syllable follows another."[16] Francis heard the chorus of creation,[17] and Bonaventure composed his theological reflections with a keen ear for this melody.[18] When summarising the major tenets of theology for student friars in the aptly named *Breviloquium*, or *Brief Word*, Bonaventure appeals to the musical motif to explain the course of the cosmos. Just as a person is unable to appreciate the loveliness of a song without following it from beginning to end, so too the beauty of the world is imperceptible to those who do not understand how divine wisdom generates, orders and governs the universe.[19] Close attention to the natural world allows humanity to heed the praise that arises from every being, both animate and inanimate, for all creatures sing of their Creator. One would have to be deaf not to hear them.[20]

In the richly textured, symbolic language of Bonaventure, every creature is then a syllable in a song, or a vestige of God, a word in the Book of Creation, a rivulet flowing from the fontal Goodness, or a seed sown into the fecund fabric of the world.[21] These multiple modes of expression disclose the perfect work of the Triune God, who is Artisan,

Author, Almsgiver and Agronomist. Indeed, everything that has being, visible and invisible, emanates from the divine source as the gracious handiwork of the Father who, through the Son and in the outpouring of the Holy Spirit, fills the universe with signs of power, wisdom and providence. From the celestial spheres to the rocks and flowers of the field, from the birds of the sky to the fish in the depths of the sea, from the angelic hosts to married couples with children, the goodness and beauty of the Trinity are displayed. All of creation is both a sacrament mediating the presence of God in a tangible fashion and an illuminated text narrating and depicting the wonders of God, who created all things through the Eternal Word, Jesus Christ. Bonaventure notes that creatures reflect the divine on at least one of three levels: vestige or footprint, image, or similitude.[22] Since creation is the free operation of the Trinity, all beings display a vestige of the threefold essence, power and presence of God. Images, for their part, are sentient beings who reflect the Father with their capacity for memory, the Son with the power of intelligence and the Holy Spirit by virtue of the will. The most intimate expressions of the Triune God are the similitudes, that is, the children of God, who are transformed by the theological virtues of faith, hope and love. To these individuals belong the stewardship of creation and the burden of restoring all their fellow creatures, which have been subjected to futility by sin through no fault of their own, to their original, pristine nature as intended. For Bonaventure, this journey of reconciliation is made foremost in the company of Christ, through whom all was created, for in the transfiguration on Mount Tabor the mediator between God and creation reveals that even rocks, plants and animals are restored in him.[23]

## ROGER BACON AND DUNS SCOTUS: REFLECTIONS ON GRACE AND GLORY IN THE NATURAL WORLD

To care for creation and embark on the journey into God requires close attention to the natural world. Two British friars, Roger Bacon (1214–94) and Duns Scotus (1266–1308), give voice to the Franciscan fascination with the myriad reflections of divine agency and purpose in the materiality of the earth. Writing from Paris at the request of Clement IV, Roger Bacon proposed in his *Opus Majus* a thorough, even radical re-organisation of the academic curriculum that promoted a serious engagement with the sciences. Often promoted as a forerunner of modern scientific method and considered by some to be an anti-establishment troublemaker, Bacon understood his project rather as a necessary preamble to the proper reading of Scripture. Gazing around the university and beyond to the widespread pulpits of Christendom, Bacon noted the poor quality of biblical studies and the pitiable preaching of his fellow mendicants. Lost to most brothers was the simple appeal to Scripture, commendation of virtue and condemnation of vice that characterised the preaching of Francis. One glaring cause behind this despicable situation was an inability or unwillingness to take the text seriously at the literal level before seeking out the spiritual meaning. Scripture speaks of the multitude of creatures brought into existence by God, and it is incumbent upon the theologian to know the literal nature of these beings, both in the particular and universal, in order to read and interpret the Scriptures as God intended on the spiritual level:

> In addition, we see that the literal sense rests in the knowledge of the nature and properties of creatures, so that by means of appropriate adaptations and similitudes the spiritual meaning can be drawn out. Saints and ancient sages alike set forth this view, and this is the true and genuine manner of explanation which the Holy Spirit taught. It is therefore necessary that a theologian know creatures well.[24]

To have this excellent knowledge of creatures demands a rigorous, disciplined examination of the natural world by religious people. Religion, according to Bacon's appeal to Cicero, is taken from the Latin, *relegere*, which means 'to re-read'.[25] Philosophy, broadly understood under the rubrics of linguistics, mathematics, optics, experiential comprehension and ethics, assists the aspiring theologian to read anew the Book of Creation and thus, understanding the truth of what is examined, approach the Creator through created realities as diverse as a magnificent rainbow and the Troglodyte race in the depths of distant Ethiopia. Together with this concern for creatures comes an emphasis on geographical location.[26] Each specific place of God's good earth generates a specific actuality, and a diversity of places produces a variety of material, animal and human realities throughout the world. While the celestial wonders of the night sky certainly proclaim the majesty and beauty of the Creator and elicit reverence, specific places on earth must also be studied and understood if we are to comprehend the sublime depths of the Bible and make our way on the road back to God. Appealing to the peripatetic imagery dear to Franciscans, Bacon notes that material roads signify spiritual roads, and that material or corporeal places, which terminate motion by providing a reason to stop, signify spiritual places.[27] There are no more important places in the world to stop and study than those found in the Holy Land. Quoting Jerome, Bacon continues, "He will have a clearer insight into the sacred Scripture who has contemplated Judea with his own eyes."[28] Of course, not everyone can make a pilgrimage to the Holy Land, but a discipline like astronomy, as a subset of mathematics, together with knowledge of languages and a close reading of travel accounts, clarifies the location, climate, aesthetics and utility of such places as Jerusalem. Guided by a firm grasp of the literal sense of the specific place mentioned in the Bible, those who re-read the world can henceforth delight in the spiritual sense of the Scriptures, that is to say, in the divine peace proffered to those who enter the Jerusalem on high.

Duns Scotus, who spent time at the universities in Oxford and Paris, mirrors the preoccupation with the particular in his celebrated doctrines of "thisness" (*haeccitas*). Simply put, Scotus underscores the gratuitous, generous and artistic power of God by accentuating the "thisness" of every individual creature and the positive knowledge of the divine derived from every being. It is important to call to mind that in the Scotistic vision of reality, creation is not tangential to divine desires but came into being due to God's wilful longing to become united with the cosmos in the Incarnation of the Word in the singular Jesus Christ. The order of grace anticipates or precedes the order of nature such that God preordained the cosmos to grace and glory in the assumption of nature by the eternal Son of God.[29] This means that from all eternity the human nature of Christ was predestined to be glorified and united with the Word. The theological consequences are stunning, since Scotus can then maintain that the Incarnation is due to the eternal goodness of God, not humanity's temporal need for a redeemer after the fall from grace in Eden. Just as God foresaw the Incarnation, so too were the divine co-lovers preordained for glory. These men and women were to be accompanied by other creatures that could assist them in loving the Creator. While there is a certain inequality of charity, in that God's desire for human-ity preceded that for other creatures, Scotus does hold that God loves all that exists, including, for example, an individual tree. There is then a wonderfully beautiful, intensely volitional dynamic in the Subtle Doctor's reflections on God's relationship to all created beings, given the contingency of the world. Everything that exists is due exclusively to the liberality and expansive love of the Creator, who chose to craft the ultimate, irreducible reality or *haeccitas* of each singular creature.[30]

## ANGELA OF FOLIGNO: A WORLD PREGNANT WITH GOD

In the summer of 1291, a devout widow of Foligno departed on a pilgrimage to Assisi, where she entered the upper basilica. To the consternation of her companions and nearby Franciscans alike, Angela (1248–1309) collapsed in an anguish-stricken heap on the pavement of the church, uttering words of wonder and love. Moments earlier she had contemplated an evocative stained-glass window – still visible today – depicting Christ presenting Francis to the world just as Mary offered Jesus. Angela soon found in the evangelical vision of Francis a path for her own life's calling, which included a keen sense of God's presence in the world. One day, when she was preparing to receive communion after confessing her sins, God offered to console her, and, as Angela recounted:

> "in a vision I beheld the fullness of God in which I beheld and comprehended the whole of creation, that is, what is on this side and what is beyond the sea, the abyss, the sea itself, and everything else. And in everything that I saw, I would perceive nothing except the presence of the power of God, and in a manner totally indescribable. And my soul, in an excess of wonder cried out, 'This world is pregnant with God!' Wherefore I understood how small the whole of creation is – that is, what is on this side and what is beyond the sea, the abyss, the sea itself, and everything else – but the power of God fills it all to overflowing".[31]

What Angela experienced and recounted is what generations have come to know: the created world is groaning, to cite St Paul, and yearning to burst forth and give birth to a marvellous manifestation of divine power. It is not surprising that her eucharistic vision followed on the heels of her decision to confess her sins, for Francis marvelled at the humility of God present in the material world and likewise responded with a commitment to do penance. Celano saw in Francis the fulfilment of the Pauline eschatological hope, and the young Bonaventure noted that the conversion of Francis freed nature to return to original innocence. Once opaque to humanity, whose eyes were darkened by fear and suspicion, creatures were called forth from the shadows by Francis and rendered transparent in the light of God's grace, and set free to reclaim their divine birthright as brothers and sisters to humanity. In this sacred exchange initiated by God in Francis, men and women rediscovered their place in the cosmos and, in the company of other creatures, revel in the goodness and beauty of the Creator. As unique, individual expressions of the Master Artisan, every creature deserved the reverential respect that Bacon and Scotus articulated in their reflections on the magnificent, glorious elements of the material world. Angela looked upward and beheld Christ offering Francis to the world, and she, together with others through the centuries, beheld in Francis an example of how and why all creatures are to lead back to God. The life and legacy of Francis remains a forceful reminder that the role of God's children is not only to be humble caretakers or stewards of creation, but indeed to be courageous liberators of their brothers and sisters in the mutuality of compassionate concern that the Creator intended from the beginning and desires at the end.

## Notes

1  Jim Morrison, Ray Manzarek, Robby Krieger and John Densmore, 'When the Music's Over', *Strange Days*, Elektra/Asylum Records, 1967. I would like to thank Ms Katherine Wrisley and Dr John W. Daniels, Jr at Flagler College for their bibliographical and editorial assistance with this chapter.
2  *A Letter to the Entire Order*, FAED, vol. I, p. 117.
3  *Test.*, ibid., p. 125.
4  *Admonition I*, ibid., pp. 128–9.
5  *Exhortation to the Praise of God*, ibid., p. 138.
6  *The Praises to Be Said at All the Hours*, ibid., p. 161.
7  *Office of the Passion*, ibid., p. 149.
8  *Canticle of the Creatures*, ibid., p. 114.
9  Thomas of Celano, *Legend for Use in the Choir*, ibid., no. 8, p. 322.
10  Bonaventure, *Commentaria in Quatuor Libros Sententiarum Magistri Petri Lombardi*, in *S. Bonaventurae Opera Omnia* (Quaracchi, 1887), vol. III, pp. 621–4.
11  Thomas Aquinas, *Summa Theologica*, trans. Fathers of the English Dominican Province (New York, 1947), vol. II/II, pp. 1287–8.
12  Bonaventure, *Commentaria*, vol. III, p. 622. Translations from the Latin are by the author unless indicated otherwise.
13  Ibid., vol. I, p. 161.
14  Ibid., vol. II, p. 384 and vol. III, p. 623.
15  Ibid., vol. II, pp. 383–4.
16  Ibid., p. 383.
17  *LM*, 9:2.
18  Bonaventure, *Commentaria*, vol. I, p. 786.
19  Bonaventure, *Breviloquium*, ed. Dominic Monti (Saint Bonaventure, 2005), pp. 10–11.
20  Bonaventure, *The Journey of the Soul into God*, ed. Philotheus Boehner (Saint Bonaventure, 1956), pp. 49–51.
21  Bonaventure, *Sermon 22*, in Timothy J. Johnson (intro., trans. and notes), *The Sunday Sermons of Saint Bonaventure* (Saint Bonaventure,

2008), pp. 272–3; Bonaventure, *Commentaria in Ecclesiastes*, c. 1, q.2, *Opera Omnia*, vol. vi, p. 16; *LM*, 9:2; Bonaventure, *The Minor Life of Saint Francis*, vol. ix, p. 5; Bonaventure, *Sermon 11*, in *The Sunday Sermons*, p. 157.

22  Bonaventure, *Breviloquium*, p. 97.

23  Bonaventure, *Sermon 16*, in *The Sunday Sermons*, pp. 216–17.

24  Roger Bacon, *The Opus Majus of Roger Bacon* (Eliborn Classics edition), ed. J. H. Bridges (London, 1900), vol. i, p. 175.

25  Roger Bacon, *Moralis Philosophia*, ed. E. Massa (Zurich, 1953), pp. 32–3.

26  Bacon, *Opus Majus*, pp. 300–2.

27  Ibid., pp. 183–4.

28  Ibid., p. 184.

29  Duns Scotus, *Ordinatio III*, d.7, q.3, in A. Wolter, 'John Duns Scotus on the Primacy and Personality of Christ' in D. McElrath (ed.), *Franciscan Christology* (Saint Bonaventure, 1980), pp. 146–59.

30  Duns Scotus, *Ordinatio II*, d.3, nos. 172, 175, 187–8, in M. B. Ingham, *Scotus for Dunces* (Saint Bonaventure, 2003), pp. 162–3.

31  *Angela of Foligno, Complete Works*, trans. and intro. P. Lachance, pref. Romana Guarnieri, Classics of Western Spirituality (New York, 1993), pp. 169–70.

**Part II**

*The heritage of Francis of Assisi*

# 10 Francis and the pursuit of learning

BERT ROEST

## INTRODUCTION

The stunning transformation of the Franciscan order from a small band of laymen into a well-organised international order of educated preachers and theologians, with schools all over Europe, took place even more quickly than was acknowledged until recently. Ignoring suggestive insights by Hilarin Felder, who in 1904 published the first monograph on this issue, many historians writing on Franciscan education have argued that the question of studies was only addressed systematically under Bonaventure, minister general (1257–73), and particularly by the constitutions of Narbonne in 1260. According to this interpretation, the creation of a school network began in earnest under the Franciscan ministers general Albert of Pisa (1239–40) and Haymo of Faversham (1240–4), to be brought to full fruition under Bonaventure.

As numerous Franciscan study houses can be traced back to the early 1220s, and Franciscan chronicles provide references to lectors and the exchange of students during the 1230s, it becomes plausible to assume that the creation of schools and provincial study houses for the training of lectors was well under way during the leadership of Elias, who governed the Franciscan order as a vicar from 1221 to 1226, and again as minister general between 1232 and 1239. This brings the problem of studies back to Francis's final years. Between his abdication of leadership of the order in 1221 and his death in 1226, Franciscan schools and study houses started to appear in Italy, Spain, France and England. Francis must have been well aware of that. All the more reason to revisit a central question among scholars looking for the authentic Franciscan ideals, namely, what Francis thought about the place of learning and the pursuit of studies in the Franciscan way of life.[1]

## FRANCIS AS THE ENEMY OF SCIENCE? IMAGES FROM THE HAGIOGRAPHICAL TRADITION

Discussions concerning Francis's views on learning have unfolded within the context of the so-called Franciscan Question, initiated by the publications of Paul Sabatier in the late nineteenth and early twentieth centuries. Sabatier perceived a huge dichotomy between the ideals of Francis and the realities of an institutionalised and increasingly learned order of clerics. Looking for the authentic voice of Francis and the early brothers, Sabatier and like-minded scholars after him put much stock in a series of writings ascribed to the circle of Francis's early companions, such as the *Anonymous of Perugia*, the *Legend of the Three Companions*, the *Assisi Compilation*, the *Deeds of Blessed Francis and His Companions* and the *Mirror of Perfection*. The discussions concerning the status of such texts, whose voices they represented and how they might be put in a proper chronological order have kept Franciscan scholars busy for more than a century.[2]

Some of these works seemingly provide first-hand testimony on Francis's qualms about the pursuit of learning, as Sabatier was keen to point out in his influential biography of Francis.[3] These concerns stand out particularly in the *Assisi Compilation* and in the *Mirror of Perfection*. Depending on one's scholarly convictions, the *Assisi Compilation* is either compiled in or around Assisi between c.1246 and 1260 or is the product of more clandestine compilatory practices in the decades following the decree from 1266 to destroy all hagiographical texts on Francis except for the now official texts written by Bonaventure. The *Mirror of Perfection* can possibly best be understood as an early fourteenth-century reworking of materials already present in the *Assisi Compilation*.[4]

Both texts seem to mirror the bewilderment of the companions about the divergence between the Franciscan way of life remembered from the early days and the direction taken by the friars leading the order during Francis's final years. Whatever the contextual problems concerning such an interpretation, it has proved to be sufficiently suggestive for followers of Sabatier to conclude that Francis was against the pursuit of studies.

The *Assisi Compilation* lends itself particularly well to creating the image of a Francis staunchly opposed to studies. First of all, the text exploits his status as an illiterate, simple-minded man, a recurrent theme in the hagiographical tradition. In this text, it is formulated to make the point that Francis's teaching, so important for the salvation of mankind, did not result from any acquired knowledge but was the inspired utterance of a man completely devoid of learning. This is framed in homiletic encounters in the presence of bishops, as well as in settings of theological dialogue, in which the learned acknowledge the inferiority of booklearning in the face of the soaring spiritual theology of the uncultured saint (CA, 10, 35–6).

Secondly, the text puts the role of learned friars in a negative light, suggesting that they aimed to bypass the directives of the *Rule* by recourse to Cardinal Hugolino. Furthermore, the world of learning is depicted as an intrinsic danger to the friar, even though a knowledge of Scripture, if properly channelled towards charity and the tasks at hand, is not condemned wholeheartedly. In the end, learning becomes an obstacle to the salvation of the friars, as well as the root cause of the ruin of the order. Hence, the faithful friar opts for a life of simplicity and renounces learning, as well as the books in which such learning is contained (CA, 18 and 47).

An ultimate key passage of the *Assisi Compilation*, which reappears in fuller form in the *Mirror of Perfection*, relates Francis's confrontation with a novice who wants to improve his knowledge of the Psalms and seeks the founder's permission to have a Psalter of his own. Francis's negative response, at odds with the permission already given by the ministers general and provincial, clearly denounces the acquisition of books and the pursuit of learning as being inimical to the minorite vocation. In this anecdote, the minister general and the minister provincial personify the machinations of clerical friars (CA, 103–5; MP, 3–5 and 72).

Scholars seeking additional ammunition did not only find this in the *Mirror of Perfection*, but could also rely on the *Second Life* by Thomas of Celano, which, unlike the latter's *First Life*, was not written as a programmatic text in the context of Francis's canonisation. Instead, the *Second Life* was based in part on the same dossiers as the *Assisi Compilation* and possibly reflects a change in attitude by its author, who was no longer portraying the deeds of a new saint but might have been looking for a man whose way of life no longer seemed easily accessible.[5]

Although less insistent than the *Assisi Compilation* and the *Mirror of Perfection*, Celano's *Second Life* does at times address the issue of learning in very cautionary tones. There is more space in this text to honour proper ecclesiastical learning among clerical friars, especially in the context of preaching (2 Cel., 163), yet learned 'curiosity' and book-collecting outside clearly defined clerical and apostolic tasks are condemned (2 Cel., 62, 189, 195). Francis asked all who entered the order to leave everything behind and offer themselves naked to the arms of the Crucified Christ. Hence, learned clerics willing to join had to sacrifice the security of their learning. Thus dispossessed, they could unconditionally surrender to the life of evangelical perfection (2 Cel., 194).

Additional fuel for Francis's negative evaluation of learning could be inferred from texts compiled by other former companions of Francis and by later generations of spiritual partisans. A case in point are the famous *Golden Sayings* ascribed to the elderly Giles of Assisi (*c*.1190–1262), which maintain that the Word of God has to be performed and not studied passively, and laments that 'Paris had destroyed Assisi', that is, that access to higher learning had compromised Francis's original intentions. Likewise, learning is presented as a major cause for the demise of the original Franciscan ideals in the poetry of the spiritually inclined polemicist–poet Jacopone da Todi (*c*.1228–1306).[6]

On the basis of such a variety of hagiographical and polemical utterances Francis could be depicted as inimical to the pursuit of science and the tendencies of clericalisation and institutionalisation related to it. This has been maintained by those convinced by Sabatier but also shines through in more moderate form in the writings of John Moorman and Raoul Manselli, who recognise the achievements of the order under Bonaventure's guidance but nurture sympathies for the ongoing struggle of spiritual factions who hankered back to the 'pristine beginnings'. Manselli in particular has revived the idea that the unofficial hagiographical corpus gives us privileged access to the views of Francis and his early companions by arguing that these texts rest on oral traditions that reach back to Francis's lifetime and that can still be identified stylistically in the texts as we have them.[7]

## FRANCIS ACCEPTING OF SCIENCE? THE LETTER TO ANTHONY OF PADUA

A number of scholars aiming to understand the adoption of scholarly interests within the order as part and parcel of the 'authentic' Franciscan life sketch a different view of Francis and the emergence of studies. Some of them, such as Hilarin Felder, proclaim that Francis understood science to be a natural sister of holy simplicity. Although Felder's interpretation of the source passages supporting this verdict might be overly optimistic, other scholars with slightly different agendas voice comparable opinions. They maintain that Francis was not opposed to theological learning as long it did not threaten the Franciscan way of life. With variations, this latter position is found in studies by Gratien de Paris, Giuseppe Abate, Kajatan Esser and, more recently, those of Teodosi Lombardi, Martino Conti, Lorenzo Di Fonzo and Faustino Ossanna. Most of these authors bypass the hagiographical tradition (except for Thomas of Celano and Bonaventure). Instead, they prefer Francis's writings, the *Rule*, the *Admonitions* and especially the letter to Anthony of Padua.[8]

The latter text, which invites the theologian–preacher Anthony of Padua to teach the friars, has been interpreted as a clear and unambiguous endorsement by Francis of Anthony's theological instruction of Franciscan friars in Bologna. Whether understood as Francis's gradual acceptance of theological learning, or as his more sudden reconciliation with studies in the order, this letter would seem to show that, by the time the *Rule* was adopted, Francis allowed studies insofar as they did not extinguish the spirit of prayer and devotion.

Sabatier pointed out that the letter was known only from late medieval manuscripts and early modern editions. In his eyes, the letter was a fabrication from a much later date to authenticate developments counter to Francis's wishes. Subsequently, scholars have brought to bear on this issue a variety of philological and historical arguments. The majority believes that the letter is authentic, or at least reflects a historical reality. The most important sceptical position to date is formulated by Pietro Maranesi, who again signals its problematical manuscript transmission and discerns a fundamental difference in tone between this letter and Francis's final *Testament*.[9]

If we accept Maranesi's reservations and do not pay overmuch attention to Francis's invitation to Anthony, we still have other options, especially when we read Francis's other writings and the hagiographical corpus devoted to him slightly differently. Then we discover that even the negative statements regarding the pursuit of (theological) science in the order are embedded in contexts of literacy, textuality and theological knowledge that belie the utter simple-mindedness and the complete renunciation of theological science read into them by Paul Sabatier.

## FRANCIS THE GIFTED 'IDIOTA'?

First of all, we can qualify Francis's own self-presentation as a simple-minded and illiterate man, for instance in his *Testament*. This self-presentation, reinforced in the hagiographical tradition, is a boon for scholars searching for the simple-minded fool of God. Studies by

Oktavian Schmucki, however, reveal that Francis had been relatively well-educated for a lay person. He had been raised in an affluent merchant's household in which vernacular literacy was a matter of course. The information available concerning the production of his writings suggests a rudimentary knowledge of Latin. With reference to remarks in the saints' lives by Thomas of Celano and Bonaventure, Schmucki claims that Francis attended the parish school of San Giorgio in his youth. There he would have received lessons in Latin, with the Psalter as a possible textbook. Hence, he was able to read Latin texts, albeit at times with the help of others, and, if needed, could express himself in a basic, Italianised Latin.[10]

The self-definition of simplicity should then first and foremost be connected to biblical precedents that underscored the evangelical self-positioning of Francis (such as the passage that depicts Peter and John as uncultured men without letters, Acts 4: 13), possibly inspired by comparable strategies in other evangelical renewal movements just before and contemporaneous with the early Friars Minor. Within the writings addressed to the order the simplicity topos could have been part of a strategy to stress the importance of humility and evangelical simplicity in all Friars Minor, whether they be learned clerics or uncultured laymen.[11]

This interpretation of the topos of simplicity fits in with Francis's conversion trajectory, which took place through an ongoing engagement with the Gospel. Even his famous use of the Bible for the so-called *sors apostolorum* technique to find divine guidance for his way of life could have been modelled on famous examples from the past to which Francis had access thanks to his participation in a literate world. His surviving writings beyond the *Rules* of 1221 and 1223 – written with the assistance of friars with a greater biblical knowledge, such as Julian of Speyer – show sufficient theological sensibilities and access to theological authorities to assume that Francis's self-representation as a simple and illiterate layman was created from a literate vantage point. A perusal of his texts shows a familiarity not only with the Psalms and the New Testament, but also with the *Rule* of St Benedict, and sayings of such theologians as Anselm of Canterbury and Bernard of Clairvaux. Not all of this should be ascribed to the influence of learned secretaries. Likewise, the same hagiographical sources that tell such a cautionary tale regarding studies and depict Francis as the uncultured but divinely inspired *idiota* also emphasise his willingness to engage in the reading, actively or passively (as a listener), of 'sacred books', for which he had apparently a very good memory.[12]

Hence, Francis's embrace of the Gospel message was not the action of a completely naïve, illiterate man. After all, this is the period of the ecclesiastical censure of various popular religious movements initiated by lay people (such as the Waldensians and the Humiliati) and the threat of Cathar dualism. Although the event is completely plastered over within the hagiographical eulogies, papal approval for the minorite evangelical project makes more sense if we assume that Innocent III encountered in Francis not just a lay enthusiast but someone with enough understanding to steer free from non-Catholic 'misinterpretations' and crude appropriations of the biblical message so as to make him into a possible partner for the pope's reform agenda.

Francis's opposition to learning would therefore never have gone so far as to allow the intrusion of heterodox or outright heretical ideas due to a lack of instruction in the tenets of Catholic faith. This concern is for instance traceable in chapter 19 of the *Rule* of 1221 and in the second chapter of the *Rule*, which urge ministers to examine the catholicity of newcomers to the order, especially in the context of Cathar and Waldensian undercurrents in contemporary forms of popular religious enthusiasm.[13]

The education of Francis before his conversion, his acceptance of basic forms of instruction to ensure the catholicity of his friars and his engagement with texts from the Christian tradition should convince us that he cannot be depicted as the proverbial simpleton opposed to any form of religious instruction. Furthermore, if we analyse the vision of the Franciscan 'golden age' as put forward by the hagiographical corpus and the so-called *Dictated Works*, we notice that Francis and the members of his brotherhood were defining themselves regularly with recourse to texts and writing. It is telling that brothers took care to note down what Francis was saying, and that Francis himself would call upon literate friars in his company to write down events and inspired utterances, as part and parcel of the creation of an authoritative textual community in which the use of biblically inspired writing and epistolary communication became a matter of course. Comparable mechanisms must have been at work in the prolonged editorial process leading to the *Rule* of 1221.[14]

Religious and spiritual formation by means of the written word also shines through in a number of Francis's other writings, such as the *Admonitions* and the *Office of the Passion*. The former testifies in and of itself to the founder's willingness to provide religious guidance to his friars. The latter text was formative for the liturgical and devotional life of the brotherhood and as such implied a thorough acculturation to the

Psalms with additional prayers (something that was reconfirmed in the liturgical guidelines to the *Rules*). It also signposts Francis's personal embrace of a more clerical, literate lifestyle, to which his use of the breviary and his ordination as Levite–deacon provides additional testimony.[15]

## THE NECESSITY OF STUDIES IN AN APOSTOLIC ORDER

It is impossible to know whether Francis harboured any views regarding studies in the very early days of his movement. Given that he tried to follow Christ's example around Assisi in total poverty, humility and devotion, living by the labour of his hands, learning cannot have been uppermost in his mind. Yet the issue of religious instruction automatically presented itself when the first better-educated clerics entered the movement and when the friars made a more fundamental choice of a life of pastoral mission instead of one of eremitical retreat.

The choice of a missionary existence, just after the brothers' return from the papal court in 1209, is reflected in various hagiographical traditions. Insofar as this was an *informed* decision, the choice of a life of mission, just after Francis had received papal approval of his way of life and right around the time the Church was coming down hard on a number of other lay initiatives, implied an acceptance of at least a measure of basic training. Although early Franciscan preaching was above all a call to repentance without much doctrinal content, some guarantees of catholicity had to be met in order for the friars to evade accusations of heresy and to be capable of debate with the Cathars. That these were serious concerns is revealed at various junctures in the earliest Franciscan historical writings.[16]

From this perspective, the acceptance of a measure of instruction may have occurred rather early, and this created the preconditions that led to the first permanent 'schools' in the early 1220s. By that time, Franciscan missionaries were meeting Muslims, and Franciscan preaching within the Christian commonwealth was moving beyond the call to repentance towards veritable preaching, or doctrinal preaching. Whatever the authenticity of the letter to Anthony of Padua as we have it now, it possibly reflects an underlying reality, namely, that Franciscan preachers and missionaries needed more efficacious theological training, and that Francis was not fundamentally opposed to it, even if he lamented the loss of initial minorite simplicity.

## THE PLACE OF STUDIES IN THE 'AUTHENTIC' WRITINGS

If what I am saying is correct, the question should not be whether Francis was totally opposed to the influx of learning in the order but rather how he felt that he could square the need for studies with his desire for evangelical poverty and humility. To answer this, we need to peruse more of Francis's surviving writings than just his alleged letter to Anthony.

Insofar as these writings address the issue of studies at all, they do not disqualify them outright but formulate concerns that the pursuit of theological studies in itself could lead to undue pride, or to a love of studies for their own sake, without humility and openness towards the gifts of the Spirit. This is stated in chapters 5 and 7 of the *Admonitions*, which probably date from the early 1220s. These passages contain stern warnings against the pursuit of studies for their own reward and without the proper attitude. Yet they acknowledge implicitly the activity of studying in the order and can only be interpreted meaningfully if we see them as attempts to steer in the right direction activities that were indeed taking place.

The issue of studies, or rather 'wisdom', is furthermore addressed metaphorically in Francis's *Salutation of the Virtues*. In this work, Queen (or Holy) Wisdom is put on a par with Sister Simplicity. Whereas Queen Wisdom thwarts the machinations of the devil, holy and pure simplicity shows the emptiness of worldly wisdom. Hence true learning is solely concerned with a sincere quest for spiritual insight into God's intentions, and its character is revealed outwardly first and foremost through one's actions. Whatever the spiritual overtones at work here, this passage seems to present the proper exercise of wisdom as a virtue but does not translate into clear-cut directives for studies in the order.[17]

Counter to what one might expect, the *Rules* of 1221 and 1223 do not provide specific guidelines regarding the pursuit of learning either. Some forms of study are implied in the chapters devoted to preachers and their proper examination by the ministers. Beyond that, both *Rules* curtail the undue acquisition of books by individual friars (as contrary to the Franciscan ideal of poverty). The third chapter of the *Rule* of 1221 simply states that clerics should only have books that were necessary for the fulfilment of their clerical tasks, and that literate lay friars could have a Psalter.[18] Furthermore, both *Rules* imply that everyone should fulfil the life of evangelical perfection by exploiting the professional skills he brought to the order. This left clerical and literate lay friars some room for honing these skills with additional training for homiletic and missionary purposes, but it did not envisage the kinds of in-depth theological training, replete with dispensations from other activities, that we know from contemporary Dominican sources, and that were beginning to take place in several Franciscan communities precisely around this period.

Chapter 10 of the more legally phrased *Rule* of 1223 seemingly introduces an additional element, much discussed in Franciscan scholarship, namely, that illiterate friars should be content with their state and not try to become literate. Those seeking evidence for Francis's fundamental opposition to learning could use this passage as proof of his ultimate objections to studies. Considering the context, however, this interpretation seems unwarranted. More inclusive interpretations are given by Kajetan Esser and Carlo Paolazzi. They argue that the passage must be seen as a clarifying consequence of the message already present in the *Rule* of 1223, namely that everybody should seek the life of evangelical perfection with the skills he brought to the task. Literate friars could work with their literate skills, but friars without reading skills should not search for literacy and scholarship, because that only served self-enhancement.[19]

At variance with this is Pietro Maranesi's argument that this passage on illiterate friars in the *Rule* of 1223, not unlike passages regarding the liturgical obligations of lay and clerical friars in chapter 3 of the same text, signals a gradual shift in attitude. In Maranesi's interpretation, the passage denies illiterate friars access to books more explicitly than earlier statements in the *Rule* of 1221. This would have resulted from Francis's realisation that the division between the illiterate friars and an elite of literate (and predominantly clerical) friars had become irreversible, and that the latter had begun to monopolise leadership roles with the full support of the papal curia. Whereas the *Rule* of 1221 had predominantly been a codification of minorite practices from earlier days, the *Rule* of 1223 was a more formal document negotiating Francis's vision with the wishes and demands of the Church through the cardinal protector and the leading friars in the order. By inserting the passage on illiterate friars, Francis would have resigned himself to the by now rather fundamental divide within the order but at the same time would have commanded more sternly than before the illiterate friars still present in the order to embrace their status, and therewith become the torch-bearers of the original Franciscan zeal, in an order now increasingly ruled by learned clerics.[20]

From Maranesi's perspective, Francis's *Testament* is a thoroughly nostalgic text, commemorating a time in which the Friar Minor was subject to all – a time that was no more, and was already in danger of being forgotten. It rephrases central desires for the authentic Franciscan life, in which the friars lived by the labours of their hands. Yet the *Testament* expresses veneration for theologians and does not condemn theological learning, conscious of the fact that as a pastoral task force within the Church supported by the papacy the order was not to survive without it.

If we follow the leads already offered by Esser and Schmucki, the passage in the *Testament* that recalls the ignorant and illiterate subservient status of Francis and his early followers is not just a nostalgic reminder but still aims to correct those learned friars who in their pursuit of studies and power had lost their humility and scorned the simplicity of the minorite life. By their desire for learning itself they had spurned the deeper spiritual insights of true knowledge, just as the high priests mentioned in the Acts of the Apostles had scorned the apostles as simple-minded men without letters.

In either case, Francis did not develop a more positive attitude towards studies towards the end of his life than before, as is suggested in the studies of Di Fonzo and Ossanna, in which the letter to Anthony stands central. Nor did Francis near the end of his life condemn studies completely. The implicit message from the *Admonitions* still stood: theological learning could be commendable and to an extent might be necessary, but undue desire for learning could destroy the evangelical virtues on which the Franciscan life was founded.

## TENTATIVE CONCLUSIONS

Francis was a relatively well-educated lay person, who opted for a life of evangelical perfection, emphasising poverty and identifying with the outcasts of society. At first sight these ideals preclude any form of study, and it can be assumed that initially Francis did not give matters of study much thought. Francis shaped his religious experience from the outset with recourse to the biblical texts and classics of the Christian tradition, and used the written word both to help constitute his movement and to communicate his convictions about Christian life to his friars and to the world at large.

As soon as missionary endeavours began to predominate within the movement – notwithstanding a great love for eremitical retreat – Francis opted implicitly for the necessity of training his friars, if only to forgo charges of heretical teaching, and to adhere to the doctrines of the

Church. Considering the historical context, it is unlikely that Francis was unaware of this consequence. It also informed his deference to clerical authority.

The emphasis on mission stimulated the influx of clerics, and there is no real evidence to suggest that Francis was fundamentally opposed to their theological learning. However, it should remain subservient to the essence of Franciscan humility and poverty, and it should not cause friars to feel in any shape or form superior to other members within the order. The latter was fundamental: learning as a 'possession' and as a source of personal pride was anathema.

Around 1220, Francis understood that tendencies of expansion and institutionalisation had gone beyond his control, up to the point that he abdicated from his leadership. From then onwards, he tried to influence matters even more forcefully with recourse to the written word, both in his editorial engagement with the *Rules* of 1221 and 1223, and with his letters and *Testament*. By then, Francis realised on the one hand that the pursuit of studies by parts of the clerical body of the order in particular was having profound repercussions and, on the other hand, that, within bounds, proper theological studies were absolutely necessary. He may have expressed the latter in his alleged letter to Anthony.

Whatever Francis's reservations, a full condemnation of studies is nowhere to be found in his writings. It is to be expected that such a condemnation does not figure in the *Rule*. Yet it is absent even in the *Testament*. That text again puts forward Francis's simple and illiterate status. This should probably be read as a biblically inspired rhetorical strategy to stress the extent to which the minorite way of life was based on divine inspiration and needed to be followed faithfully. Yet that same text also expresses veneration for priests, theologians and theological knowledge.

Although not an enemy of studies in the absolute sense, Francis never wanted his brothers to make theological studies their core activity. That shows to what extent he still wished to keep his distance from the Dominican model, where studies from the outset shaped the daily life of friars. By the early 1220s, Francis had first-hand experience of the Dominican lifestyle. Although he respected it, he did not feel inclined for his order to emulate that way of life to the full. In his eyes, there remained a place for lay friars and for forms of manual labour unconnected to pastoral ministry.

Still during his lifetime, Franciscans began to establish schools and seek out universities, and it became more common to provide in-depth theological training to friars designated for pastoral and missionary tasks. With this in mind, it remains tempting to read Celano's *Second Life* and the 'unofficial' hagiographical accounts based on dossiers compiled by Leo and his fellow companions as direct evidence for Francis's condemnation of studies at the very end of his life. This was Sabatier's position, who situated some of these texts far too early. This view has again found support from those inspired by Raoul Manselli's assertion that these texts, even when compiled much later, contain remnants of genuine eyewitness accounts of the real Francis.

I would argue, however, that the historical reality is more complex. All these hagiographical writings were put to parchment after twenty to eighty years of additional developments. Even if these texts incorporated oral memories of the 'pristine' beginnings, this does not mean that such cultivated memories, put down in writing between the 1240s and the early fourteenth century, can be equated without further ado with the historical realities of Francis's last years. Following Maurice Halbwachs, modern research on the construction of social memory in specific groups highlights the influence of contemporary interests on the content of what is remembered. Based on this, we should be aware of the fact that the 'memories' of Francis and his 'sayings' transformed into these textual (hi)stories were remembered in light of the stakes of the historical moment in which they were put to parchment.[21]

In short, the agenda of these texts may have had as much to do with events from the 1240s and after as with the Franciscan world of the mid 1220s. Whatever their message, these texts do not provide privileged access to the mind of Francis in his final years. For that, the writings of Francis himself remain our best option. It should not deter us that they only give us tentative answers.

The non-official hagiographical corpus emerged in an order that had witnessed enormous changes: it had seen the dismissal of Elias, which resulted in the further curtailment of the lay voice in the order; it had seen the progressive acceptance of privileges, and an increasing inequality in power and lifestyle between a learned Franciscan elite and the rank and file. That remains the most probable historical context to interpret the at times polemical message of the unofficial hagiographical tradition.

Under the leadership of Elias, the order was guided more in line with some of the wishes of Francis than is sometimes assumed. Whatever his faults, emphasised and maybe invented by clerical Franciscan sources from the later thirteenth century and after, Elias had maintained a good relationship with Clare and with at least some of the original companions. This could indicate that in the eyes of several men and women once close to Francis, the policies of Elias were not a complete betrayal.

Elias had not been among the party of friars who asked the pope to nullify the *Testament* in 1230. That was done under the reign of John Parenti (1227–32), when Elias was guiding the construction of the Assisi basilica. Under Elias (elected in 1232 against the wishes of the clerical elite), the order might not have observed the life of poverty as Francis envisaged it, yet it adhered to the *Testament*'s central command not to add glosses to the *Rule*. Elias also held clericalisation at bay. It was only after his deposition in May 1239 that the order (now led by Albert of Pisa, Haymo of Faversham and their circle of theologians) created new constitutions which marginalised the position of lay friars.

Whereas Elias adhered to the *Testament*'s command to follow the *Rule* without glossing, he also stimulated the development of studies, as Salimbene later had to admit rather reluctantly. This could imply that within the circles around Elias that still cherished the legacy of Francis, the creation of schools and study houses was deemed acceptable. Within limits these friars may have thought (correctly or not) that this could be reconciled with the wishes of the founder–saint.[22]

When highly educated clerical factions took control of the order in and after 1239, promptly began to issue constitutions that sanctioned the creation of strict hierarchies and pursued policies that disqualified older ways of life, some companions of old reached for their pens to denounce the pursuit of learning. By then, theological scholarship had come to stand for everything that was undercutting older ideals of evangelical poverty, humility and fraternal equality: Paris had destroyed Assisi.

## Notes

1 Cf. H. Felder, *Geschichte der wissenschaftlichen Studien im Franziskanerorden bis um die Mitte des 13. Jahrhunderts* (Freiburg im Breisgau, 1904); B. Fajdek, 'Gli studi nell'ordine dei frati minori secondo le costituzioni di Narbona di San Bonaventura', *Vita Minorum: Rivista di spiritualità francescana*, 62 (1991), 527–34; B. Roest, 'The Franciscan School System: Re-Assessing the Early Evidence (ca. 1220–1260)', in M. Robson and J. Röhrkasten (eds.), *Franciscan Organization in the Medicant Context: Formal and Informal Structures of the Friars' Lives and Ministry in the Middle Ages*, Vita Regularis. Ordnungen and Deutungen Religiosen Lebens im Mittelalter, 44 (Berlin, 2010), pp. 253–79.

2 Cf. F. Accrocca, *Francesco e le sue immagini: Momenti della evoluzione della coscienza storica dei frati minori (secoli XIII–XVI)*, Studi Antoniani, 27 (Padua, 1997); J. Dalarun, *La malavventura di Francesco*

*d'Assisi*, Fonti e ricerche, 10 (Milan, 1996); L. Pellegrini, *Frate Francesco e i suoi agiografi*, Collana della società internazionale di studi francescani diretta da Enrico Menestò e Stefano Brufani, Saggi, 8 (Assisi, 2004); J. Dalarun, *Vers une résolution de la question franciscaine: La légende ombrienne de Thomas de Celano* (Paris, 2007).

3  P. Sabatier, *Vie de s. François: Edition définitive* (Paris, 1931), pp. 371–89.
4  Cf. Dalarun, *La malavventura*, pp. 140–50. F. Accrocca, 'Oltre Sabatier: La nuova edizione dello *Speculum perfectionis*', *Miscellanea Francescana*, 106–7:3–4 (2007), 504–28.
5  Cf. Dalarun, *La malavventura*, pp. 118f.
6  *Dicta beati Aegidii Assisienses*, ed. PP. Collegi S. Bonaventurae, 2nd edn (Quaracchi, 1939), pp. 55–7, 91: '*Parisius, Parisius, ipse destruis ordinem sancti Francisci*.' Among the poems of Jacopone, see esp. *Laude* XXXI: 'Tale qual è: non c'è religione/Mal vedemmo Parisi, c'hane destrutto Ascisi:/co la lor lettoria, messo l'o en mala via.' Jacopone da Todi, *Laudi, Trattato e Detti*, ed. Franca Ageno (Florence, 1953), pp. 113f.
7  J. Moorman, *The Sources for the Life of St Francis of Assisi* (Manchester, 1940); J. Moorman, *A History of the Franciscan Order from its Origins to the Year 1517* (Oxford, 1968); R. Manselli, *Nos qui cum eo fuimus: Contributo alla questione francescana*, Bibliotheca Seraphico-Capuccina cura instituti historici ord. Fr. Min. Cappuccinorum, 28 (Rome, 1980).
8  Gratien de Paris, *Histoire de la fondation et de l'évolution de l'ordre des Frères Mineurs au XIIIe siècle* (Paris, 1928), p. 96; G. Abate, 'S. Antonio maestro di sacra teologia', in *S. Antonio dottore della chiesa. Atti delle settimane antoniane tenute a Roma e a Padova nel 1946* (Vatican City, 1947), pp. 265–94; K. Esser, 'Der Brief des hl. Franziskus an den hl. Antonius von Padua', in E. Kurten and I. de Villapadierna (eds.), *Studien zu den Opuscula des hl. Franziskus von Assisi*, Subsidia scientifica franciscalia, 4 (Rome, 1973), pp. 43–58; K. Esser, 'Studium und Wissenschaft im Geiste des hl. Franziskus von Assisi', *Wissenschaft und Weisheit*, 39 (1976), 26–41; T. Lombardi, 'Sant'Antonio di Padova maestro di teologia a Bologna: Il problema degli studi agli inizi dell'ordine francescano', *Il Santo* (1982), 797–818; M. Conti, 'Lo sviluppo degli studi e la clericalizzazione dell'ordine', *Antonianum*, 57 (1982), 321–46; L. Di Fonzo, 'L'apostolato intellettuale, componente essenziale del carisma francescano-conventuale', *Miscellanea Francescana*, 94 (1994), 568–88; F. Ossanna, 'Il senso della teologia nell'Ordine francescano: La lettera di Francesco ad Antonio', *Miscellanea Francescana*, 94 (1994), 505–15.
9  P. Sabatier, 'Examen de quelques travaux récents sur les opuscules de saint François', *Opuscules de critique historique*, 11 (1904), 117–61. Cf. C. Paolazzi, 'Francesco, la teologia e la "Lettera a frate Antonio"', in G. Ravaglia (ed.), *Antonio uomo evangelico*, Atti del convegno di studi (Bologna, 22–3 febbraio 1996) (Padua, 1997), pp. 39–61. Cf. P. Maranesi, *Nescientes Litteras: L'Ammonizione della regola francescana e la questione degli studi nell'ordine (sec. xiii–xvi)*, Bibliotheca

Seraphico-Capuccina cura instituti historici ord. Fr. Min. Cappuccinorum, 61 (Rome, 2000), pp. 39–43. Cf. 2 Cel., 163.

10  O.Schmucki, '"Ignorans sum et idiota". Das Ausmass der schulischen Bildung des hl. Franziskus von Assisi', in *Studia historico-ecclesiastica. Festgabe für prof. Luchesius G. Spätling OFM* (Rome, 1977), pp. 283–310.

11  Ibid., pp. 291, 303f.

12  N. Scivoletto, 'Problemi di lingua e di stile degli scritti latini di san Francesco', in *Francesco d'Assisi e francescanesimo dal 1216 al 1226, Atti del IV convegno internazionale Assisi, 15–17 ottobre 1976* (Assisi, 1977), pp. 101–24, esp. pp. 115–18. Cf. 2 Cel., 102.

13  RNB, 19; *Rule*, II. See K. Esser, *Anfänge und ursprüngliche Zielsetzungen des Ordens der Minderbrüder* (Leiden, 1966), pp. 150–2.

14  References to a scribal culture constituting the textual community of the friars can be found in the *Dictated Works* (*Opuscula Dictata*, no. viii – *De vera et perfecta laetitia*). Comparable references can be found in CA, 12. Cf. M. F. Cusato, 'An Unexplored Influence on the *Epistola ad fideles* of Francis of Assisi: The *Epistola universis Christi fidelibus* of Joachim of Fiore', *FS*, 61 (2003), pp. 253–78. For literature on the *Rule* of 1221 see D. Flood, *Die Regula non bullata der Minderbrüder*, Franziskanische Forschungen, 19 (Werl im Westfalen, 1967); K. Esser, *Textkritische Untersuchungen zur Regula non bullata der Minderbrüder*, Spicilegium Bonaventurianum, 9 (Grottaferrata, 1974); D. Flood, 'Regulam melius observare', in *Verba Domini mei. Gli Opuscula di Francesco d'Assisi a 25 anni dalla edizione di Kajatan Esser, OFM* (Rome, 2003), pp. 329–61; C. Paolazzi, 'La "Regula non bullata" dei Frati Minori (1221) dallo "Stemma codicum" al testo critico', *AFH*, 100 (2007), 5–148.

15  Anthonius van Dijk, 'The Breviary of Saint Francis', *FS*, 9 (1949), 13–40; P. Messa, 'Beatus Franciscus acquisivit hoc Breviarium', in Cesare Vaiani (ed.), *Domini vestigia sequi. Miscellanea offerta a P. Giovanni M. Boccali*, Studi e Ricerche, 15 (Assisi, 2003), pp. 133–79; A. Callabaut, 'Saint François lévite', *AFH*, 20 (1927), 193–6.

16  See especially Esser, *Anfänge und ursprüngliche Zielsetzungen*, pp. 204–5.

17  *Salutatio Virtutum, Fontes Franciscani*, Medioevo francescano, 2 (Assisi, 1995), p. 223. Cf. Esser, 'Studium und Wissenschaft', 34–6.

18  Scholars argue whether the *Rule* of 1221 intends that clerics could have books for liturgical purposes, or more generally books necessary to fulfil their tasks. I follow the latter interpretation. See C. Paolazzi, 'I frati minori e i libri: Per l'esegesi di "Ad implendum eorum Officium" (RNB, III, 7) e "Nescientes litteras" (RNB, III, 9; X, 7)', *AFH*, 97 (2004), 3–59, esp. 14–31.

19  Esser, 'Studium und Wissenschaft', 36–7, argues that the 'nescientes litteras' passage in the *Rule* of 1221 is similar to the 'nescientibus litteras librum habere non liceat' in the third chapter of the *Regula non bullata*. Paolazzi's analysis of these two passages is similar. Paolazzi, 'I frati minori e i libri', 44–7.

20 Maranesi, *Nescientes Litteras*, pp. 29–37, 60–5. The appearance of the lay–clerical divide at this juncture is denied by Martino Conti. Cf. Conti, 'Lo sviluppo degli studi', 323–9.

21 M. Halbwachs, *La mémoire collective* (Paris, 1950). He and successors suggest that memory can best be understood as a sieve or a distorting lens, bent on preserving from or finding in the past what underscores a specific faction's sense of identity in the here and now.

22 G. Barone, 'Elias von Cortona und Franziskus', in D. R. Bauer *et al.* (eds.), *Franziskus von Assisi: Das Bild des Heiligen aus neuer Sicht*, Beihefte zum Archiv für Kulturgeschichte, 54 (Cologne–Weimar–Vienna, 2005), pp. 183–94. *The Chronicle of Salimbene de Adam* acknowledges Elias's promotion of theological studies: Salimbene, 83.

## 11 The early Franciscans and the towns and cities

JENS RÖHRKASTEN

As the son of a successful merchant, Francesco Bernardone grew up in a city, enjoying his father's wealth and social status. He was formed by an urban style of life which included distinctive entertainments and festivities, and his training and education prepared him for a world of commerce which was centred on towns. He took on this role in his early 20s at the latest, when he was following in his father's footsteps, e.g., transporting bales of cloth from Assisi to nearby towns for sale there (1 Cel., 8). Thomas of Celano describes him in this phase of his life as an urban dweller who lacked any sense of the beauties of nature (1 Cel., 3). All this changed with his conversion, which included not only rejection of his social status and breaking with his family, but also abandonment of his urban lifestyle and indeed departure from the town of Assisi itself (1 Cel., 16). Later in the thirteenth century the symbolic value of abandoning urban life in favour of religion was underlined by Bonaventure of Bagnoregio, Paris master and minister general of the order, who, in a commentary on the Gospel of Luke, stated: 'Travelling into the desert and abandoning the town means abandoning the secular and entering the life of religion.'[1]

After this break Francis's former peers were not automatically supportive. The *Legend of the Three Companions* reports that begging trips into his home town by Francis and his first companions were met with criticism and yielded few results (3 Soc., 35). This did not disturb Francis, who was now pursuing a life of poverty, shunning normal habitations and dwelling in woods, abandoned churches and religious houses for as long as they offered shelter (1 Cel., 6). Initially he led the life of a hermit, without fixed abode; by the time he was joined by his first followers, he was staying at Rivo Torto outside Assisi, and then later mostly at the abandoned church of Santa Maria degli Angeli. The early friars lived likewise in chapels and small churches, in huts and hermitages, and even in caves – in any case, outside urban settlements. When the friars were entrusted with their first mission, Francis sent them to different parts of the world, not specifically to towns (1 Cel., 29).

Emanating from the urban culture of early thirteenth-century Italy, rejection of the town was also a rejection of urban values, including the rivalries and faction fighting which characterised contemporary political life. When the Pisans captured a Franciscan in 1225 because they regarded him as a citizen of Lucca, he received papal support in the form of a letter which explained that his entry into religious life coincided with a withdrawal from the secular world.[2] Francis himself is said to have made this point in Perugia when the local elite disturbed his sermon: he had been called by God, and they should not regard him merely as a man of Assisi.[3] Abandoning towns also had a symbolical meaning.

Although Francis never seems to have resided in a town for any length of time after his departure from Assisi, he was a frequent visitor of urban centres in Italy and other parts of the Mediterranean after he had begun his pastoral work of preaching his simple but very powerful sermons. Jacques de Vitry gave a description of the Franciscans he encountered in 1216: they were hermits, living in remote places, but they were active in towns during the day.[4] Francis himself had experienced the problems posed by a lack of any supplies: when he returned with his companions from the meeting with Innocent III in Rome through the valley of Spoleto, they were not able to refresh and supply themselves because of their remote base (1 Cel., 34). Even at this early stage, when the whole community consisted of only twelve friars, dependence on the support provided by an urban environment became painfully obvious. In addition, urban centres offered the audience for sermons and for Francis's sometimes theatrical appearances, when he would confess his weaknesses to large crowds of spectators. For these reasons the break with towns was never complete or permanent. Francis's retreat from Assisi was both practical and symbolic, but as soon as he felt himself compelled to preach the Gospel he returned to Assisi. Francis himself decided to spend much time in the vicinity of his home town, where he could preach and in turn draw on the resources offered by its economy without being part of its commercial organisation.[5] This ambivalence between a preference for the eremitical life coupled with a rejection of towns on the one hand and the convenience of reaching large urban audiences for their apostolic work while enjoying the material support offered by towns on the other remained characteristic of Franciscan groups in Tuscany and other parts of central Italy until the middle of the thirteenth century and beyond.[6] However, the predominant trend in the expanding community was different: it was seen as desirable to be close to urban populations, also at night, and not just by the friars but also by their urban supporters. The *vita* of Bernard of Quintavalle illustrates the first steps of this process, the Franciscan settlement in towns: after their attempt to find shelter in one of the rich houses of Florence had failed, Bernard and his companion spent the night in the porch of the building, whose master and mistress regarded and treated them as potential thieves. Their error of judgement was only revealed early the next morning when the woman, who had refused to admit the two friars at night, discovered them at prayer in the local parish church. Far from being ordinary vagabonds, the two turned out to be deeply devout men, and her surprise was all the greater when she observed that they even refused the alms offered them by another citizen. Their absolute refusal to accept coins demanded an explanation, and so the two friars were able to explain their beliefs and purpose. Their credentials thus established, the two were then offered shelter in the house which had previously been closed to them, and their story began to spread through the town.[7] Elsewhere Franciscan settlements also began with the offer of shelter in private houses or in empty buildings. In Mühlhausen, in Thuringia, the local count assigned the first four friars in the town an unfinished house in the hope that they would build the missing roof, in the meantime offering them the use of a cellar in his castle. Here the four were content to live for a year without making any effort to finish the building assigned to them, after which the nobleman withdrew his support.[8]

The transition from an offer of temporary shelter for a small number of friars to the provision of permanent urban residences marked a significant step in the order's development, and it was not a smooth process. It is difficult to say whether we are dealing with a gradual change, as the *Legend of the Three Companions* suggests, or whether the move into towns was the result of systematic planning.[9] Both are possible, because the changes affecting the early Franciscan community were rapid and, once they had been sent out to different countries, small groups of friars were acting on their own, hundreds of miles apart and remote from the centre at the Porziuncula, confronted with different conditions and challenges. If an episode related in the *Second Life* by Thomas of Celano and in the *Mirror of Perfection* can be believed, Francis – as ever aware of the changes affecting the order – remained very sceptical of the minorites' urban presence. Travelling to Bologna on his return from Egypt, he heard that the friars had just constructed a new house there; when he became aware that they were associated with the ownership of the property, he immediately left the town and ordered them all out.[10] For Francis, a permanent presence in an urban centre held the danger of becoming subject to the centre's prevalent norms, so departure from the town and a return to an itinerant lifestyle were necessary to preserve the original ideal. Were not the friars to serve the lord as pilgrims and vagrants? This attitude survived especially in central Italy, where small groups of Franciscans continued to live as hermits or itinerant preachers. Stories about Francis's own reluctance to accept urban dwellings for his friars were particularly popular among these groups, although much of the subsequent discussion centred on poverty and the legal status of conventual buildings rather than their location. Nevertheless, tensions over friars' permanent residences in towns led Bonaventure to address the issue and to justify their presence in urban centres.

Even if the story of Francis in Bologna is apocryphal, it is well documented; the expansion of the Franciscan order throughout Europe was based on urban centres. For the first Franciscan travellers who explored new regions, towns served as destinations, as meeting-places and as the basis for future activities. Franciscan convents were an urban feature. This did not mean that the friars restricted their pastoral work to towns. Instead, they created provinces, which were districts with defined borders. Their pastoral responsibilities extended to the whole of the population within the boundaries of the provinces, which were further subdivided into custodies. The topographical key to the often extensive provinces and custodies was the towns. Each of the Franciscan convents in these territorial units developed a district from which it could obtain the required economic and material support. These so-called boundaries were just as well organised as the provinces and the custodies, and they also represented the areas on which each Franciscan community focused its pastoral work. The Franciscans, as well as the other mendicant orders (the Dominicans and, from the middle of the thirteenth century, also the Carmelites and the Austin Friars), began to focus on towns and cities to such a degree that they came to be regarded as an entirely urban phenomenon. The change is reflected in the *Rule* of 1221, with its reference to 'places' which are seen as different from the hermitages. Here the friars are admonished not to acquire the ownership of a 'place', whatever its nature.

Following initial journeys to France and Spain, a more determined effort to transplant the friars into other parts of Europe was made in 1219, when a decision was taken to send missions into France,

Germany, Hungary and Spain, as well as into those parts of Italy which had not yet been visited.[11] While the friars sent to Germany and Hungary met with a hostile reception, partly because they were unable to communicate with the local inhabitants, the missions to France and Spain were a success. By 1233 there were more than twenty Franciscan houses in French towns, among them such important centres as Amiens, Beauvais, Chartres, Meaux, Orléans, Paris, Rouen, Soissons and Troyes. Among the early houses in Spain were Barcelona, Gerona and Vic. In some of the larger cities, such as London, the newly arrived minorites found Dominican friars already in place, and in some instances the Friars Preacher provided valuable assistance. With the emergence of other mendicant orders in the course of the thirteenth century, especially the Carmelites and the Austin Friars, many cities could boast a substantial mendicant presence, with four or even more convents by the later thirteenth century. This reflected the economic potential of cities, where even those religious could survive who refused an economic basis; it was also an indication of the inhabitants' willingness to provide sustained material support for a new form of religious life. In a number of European cities the Franciscans were invited to remain, were provided with accommodation by prominent citizens and were granted essential support by the local bishop, or had convent buildings financed by members of the nobility or even royalty.

After the failure of the missions to Germany and Hungary a new attempt was made in 1221, when a large group of friars under a native speaker, Caesar of Speyer, was sent north of the Alps. Travelling in groups, the friars assembled in Augsburg, from where they moved on into the central towns, to Würzburg and also to Mainz, Worms, Speyer and Strassburg. Not long afterwards the first Franciscans were in Cologne, the largest town in the German lands. Three years later the first Franciscans arrived in England, where – as in the case of the other regions – they established a presence in key towns: having arrived at Dover they walked to Canterbury, London and Oxford, the kingdom's religious, political, economic and intellectual capitals. Even during the lifetime of St Francis the order was undergoing a noticeable change which was visible to all: the minorites began to establish urban residences. This expansion and transition coincided with a change in the life of Francis of Assisi, who began to withdraw from the leadership of the order after his return from Egypt in 1219/20.

The death of Francis seems to have had no impact on the order's development, apart from providing the community with a symbol which stood for a radical religious ideal. Roughly coinciding with

Francis's canonisation in 1228 was a further expansion, this time from the German province into Bohemia, Hungary and Poland, and then into Denmark and the less urbanised kingdom of Norway. Friars from the English province soon went north to Scotland, where they could initially be found in Berwick, and to Ireland, where they established convents in Dublin and Limerick. The order's expansion required a rearrangement of its territorial organisation, so that different phases of development can be found in the different regions. In 1217, when Franciscans were also sent into France, Provence, Spain and the Holy Land, six districts were established in Italy. Between 1227 and 1233 the province in the Iberian Peninsula was subdivided into the new districts of Castile, Aragon and Santiago. The German province was subdivided in 1230 into the new units of Saxony and Upper Germany. Probably in 1239 the latter was again subdivided into the provinces of Cologne and Upper Rhine.[12] Within ten years of St Francis's death the order had become a truly international organisation. Its convents, which could be found in all parts of Europe, were generally located in towns.

In this context two important aspects need to be considered. First, there were significant differences in the level of urbanisation within Europe, both in terms of the density of towns and the degree of their development as multifunctional centres. Economically vibrant areas of high urban density in the north of Italy, the Rhineland, Flanders and the north of France contrasted with regions where towns were rare, like the north of Germany, and the eastern Baltic, where urban growth was just beginning in the twelfth century, or Scotland and large parts of Ireland, where urban development had made important advances under the Vikings, the Anglo-Normans and the Scandinavian kingdoms.[13] Small urban centres were hardly able to sustain a religious community which drew part of its legitimacy from its claim to poverty. On the other hand, a number of Franciscan hermitages survived in central Italy. Even in areas with developed urban networks towns differed in their nature and wealth, as well as in their political organisation. Did the citizens enjoy a high degree of independence – this was the situation in many northern Italian towns and in the imperial towns (*Reichsstädte*) of the German lands – or were they under the control of a powerful secular or ecclesiastical lord? In the latter case mere popular appeal was not sufficient for a Franciscan settlement: the friars also had to win over the powerful, and this is reflected in their cultivation of good relations with royalty, an exception being the territories controlled by the Hohenstaufen dynasty, where royal support became significant only in the second half of the thirteenth century when new families had taken control of southern Italy and Germany. Other significant differences can be found in the ecclesiastical structures. In England some towns, like Boston, contained only one parish, while the parochial structure in others, such as London, with more than a hundred parishes, was far more complex. In almost all towns the minorites also found other, pre-existing ecclesiastical institutions, hospitals, houses of canons and sometimes monasteries. For the Franciscans this meant that they had to adapt to a variety of conditions. During the order's expansion they tended to move into the larger towns first, although exceptions were possible. In central Italy Franciscans were also present in smaller towns from early on, the small convents serving as staging posts, facilitating communication within the community. Secondly, consideration needs to be given to foundation dates. There was a certain temptation for convents to date their origins as early as possible. Despite the relatively good biographical information on the order's founder, not all of the early abodes of Francis and his followers are known. The Porziuncula became the order's centre, and it can be regarded as the oldest Franciscan convent. On their journeys, initially though Italy but then also through France, Spain and parts of the Balkans, Francis and his early followers are certain to have visited many towns, and it is equally plausible that they would have remained in them for a period of time. Although such visits did not establish a permanent Franciscan presence, there was a tendency to date a minorite presence in the location from that time onwards. Such a temptation was particularly strong when St Francis himself could be claimed as the founder of the house. Among the convents which laid claim to such a spectacular pedigree were Barcelona, Cervera, Gerona, Lerida and Perpignan. While the foundation of the first Franciscan house in Limoges can be safely attributed to St Anthony of Padua, it is not always possible to prove early foundation dates on the evidence of the available sources. Historians tend to operate on the basis of the first documentary reference, well aware that such a source may refer to an already well-established convent with origins going much further back. It has to be accepted that the first Franciscan urban residences were often small and provisional. The friars' refusal to accept ownership also contributed to the fact that they did not leave a trace in contemporary records. Many foundation dates of Franciscan convents are simply not known.

The Franciscans began to have houses in towns from the early 1220s onwards at the latest. These were often private and provisional dwellings of poor quality and in unfavourable locations: a run-down house in London, an old synagogue in Cambridge, the local leper hospital in Erfurt.[14] The order's success in attracting novices soon rendered these structures unsuitable. Within a decade this simple accommodation gave way to religious precincts with their own chapels and convent buildings. Their development into proper convents was a complex process. The friars had to find the necessary support, and they had to decide where and how their convent would be built. Apart from material help they also needed legal assistance from outsiders, because they refused to enter into legal relationships with the former property owners. The property was held for them by the papacy or by a secular authority, or sometimes by the urban government. There were not just logistical and economic considerations: the process also led to controversy within the order. The initial architectural guidelines were vague, and the friars were confronted with citizens who were keen to show their appreciation of the new piety by providing them with splendid buildings. When the Franciscans of Erfurt were to leave the leper hospital which had served as their first accommodation, one of them, Jordan of Giano, was asked whether they would need a cloister. Jordan's reply that he did not know what a cloister was and that a small house with easy access to water would be sufficient has been cited many times.[15] In the English province different ministers provincial seem to have followed different policies. In the time of Agnellus of Pisa an infirmary was built in the Oxford convent which hardly exceeded the height of a person. On the other hand, the mud walls in the first dormitory of the London Greyfriars were replaced with stone structures. Under Haymo of Faversham attempts were made to increase the precinct areas so that the friars could supply themselves with food from their own gardens. Tendencies to replace provisional structures with proper stone buildings were not accepted by all. The roof of the Franciscan church had to be removed because its architecture was seen as contravening the order's ideals and structural changes had to be made to the cloister. When the minister provincial who had demanded these changes was threatened with a reprimand because the London convent was not properly enclosed, he replied that he had not joined the order to build walls.

The creation of proper monastic precincts for the Franciscans created problems for the order. Within two years of Francis's death the foundation stone of a large burial church for the saint was laid in Assisi by Gregory IX. This happened at a time when many of the friars' buildings in other towns were still provisional. Founders, benefactors and secular rulers were keen to show their appreciation of the friars by providing them with their own churches and suitable accommodation, while proud citizens who wanted to display the wealth and status of their commune planned magnificent public buildings. Franciscan churches could be part of such topographical and architectural programmes, and local ambitions did not always coincide with the friars' spiritual ideals. Reporting on the construction of the friars' house at Paris, Thomas of Eccleston wrote that to many of his brethren its dimensions seemed to be irreconcilable with the order's ideals of poverty. Adding that the roof of the new building collapsed when the friars were about to enter, he presented the event as a divine judgement against decadence. By 1260 at the latest the order's constitutions provided guidelines on architectural planning, imposing restrictions on vaulted roofs in the churches, on decorated windows and on painted walls.

In the larger towns the creation of a religious precinct could be a lengthy process. The case of London may serve as an example. After a year in temporary accommodation, the Franciscans moved to the site which was to become the city's Greyfriars' convent in the summer of 1225.[16] Less than twenty years later a church had been constructed, while the area of the friary was still expanding. This process of land acquisition continued until the middle of the fourteenth century. By this time a large and magnificent second convent church, begun in the first decade of the fourteenth century, had already been completed. The long delay can probably be explained by the fact that the convent was created piecemeal in an area which had already been built up. This meant that individual plots of land had to be gradually collected before a new construction phase could begin. In England these processes can be reconstructed, because in November 1279 King Edward I issued the statute *De viris religiosis* which prohibited the donation or sale of real estate to the clergy. Despite its draconian character, the legislation did not impose a blanket ban on such transactions. Events in the following decades show that they were still possible, if a royal licence could be obtained. Such licences were available if the case had been investigated by a royal official in the locality. For this purpose the official was to assemble a jury which had to provide relevant information, e.g., concerning the impact on royal rights and incomes or the creation of public nuisances and inconvenience. These inquests were submitted to the royal chancery in writing, and the surviving sources show that the Franciscan house in York, founded c.1230, was still developing its precinct in 1288. Oxford was still being enlarged in 1319, and the house at Cambridge, whose origins are coterminous with those of York, was still receiving property in 1353. It is true that conditions had changed when this grant was made because the high mortality rates due to the

Black Death which swept through England in 1348–9 must have had an impact on the demand for land in towns, and mendicant convents generally seem to have needed additional space for burials, but the situation in England had its parallels in other provinces. The Franciscan convent of Paderborn, founded in the first half of the thirteenth century, was still being enlarged in the 1320s. The house in Höxter, also situated in Westphalia, developed over at least half a century, and the creation of the Franciscan precinct in Nuremberg is thought to have taken from *c.*1228 to 1294. The construction of the Franciscan church of Würzburg alone is thought to have taken forty years.[17]

Even discounting natural disasters like the fires which destroyed the Franciscan churches of Bergen and Roscommon, there were different reasons for such delays.[18] Urban growth in the thirteenth century resulted in a high demand for real estate, with correspondingly high prices. The necessary funds would not always have been available, because financial support is likely to have fluctuated. In the case of ecclesiastical urban lords – a famous case is the Benedictines of Bury St Edmunds – concern about the infringement of privileges caused a delay.[19] Another type of obstacle was caused by the bitter rift between Emperor Frederik II and the papacy. After the emperor's second excommunication in 1239, a ban publicised by the mendicants, measures were taken against the Franciscans in Sicily and southern Italy. The emperor, Frederick II, regarded the friars as too close to Innocent IV, and this impeded their settlement in imperial lands. Their house at Palermo was dissolved, only to be reconstituted after 1250, the year of Frederick II's death.[20] While the rift between empire and papacy between 1239 and 1250 may have also affected a number of convents in Germany, political conditions were not the factor with the greatest impact on Franciscan urban development: that probably consisted of changes in urban topography and in the responses of the urban population to the minorites. Franciscan sites which had been sufficient for a small group of friars and their modest following soon became inadequate because Franciscan preachers attracted large congregations in the churches and an increasing number of novices needed to be catered for. In addition, the Franciscans were often not the only mendicant convent in the host town. In order to distribute more evenly the burden of a religious house of this type, Pope Clement IV introduced a *Rule* in 1265 prescribing a minimum distance of 300 rods (*cannae*) between mendicant convents. In many towns these factors led to the relocation of Franciscan friaries. The identification and purchase of a new area and the complete reconstruction of church and convent buildings were complicated and demanding tasks, although the available evidence shows that the friars were often keen to make use of valuable building material from their old site. Relocations extended the phase of Franciscan urban settlement – and some convents, such as that of Limoges, were even relocated more than once.

Although the urban landscape of thirteenth-century Europe is varied, it has been possible to identify patterns in the minorites' topographical settlement. The first Franciscans did not automatically find accommodation within towns: they sometimes had to remain within the suburbs, outside the walls. Even though this gave them welcome proximity to the urban population in areas not automatically integrated into the towns' parish system, the need for security and perhaps also a desire for greater proximity to the wealthier groups of citizens led to a move towards the area within the fortifications, often close or even immediately adjacent to the town walls. The case of Arezzo, where the Franciscans relocated outside the town, is rather uncommon. Franciscan convents located next to the town walls usually had their church facing the town and their conventual buildings in the more secluded and quiet area between the church and the walls. Locations near a river were favoured. When such places could not be obtained, the friars were often keen to develop aqueducts in order to have independent water supplies. Franciscan churches tended to be spacious but plain, the conventual buildings functional rather than ostentatious. However, there were notable exceptions: by the mid fourteenth century the order also had a number of magnificent churches, e.g., Santa Croce in Florence, and in Siena, Parma and Mantua, as well as in London. These buildings were not necessarily desired by the friars themselves, but they represented expressions of piety and shows of status by wealthy benefactors. Having become part of urban society, the Franciscans could be subject to pressures exerted by their supporters.

The fact that Franciscan convents and churches were financed by largely secular benefactors, and the friars' principled decision not to claim ownership of the lands and buildings in their use, gave them a particular status. Franciscan churches became multifunctional sacred spaces: they were places of worship, but they could be used for many other purposes as well. As a matter of principle they were open to the population as a whole. They could provide the neutral ground needed in cases of arbitration; they could be used as places of safe deposit for treasure, or as schools or archives. Given that they were often the largest available location in the town, they became meeting places for town councils, temporary residences for visiting members of the aristocracy and venues for diplomatic negotiations, or they could provide the background for public festivities, reflecting the mutual bond between community and friars. It was not uncommon for commercial transactions to be conducted in Franciscan churches or for them to be named as venues for the repayment of debts. Within a matter of decades church and convent became constituent elements of their host towns, part of the local topography, many of the friars having been recruited from the local population, rather than places which represented a radical and new form of Christianity.

The Franciscans' remarkable success needs to be explained. The Franciscans came to the towns to preach and to offer a living example of the apostolic life to a population largely subject to the demands of intense commercial development. Effective preachers were often confronted with requests to hear confession after their sermons, and these pastoral duties formed the core of the friars' activities. Having renounced all worldly possessions, Franciscans were ideally suited to the role of mediator, and the devotion they inspired led to peace proclamations in some Italian communities in the 1230s. The inspiration provided by them led to the formation of female as well as male lay communities. These were linked to Franciscan priests who acted as their confessors and advisors. Minorite priests were entrusted to celebrate Mass and to say prayers for the dead. These services, which had been the preserve of the elite, were not extended to much larger sections of the population. Franciscan churches, cloisters and cemeteries, those of the male as well as of the female order, became burial grounds for members of the laity, and important families paid for their own memorial chapels. For the convents this was an important source of income, and it seems that they had to accept the architectural taste of the families whose building activities gradually altered the interior space of the churches, including windows and furnishings. However, the offer of burial space and the provision of memorial Masses could infringe parochial rights, and there were tensions, even open conflict, between members of the secular clergy and the friars, until a formula for a just distribution of financial proceeds was found by Boniface VIII (on 18 February 1300). Even though the legal settlement did not automatically represent the end of the dispute, such tensions were never universal. In fact, relations between the friars and secular priests could be close, and numerous late medieval wills made by secular priests contained bequests to the Franciscans. There is another dimension to the issue. In their writings, medieval historians tended to focus on the unusual rather than the ordinary, on disputes rather than the routine.

Hence, a harmonious co-existence of secular clergy and mendicants in a town is not so strongly reflected in the sources as '*scandalum*' and public quarrels.

The symbiosis between towns and mendicant orders led Jacques le Goff in 1968 to chart the distribution of friaries when he initiated an enquiry into the urban development of medieval France. His working hypothesis was a correlation between the map of medieval French towns and the map of mendicant houses in France: it was assumed that no mendicant convent could be found outside an urban centre, and that there was no town without a religious house of this type.[21] This method was intended to identify the towns and also to trace their development. The foundations were to be charted chronologically to reflect urban development. This survey of mendicant houses aimed not just to reveal urban development, however, but also to reflect urban hierarchy. The potential to support one or more mendicant houses depended on the size and on the commercial role of an urban centre. The major cities usually accommodated several such convents; the number of mendicant houses in smaller towns was correspondingly lower. Although numbers fluctuated, there were eleven houses of friars in Paris and seven in London in the late thirteenth century. While research into French urban development had been the original intention, the project also raised important questions about mendicant convents. Were there patterns concerning their location in towns? Was it possible to obtain information about the number of friars living in them? What could be established about their religious, social and political contexts?

Although the project, which was based on the borders of the modern French Republic rather than on the boundaries of the medieval mendicant provinces, produced a number of interesting results and observations on the topography of mendicant houses, their social composition, their roles in urban society and the phases of their development, there were also problems. There was a suspicion that a survey of mendicant houses was perhaps not the best way to trace the urbanisation of France. It appeared that insufficient attention had been given to the mendicants' relations with the rural population when it emerged that they also drew significant support from the countryside. Other criteria, such as the state of urban defences or economic and financial power, offered themselves as better indicators. In addition, it seemed that the urban phenomenon was not restricted to the larger towns, but that much smaller settlements could also have an urban character even though they lacked the presence of a mendicant house.[22]

CONCLUSION

The Franciscan move into towns was not lost on the general public, and it also led to dissent within the order. The Franciscan minister general Bonaventure addressed the question of why the minorites were present in towns and cities. According to him, there were three reasons: first, it was necessary to be close to the laity in order to provide an example; secondly, he pointed out that his friars depended on the material support provided by a town; and, thirdly, the friars needed the protection offered by towns. This was not the only criticism addressed by Bonaventure. He also dealt with another, potentially even more difficult question: why did the minorites need such large convents and churches? In the cities, he argued, the friars needed space so that they could develop proper convents with cloisters, infirmaries and also gardens so that they could grow their own food. Space too was needed for their work and for their studies, as well as for the recreation of those who were returning from long journeys. In other words, in the cramped conditions of medieval towns the friars needed air to breathe.[23] Despite St Francis's ambivalent relationship to urban life and culture, the Franciscans were an important factor in later medieval urban development. Their convents and churches were widely used by the public, and their pastoral activities enriched urban culture.

## Notes

1 *Illud autem iter in desertum et egressus de civitate significat egressum vitae saecularis et ingressum religionis*, in *S. Bonaventurae Opera Omnia* (Quaracchi, 1895), vol. VII, p. 111.

2 *Bullarium Franciscanum*, ed. J. H. Sbaralea (Rome, 1759), vol. I, p. 23, no. XXII, 4 October 1225.

3 R. Brentano, 'Do Not Say that This is a Man from Assisi', in P. Findlen, M. Fontaine and D. Osheim (eds.), *Beyond Florence: The Contours of Medieval and Early Modern Italy* (Stanford, 2003), pp. 72–80, at p. 72; R. B. Brooke (ed.), *Scripta Leonis, Rufini et Angeli Sociorum S. Francisci. The Writings of Leo, Rufino and Angelo, Companions of St Francis*, OMT (Oxford 1970), pp. 150–1.

4 'De die intrant civitates et villas, ut aliquos lucrifaciant operam dantes actione; nocte vero revertuntur ad heremum vel loca solitaria vacantes contemplationi.' R. B. C. Huygens (ed.), *Lettres de Jacques de Vitry* (Leiden, 1960), pp. 75–6.

5 D. Flood, 'The Domestication of the Franciscan Movement', *Franziskanische Studien*, 60 (1978), 311–37, at 312.

6 *Eremitismo nel francescanesimo medievale*, Atti del XVII convegno della società internazionale di studi francescani, Assisi 1989 (Assisi 1991).

7 *Chronica XXIV Generalium Ordinis Minorum,* in *Analecta Franciscana* (Quaracchi, 1928), vol. III, pp. 37–8; also T. Desbonnets (ed.),
*Legenda Trium Sociorum:* (cf. n. 5) at pp. 117–18.

8 Jordan of Giano, nos. 45, 52.

9 3 Soc., 60.

10 2 Cel., 58. P. Sabatier (ed.), *Le Speculum Perfectionis ou Mémoires de
frère Léon,* British Society for Franciscan Studies, 13 (Manchester,
1928), p. 20.

11 Jordan of Giano, nos. 3, 21.

12 H. Golubovich, 'Series provinciarum ordinis fratrum minorum, saec.
XIII et XIV', *AFH,* I (1908), 1–22, at 2–5, 11; H. Lippens, 'Circa divisio-
nem Provinciae Rheni disquisitio (1246–1264)', *AFH,* 48 (1955), 217–24.

13 F. J. Cotter, *The Friars Minor in Ireland from Their Arrival to 1400,* ed.
R. A. McKelvie, Franciscan Institute Publications, History Series, 7
(St Bonaventure, 1994), p. 9.

14 Thomas of Eccleston, c. 2, 101–2, c. 4, 114–15; C. L. Kingsford, *The Grey
Friars of London* (Aberdeen, 1915), p. 145.

15 Jordan of Giano, nos. 43, 51.

16 J. Röhrkasten, *The Mendicant Houses of Medieval London 1221–1539,*
Vita Regularis, 21 (Münster, 2004), c.1.

17 R. Pieper, *Die Kirchen der Bettelorden in Westfalen: Baukunst im Span-
nungsfeld zwischen Landespolitik, Stadt und Orden im 13. und 14.
Jahrhundert;* Franziskanische Forschungen, 39 (Werl, 1993), pp. 67–8;
U. Schmidt, *Das ehemalige Franziskanerkloster in Nürnberg* (Nurem-
berg, 1913), p. 4; H. Konow, *Die Baukunst der Bettelorden am Oberrhein*
(Berlin, 1954), p. 9.

18 B. E. Bendixen, 'Das Franziskanerkloster zu Bergen in Norwegen', *Franziskanische Studien,* I (1914), 204–29, at 205, 209; Cotter, *The Friars
Minor in Ireland,* p. 20.

19 J. Röhrkasten, 'The Creation and Early History of the Franciscan Cus-
tody of Cambridge', in M. Robson and J. Röhrkasten (eds.), *Canterbury
Studies in Franciscan History* (Canterbury, 2008), vol. I, pp. 51–81;
F. M. Delorme, 'Les Cordeliers dans le Limousin aux XIIIᵉ–XVᵉ siècles',
*AFH,* 32 (1939), 201–59; 33 (1940), 114–60.

20 G. Leanti, 'L'ordine Francescano in Sicilia nei secoli XIII e XIV', *Miscellanea Francescana,* 37 (1937), 547–74, at 563–4.

21 J. Le Goff, 'Apostolat mendiant et fait urbain dans la France médiévale:
l'implantation des ordres mendiants', *Annales ESC,* 22 (1968), 335–52,
at 337.

22 J. Le Goff, 'Ordres mendiants et urbanisation dans la France médiévale',
*Annales ESC,* 25 (1970), 924–46.

23 *S. Bonaventurae Opera Omnia* (Quaracchi, 1898), vol. VIII, p. 341:
'Religiosi vero, qui in cellarum reclusoriis religantur, nisi aliquam
interius habeant aeris recreationem, cito languescentes tabescunt et
ad studia spiritualia inhabiles efficiuntur, ita quod nec sibi nec aliis
proficiunt in devotionis internae profectu, in sapientiae intellectu, in
virtutum exemplis et in doctrina salutis.'

# 12  The Third Order of Francis

INGRID PETERSON

The Third Order of St Francis developed from the lay penitential movement of the Middle Ages. As literacy spread and the religious needs
of the faithful shifted, the general population began to seek ways to
live the Gospel with greater intensity. These laity became known as
penitents, because they had undergone dramatic conversion experiences.
The way of penance was understood in the biblical sense as *metánoia*, a
reversal of values and behaviour. In his *Testament*, Francis describes
his life in terms of such a reversal: his earlier 'life in sin' among the
townspeople of Assisi and his later 'life of penance'. Penance was not
about asceticism or repentance within the sacramental system; instead, it
meant imitation of the way of the apostles, who shared their goods and
identified with the poor Christ by caring for those in need.

When Francis 'left the world', he abandoned his reliance on the
values subscribed to by society within the flourishing urban centres.
While about 90 per cent of the people lived at or below subsistence
level, the rising merchant class was beginning to challenge the domin-
ance of the landholders. This world of accumulated wealth, ownership,
power and prestige is the world Francis left. Instead, he sought an
alternative world in a social system rooted in the Gospel and its concern for each person, especially the poor and outcast. Francis's efforts
were reinforced by Assisi's Freedom Charter of 1210, which shifted
power from the nobility back to the common folk.

Because the concept of penance was so prevalent in the twelfth and
thirteenth centuries, it influenced how Francis, Clare and their followers shaped their lives. And because Francis described his new life as a
way of penance, his early followers became known as the Penitents
from Assisi. These followers were viewed as a brotherhood of penitents,
and St Clare was considered an abbess of penitents. Her life of penance
was marked by a radical separation from the values of her family in
order to develop a deeper relationship with God and to attend to the
needs of the unfortunate about her. Both Francis and Clare placed

a positive emphasis on the God who became human, suffered and died to bring others to the fullness of life. They understood penance as a way towards the riches of a life in God instead of in material wealth.

The lay penitential life was widespread by the time of Francis and Clare. In the eleventh century, it became a prevalent way of holiness for those outside traditional religious life. Jacques de Vitry's *vita* of Marie Oignies (1177–1213), written as early as 1215, provides an insight into the penitential way of life.[1] Marie lived in the region of the Low Countries stretching from Liège to Brabant and Flanders, where the Beguines first appeared sometime between 1170 and 1180. Married at 14, she lived with her husband in a leper colony, where they devoted themselves to care for the sick and destitute. Marie's spirituality centred on the humanity of Christ, love of poverty and charitable works. Initially formed for persons who were waiting to be received into the Church, their way of penance attracted others to conversion.

Lay penitents who lived in their own homes began to bond as communities and to meet social needs. Peter Waldo (1140–1218), a wealthy merchant from Lyons who chose to live as a poor beggar, was one of those early penitents who gathered followers. Robert Stewart describes how Waldo's conversion stemmed from the story of St Alexis, a wealthy man who chose to live as a poor beggar.[2]

Waldo sold his possessions, made provision for his wife and children, and gave the remainder of his resources to the poor. Upon making a vow to model his life upon that of the early apostles, he began to gather followers. They renounced their possessions, lived on alms, preached a message of conversion, and urged others to adopt voluntary poverty and to follow the poor Christ. Lester Little suggests, however, that their example and good works as laity threatened the clergy, even seeming to imply that priests were not essential to Christian society.[3]

Inevitably a conflict with the clergy arose, causing Waldo and his followers to seek approval for their way of life in 1179. Commonly known as Waldensians after their leader, they received a blessing and papal approval for their form of voluntary poverty but were restricted to preaching only with the permission of the local bishop. In their time, they were known as the Poor of Lyons, the Poor of Lombardy or the Poor of God. The Waldensians evolved into two distinct groups: the *perfecti*, who were ordained and took evangelical vows, and the *credentes*, who lived in their own homes, practised a life of penance and supported the preaching group with alms.

The Humiliati, meanwhile, lived in lay communities and, in contrast to the Waldensians, wandered to preach in an itinerant lifestyle.

From Lombardy, the Humiliati constituted another group of laymen. They were popular with artisans who wished to live the Gospel while continuing to practise their professions and trades. A chronicler of the time described the Humiliati as 'citizens who, though living at home with their families, had chosen for themselves a certain form of religious life: they abstained from lying or taking lawsuits, pledging to do battle for the Christian faith'.[4] Although they were: Initially condemned, Innocent III reversed their censure, added a juridical structure and approved their movement.

Following their papal endorsement, the Humiliati were divided into three orders: two for clerics and laymen leading a monastic form of life in community, and a third for those who lived in the world under a programme of life called a *propositum*. The term 'tertiary' was used for the third form of Humiliati. It has continued to be used throughout the centuries for those who belong to a third order. The group of married Humiliati lived a simple life in their own homes but were not required to dispose of their possessions. The preaching group of Humiliati were sanctioned by the pope to preach on morals but not on church doctrine, the explanation of which was reserved for the clergy. The Humiliati became known for supporting their local communities and aiding the poor.

Omobono of Cremona was a merchant with the Humiliati distinguished by his piety, dedication to the poor and ardent struggle against heresy. He was a prosperous tailor and merchant who established a wide reputation for his honesty. His name is derived from the Latin *homo bonus*, 'the good man'. He believed that God had allowed him to work in order for him to support those living in poverty. Shortly after Omobono's death in 1197 he was canonised by Innocent III, who described him as 'a father of the poor', 'consoler of the afflicted' and 'a man good in name and deed'. It was after his canonisation in 1201 that the pope endorsed the Humiliati by giving the tertiaries a *propositum*. Vauchez points to the importance of this document as the Church's first official recognition of a religious institution within the penitential movement.[5] Penitents set out to gain salvation as persons faithful to the requirements of the laity, dedicating themselves to their own families and work while aiding the indigent.

The ideals of the apostolic movement and voluntary poverty were closely intermingled with the heretical movements of the twelfth century.[6] Herbert Grundmann contends that all the religious movements of the medieval Church were eventually confronted with two options.[7] They either adopted the hierarchy's fixed forms as an established order or separated themselves from the ecclesiastical *Rules* and broke with the Church to become a sect, that is, they became heretical. The early heretics of Cologne and southern France claimed they represented the true Church of the poor Christ, for they held all their goods in common, in contrast to the Catholic clergy, who piled up wealth and private property. That they rejected both the hierarchy and the sacramental system brought them into constant conflict with the Church.

The Cathars were one such heretical movement, believing in a dualistic universe in which the God of the New Testament who ruled over the spiritual realm was in conflict with Satan, the evil God who ruled over matter. Similar systems of belief arose in various geographical locations in different forms, and with names such as the Albigensians and Bogomils. The persecution of the Inquisition and the efforts of Innocent III and his successors had halted the spread of the Cathars by the fifteenth century. In the midst of such rampant heretical movements a few itinerant preachers, such as Robert of Arbrissel in France, became licensed to preach. In time, Arbrissel, Bernard of Thiron, Vitalis of Savigny and Norbert of Zanten all founded ecclesiastical orders.[8] M.-D. Chenu claims that the lay groups who were not tightly bound by the institutional frameworks of the Church were, paradoxically, in a better position than the monastics to initiate an authentic return to the Gospel life.[9]

## FRANCIS'S 1209 AND 1220 EXHORTATIONS TO THE PENITENTS

Francis identified himself as a lay penitent whose conversion led him from a life centred on worldly desires to a radical change focused on the Gospel. God's imperceptible action within his soul brought him to practise penance, charity, humility, service, prayer, fasting, abstinence and restitution. In granting Francis oral approval for his way of life in 1209 Innocent III recognised the blessings of his way of penance. Francis acknowledged all 'those who do penance' and established a bond with them in 1209 and again in 1220 by composing two documents known as the *Earlier* and *Later Exhortations*. He bestowed a blessing on those who persevere in penance, mentioning both men and women.

The early document describing the way of life that Francis prescribed for the lay penitents, popularly known as the *Letter to the Faithful*, and dated between 1209 and 1215, appears in the latest edition of the primary sources, entitled the *Earlier Exhortation to the*

*Brothers and Sisters of Penance.*[10] Kajetan Esser conferred the title of *The First Version of the Letter to the Faithful* on the Volterra text. When a new English translation was published in *Francis of Assisi: Early Documents* in 1999, it was entitled the *Earlier Exhortation*, with the explanation that it is 'more correctly seen as an exhortation to those first penitents who came to Francis to share his gospel way of life'.

This simple form of life is the foundational document of the Third Order, for it describes a way of 'doing penance' in the lay life. The *Earlier Exhortation* insists that a life of penance begins with the action of God in the soul. It describes new deeds, a new way of 'doing'. A life of penance begins with an interior change of attitude that is expressed by producing 'worthy fruits of penance'. Francis explains that those who do penance love God and neighbour, resist the tendencies of their fallen nature, partake of the Body of Christ, and act and live in conformity with their conversion. The penitential life does not begin with adopting norms or practices of penance. It begins with a movement of the heart that leads to action.

The *Later Exhortation* reiterates the essence and vision of Franciscan life. Stewart provides a scholarly discussion of the name and date, along with a historical-critical analysis and comparison of the *Earlier Exhortation to the Brothers and Sisters of Penance* and the *Later Admonition and Exhortation to the Brothers and Sisters of Penance*. The Latin text and an English translation of Francis's *Exhortation to the Faithful* are found in a *History of the Third Order Rule: A Source Book.*[11] Francis begins by reviewing the elements that characterise the penitential movement: charity, humility, service, prayer, fasting, abstinence and restitution of goods acquired unjustly. He urges his followers to be mindful of certain obligations to avoid falling into heresy, once again emphasising actions that embody penance. David Flood explains that 'Franciscanism is not a set of ascetical disciplines. It is a way of dealing with the universe. One does not bend oneself to law and rule; one catches on to the rhythm of things . . . One goes through the steps in order to dance; and soon one is dancing and forgets the steps . . . Francis emphasises doing.'[12] Francis builds his understanding of penance on the conviction that people change by doing. The *Later Exhortation* concludes by describing the blessings of the way of penance as a new sensibility. This text is dated around 1220 and given the full title *Later Admonition and Exhortation to the Brothers and Sisters of Penance (Second Version of the Letter to the Faithful)* in *Francis of Assisi: Early Documents.*[13]

Thomas of Celano in his *First Life of St Francis* portrays the eagerness of the people of Francis's time to embrace the movement he inspired:

> Men ran, women also ran, clerics hurried and religious rushed to hear the holy one of God, who seemed to everyone a person from another age. People of all ages and both sexes hurried to behold the wonders which the Lord worked anew in the world through his servant ... Many people, well-born and lowly, cleric and lay, driven by divine inspiration, began to come to St Francis, for they desired to serve under his constant training and leadership. . . To all, he gave a norm of life and to those of every rank he sincerely pointed out the way of salvation.
>
> (1 Cel., nos. 36–7)

Certain persons stand out who caught on to the message of Francis. The mutual fondness between Francis and the noblewoman Lady Jacopa dei Settesoli is memorialised by her burial in the lower basilica di San Francesco in Assisi. According to *The Treatise on the Miracles of Thomas Celano*, Pressede was another woman distinguished by her piety. Francis 'received her to obedience, and with pious devotion gave her the habit of Religion, that is, the tunic and the cord' (3 Cel., no. 181). According to tradition, Luchesio, a merchant from Poggibonsi, and his wife Buonadonna (d. 1260) were the first married couple to be blessed by Francis as penitents. They converted from a prosperous life and began to care for the poor in their region.[14]

It is difficult to identify the early adherents of the Third Order, or tertiaries, because the boundaries were extraordinarily porous. The early followers of Francis's way of penance did not join an organisation as members, or take vows; they simply lived according to Francis's exhortation to 'do penance'. A diversity of persons, married and single, kings and queens, wealthy and poor, hermits and those actively involved in society, all followed the way of Francis through the Third Order. Married into the court of Thuringia, Elizabeth of Hungary (1207–31) tapped into the royal coffers to alleviate the misery of her people. Her acts of charity, intense spiritual life and widespread popularity led to her canonisation three years after her death. Elizabeth has been named the patron of the Third Order.

Other unmarried laywomen took up the penitential life in a variety of forms that included penance, prayer and service. Douceline of Digne (1214–74), sister of the friar Hugh of Digne, formed a beginage at Hyères which also was promoted by Jacques de Vitry. Veridiana of Castel

Fiorento (1182–1242) lived in a cell as an anchoress attached to the chapel of St Anthony in Florence. Umiliana of Cerchi (1219–46), whose extraordinary generosity was not understood by her husband, engaged her sister-in-law to assist in sharing their wealth with the poor of Florence in accord with the precepts of Francis. Although in her teens, Rose of Viterbo (1233–51) preached in the streets against the emperor, causing Rose and her family to be exiled from the city. Angela of Foligno (1248–1309) left an extensive record of her mystical experiences of God which reflect the influence of the Spiritual Franciscans.[15] The lives of these women were marked by extreme asceticism and miracles, essential attributes in order for women of the time to be canonised.[16]

As for high-born men affected by Francis's message, St Louis IX (c.1214–70), crowned king of France at the age of 12, was educated by Francis's brothers and became a penitent known for promoting learning, founding hospitals and churches, and responding to the needs of the poor in his provinces. He exemplified peace and justice as a civil administrator and was called upon by other leaders to negotiate peace. Louis was canonised in 1297 by Pope Nicholas IV. The nobleman Ivo of Britanny (1253–1303) became known as an advocate for the poor. He studied theology, and canon and civil law, and was ordained priest for the diocese of Tréquier in France. As a judge in the ecclesiastical courts, he affiliated with the Franciscan lay penitents and established a reputation for helping the poor, widowed and orphans to receive a fair hearing. Ivo was canonised in 1347.

## CARDINAL HUGOLINO'S 1221 MEMORIALE PROPOSITI AND POPE NICHOLAS IV'S 1289 SUPRA MONTEM

The rise of the mendicant orders caused the penitential movement to spread after 1220. Both Francis and Dominic called lay communities to penitence. This spread of the penitential movement led Cardinal Hugolino to organise fraternities in Italy through his *Memoriale propositi* (1221), a document describing their status and obligations. Cardinal Hugolino was a papal legate of Honorius III and an imperial representative of the emperor, Frederick II. Following the decrees of the fourth Lateran Council in 1215, Hugolino (as Gregory IX) attempted to regulate the penitential movement by bringing it into the official church, as Honorius III had earlier done with the *propositum* of the Humiliati. Rather than use Francis's biblical language of the *Exhortation*, the *Memoriale propositi* employs juridical language to describe penance.

In studying the differences between the texts of Francis and Gregory and the similarity of the *Memoriale propositi* to the documents given to other penitential groups, Esser concluded there was nothing particularly Franciscan about it.[17] However, Pazzelli held that while their styles differ, they both have the same spirit.[18] Whatever its nuances, the *Memoriale propositi* proposed a way of life similar to that approved by the Church for other groups of medieval penitents. It prescribed that penitents wear robes made of poor, undyed fabric, which indicated their entrance into the penitential life. They were instructed to fast more frequently than the faithful and, if literate, to recite the seven canonical hours daily. If they were unable to read, they could substitute a defined number of Our Fathers and Glory Bes. They were required to go to confession and receive communion three times a year. They were forbidden to take solemn oaths or bear arms, a practice which soon brought them into conflict with the public authorities, especially in the Italian communes.

Because Francis did not provide a canonical *Rule* text for the Third Order, the *Rules* used by both the secular and regular branches have been subject to periodic updating. While the existence of the Third Order is anchored in Francis's *Exhortation* of nearly a century earlier, its canonical foundation begins in 1289 with the *Rule* of Nicholas IV. The first Franciscan pope, Nicholas IV, began to receive requests from local groups of penitents for official approval of their *Rule*. In response, he issued the bull *Supra montem* in 1289. It refers to Francis as *institutor*, and it distinguishes his way of life as an order. Nicholas IV's *Rule* is important because it gave papal approval to the Third Order, although it created uncertainty about which branch of the order it was intended to direct, the married, lay men and women who lived in their homes or those who took vows and lived in community.

Stewart demonstrates how the *Rule* of 1289 follows the *Memoriale propositi* but rearranges the content to follow the general order of other religious *Rules*. One difference is that the *Rule* of 1289 declares that the visitor to the houses of penitents be selected from the Friars Minor. This prescription was disputed, because it seemed to place the Franciscan penitents under the jurisdiction of the friars and to add a clerical order as another layer of authority. Edith Pásztor argues that the *Rule* of 1289 made the Franciscan penitents distinctive in calling them to 'be Catholics', declaring them orthodox and giving them an important place in the Church as opponents of heresy. In mitigating the prohibition against arms in the *Memoriale propositi*, the penitents were drawn into the political struggles of the Church during the Crusades.

Stewart concludes that the *Rule* of 1289 construes Francis's charism of penance as a service of orthodoxy. After the introduction of the Third Order *Rule* of Nicholas IV, tertiaries continued their good works within the juridical framework of the Church. Blessed Ramon Llull (1235–1315), a married tertiary, worked among the Islamic people of North Africa.

The Blessed Delphine of Pumicel (*c.*1283–*c.*1360) and St Elzéar of Sabran (1285–1325) are the only Franciscan couple recognised in the Church's canon of the beatified and canonised. They were nobles from Provence. King Charles II betrothed Delphine, a 12-year-old orphan who had made a private vow of chastity, to Elzéar when he was 10. They entered into a 'spiritual marriage' in which conjugal relations were renounced with the consent of both parties. Such a medieval practice was often linked to the Franciscan practice of penance. Upon the death of his father, Elzéar, at the age of 23 began to manage his estates in the kingdom of Naples. Elzéar and Delphine raised the moral level of the court and insisted that their household attend daily Mass, go to weekly confession, avoid gambling, keep the peace and seek forgiveness from one another. They maintained lifelong connections with the Franciscan friars and, according to tradition, were received into the Third Order in Naples while serving in the court of Queen Sancha and King Robert. Elzéar was canonised in 1369 by his uncle, Pope Urban V (1362–70). The ideal of a virginal marriage had fallen out of favour with the Church by 1664 when Delphine was beatified, so she was never canonised.

During the fourteenth century the papacy continued to steer the laity away from the widely popular penitential movement and into the service of the Church. The confraternities of penitents became absorbed by the Third Order, which began to recruit women members. The first official document institutionalising the communal form of life of the women of the Third Order was given in 1324 to Angelina Montegiove by John XXII.[19] After the women of the Third Order became regularised, they often became semi-cloistered. Vauchez holds that, as a consequence, the originality of the medieval lay movement was essentially lost until the reforms adopted in the sixteenth and seventeenth centuries. The interim period is fraught with tensions between laity and clergy, the male hierarchy and groups of female religious. In 1428, Martin V created additional internal dissent through *Licet inter coetera*, a bull placing all tertiaries under the direction of the minister general of the Friars Minor. His successor, Eugene IV, revoked his controversial disposition.

In the fifteenth century tertiary communities of men and women began to unite by forming federations, congregations or chapters. In 1439, the Belgian Congregation of Zepperan and the Dutch Chapter of Utrecht joined seventy groups of men and women with religious vows who elected their own minister general.[20] In 1447, Nicholas V's similar effort made to unify the Italian men's communities failed. Although his intention had been to centralise the brotherhoods, the move was perceived as a threat to their autonomy. At the same time, the Great Schism resulted in further disunity.[21] The 1521 *Rule* of Leo X unified the male and female communities under vows by introducing one *Rule* for both the 'brothers and sisters'. It also established new titles for the heads of their houses: 'minister' for the men's communities and 'mother' for the women's. When many Franciscan women's congregations revised their constitutions following the second Vatican Council, they adopted the term 'minister' for their elected leaders.

### 'RULES' FOR THE THIRD ORDER SECULAR

In time, updated versions of their *Rules* were given to both branches of the Third Order. Each of these *Rules* was an adaptation to accommodate their times. Thus it is that the remaining history of the Third Order is traced through division and revision. Secular Franciscans may be married or single, in contrast to the men and women of the Third Order Regular, who are celibate. According to canon 303 in the Code of Canon Law, Secular Orders are 'Associations whose members share in the spirit of some religious institute while in secular life, lead an apostolic life, and strive for Christian perfection'. Like all orders, they follow an approved *Rule* and, after a period of novitiate, make a formal profession and experience communal life through regular monthly meetings. Secular Franciscans are organised into fraternities at local, regional, national and international levels. They are governed by the *Rule*, the constitutions, the ritual and statutes, and meet regularly. Secular Franciscans include Anglican, Lutheran and Roman Catholic provinces around the world. It is estimated that today there are more than 1.5 million secular Franciscans.

In 1883, Leo XIII issued *Misericors Dei filius*, a *Rule* specifically for the members of the Franciscan secular Third Order who did not live under evangelical vows in a religious community. A member of the Third Order Secular, Leo XIII attempted to broaden the requirements for their membership by writing this revised *Rule* for them. It simply required that its members wear a small, concealed scapular, observe the commandments, avoid extremes of extravagance and style, be temperate in food and dress, fast two days a year, and the recitation of the Our Father, Hail Mary and Glory Be to the Father twelve times. His *Rule* re-emphasised the Third Order's original roots in the penitential movement by encouraging members to deepen their faith and engage in social action. Leo XIII's revision of 1883 succeeded in drawing many to a deeper faith. It is estimated that 2.5 million tertiaries were active by the early twentieth century. However, in reducing the number of prescriptions and some difficult demands, the *Rule* of 1883 changed the nature of the order. Leo XIII suggested a different identity for the secular branch of the Third Order from that which it had in the thirteenth century.

Following the second Vatican Council, the *Rules* for the Third Order Secular and the Third Order Regular were updated and rewritten by members of their orders. Both new *Rules* received papal approval soon after completion and are are prefaced with Francis's *Earlier Exhortation* to anchor the orders to their inspiration in Francis. The Third Order continues to consist of two expressions. Paul VI approved the *Rule* of the Secular Franciscan Order in 1978. It follows the guidelines of the International Obediential Congress of the Secular Franciscan Order (SFO) held in Assisi in 1969. At that time the title of the Secular Franciscan Order was adopted as the title of the secular branch of the Third Order.

The *Rule* was revised to encourage Secular Franciscans to respond to the need for social action. It expresses the mission of the lay vocation through single or family life, work to provide a daily livelihood and the practice of the beatitudes following the beneficence of Francis. The spirit of the 1978 *Rule* is expressed in Article 4: 'The Rule and life of the Secular Franciscan is this: To observe the Gospel of our Lord Jesus Christ by following the example of St Francis of Assisi, who made Christ the inspiration and centre of his life with God and people.' The *Rule* requires its members to dedicate themselves to careful reading of the Gospel, going from the Gospel to life and life to the Gospel.

'RULES' FOR THE THIRD ORDER REGULAR

Both dimensions of the Third Order value prayer, simplicity, concern for the poor, care for creation and peacemaking. They both exemplify what it means to 'do penance' for the sake of the Gospel. Members of the Third Order Regular hold their material goods in common to share with those in need, while Secular Franciscans retain the ownership of their goods. Each separate congregation of brothers and sisters has a central administration governing its separate houses. Both orders are about more than apostolic work. Following the example of St Francis, patron saint of ecology, they have collaborated in recent years with political agencies opposing exploitation of the environment in ways that place hardships on the poor. Many members are in the forefront of public life. They work to promote a civilisation that respects the dignity of the human person, the universal call to holiness and the theology of the lay vocation. They promote a climate of fraternity among all peoples and religious for the common good. In short, the Third Order Regular is about every aspect of Gospel life.

Leo X issued the bull *Inter coetera* specifically for the vowed members. At the beginning of the sixteenth century the Roman curia attempted to provide greater uniformity within the Franciscan movements of Third Order men and women. Because the 1289 *Rule* of Nicholas IV did not mention community life or the evangelical vows, the Third Order groups of men and women had become predominantly lay. The reform of the fifth Lateran Council (1512–17) prompted the 1521 *Rule* of Leo X addressed to 'The Brothers and Sisters of the Third Order of Blessed Francis, living in congregations under the three essential vows'. It emphasised penance as the fundamental characteristic of the Third Order. Whereas the *Rule* of Nicholas IV had guided all the dimensions of the Third Order, Leo separated the order into two distinct branches, one for the Third Order Secular (TOS) and another for the Third Order Regular (TOR). However, Leo's *Rule* did not take into account the Third Order groups that received pontifical recognition in the fifteenth century. Since Leo X's *Rule* implied the Friars Minor had jurisdiction over the Third Order, the ambiguity of whether the papacy or friars had jurisdiction remained troublesome.

The new 1917 Code of Canon Law required religious orders and congregations to adapt to its legislation. Leo's *Rule* was contrary to some points of the new code which were unsuitable for congregations that originated in dioceses that had approved their constitutions. Unlike Leo X's *Rule*, the 1927 *Rule* was written for both male and female religious. It was edited by the generals of the four Franciscan orders.[22] In 1927, Pius XI issued *Rerum condicio* for the brothers and sisters of the Third Order Regular which was promulgated at the time of the 700th anniversary of St Francis's death. The introduction proclaims it 'a new *Rule*, more thoroughly pervaded with the Franciscan spirit and in harmony with the modern Law of the church'. Chapter 1 draws from the *Rule* of the Friars Minor to describe its purpose. It frequently refers to the penitential life and the following of Francis, and concludes with the blessing of Francis. However, in a later commentary, Esser noted that many congregations were already stabilised and made little effort to conform to the spirit of the new *Rule*.

A twentieth-century effort to renew the Third Order Regular on its foundation in the penitential movement began with a study project by twenty-five Franciscan congregations in France and Belgium that had become dissatisfied with the way the tenets of Franciscan spirituality had been presented by Pius XI. Alternative versions were later proposed by Dutch and German sisters. This work preceded the Fourth Interobediential Congress of the Third Order Regular held in 1974 in Madrid. The congress was called following the close of the second Vatican Council to promote communication between the Third Order congregations of men and women. The Madrid congress revolved around the recovery of the Third Order identity as a penitential movement. The discussions on the purpose of the order, prayer life, the practice of poverty, obedience, consecrated celibacy and peace were described in 'A Statement of Understanding of Franciscan Penitential Life'.[23] This work led to the revision of the *Rule and Life of the Brothers and Sisters of the Third Order Regular*. Pope John Paul II (1978–2005) approved the new *Rule, Franciscanum vitae propositum*, on 8 December 1982, which required its members to live in community, to profess the evangelical vows and to dedicate themselves to the service of others.

After the completion of the recently revised *Rules* for the secular and regular branches of the Third Order, separate histories were prepared to trace their development. Robert Stewart's history of the Third Order Secular, *'De illis qui faciunt Penitentiam', The Rule of the Secular Franciscan Order: Origins, Development, Interpretation*, was published in 1991. A further study, edited by Carney, Godet-Calogeras and Kush, *The History of the Third Order Rule: A Source Book*, was published in 2008. Both of these recent studies are valuable because they provide English translations and commentaries on the historical Franciscan and ecclesiastical documents that have shaped their orders. Marie-Benoît Lucbernet's contemporary commentary on the Third Order *Rule* in *The History of the Third Order Rule* describes it as a spiritual text that inspires conversion, a reference text that facilitates unity and a prophetic text.[24]

In 1985, an International Franciscan Conference (CFI) was established as a permanent group to bring the male and female groups to a shared understanding of what it means to belong to the Third Order Regular. Their statutes describe their goals as being to foster communication and solidarity among member groups and to collaborate with the First and Second Orders and the SFO. Throughout its diverse history, the constitutive elements of Francis's vision for the Brothers and Sisters of Penance endure: poverty, minority, penance–conversion and prayer–contemplation. However, penance remains the primary characteristic of the Third Order. Despite its diverse forms of secular and communal life, the Third Order remains true to the spiritual ideals of Francis.

### Notes

1   Jacques de Vitry, *The Life of Marie of Oignies*, trans. M. H. King, Peregrina Translation Series, 3 (Toronto, 1989).
2   R. M. Stewart, *'De illis qui faciunt Penitentiam'*, *The Rule of the Secular Franciscan Order: Origins, Development, Interpretation* Bibliotheca Seraphico-Capuccina cura instituti historici ord. Fr. Min. Capuccinorum, 39 (Rome, 1991), pp. 113–15.
3   L. K. Little, *Religious Poverty and a Market Economy* (Ithaca, 1978), p. 127.
4   A. Vauchez, *The Laity in the Middle Ages: Religious Beliefs and Devotional Practices*, ed. D. Bornstein, trans. from the French, *Les Laïcs au Moyen Âge: pratiques et expériences religieuses*, by M. J. Schneider (Notre Dame, 1993), p. 120.
5   Ibid., pp. 120–1.
6   H. Grundmann, *Religious Movements in the Middle Ages*: *The Historical Links between Heresy, the Mendicant Orders, and the Women's Religious Movement in the Twelfth and Thirteenth Century, and the Historical Foundation of German Mysticism* (London, 1995), p. 9.
7   Ibid., p. 1.
8   Ibid., p. 19.
9   M.-D. Chenu, *Nature, Man and Society in the Twelfth Century: Essays on the New Theological Perspectives in the Latin West*, trans. J. Taylor and L. Little (Chicago, 1968), p. 219.
10  See *FAED*, vol. 1, pp. 41–4.
11  Stewart, *'De illis'*, pp. 135–83; M. Carney, J. F. Godet-Calogeras and S. Kush (eds.), *History of the Third Order Rule: A Source Book*. (St Bonaventure, 2008), pp. 42–51.
12  D. Flood, *The Commonitorium*, 3 (1980) 20, n. 2, in Stewart, *'De illis'*, p. 180, n. 127.
13  *FAED*, vol. 1, pp. 45–51.
14  See I. Peterson, 'Thirteenth-Century Penitential Women: Franciscan Life in the Secular World', *Studies in Spirituality*, 12 (2002), 43–60.
15  *Angela of Foligno, Complete Works*, trans. and intro. P. Lachance, pref. Romana Guarnieri, Classics of Western Spirituality (New York, 1993).
16  D. Weinstein and R. M. Bell, *Saints and Society: The Two Worlds of Western Christendom, 1000–1700* (Chicago, 1982), pp. 34–6.
17  K. Esser, 'Un documento dell'inizio' del duecento sui penitenti', in M. D'Alatri (ed.), *I Frati penitenti di san Francesco nella società del due e trecento* (Rome, 1977). in Stewart, *Rule of the Secular Franciscan Order*, p. 199.

18 R. Pazzelli, *St Francis and the Third Order: St Francis and the Pre-Franciscan Penitential Movement* (Quincy, 1989), pp. 113–14.

19 See R. A. McKelvie, *Retrieving a Living Tradition: Angelina of Montegiove, Franciscan, Tertiary, Beguine.* (St Bonaventure, 1997).

20 W. J. Short, 'Brothers and Sisters of Penance', in Short, *The Franciscans* (Wilmington, Del., 1989), p. 90.

21 L. I. Aspurz, *Franciscan History: The Three Orders of St Francis of Assisi*, trans. Patricia Ross (Chicago, 1982), p. 514.

22 The four Franciscan orders are known today as the order of Friars Minor, the order of St Clare, the Third Order Regular of St Francis and the Secular Franciscan Order (formerly known as the Third Order Secular).

23 'A Statement of Understanding of Franciscan Penitential Life, Inter-Obediential Congress, Madrid, 1974', in Carney et al. (eds.), *History of the Third Order Rule*, pp. 196–200.

24 M.-B. Lucbernet, '"Rule and Life" of 1982: A Turning Point in our History', in Carney et al. (eds.), *History of the Third Order Rule*, p. 502.

## 13 Franciscan ideals and the royal family of France (1226–1328)

SEAN L. FIELD

In 2004, the French publishing house Gallimard published *Héros du Moyen Âge: le saint et le roi*, a 1,318-page tome combining two recent works by Jacques Le Goff, one about Francis of Assisi and the other Louis IX of France. The subtitle is slightly misleading, since both 'heroes' were in fact recognised as saints after Louis's canonisation in 1297. Nevertheless, it is no surprise that Le Goff would find these two men intriguing, or that Gallimard would pair them, for they were two of the thirteenth century's emblematic figures, linked by the influence that Franciscan ideals had on Louis, his family and his Capetian descendants.

This influence is undeniable but difficult to pin down, for several reasons. First, there is the problem of defining 'Franciscan ideals'. Francis's admirers and modern scholars have long argued over who he 'really was' and how his message should best be interpreted. Thus, we cannot simply ask whether the French royal court followed one predetermined model arbitrarily defined as Franciscan. Secondly, there is the problem of disentangling Franciscan piety from other related strands. The French court fostered close ties to many different orders and branches of the Church. It would therefore be disingenuous to ascribe every Capetian impulse towards piety, simplicity or humility to Franciscan influence. Searching for Franciscan influence requires close attention to actual interaction between royal figures and leading Franciscans and to structural links built up between court and order.

Yet there is no shortage of evidence to sift through. By the end of the Capetian era, the French royal family had founded and supported numerous Franciscan houses, royal women generally employed Franciscans as confessors and indeed St Louis himself was increasingly remembered in strongly Franciscan terms. Louis and his generation of French royalty absorbed Francis's model of apostolic piety, developed crucial relationships with leading Franciscans in Paris and at times made decisions based on the influence of Franciscan advisors. By the end of the Capetian period, the French court's distinctive brand of piety was in part an adaptation of Franciscan ideals. In particular, it was women who become most closely tied to Franciscans, who patronised the order's communities and who were often most emphatic in tying Franciscan models to Capetian sanctity. Other European courts, notably in eastern and central Europe, developed a similar link between female spirituality and Franciscan influence.[1] But Paris was a crucial meeting-point for royal ideology and *minoritas* ('lesserness', or simply humility), creating a distinctive mix that was then broadcast through space and time.

## LOUIS IX: EARLY CONTACTS AND THE CRUSADE

The earliest contacts between Franciscans and the royal court must have occurred in the 1220s, although their exact nature is somewhat obscure. For instance, claims that Queen Blanche of Castile (1188–1252) entrusted Louis IX's childhood education to friars are unsubstantiated by any contemporary evidence.[2] But Blanche and Louis IX would seem to have been aware of Francis by the time of the latter's death, since Thomas of Celano depicts the 'king and queen and all the magnates of France' at that time rushing to venerate the simple pillow that Francis had used in his (presumably last) illness (1 Cel., 120). Moreover, it is likely that the royal court supported the first ministers provincial of France and may also have enjoyed early contacts with the first Franciscan masters of theology at the University of Paris, Alexander of Hales and Jean de la Rochelle. Julian of Speyer, the author of a life of and office for St Francis, is said (at least in a late fourteenth-century source) to have been a master of song at the French court before his conversion to the order around 1227.[3]

If the earliest evidence is sketchy, the royal court had certainly developed deep-rooted ties to the order by the time Louis IX departed for his Crusade in 1248. By the early part of that decade Louis had entrusted Franciscans with a role in voyaging to Constantinople to purchase relics of the passion,[4] and in 1247–8 Franciscans were among the main agents he employed as his *enquêteurs* – royal agents empowered to address complaints about the previous conduct of royal officials.[5] Moreover, Louis probably worked with Innocent IV to get the Franciscan Eudes Rigaud appointed archbishop of Rouen in March 1248.[6] Since Eudes had succeeded to the chair of theology at Paris in 1245, Louis would surely have known him at least by reputation. At about the same time, Louis instituted three solemn feast days in honour of the relics of the passion which he had installed in the newly built Sainte-Chapelle (consecrated in April 1248, with Eudes Rigaud among the prelates in attendance). He assigned liturgical oversight for one of the three to the Franciscans of Paris, and since the brother who had celebrated Mass would afterwards eat with the king, evidently Louis was in the habit of taking meals with friars by this time.[7]

These bits of anecdotal evidence suggest that by 1248 Louis trusted Franciscans to act as quasi-governmental agents, helped to promote them to high ecclesiastical office and associated them with his most cherished projects. These early personal connections bore institutional fruit. Louis chose Friars Minor and Preacher as his main *enquêteurs*, for example, not merely because he respected them personally, but because their rejection of money and disdain for worldly advancement made them the perfect instruments for his own attempts at instilling justice and promoting reform.[8]

Not surprisingly, then, Louis's departure for his Crusade in the summer of 1248 provides the first really dramatic example of the royal family's personal attitudes towards the Friars Minor (*fratres minores*). After departing from Paris in June, Louis paused at Sens, where the Franciscans were holding their provincial chapter. According to Salimbene, who was present, Louis and his younger brothers Alfonse, Robert and Charles approached on foot dressed in simple pilgrims' garb, and the Franciscans, led by Eudes Rigaud himself, rushed out to meet them. The king then asked for prayers for the royal family, and later the king and his brothers dined with Eudes while John of Parma, minister general, and Geoffrey of Brie, minister provincial, and all the custodians, definitors and delegates ate at separate tables in the refectory. The royal siblings paid particular honour to John of Parma in apparent deference to his reputation for holiness. Nor was this the end of Louis's contacts with Franciscans on his outward journey to the Holy Land. Salimbene recorded Louis's frequent visits to Friars Minor (as well as other religious) as he moved south, particularly at Vézelay, where Louis humbly sat on the ground in the dust and formed a circle of his own brothers and Franciscans around him and again asked for prayers.[9] Although Salimbene's interest in highlighting Franciscan matters inevitably colours our perception, nevertheless it appears that Louis consciously sought to project an aura of Franciscan humility around his pilgrim's persona and associated himself with Franciscan prayers as he prepared for his attack on Egypt. Indeed, Francis's mission to al-Malik-al-Kâmil in 1219 may well have formed part of Louis's frame of reference for his new campaign in the same region.

Unfortunately, Louis's Crusade was a disaster in practical terms. After taking Damietta, the crusaders were soundly defeated and Louis himself captured. By the time of his return to France in 1254, Louis was a changed man. He took the Crusade's failure to heart, blaming the defeat on his own sins. He undertook a series of governmental reforms (including the appointment of new *enquêteurs*, about half of whom were mendicants), and the penitential streak in his piety became more pronounced.[10] If any single episode helped shape the more intense personal religiosity of the last phase of his life, it may well have been his encounter with the Franciscan Hugh of Digne, known as a holy man. Upon his return in July, Louis landed at Hyères and sent for Hugh, who arrived with a crowd of men and women following him. Hugh's sermon warned Louis that there were too many religious gathered at his court and enjoying the good life, and he admonished him to listen to the wishes of his people and beware, lest God deprive him of his life and kingdom if he did not do justice. Louis was moved enough to ask Hugh several times to stay with him, but Hugh took his own advice and departed.[11]

These two encounters with Franciscans at pivotal moments on his voyages to and from the Holy Land framed Louis's Crusade, helping to shape its meaning in his mind and steering him towards a model of personal simplicity and stern renunciation. In this light it is not surprising that the ties between the royal court and Franciscan advisors grew ever stronger after 1254. One gets the impression that Louis would have been greeted as a friend as well as a sovereign at the *grand couvent* – as well he might, since he had helped the brothers secure this Left-Bank residence as early as 1230 and provided crucial funds for further building in the 1250s.

## TEACHERS AND PREACHERS

Among those residing in this house were the order's most illustrious masters of theology. The string of men who occupied the Franciscan chair of theology in the two decades after 1245 includes Eudes Rigaud, William of Meliton, Bonaventure, Gilbert of Tournai, Eudes of Rosny, William of Harcombourg and Eustache of Arras. All of them are known to have offered advice, consultation or preaching to the royal family. The most immediate interpreters of Franciscan ideals for the Capetian court were thus the intellectual and theological leaders of the order at Paris.

Eudes Rigaud in particular may have been 'the closest personal companion Louis ever had'.[12] He preached in front of the king, enjoyed his hospitality at royal residences, celebrated the weddings of at least two of Louis's children, and attended royal funerals and baptisms. Most tellingly, Louis called Eudes to his side when ill and dealing with the loss of his eldest son, Louis. In more practical matters, Eudes helped negotiate the landmark treaty with England in 1259, sat in the Parlement of Paris and preached Louis's second Crusade. He took the cross himself in 1267 and departed with Louis in summer 1270.[13] Eudes was probably present at Louis's death in Tunis that August and was one of the executors of his will. Indeed, in the ensuing confusion of the mass illness that swept through the royal entourage, Philip III named Eudes principal counsellor to his brother should the latter have to assume the regency.[14] For Louis, Eudes must have embodied Franciscanism, as a dedicated churchman who worked tirelessly, provided comfort and counsel, and supported the king in his most cherished endeavours. This was no abstract ideal but a flesh-and-blood example of the legacy of St Francis readily available as a model to the king.

Bonaventure had also extended contacts with the court. He preached frequently to the king and his family between 1254 and 1270, even structuring some of his sermons in response to requests for explanations of specific biblical passages from Louis, his wife Marguerite and their daughter Isabelle. Several contemporary anecdotes describe Louis's conversations with Bonaventure. In one, Louis asked him if it would be better not to exist at all rather than to sin and offend God. The two future saints agreed that not to exist would be preferable to offending the Lord, even for a king. In another episode, after the death of Louis's eldest son in 1260, he explained to Bonaventure that even though he had loved his son dearly, he would not wish that he had avoided death, since that would be to rebel against the will of God.[15] In intimate moments such as this, we see the king working through the most emotional and profound elements of his spirituality with the leading Franciscan theologian of his day.

Other Franciscans played similar, if less personal, advisory roles. Gilbert of Tournai, for example, wrote an important treatise of political and moral exhortation for Louis in 1259. The *Eruditio regum et principum* is actually a series of three letters addressed to Louis, offering instruction on the piety, discipline and justice necessary to princes, but also explicitly commenting on the Crusade's defeat and blaming it on the vices of the French people and crusaders.[16] Eustache of Arras and the more obscure William of Ligny preached before the royal family as well.[17] Moreover, university masters were not the only influential Franciscans with ties to the court. Jean of Samois is also known to have preached to Louis in the Sainte-Chapelle,[18] and Mansuetus of Castiglione Fiorentino co-operated with Louis on negotiations with England in 1258–9 so successfully that Louis rewarded him with a precious relic of the Crown of Thorns.[19]

Louis's gravitation towards the mendicant orders publicly solidified during the battles between seculars and mendicants at the University of Paris. In the early 1250s secular masters protesting against the influence of the mendicants were able to garner the support of Innocent IV, largely because of the untimely publication of the Parisian Franciscan Gerard of Borgo San Donnino's radically Joachite *Introduction to the Eternal Gospel*. Alarmed at this book's suggestion that in the coming 'age of the Holy Spirit' the Church hierarchy might become superfluous, Innocent limited mendicant privileges as preachers and confessors. Although these limitations were quickly rescinded by Alexander IV, the battle dragged on until June 1256, when the secular master William of Saint-Amour attacked Louis's attempts to make peace in this dispute and mocked him for modelling his own penitential behaviour too closely on that of the mendicants. When Alexander IV deprived William of his benefices and expelled him from France a few months later, the pope acknowledged that he was acting in accordance with Louis's wishes.[20] Thus, by 1255 Louis was perceived by some as a 'mendicant' king, one who was closely, even dangerously, tied to the Friars Minor and Preacher. From this perception sprang the contemporary vein of mockery publicised by the poet Rutebeuf, who a few years later openly decried Louis's dependence on the friars. For better or worse, by 1256 Louis's moderation in dress, quasi-monastic routine of prayer and devotion, and penitential outlook were seen as mendicant in inspiration.

This larger context is a reminder that although the appeal of Franciscan humility was central to Louis's spirituality, his affinity with apostolic ideals was not solely Franciscan in its inspiration. His ties to Dominicans and other mendicant orders were also notable. Thus, while the king's conscious embrace of friars among his closest collaborators was crucial to the rise of Franciscan forms of piety at court, in order to find a sphere where the Franciscans held nearly exclusive sway it is necessary to turn to the personal and institutional relationships they developed with Capetian women.

### ISABELLE OF FRANCE: SETTING THE MOULD

Here the pattern was established by Louis's younger sister Isabelle (1225–70), a princess who rejected several proposed marriages in favour of a life of pious virginity. Her reputation was clearly spreading by 1253, when Innocent IV wrote a letter praising and confirming her choice of virginity. Shortly thereafter, in May 1254, he asked Geoffrey of Brie to grant Isabelle's request for Franciscan confessors, a role subsequently filled by Eudes of Rosny. In 1256, Alexander IV sent her a letter of effusive praise, in which he noted the 'glowing accounts' of her conduct emanating from Franciscans close to the royal court.[21]

Isabelle is the first example of a member of the royal family to develop so close, exclusive and well-publicised a relationship with the friars. Nor was it coincidental that ultimately royal women most fully embraced a Franciscan identity. While kings less saintly than Louis IX might remain too invested in the realities of political power to portray themselves as followers of Francis, pious queens and princesses could more easily gravitate towards a model of visible humility.[22]

One way in which Isabelle provided a focus for future relations with the order was through her sponsorship of the *sorores minores* (Lesser Sisters), a distinctive branch of the Franciscan 'family' that attracted royal women's involvement over succeeding centuries. About 1254–5 plans for her new female Franciscan abbey – the first in the region of Paris – came together. Construction began around 1256, when she was joined by Louis, his queen and their eldest son, Louis, in laying the first stone of the house known as 'The Humility of Our Lady', or more familiarly as 'Longchamp' (in the modern Bois de Boulogne on the western edge of Paris). Over the next two years, she and her team of Franciscan masters (Bonaventure, Eudes of Rosny, William of Meliton, William of Harcombourg, Geoffrey of Vierzon) composed a new *Rule* for the house. Isabelle's contemporary biographer, Agnes of Harcourt, recalled that the brothers had gathered in Isabelle's chambers to do this work – an intimate picture of the kind of meeting that tied friars to French royalty. The *Rule* was first approved by Alexander IV in 1259, and a new version, revised according to Isabelle's desires, was granted by Urban IV in 1263.[23]

The nuns' entrance actually provided the setting for the most specific example we have of Louis's admiration for Sts Francis and Clare. Soon after the nuns' enclosure in June 1260 Louis entered the abbey with Isabelle and sat down with the nuns in chapter. From this position of humility, 'he gave the first sermon and teaching' the nuns had experienced at Longchamp.

> He said that we ought to take as our example Monseigneur St Francis and Madame St Clare and other saints who lived with such sanctity

and perfection, and that we should begin so high that the others who would come after us would not be able to equal us, and that we should be a mirror to all the other women of religion and lead such a life that others could take it as a good example.[24]

Louis was here drawing attention to Francis and Clare's exemplary power, to be perpetuated by the nuns of this royal, Franciscan foundation. Fascinatingly, Louis's mirror imagery is very much like that employed by the recently canonised Clare.[25]

Louis's passionate preaching demonstrated that the royal family had a great deal invested in this new community. Not surprisingly, then, Longchamp became a further centre of Parisian Franciscan life. In addition to the less prominent Franciscan brothers who resided there, Eudes Rigaud preached there at least once, Bonaventure almost certainly did too,[26] and Eustache of Arras delivered a sermon there in the presence of the king.[27] Eudes of Rosny must have been a frequent visitor as Isabelle's confessor, and it seems likely that other brothers associated with court and university would have travelled from Paris from time to time as well. At the time of Isabelle's death in 1270 Louis, as well as numerous Franciscans, attended the rituals around her interment. Isabelle had remained a laywoman to the end of her life, but her burial at Longchamp in the habit of a Franciscan nun emphasised a fusion of royal and Franciscan piety.

Just as importantly, Isabelle's specific vision of female Franciscanism provided a model for subsequent royal women. She insisted that her nuns be known as *sorores minores* and emphasised humility rather than absolute poverty as the defining attribute associated with Longchamp. This version of *minoritas* was evidently attractive to other royal women who wished to display piety and humility as well as patronage. Most of the early houses that adopted Longchamp's *Rule* were tied to the royal family. The female Franciscans of Provins gained permission to follow this *Rule* as early as 1264, with the support of Thibaud V of Champagne, who was married to Louis IX's daughter Isabelle. Most influentially, the new community of Saint-Marcel (or Lourcines) just outside Paris was founded by this same Isabelle and her mother. Other houses such as La-Garde-de-Notre-Dame (at La Guiche) and Nogent-l'Artaud were instituted by Capetian princesses before 1300, and Philip IV himself founded Moncel. Thus, by the end of the thirteenth century Capetian women could look to Isabelle's order of *sorores minores* as a place where royal patronage met female Franciscanism.

A second way that Isabelle set an influential example was through her explicit request for Franciscan confessors. Here again her preferences mirror those of her brother but move beyond them in a way that sets a gendered pattern. Louis IX had also favoured mendicants as confessors. Only one Franciscan confessor to Louis is known by name: John of Mons filled this role around the time of Louis's second Crusade and death, and after his death subsequent Capetian kings uniformly chose Dominicans in this capacity.[28,29] Their wives and daughters, however, favoured Franciscans.

### ROYAL WOMEN: PATTERNS OF PATRONAGE

Queen Marguerite and her daughters offer strong early examples of royal women who had known Isabelle and then centred their own devotions around Franciscan spirituality, patronised Saint-Marcel and Longchamp, and confessed to Franciscans.[30] John of Mons heard Marguerite's confessions as well as her husband's, and after 1277 Marguerite's confessor and executor was the Franciscan William of Saint-Pathus. The queen was also involved with Longchamp's fortunes from its very inception. Agnes of Harcourt makes it clear that Marguerite visited and conversed with the nuns frequently, sometimes relating the stories about Isabelle and her miracles that found their way into Agnes's biography. Marguerite in her widowhood devoted her resources to the development of Saint-Marcel. Together with her daughter Isabelle, Marguerite fostered this community in its beginnings at Troyes and then acted as its primary patron when the nuns moved to Saint-Marcel by 1289. She built herself a residence there and at her death left it to the nuns with the provision that her daughter Blanche (de la Cerda) be granted its use during her lifetime. Blanche, for her part, stayed at Longchamp after the death of her husband, then retired to Saint-Marcel after 1289 and spent most of her time there until her death in 1320. Like her mother, she employed William of Saint-Pathus as her confessor. Unlike her mother, she was actually buried at Saint-Marcel in the Franciscan habit.

Subsequent generations of Capetian women followed this model. Although there were exceptions, most queens of France had Franciscan confessors throughout the mid fourteenth century. For example, Jeanne of Navarre (d. 1305), Philip IV's queen, chose as her confessor and executor the Franciscan Durand of Champagne;[31] Philip V's wife, Jeanne of Burgundy, had the Franciscan Jean Viel; and somewhat later Jeanne of Burgundy (wife of Philip VI; d. 1348) chose several Friars Minor.[32]

These same women supported Longchamp and Saint-Marcel, some-times in causes that united multiple queens – for instance, the dowager queens Marguerite of Provence and Marie of Brabant joined with the current queen, Jeanne of Navarre, to petition for privileges on behalf of Saint-Marcel in the 1290s. These queens and their entourages obtained specific permission to enter and reside at the two abbeys, and indeed some retired there, following the model of Marguerite of Provence and Blanche de la Cerda. For example, Isabelle of Valois, daughter of Charles of Valois and mother of Queen Jeanne of Bourbon, retired to Saint-Marcel in her widowhood.

Other royal women actually professed as Franciscan nuns. Among royal relations, two nieces of Marie of Brabant (Jeanne and Marguerite of Brabant) entered Longchamp in 1301 and 1303. More directly, Philip V and Jeanne of Burgundy's daughter Blanche became a nun at Longchamp – the first time a royal woman had actually become a Franciscan, and indeed the first time the child of a king of France had joined a mendicant order. Her entry in 1319 was a grand ceremony, with her mother and father, her uncle Charles of Valois, other members of the royal family, the archbishop of Reims and the Franciscan master of theology, Nicolas of Lyra, all present. Her cousin Jeanne, daughter of Jeanne of France the queen of Navarre, entered the same year. Just as strikingly, Louis X's illegitimate daughter Eudeline became abbess at Saint-Marcel between 1334 and 1339.

As these houses developed their ties to royal women, Longchamp and Saint-Marcel fused Capetian memory with Franciscan piety. At Saint-Marcel, for instance, the nuns prayed for the souls of Marguerite of Provence and her daughter Blanche, and at Longchamp for Blanche of Castile, Louis IX, Isabelle of France and a host of other royal family members. Queen Jeanne of Burgundy's heart was even interred at Longchamp, near the site of her daughter's eventual tomb. Beyond formal liturgical remembrance, royal women further made themselves part of the fabric of Franciscan life in these communities by their robes, wedding gowns and fine clothing materials, which were then turned into vestments and altar clothes, and put to other ornamental and liturgical uses.[33]

Thus, female Franciscan abbeys reinforced a circular flow of piety. Franciscan confessors no doubt encouraged royal women's ties with Franciscan nuns, and close links with female Franciscan communities reinforced a desire to seek out Franciscan advisors and Franciscan modes of spirituality. When a queen or princess visited a relative at Longchamp or Saint-Marcel, she returned to court with interlaced images of Franciscan and Capetian piety, and perhaps envisioned her own eventual retirement or burial there. Indeed, many royal women chose burial at Franciscan houses. In turn, male Franciscans understood that Capetian queens could be their best allies at court. A dramatic example is the radically controversial Franciscan Bernard Délicieux, who sought help from Queen Jeanne of Navarre in his campaign against Dominican inquisitors in Carcassonne in 1304.[34]

The ties between Franciscans and royal women were also manifest in direct advice literature written by male friars for queens and princesses. Gilbert of Tournai wrote a tract for Isabelle of France that emphasised virginity but also stressed the importance of humility, and suggested that the daughters of French kings enjoyed a kind of celestial inheritance, a transmission of virtues through the female blood line that made them particular embodiments of charitable love and, perhaps by extension, *minoritas*.[35] Other friars followed Gilbert's example. Bonaventure may have written his *De regimine animae* for Blanche de la Cerda, while Durand of Champagne wrote the *Speculum dominarum* for Jeanne of Navarre, and he or another Franciscan translated it into French at her request.

## CAPETIAN SANCITY, FRANCISCAN SANCITY

This creation of texts could also be a two-way street, as Capetians – particularly women – actively commissioned specific works of hagiography from their Franciscan confessors or advisors. In particular, this dynamic played a larger role in the reshaping of Louis IX's saintly image. We have seen how Louis was influenced by Franciscans and the order's ideals in his lifetime. Now the relationship came full circle, as Franciscans promoted the cult of St Louis in ways that held Louis up as a model of Franciscan humility for a royal, and often female, audience.

Around 1302 Blanche de la Cerda asked William of Saint-Pathus to compose a new life of Louis. William used the existing records of Louis's canonisation hearings from 1282 to 1283, a copy of which was housed at the Franciscan convent in Paris. Although he was faithful to his sources, William was strongly influenced by the model of Bonaventure's *Major Life* in form and method, and highlighted elements in Louis's piety such as dispensing alms and devout prayer that fit Franciscan ideals.[36]

The Franciscan liturgical office for Louis, known as *Francorum rex* and composed after 1299, even more explicitly constructs Louis as a new Francis by borrowing from the office of St Francis (*Franciscus vir catholicus*) by Julian of Speyer. Just as the latter emphasised Francis's rejection of worldly goods, the new office for Louis stressed his rejection of earthly glory in favour of the Crusade. Indeed, *Francorum rex* took language directly from *Franciscus vir*, emphasising the way Louis's life fitted into Francis's pattern.[37] Moreover, it has recently been shown that Agnes of Harcourt's *Life of Isabelle* took its opening material nearly verbatim from a French prose life of Elizabeth of Hungary, herself an earlier royal woman strongly influenced by Franciscan ideals.[38] Just as William drew on language from the *Major Life* to present Louis as a 'new Francis', so Agnes hinted that the king's sister was a new Elizabeth. In these models, Franciscan exemplars were textually translated into Capetian sanctity.

## OUTSIDE PARIS

The Capetian adoption of Franciscan models of piety had implications that stretched across generations, as branches of the royal family spread out and reflected the model of the French court. In some instances, it was French princesses whose marriages exported a gendered preference for Franciscan ideals. A good example is Isabella of France, the daughter of Philip IV and Jeanne of Navarre, who married Edward II in 1308. She supported the male and female Franciscan communities of London and Ware, visited Saint-Marcel when back in Paris in 1325, listened to Franciscan preachers, employed Franciscan confessors and was buried at London Greyfriars in 1358, eventually with her daughter and granddaughter interred nearby. Among her closest associates were French-born widows such as Marie of Saint-Pol, who was an even stronger patron of female Franciscanism in England.[39] French connections such as these led to all Franciscan women in England following the *Rule* of the *sorores minores* created by Isabelle of France for Longchamp, and where a 'French' model of royal, female gravitation to the Franciscans was firmly in evidence.

Male members of the cadet branches of the Capetian family were also important in this process. A particularly intriguing example is Louis IX's younger brother Charles of Anjou. This ambitious prince became count of Provence through his marriage to Beatrice of Provence in 1246 and conquered the kingdom of Sicily as a papal champion by 1266. There are some early hints of Charles's interest in Franciscan models. Salimbene describes him at the Franciscan house in Vézelay in 1248 praying so fervently that the rest of the royal entourage had to wait patiently for him to finish.[40] The most intimate evidence for Charles's impression of Franciscan spirituality, however, comes from his interaction with the Provençal holy woman Douceline of Digne. Douceline was the sister of Hugh, whose preaching made such an impact on Louis IX in 1254, and the foundress of the first two Beguine communities in Provence. Her version of Beguine life fused communal living for chaste laywomen with ardent Franciscan piety. The contemporary *Life of Douceline* makes her devotion to Francis explicit, and her advisors were Franciscans such as John of Parma with Joachite and 'spiritual' leanings. According to this *Life*, Charles had heard many bad things about the Franciscans and banished them from his good graces.[41] But then when Countess Beatrice was in danger of dying in childbirth, she dreamed that a Beguine helped save her. When Charles discovered that this must be 'Hugh of Digne's sister' and heard of her virtues, he sent for Douceline, and the countess delivered safely. Not only did the count and countess then develop a particular devotion to Douceline, but as a result Charles restored the Franciscans to his favour, supported Douceline's communities with alms, and tested her ecstatic raptures to his own satisfaction. Later, around 1263 when Charles was contemplating his invasion of Sicily, he consulted Douceline. She informed him that God, the Virgin and St Francis favoured his expedition, and after his victory he paid her even greater devotion. But Douceline also chastised him and threatened God's wrath when he was ungrateful for divine gifts, and wrote to him to this effect, warning that ingratitude would lead to reversals of fortune (the *Life of Douceline* attributes the Sicilian Vespers to this cause!).

## CONCLUSION

Later Franciscans sought to claim that Louis IX had formally joined the Franciscan Third Order, or that his sister Isabelle had been a nun at Longchamp. Neither claim had a basis in fact, but they demonstrate the way a Franciscan identity had come to seem compatible with royal piety. From the first contacts early in the reign of Louis IX and the strong personal relationships developed by the king and his sister, the alliance between the powerful Capetians and the humble *fratres* and *sorores minores* developed institutional ties that made it routine for friars to act as royal agents and Franciscans to be the closest advisors to queens and princesses. These ties had become evident by the time of Louis's first Crusade and had grown into particularly close relationships between the royal family and the Franciscan masters of theology in Paris by the 1250s and 1260s. Following the model of Isabelle of France, it was royal women who did the most to expand and strengthen these ties over succeeding decades, by patronising the *sorores minores* and utilising Franciscans as confessors. At the same time, daughters and younger sons from the Capetian line reproduced their family's brand of Franciscan-tinged piety as they left France for other realms. By the 1320s, when Philip V had travelled to Longchamp to die a pious death near his daughter the Franciscan nun, and his wife had elected burial for her heart at the same house, Franciscan *minoritas* had come to form an important element in the self-projection of French royal piety and the court's conception of the virtues that should be embodied by a holy ruling family.

## Notes

1  G. Klaniczay, *Holy Rulers and Blessed Princesses: Dynastic Cults in Medieval Central Europe*, trans. É. Pálmae (Cambridge, 2002).

2  L. K. Little, 'Saint Louis' Involvement with the Friars', *Church History*, 33 (1964), 125–48, at 127.

3  See J. M. Miskuly, 'Julian of Speyer: Life of St Francis (*Vita sancti Francisci*)', *Franciscan Studies*, 49 (1989), 93–174, at 93–4.

4  E. Miller, 'Review of Exuviae Sacrae Constantinopolitanae', *Journal des Savants* (1878), 292–309 and 389–403, at 302–3.

5  W. C. Jordan, *Louis IX and the Challenge of the Crusade* (Princeton, 1979), p. 53.

6  Salimbene, p. 441; A. J. Davis, *The Holy Bureaucrat: Eudes Rigaud and Religious Reform in Thirteenth-Century Normandy* (Ithaca, 2006), pp. 31–2.

7  H.-F. Delaborde, *Vie de saint Louis par Guillaume de Saint-Pathus, confesseur de la reine Marguerite* (Paris, 1899), pp. 41–2.

8  C. H. Lawrence, *The Friars: The Impact of the Early Mendicant Movement on Western Society* (New York and London, 1994), c. 9; Jordan, *Challenge*, pp. 53–5; W. C. Jordan, 'Anti-Corruption Campaigns in Thirteenth-Century Europe', *Journal of Medieval History*, 35 (2009), 204–19.

9  Salimbene, pp. 212–15; 464; 305; 215–16.

10  Jordan, *Challenge*, c. 6.

11  J. Monfrin (ed.), *Joinville, Vie de saint Louis* (Paris, 1995), pp. 657–60.

12  Little, 'Saint Louis' Involvement with the Friars', 132.

13  A. Callebaut, 'La Deuxième Croisade de S. Louis et les Franciscains', *La France franciscaine*, 5 (1922), 282–8.

14  Davis, *The Holy Bureaucrat*, pp. 157–73.

15  J. G. Bougerol, 'Saint Bonaventure et le roi saint Louis', in *S. Bonaventura 1274–1974* (Grottaferrata, 1973), vol. II, pp. 469–89.

16   J. Le Goff, *Saint Louis*, trans. G. Evan Gollard (Notre Dame, Ind., 2009), pp. 321–8.

17   J. G. Bougerol, 'Sermons inédits de maîtres franciscains du XIIIe siècle', *AFH*, 81 (1988), 17–49, at 21.

18   M. C. Gaposchkin, *The Making of Saint Louis: Kingship, Sanctity, and Crusade in the Later Middle Ages* (Ithaca, NY and London, 2008), p. 156.

19   S. L. Field, *Isabelle of France: Capetian Sanctity and Franciscan Identity in the Thirteenth Century* (Notre Dame, Ind., 2006), pp. 71–2.

20   Little, 'Saint Louis' Involvement with the Friars', 136–43.

21   Field, *Isabelle of France*, pp. 42–59.

22   Gaposchkin, *The Making of Saint Louis*, p. 156.

23   Field, *Isabelle of France*, cc. 3, 4.

24   S. L. Field (ed. and trans.), *The Writings of Agnes of Harcourt: The Life of Isabelle of France and the Letter on Louis IX and Longchamp* (Notre Dame, Ind., 2003), p. 47.

25   R. J. Armstrong, *Clare of Assisi: Early Documents, Revised and Expanded*, (New York, 2006), pp. 59–65, at p. 61. On the authenticity of the *Testament*, see L. S. Knox, *Creating Clare of Assisi: Female Franciscan Identities in Later Medieval Italy*, The Medieval Franciscans, 5 (Leiden, 2008), pp. 9–14.

26   J. G. Bougerol, *Saint Bonaventure, Sermons de tempore* (Paris, 1990), pp. 274–5 (a sermon that must have been preached at Longchamp).

27   Bougerol, 'Sermons inédits de maîtres franciscains du XIIIe siècle', 21.

28   Little, 'Saint Louis' Involvement with the Friars', 128.

29   X. de la Selle, *Le Service des âmes à la cour: confesseurs et aumôniers des rois de France du XIIIe au XVe siècle*, Mémoires et documents de l'École des chartes 43 (Paris, 1995).

30   A.-H. Allirot, 'Longchamp et Lourcine, deux abbayes féminines et royales dans la construction de la mémoire capétienne', *Revue d'histoire de l'église de France*, 94 (2008), 23–38.

31   M. J. P. Robson, 'Queen Isabella (c.1295–1358) and the Greyfriars: An Example of Royal Patronage Based on Her Accounts for 1357–1358', *FS*, 65 (2007), 325–48, at 328.

32   X. de la Selle, *Confesseurs et aumôniers des rois de France du XIIIe au XVe siècle* (Paris, 1995), pp. 310–11.

33   For this and two preceeding paragraphs, see Allirot, 'Longchamp et Lourcine', 28–36.

34   A. Friedlander, *The Hammer of the Inquisitors: Brother Bernard Délicieux and the Struggle against the Inquisition in Fourteenth-Century France* (Leiden and Boston, 2000), p. 223.

35   A. H. Allirot, 'Filiae regis Francorum: princesses royales, mémoire de saint Louis et conscience dynastique (de 1270 à la fin du XIVe siècle)', Thèse de doctorat, Université Paris X-Nanterre, 2007, p. 310; S. L. Field, 'Gilbert of Tournai's Letter to Isabelle of France: An Edition of the Complete Text', *Mediaeval Studies*, 65 (2003), 57–97.

36   Gaposchkin, *The Making of Saint Louis*, pp. 38, 156–8; C. Frugoni, 'Saint Louis et saint François', *Medievales*, 34 (1998), 35–8.

37 Gaposchkin, *The Making of Saint Louis*, pp. 158–68; M. C. Gaposchkin, 'Louis IX et la mémoire liturgique', *Revue d'histoire d'l'église de France*, 95 (2009), 23–34, at 32–3.

38 L. Seláf, 'Párhuzamos Életrajzok: Szent Erzsébet és Isabelle de France Legendái', in V. Kapisztrán OFM (ed.), *Árpád-házi Szent Erzsébet kultusza a 13–16. Században*, Studia Franciscana Hungarika 2 (Budapest, 2009), pp. 141–50.

39 S. L. Field, 'Marie of Saint-Pol and Her Books', *The English Historical Review*, 125 (2010), 255–78.

40 Salimbene, p. 216.

41 H. J. Grieco, 'Franciscan Inquisition and Mendicant Rivalry in Mid Thirteenth-Century Marseilles', *Journal of Medieval History*, 34 (2008), 275–90, at 279; J. Chiffoleau, 'Les Mendiants, le prince et l'hérésie à Marseille vers 1260', *Provence historique*, 36 (1986), 3–19. *I thank Cecilia Gaposchkin and Adam J. Davis for their criticisms.*

## 14 Franciscans as papal and royal envoys to the Tartars (1245–1255)

PETER JACKSON

### INTRODUCTION

Gregory IX, a keen patron of the newly founded mendicant orders, increasingly resorted to them as instruments of papal authority, notably as Crusade preachers and as diplomatic envoys. And towards the end of his pontificate, these developments received an unexpected boost from the appearance of the Mongols (more commonly known as 'Tartars') on the horizons of the Latin world. The Mongols were engaged in a mission of world conquest that they believed to have been entrusted by heaven to the empire's founder, Chinggis Khan (d. 1227), and campaigns headed by his senior grandson, Batu, reduced the nomadic tribes of the Eurasian steppe and the principalities of the Rus, and in 1241–2 devastated Poland, Moravia and Hungary. In the course of this first attack on Latin Christian territory, the mendicants suffered alongside other sections of the Catholic Church. Friars were among those massacred; and, according to the Franciscan guardian of Prague, the invaders had destroyed at least two of the Franciscan custodies in eastern Europe.[1]

When Innocent IV convened the Council of Lyons (1245), the most recent – and the most accurate – intelligence concerning the Mongols had been provided by an émigré Russian ecclesiastic named Peter. It seems that Peter's responses to the questions put to him by the pope and the cardinals served as a framework around which at least one of the papal ambassadors to the Mongols would structure his own report; and certainly his statement that the Mongols received envoys favourably (*benigne*) and sent them back promptly must have encouraged the curia to enter into diplomatic relations with the newcomers.[2,3]

### THE PAPAL AMBASSADORS

In April 1245, even before the council assembled, Innocent IV dispatched three embassies to the Mongol world – one through eastern

Europe and two by way of the Near East, where other Mongol forces had recently made their appearance during the years 1242–4, defeating the Seljük sultan of Anatolia (Rûm) and demanding the submission of the Latin principality of Antioch. The pope may here have been acting upon information supplied by Peter, who had spoken of three distinct Mongol armies operating respectively against the Egyptians, the Turks (that is, the Seljüks), and the Hungarians and Poles.[4]

For our purposes, the most important of these embassies was led by the Franciscan John of Plano Carpini (Pian di Carpine), who headed due east from Lyons for the Pontic steppes. As a former guardian of Saxony, minister provincial for the entire province of Germany and, most recently, a papal penitentiary, Carpini possessed a wealth of spiritual and administrative experience and, no doubt just as importantly, was personally acquainted with certain Catholic rulers in eastern Europe, in particular King Wenceslaus (Vaclav) I of Bohemia. Innocent had at first intended, it seems, to send other Franciscans to the Mongols in the Near East; but in the event he deputed two groups of Dominicans for this task, headed respectively by André of Longjumeau and the Lombard Ascelin.[5]

On the Bohemian king's advice, Carpini and his colleague, the Czech Stephen (or Ceslaus), visited various princes in Poland, where they were joined by a Polish Franciscan named Benedict as interpreter. They then moved on via the Russian principalities of Galicia (Halicz) and Kiev into the steppes, where Mongol commanders forwarded them to Batu's headquarters on the Volga. Stephen had already remained behind at the first Mongol camp because of poor health.[6] The party now had to leave others among themselves, whom Carpini elsewhere terms 'companions and servants', at Batu's encampment while he and Benedict were sent on to the court of the kaghan-elect Güyüg in Mongolia.[7] We are not told whether Carpini's instructions coincided with those of Ascelin, which were to deliver the pope's message to the first Mongol army he encountered and to which the Dominican adhered rigidly, refusing to travel onwards to Güyüg's headquarters. The two Franciscans, by contrast, apparently raised no objection to this unexpected extension of their journey. Carpini's somewhat depleted party was therefore the only one to travel almost the entire breadth of Asia to the centre of the Mongol empire; it was also the first to report back to the pope. For both reasons, it seems to have created a greater sensation on its return to Latin Europe than did its Dominican counterparts.

As far as we can tell, each group carried with it four papal bulls. *Cum hora undecima*, which Gregory IX had dispatched in 1235 to a

Dominican friar operating in Muslim Syria, was reissued, with fuller privileges for the friars and with a list of addressees extended to embrace the Franciscans dwelling among a host of peoples, including Greeks, 'pagans', Ethiopians, Nubians, Goths (in the Crimea), Zicchians (south-east of the Sea of Azov), 'Ruthenians' (Russians), Nestorians, Georgians and Armenians. Two further bulls were addressed to the 'king' of the Mongols and his people. *Cum non solum* urged them to desist from their campaigns of devastation, warning them of the vengeance of God and enquiring about the reasons for their destructive conduct and their future intentions; *Dei patris immensa* presented the Mongols with an outline of the tenets of the Christian faith. The fourth and last bull, *Cum simus super*, appealed to the clergy of other confessions, particularly the Greeks and the Russians, to restore the unity of the Church by acknowledging Roman primacy. Indeed, the pope's biographer, Niccolò da Calvi, depicts Innocent as dispatching missions to a host of peoples both pagan and schismatic, among which Carpini's party and the embassies sent to 'the sultans of Egypt (*Babilonie*) and Anatolia (*Iconium*)' were just three.[8] Carpini describes himself as 'envoy of the apostolic see to the Tartars and other nations of the East'.[9]

The purpose behind these embassies, then, was not merely diplomatic contact with the Mongols. Just as the two Dominican parties seem to have spent a considerable time in negotiations with the Muslim powers through whose territories they passed, so Carpini's route took him to the court of one of the leading Russian princes, Daniil of Galicia and Volynia. In Daniil's absence on a visit to Batu, his brother Vasil'ko summoned the bishops, to whom the friars read a papal letter urging them 'to return to the unity of Holy Mother Church' – in other words, *Cum simus super*.[10] It is possible that Innocent was endeavouring to capitalise on the predicament of communities – whether non-Latin Christian or Muslim – which were immediately threatened by the Mongol advance, and hoping to bring them into the Catholic fold with the promise of military assistance. The embassies to the Mongols were accordingly part of a much wider campaign of evangelism; each friar was acting in a dual capacity, as a diplomatic envoy and as a missionary for the Roman Church.

Innocent may well have remained in ignorance of the progress of the embassies for some time. Carpini gave the companions he left at Batu's headquarters a letter for the pope, on the understanding that the Mongols were sending them back to Lyons. In the event they got no further than the encampment of the Mongol commander Mochi, just east of the River Dnieper, and were kept there as hostages until permitted to rejoin Carpini on his return journey.[11] Receiving no word of the friars, therefore, Innocent evidently concluded they were lost, and this was surely why he sent another mission (this time comprising Dominicans) to Halicz in 1246.[12]

It is unlikely that the pope had high expectations regarding the Mongol response to his messages; he may have set greater store by the other commissions entrusted to his envoys. Carpini himself says that he chose to proceed first to the Tartars, which suggests that Innocent had left it to his envoys to decide on their priorities.[13] It is extremely improbable that the pope, as has been claimed, envisaged an alliance with the Mongols against the Muslims of the Near East. What is not in doubt is that he had ordered those friars who visited the Mongol world to obtain as much intelligence as they could – in other words, to spy.[14]

The various missions returned to Lyons in the course of 1247–8. Carpini's party was the first. Having witnessed the enthronement of the Kaghan Güyüg in August 1246, the party retraced its steps via Kiev, where the inhabitants came out to greet them as if they had risen from the dead, and the court of the Hungarian King Béla IV, who had a stronger interest than most in accumulating information on the Mongols.[15] Thereafter they revisited Daniil and Vasil'ko, whose clergy solemnly acknowledged the primacy of Rome; in 1253 Daniil would be rewarded with a coronation at the hands of a papal legate (although he subsequently despaired of western aid and submitted to the Mongols). Yet the pope can otherwise have derived little reassurance from the result of his embassies. Carpini brought back a great deal of information on the Mongols, their lifestyle and customs, and their methods of warfare; he even included recommendations as to how best to resist a future attack. But he also reported that they had withdrawn from Europe in 1242 only because of the death of the Kaghan Ögödei, and that Güyüg was already planning a fresh expedition against the west.[16] He and Ascelin both returned with ultimatums from Güyüg requiring the pope's submission; in addition, Ascelin brought a menacing letter from the Mongol general Baiju, stationed in Armenia.

## WILLIAM OF RUBRUCK'S MISSION

Following Carpini's return to Lyons in October 1247, Pope Innocent sent him on a mission to Louis IX of France, with the aim, no doubt, of keeping the king fully informed in advance of his impending Crusade.[17] But while on Cyprus in December 1248, preparing for his invasion of

Egypt, Louis received an embassy from the Mongol general Eljigidei in Iran which bore a cordial message and assured him of the Christian faith not only of Eljigidei himself but also of the Kaghan Güyüg. This contrasted so sharply with the overbearing tone of previous communications from the Mongols that the king early in 1249 dispatched back his own envoys, headed by the Dominican André of Longjumeau (previously one of the pope's ambassadors).[18] Güyüg having died in 1248, they were received by his widow, who forwarded them in 1251 with a demand for the king's submission; according to his biographer Joinville, Louis deeply regretted having sent the embassy.[19] It was on account of André of Longjumeau's recent experience that when William of Rubruck, a Franciscan in Louis's entourage, left Palestine for the Mongol world, he was at pains to avoid giving any impression that he was the king's ambassador.

Rubruck's *Itinerarium* opens with his entry into the Black Sea in May 1253, after he had been joined in Constantinople by another Franciscan, Bartholomew of Cremona. Bartholomew was possibly selected because he knew Greek, having participated in a mission to Constantinople headed by 'Friar Thomas, our Minister' – namely, the minister provincial in the Holy Land, who is known to have accompanied John of Parma, minister general, on an embassy to the court of the Greek emperor of Nicaea.[20]

Rubruck's mission was a personal one. He made it clear that he was no envoy in a sermon he preached in the cathedral of Hagia Sophia at Constantinople, and he continued at intervals to emphasise this fact.[21] One of his aims was to make contact with Batu's son Sartaq, reports of whose conversion to Christianity had reached the crusading army in the Holy Land. He also wished to preach the Gospel to the Mongols at large. Nevertheless, his chief purpose, he tells us, was to minister to the spiritual needs of a community of German miners who had been enslaved in Hungary in 1241–2 and were now employed in Central Asia.[22] He carried a letter of introduction from King Louis, which asked permission for him to remain in Mongol territory in order to preach, and also a message from the Latin Emperor Baldwin II of Constantinople to the nearest Mongol commander, requesting safe conduct through the Pontic steppe. And, like Carpini, he was under orders to write down everything he saw; Rubruck too was, *inter alia*, a spy.[23]

On returning to Syria in 1255, Rubruck discovered that Louis had gone home. Ordered by the Franciscan minister provincial in Syria to put his report in writing, he asked the king to obtain permission for him to travel to France. We know that he subsequently did so, since the

English Franciscan Roger Bacon met him there (see below). Yet he had little to report to Louis by way of achievement. He had failed to make contact with the German slaves, who had been moved hundreds of miles to the east. He was disappointed in Sartaq; indeed, he did not believe the prince was a Christian, or, at the very least, disclaimed any knowledge of whether Sartaq was a Christian or not.[24] His attempts at evangelism were doomed by the inadequacy of the interpreter whom the party had acquired in Constantinople, a man Rubruck describes as 'neither intelligent nor articulate' and whom even the Mongols at the kaghan's headquarters regarded as good for nothing.[25] It was not until the party had spent several weeks in Möngke's entourage that Rubruck acquired as his interpreter the foster-son of the Parisian goldsmith Guillaume Buchier, who translated for him in a public religious debate between Christians, Muslims and Buddhists that had been convened on the kaghan's orders. If we are to believe both Rubruck and Bacon, the friar's performance in this confrontation was a *tour de force*. He allegedly vanquished his Buddhist opponent and won from the Muslims the sweet triumph of an acknowledgement that everything in the Gospel was true and that they prayed for a Christian death; recent scholarship has challenged the accuracy of these reminiscences.[26] Nor did Rubruck have any conversions to report. He tells us that he had baptised in all 'six souls' – and even these may have been Nestorian Christians who embraced the Latin rite.[27] When leaving Möngke, he asked the kaghan's permission to return at some future date in order to preach the Gospel to the German slaves and their offspring, and this was granted on condition that his superiors agreed.[28] It is possible, although we have no evidence, that he travelled to eastern Asia a second time and spent the rest of his life there.

## DIPLOMATIC MISAPPREHENSIONS

Archbishop Peter was to some degree correct. The Mongols did welcome ambassadors; but the brief summary of his report that has survived fails to do justice to the difficulties posed by Mongol diplomatic usage. It was not so much a matter of unfamiliar and suspect rituals, such as that of purification by passing between two fires, with which Carpini and his companions were ready to comply. They also duly genuflected three times at the threshhold of a Mongol commander's tent; and, according to Benedict, they even bowed their heads before an effigy of Chinggis Khan (although Carpini is silent in this context).[29] The contrast with the recalcitrance of Ascelin and his colleagues regarding Mongol protocol at Baiju's encampment could not have been more marked.

The root of the problem was essentially the Mongols' programme of world conquest. They made peace only with those who yielded to them and accepted their proper place in the Mongol empire; it was thus by no means illogical that in the Mongols' vocabulary the Turkish term *el/il* denoted both 'peace' and 'submission'.[30] Any prince who sent envoys to them had *ipso facto* embarked on the process of accepting the kaghan's sovereignty. It is perhaps pointless to ask whether this was a matter of conviction or merely of convenience. But the assumption would certainly have given the Mongols a sense of moral rectitude had it subsequently proved necessary to attack the prince in question. The notion that the pope was offering them submission was especially attractive; it appears that they were already familiar with his exalted status, viewing him at this juncture as a major potentate and the overlord of a number of subject kings.[31]

In this context, the letters that both Carpini and Rubruck carried, and their own attempts at explanation, gave rise to confusion over the character of the mission. Innocent IV's bull *Cum non solum* voiced the desire for 'all to live in the unity of peace' and requested the Mongols to 'engage in fruitful discourse ... especially on those matters that pertain to peace'.[32] On first reaching a Mongol encampment, Carpini and his colleagues assured the chief men there that the pope desired all Christians to be on friendly terms with the Mongols and be at peace with them; it was his desire, moreover, that 'the Tartars be great before God in Heaven'.[33] The inadvertent ambiguity of Innocent IV's language was picked up by the Kaghan Güyüg, who believed that the pope was yielding to the Mongols. 'Having taken counsel about having peace with us', began his reply, 'you have sent us a plea of submission.'[34] Carpini's own conciliatory conduct appeared to corroborate this impression.

Rubruck, for his part, soon found that his unofficial status threatened to undermine the progress of his mission. Warned at the Crimean port of Soldaia (Sudak) that unless he was an ambassador he would not be granted safe conduct through Mongol territory, he used ambivalent language in dealing with the prefects of the town, allowing them to believe that he was travelling as the French king's own envoy. The fact that Louis was sending with the friars his own clerk, Gosset, with alms to support them on their journey, must further have muddied the waters.[35] And the missive that the king had entrusted to them was likewise calculated to mislead the Mongols, for it was clearly more than a simple letter of introduction. Although it has not survived, we know something of its tone and contents from scattered references to it in the *Itinerarium*. Louis felicitated Sartaq on his conversion to Christianity and urged him to be a friend to all Christians, to exalt the cross and to be an enemy to all its foes.[36] Rubruck later suspected that the Armenians who translated the letter had given it a more forceful rendering – in the hope, perhaps, that Latin–Mongol collaboration would bring disaster on the Muslim enemy.

As a consequence, the Mongols concluded that the French king was asking for military assistance from them, and Sartaq, viewing the mission as problematic, sent Rubruck to his father, Batu.[37] Batu decided to send the clerk Gosset back to his son, presumably as a hostage, dispatched the two friars and their interpreter to the Kaghan Möngke in Mongolia, and followed this up with his own letter to the kaghan. On his arrival in Möngke's encampment, Rubruck was asked whether he came to make peace. When in response he denied that King Louis was at war with the Mongols, they asked in bewilderment why he had undertaken the journey, if not to make peace. Rubruck's incomprehension of the issue at stake is clear from his statement, in the kaghan's presence, that the friars had brought 'a message of peace' for Sartaq from Louis.[38] His choice of expression was open to the same misinterpretation as the phrases used by Innocent IV and Carpini almost a decade previously.

The shift in Mongol perceptions can be illustrated by the friars' reception. At Sartaq's camp they had initially been exempt, as holy men, from making the triple genuflection before the prince, whereas at both Batu and Möngke's headquarters they were made to perform it – that is to say, they were treated as envoys.[39] At the kaghan's court it was finally accepted that Rubruck was no ambassador; in any case, as he later discovered, Batu's letter had been mislaid, and Möngke had forgotten its drift.[40] Ironically, when responding to King Louis, Möngke employed Rubruck as his own envoy. In this capacity the friar conveyed yet another Mongol ultimatum, which denounced Eljigidei's envoy of 1248–9 as a charlatan and required the French king's submission.

## THE DRAWBACKS OF POVERTY

The friars' purposes were also undermined by the prescriptions of their order. Rubruck subsequently learned that Carpini and his colleagues had adapted their Franciscan garb in order not to incur the contempt of their hosts.[41] A related handicap was the inadequacy of the gifts they carried. As Carpini had admitted at the encampments of Kerancha and Batu, the pope had sent no presents; all the friars could offer was what they had for their own needs, together with furs that they had purchased in Poland on Vasil'ko's advice. But they were pestered for gifts at every encampment at which they halted and also suffered from pilfering at the hands of their escort, with the result that they ran out and had virtually nothing left to present to Güyüg at his enthronement. Since they brought no tribute, in accordance with Mongol practice they were given only meagre provisions.[42]

Rubruck had purchased in Constantinople some fruit, wine and 'biscuit' to present to Sartaq; otherwise, what his party carried was designed, again, only for their own sustenance.[43] As he told both the commander of the first Mongol camp he reached and Sartaq's chief secretary, he and his colleague were debarred from owning possessions and therefore had no gifts for them, and he had likewise to confess later to the kaghan that the party had brought no gold or silver. This hardly enhanced their stock in the eyes of their hosts, who were on the lookout particularly for valuable cloth.[44] On their outward journey the friars were repeatedly harassed for gifts and obliged to share their poor rations both with the Mongols and with the Mongols' starving slaves.[45] Rubruck himself was conscious that he and Bartholomew, clad in their habits and with bare heads and feet, presented quite a spectacle at both Batu's encampment and the kaghan's. Even the Mongol guide who escorted the two Franciscans from Batu to the kaghan took no pains to mask his contempt for them, at least until he realised that their prayers could be of benefit to himself and to others.[46]

It was in part for these reasons that when, on his return through Armenia, Rubruck encountered a group of Dominicans he warned them that no heed would be paid to them if their sole aim was to preach, and that in his report he recommended that no more friars be sent to the Mongols; rather, a bishop should be selected as ambassador and should travel in some style.[47] Certainly an official ambassador would have been entitled to address the kaghan without being restricted to answering his questions.[48] Unfortunately, Rubruck was ignoring the fact that even an envoy of this exalted rank would have encountered many of the same problems as did humble mendicants; nor would a bishop necessarily have proved any more successful at preaching the Gospel to his Mongol hosts.

## THE CIRCULATION AND QUALITY OF THE FRANCISCANS' REPORTS

Carpini's report to the pope has not survived; the manuscripts of his *History of the Mongols* that have come down to us are addressed to 'all

Christ's faithful'. His mission appears to have enjoyed considerable publicity. The Franciscan Salimbene de Adam, who as a young man met Carpini twice, just prior to his return to the pope and again following his visit to Louis IX, describes him as exhibiting his book at Franciscan houses and amplifying its contents by word of mouth in response to questions.[49] And Carpini himself tells us that even while the friars were travelling back through eastern Europe his as yet incomplete report was being borrowed and abridged versions being produced.[50] One of these was certainly the 'Tartar Relation', drafted in Poland in July 1247 by a Franciscan who calls himself 'C. de Bridia' and addressed to his superior, Minister Provincial Bogusław. De Bridia was in all likelihood one of the group that had been left at Mochi's encampment on the outward journey and rejoined Carpini only in the course of his return.[51] The 'Tartar Relation' is therefore to some extent a first-hand account in its own right, even though the author also lifted extensive passages from Carpini's *History of the Mongols*.

The *History* has reached us in two versions, of which the later one (less well represented in the manuscript tradition) includes an additional chapter narrating the journey and a number of other changes and interpolations, designed to place stronger emphasis upon the danger posed by the Mongols.[52] We also have a second, relatively brief narrative of the mission, which Benedict dictated to a *scholasticus* in Cologne on the friars' return in the early autumn of 1247 but which carries no dedication. The 'Tartar Relation' has survived in only two manuscripts.[53] We owe it to the Dominican encyclopaedist Vincent of Beauvais, who was closely associated with the French royal court, that Carpini's findings circulated as widely as they did. He incorporated a considerable proportion of the first recension – along with sections of the *Historia Tartarorum*, the report of Ascelin's mission by Simon de Saint-Quentin – in his *Speculum Historiale* (c.1253).

By contrast, Rubruck's *Itinerarium* was destined simply for King Louis and appears to have fared even less well than Carpini's report. Bacon is the only person known for certain to have read it. He met Rubruck, probably in Paris several years later, discussed his report with him and inserted in his own *Opus Maius* (c.1267) not simply material from the *Itinerarium*, primarily of geographical interest, but also one or two details gleaned from its author by word of mouth.[54] Even Bacon's work had only a narrow circulation, however; and otherwise Rubruck's account languished in oblivion until it was unearthed by Hakluyt in the late sixteenth century. We may well be indebted to Bacon that it survived at all, since the few principal manuscripts are all of English provenance.[55]

What of the quality of the respective accounts? Carpini and Rubruck stand head and shoulders above any of the other contemporaries who wrote about the Mongols – and indeed above other thirteenth-century reports in general. Both alike furnish rich ethnographic data regarding peoples of whose existence the west had hitherto never even heard. But in texture they differ sharply from one another. Carpini's *History* has all the cool precision and rational structure to be expected of a diplomatic report. A significant proportion is devoted, naturally, to military matters: Mongol weaponry and tactics and the best means of resistance. He included a chapter on the Mongols' good qualities, even though he also described their vices as beyond enumeration and left his readers in no doubt as to the danger they posed.[56] He steered clear of lurid generalisations about the Mongols' cannibalism, of the sort that had been current in Europe since 1241, observing merely that they had been known to eat human flesh in dire emergency.[57]

Rubruck's highly vivid and readable *Itinerarium* appears much less systematic because the work is essentially a lengthy narrative of his experiences, though incorporating specific chapters on the Mongols' lifestyle and customs, on the Buddhist religion (previously unknown) and on shamanistic practices. He was more discursive than Carpini, interpreting his commission from King Louis in extremely broad terms. He furnishes details about not merely peoples, their religion and their mores, notably providing the first western description of the written characters and paper money used in China, but also fauna and flora. Here the west could first have learned of the yak, of the wild ass or *qulan* and of the great horned sheep, the *ovis Poli*, whose scientific name today associates it, unjustly, with the more celebrated Venetian traveller of the next generation.[58] One advantage Rubruck possessed over Carpini was his readiness to challenge received wisdom. He corrects the erroneous impression, current since antiquity, that the Caspian Sea was a gulf linked with the ocean; and upon learning that the monstrous peoples described by venerable authors like Isidore and Solinus had never been sighted, he began to doubt their existence.[59]

Where both reports were wanting was in their appraisal of the Mongols' military capacity. On his outward journey Carpini had been briefed by Vasil'ko, who drew on information supplied by his own envoys to the Mongols; and in the Far East the friar spoke with Rus princes and with their retinues, of whom several members are listed in his final chapter.[60] But for the most part, his informants tended to be expatriate European Christians. Almost at the very beginning of his report, he claims that what he has written is based either on personal observation or on the testimony of Christian captives who are to be relied upon.[61] Twice, when furnishing details of Asian folklore, he cites Russian clerics who had lived among the Mongols for a long time, specifying on the latter occasion that he had met them in the kaghan's encampment.[62] He was also indebted to enslaved Europeans such as the Russian goldsmith Cosmas, who gave the friars invaluable support, and others, including Hungarians, some of whom had been domiciled within the Mongol empire for as long as twenty years.[63] Rubruck had less to say on military matters. But in his case, too, much of the information he obtained came from western European slaves who had been carried off from Hungary in the course of the great invasion of 1241–2. He encountered Hungarians in Batu's following; and in the kaghan's encampment he found a woman from Metz and the Parisian goldsmith Guillaume Buchier and his wife – not to mention an Englishman named Basil and 'a great crowd of Christians – Hungarians, Russians, Alans, Georgians and Armenians'.[64]

*Déracinés* like this naturally longed for deliverance and dreamed that it might reach them through a victorious Catholic army. They therefore played down the Mongols' military strength, both numerical and technical, emphasised the conquerors' vulnerability to revolt by peoples they had subjugated and simply invented Mongol apprehensions about Latin power. Hence, Carpini alleges that the Mongols feared no country on earth apart from Christendom, and that they were numerically fewer and, on an individual level, physically weaker than the Christian nations. He had been told by non-Mongols serving in the imperial forces that in the event of a confrontation with a European army they would willingly mutiny against their masters.[65] Rubruck in turn was careful to mention all those peoples who were still resisting the conquerors.[66] He believed that if the Franks were prepared to tolerate the conditions in which the Mongols lived, they could reduce the whole world.[67] He assured King Louis that if the Mongols themselves learned that the pope was proclaiming a Crusade against them, they would all retire into their wilderness.[68] They had never yet conquered any nation by dint of strength, but only by subterfuge.[69] For him, they were 'no people' and 'a foolish nation' (Deuteronomy 32:21), inferior in power to the fifth-century Huns, whose sway had extended much deeper into Europe – ignoring, of course, the fact that the centre of gravity of Attila's dominions had lain a few thousand miles west of that of the Mongol empire.[70] Carpini had written of his informants, 'They told us about everything willingly and sometimes without being asked, for they knew what we wanted.'[71] Clearly such intelligence, and the use the friars made of it, comprised not merely factual information but also an over-sanguine assessment of the enemy's weaknesses in relation to the Latin world.

## CONCLUSION

In view of the scope and detailed character of their reports, these early missions to the Mongol world admirably fulfilled their purpose of gathering intelligence – of particular importance in Carpini's case. They did not, however, achieve their other aims – whether to deflect the Mongols from further attacks on Christendom or to spread the Gospel. For this there were a number of reasons. One was that the ideal espoused by the friars, that of voluntary (and conspicuous) poverty and abstinence, was absolutely alien to the Mongols, and risked destroying any credit they might enjoy with their hosts. Another reason – and at least as important – was their failure to grasp the implications of the Mongol world-view, namely that the Mongols did not negotiate on equal terms with independent rulers; they had no equals, only subjects or enemies. Carpini and his colleagues seem never to have been aware that their arrival at Güyüg's headquarters betokened a gesture of submission on the pope's part. Unlike Carpini, Rubruck did not set out as an ambassador; rather, he had that status thrust upon him. His reluctance at Soldaia to jeopardise his mission meant that the Mongols treated him as an envoy until he reached Möngke's court; and he travelled back to the west as the kaghan's own ambassador. Both circumstances played an important role in frustrating his evangelistic purpose.

As far as their writings are concerned, the friars courted the risk of misleading their readers by peddling the notion that the Mongols were significantly less formidable than previously thought and stood in fear of western Christian armies. Yet to charge these observers with deceit is to ignore the heavy pressure to which they were subject. Given the presumed imminence of further Mongol attacks on eastern Europe, it was vital to put heart into their fellow Latins in order to maximise resistance. Too much was at stake for them to furnish a more realistic picture.

## Notes

1 Jordan, vicar of the Franciscan province of Bohemia, to all Christ's faithful, 10 April 1242, in Matthew Paris, *Chronica Majora*, 7 vols., ed. H. R. Luard, Rolls Series, 57 (London, 1872–83), vol. VI, p. 81.

2 G. A. Bezzola, *Die Mongolen in abendländischer Sicht (1220–1270): Ein Beitrag zur Frage der Völkerbegegnungen* (Berne and Munich, 1974), pp. 124–49; J. K. Hyde, 'Ethnographers in Search of an Audience', in D. Waley (ed.), *Literacy and Its Uses: Studies on Late Medieval Italy* (Manchester, 1993), pp. 162–216, at pp. 177–8, is more non-committal.

3 'Annales monasterii de Burton', ed. H. R. Luard in *Annales Monastici*, 5 vols., Rolls Series, 36 (London, 1864–9, 5 vols), vol. i, p. 274.

4 Ibid., p. 273.

5 On these two embassies, see Igor de Rachewiltz, *Papal Envoys to the Great Khans* (London, 1971), pp. 112–18.

6 C. Dawson, *The Mongol Mission: Narratives and Letters of the Franciscan Missionaries in Mongolia and China in the Thirteenth and Fourteenth Centuries* (New York, 1980), p. 79.

7 Ibid., pp. 57, 69.

8 P. Jackson, *The Mongols and the West, 1221–1410* (Harlow, 2005), p. 93.

9 Dawson, *Mongol Mission*, p. 3.

10 Ibid., p. 51.

11 Ibid., pp. 57, 69.

12 J. Richard, *La Papauté et les missions d'Orient au Moyen Âge (XIIIe–XVe siècles)* (Rome, 1977), p. 71, n. 27.

13 Dawson, *Mongol Mission*, p. 3, cf. also p. 50.

14 Ibid., pp. 3–4, 66.

15 Ibid., p. 70; D. Sinor, 'John of Plano Carpini's Return from the Mongols: New Light from a Luxemburg Manuscript', *Journal of the Royal Asiatic Society* (1957), 193–206, at 202–6, reprinted in Sinor, *Inner Asia and Its Contacts with Medieval Europe* (London, 1977).

16 Dawson, *Mongol Mission*, p. 65.

17 Salimbene, pp. 196–7, 200–3.

18 On this embassy, see de Rachewiltz, *Papal Envoys*, pp. 121–4.

19 J. de Joinville, *Vie de saint Louis*, in *Joinville and Villehardouin: Chronicles of the Crusades*, trans. C. Smith (London, 2008), p. 267.

20 P. Jackson (ed.), *William of Rubruck Itinerarium: His Journey to the Court of the Great Khan Möngke*, trans. Jackson and D. Morgan, Hakluyt Society, 2nd series, 173 (London, 1990), p. 175.

21 Ibid., pp. 66–7; 97.

22 Ibid., pp. 67, 229, 226.

23 Ibid., pp. 119, 179, 230, 98; 59.

24 Ibid., pp. 144–6, 68, 122, 126.

25 Ibid., pp. 101, 108, 141–2, 156, 167; 183.

26 Ibid., pp. 232–4; B. Z. Kedar, 'The Multilateral Disputation at the Court of the Grand Qan Möngke, 1254', in H. Lazarus-Yafeh, M. R. Cohen, S. Somekh and S. H. Griffith (eds.), *The Majlis: Interreligious Encounters in Medieval Islam* (Wiesbaden, 1999), pp. 162–83.

27 Jackson (ed.), *Itinerarium*, p. 253.

28 Ibid., p. 238.

29 Dawson, *Mongol Mission*, pp. 14, 56, 80, 54–5.

30   A. Mostaert and F. W. Cleaves, 'Trois documents mongols des archives secrètes vaticanes', *Harvard Journal of Asiatic Studies*, 15 (1952), 419–506, at 485, 492–3.

31   Jackson, *The Mongols and the West*, p. 135.

32   K.-E. Lupprian, *Die Beziehungen der Päpste zu islamischen und mongolischen Herrschern im 13. Jahrhundert* (Rome, 1981), pp. 147, 148 (no. 21); cf. trans. in Dawson, *Mongol Mission*, p. 76.

33   Dawson, *Mongol Mission*, p. 53.

34   P. Pelliot, 'Les Mongols et la papauté', part 1, *Revue de l'Orient Chrétien*, 23 (1922–3), 3–30: see Persian text of Güyüg's letter at 17, lines 5–7 (French trans. at 18–19); English trans. in de Rachewiltz, *Papal Envoys*, appendix, p. 213.

35   Jackson (ed.), *Itinerarium*, pp. 66–8; 134.

36   Ibid., p. 132.

37   Ibid., pp. 171, 119.

38   Ibid., 172, 179.

39   Ibid., pp. 117, 133, 179.

40   Ibid., pp. 230, 250, 229.

41   Ibid., p. 132.

42   Dawson, *Mongol Mission*, pp. 56, 51; 64–6; also 27.

43   Jackson (ed.), *Itinerarium*, p. 68.

44   Ibid., pp. 101, 115, 179, 100.

45   Ibid., pp. 188, 207–8.

46   Ibid., pp. 132, 173, 141.

47   Ibid., pp. 271, 278.

48   Ibid., pp. 237, 278.

49   Salimbene, pp. 196–201.

50   Dawson, *Mongol Mission*, pp. 71–2.

51   M. Plezia, 'L'Apport de la Pologne à l'exploration de l'Asie centrale au milieu du XIIIe siècle', *Acta Poloniae Historica*, 22 (1970), 18–35, at 20–1.

52   D. Ostrowski, 'Second-Redaction Additions in Carpini's *Ystoria Mongalorum*', in F. E. Sysyn (ed.), *Adelphotes: A Tribute to Omeljan Pritsak by His Students*, Harvard Ukrainian Studies 14, pts. 3–4 (Cambridge, Mass., 1990), pp. 522–50.

53   In Yale (the MS used for the printed edition) and in Lucerne (only recently discovered): G. G. Guzman, 'The Vinland Map Controversy and the Discovery of a Second Version of the *Tartar Relation*: The Authenticity of the 1339 Text', *Terrae Incognitae*, 38 (2006), 19–25.

54   J. Charpentier, 'William of Rubruck and Roger Bacon', in A. Wallén (ed.), *Hyllningsskrift tillägnad Sven Hedin på hans 70-årsdag den 19. febr. 1935* (Stockholm, 1935), pp. 255–67.

55   P. Chiesa, 'Testo e tradizione dell'"Itinerarium" di Guglielmo di Rubruck', *Filologia Latina*, 15 (2008), 133–216, esp. 193.

56   Dawson, *Mongol Mission*, pp. 14–15, 16; Hyde, 'Ethnographers', pp. 173–6, 178–83. For a different appraisal of the two reports, see F. Fernández-Armesto, 'Medieval Ethnography', *Journal of the Anthropological Society of Oxford*, 13 (1982), 275–86.

57 Dawson, *Mongol Mission*, p. 21.
58 Jackson (ed.), *Itinerarium*, pp. 158, 142, 85.
59 Ibid., pp. 129, 201.
60 Dawson, *Mongol Mission*, pp. 51, 70–1.
61 Ibid., pp. 4, 71.
62 Ibid., pp. 23, 31.
63 Ibid., p. 66.
64 Jackson (ed.), *Itinerarium*, pp. 135; 182, 242, 203, 212, 232, 240, 245, 212, 213.
65 Dawson, *Mongol Mission*, pp. 44, 49.
66 Jackson (ed.), *Itinerarium*, pp. 65, 112, 161, 259.
67 Ibid., p. 278.
68 Ibid., p. 107.
69 Ibid., p. 227.
70 Ibid., p. 139.
71 Dawson, *Mongol Mission*, p. 66.

## 15  Franciscan missions

E. RANDOLPH DANIEL

Brother Giles of Assisi was the first Franciscan to go as a missionary to the Muslims. He had become one of Francis's companions on 23 April 1208, joining soon after Bernard of Quintavalle. According to Thomas of Celano

> [Giles] lived for a long time: he was holy, living justly and piously. He left us examples of perfect obedience, work, including work with his hands, solitary life and holy contemplation.[1]

In 1209, when the number of brothers had increased to eight, Francis sent them out in pairs. Bernard and Giles journeyed to Santiago de Compostela, the pilgrimage site in Galicia in the north-west of the Iberian peninsula, where the apostle James, son of Zebedee and brother of John, was reputed to be buried. Santiago, as the Iberians called him, had become a rallying cry of the Christian warriors who since the eleventh century had fought in the Reconquest, the struggle to reconquer and christianise the peninsula from the northern mountains southwards.[2]

According to the *Shorter Life of Giles*, he returned to Assisi from Santiago and then went to the shrine of St Michael on Monte Gargano and that of St Nicholas at Bari. Leo adds:

> As [Giles] went about the world he urged men and women to fear and love the creator of heaven and earth and to do penance for their sins. One day, when he was thoroughly worn out and suffering from hunger, he slept by the roadside. He was awakened from sleep by the favour of God, who does not abandon those whose hope is in him, and Giles found half a loaf at his head. Giving thanks to God he ate and was sustained.[3]

Sometime after his return from Santiago, Giles received permission to take a companion with him on a pilgrimage to the Holy Places in Palestine. While he was delayed in Brindisi waiting for a boat, Giles obtained a water jug, filled it with water and went through the streets crying out, 'Who wants to buy water?' In exchange for the water Giles got the necessities that he and his companion needed. After his visit to the burial place of Jesus and the other holy sites, Giles stayed in Acre. There he obtained straw with which he made baskets of the kind that were used in that town. He also helped carry the corpses of the dead to the cemetery, and he ferried water from the wells to people's homes in exchange for food and shelter. When his labour failed to obtain bread and lodging, Giles turned to the table of the Lord, begging alms from door to door.[4]

The dying Francis spoke about the earliest days of the brotherhood, saying in his *Testament*:

> And those who came to receive life gave whatever they had to the poor and were content with one tunic, patched inside and out, with a cord and short trousers. We desired nothing more...and we were simple and subject to all. I worked with my hands and I still desire to work; and I earnestly desire all brothers to give themselves to honest work. Let those who do not know how to work learn, not from desire to receive wages, but for example and to avoid idleness. And when we are not paid for our work, let us have recourse to the table of the Lord, begging alms from door to door.

Brother Leo, if he was indeed the author of the *Longer Life of Giles*, clearly had Francis's *Testament* in mind when he wrote there that Giles 'turned to the table of the Lord', but Giles was also probably one of the examples that Francis had in mind when he dictated his *Testament*. As already explained, Giles performed the most menial tasks. By devoting himself to such work Giles was, to quote Francis, 'simple and subject to all'. Having given up all of his possessions, Giles subsisted by working with his hands and by begging alms. A lay brother, he employed simple and direct langue to call people to repent. His manner was gentle, and it was primarily by means of his voluntary poverty, his humility and his willingness to work that he proclaimed the Gospel. When he saw an opportunity, he was willing to call Christians, and presumably Muslims, to repentance. If he ever went to a mosque or public market and loudly and vocally denounced Muhammad and the Qur'an the incident has escaped mention, and everything that we know about Giles makes such an incident unlikely.

In 1212, Francis himself had set out for Syria 'to preach the Christian faith and repentance to the Saracens and other non-believers'. However, contrary winds made it impossible for him to find a ship going to Syria, so he had to return to Assisi. Shortly after this he decided to go to Morocco to preach the Gospel to its Almohad ruler. He became seriously ill in Spain and once again had to turn back. In 1219, Francis travelled to Egypt, where the army of the fifth Crusade was battling the Muslims. Francis succeeded in obtaining an audience with the sultan, al-Malik-al-Kâmil. Accounts of this audience differ significantly one from another. We cannot know with any certainty what Francis said, except that he impressed al-Kâmal with his humility, his poverty and his attitude of submission. Clearly, Francis refrained from saying anything that would have caused him to be seized and condemned. Thus, although Thomas of Celano steadfastly maintains that Francis was driven to go to the Muslims by his desire for martyrdom, Francis did nothing in Egypt that would have compelled the sultan to order his execution. Francis did not condemn Muhammad or the Qur'an.[5]

Francis went from Egypt to Syria. Problems had arisen among the friars while Francis was in Egypt, and word of these reached him at Acre. Taking Brother Elias, who had been minister provincial of the Holy Land since 1217, Peter Catania and Caesar of Speyer, Francis journeyed back to Italy, probably in 1220. Once there Francis asked Caesar to work with him on enlarging and polishing the *Rule* of 1221 (or RNB).[6] Among the changes was the insertion of a chapter headed 'Those Going among the Saracens and Other Non-believers', in which it says:

> The Lord says: 'Behold I am sending you like sheep in the midst of wolves.' Therefore 'be prudent as serpents and simple as doves' [Matthew 10: 16]. Let any brother, then, who desires by divine inspiration to go among the Saracens and other non-believers go with the permission of his minister and servant. If he sees they are fit to be sent, the minister may give them permission and not oppose them, for he will be bound to render an accounting to the Lord if he has proceeded without discernment in this and other matters. As for the brothers who go, they can live spiritually among the Saracens and non-believers in two ways. One way is not to engage in arguments or disputes but to be subject to every human creature for God's sake and to acknowledge that they are Christians. The other way is to announce the word of God, when they see it pleases the Lord, in order that [non-believers] may believe in almighty God, the Father, the Son and the Holy Spirit...and be baptised... Wherever they may be, let all my brothers remember that they have given themselves and abandoned their bodies to the Lord

Jesus Christ. For love of him, they must make themselves vulnerable to their enemies, both visible and invisible.

(RNB, 16)

This new chapter 16 does two things. First, it provides a means by which friars who wanted to go as missionaries could be examined as to their aptitude for mission. The ministers were given no guidelines to use in making decisions but were simply warned that God would judge them on the basis of their choices. Neither the Benedictine *Rule* nor the Augustinian *Rule* for canons had had such a chapter, and Francis was effectively breaking new ground here.

Secondly, Francis instructs the brothers who get permission that they should be on their best behaviour among the Muslims and the non-believers. The primary duty of the brothers among the latter is 'not to engage in arguments or disputes' but to be subject to the people around them while letting them know that the friars are Christians. Instead of provoking arguments, the brothers are to act as Giles had done, to take on the most humiliating of tasks, carrying water jars and coffins for example, in return for daily sustenance. The brothers are, in other words, to be truly brothers *minor*, lesser brothers, the meekest of the meek and the poorest of the poor. Only when they see that Muslims and non-believers are favourably disposed to listen are the Franciscans to urge repentance. Francis is discouraging, if not forbidding, such tactics as publicly denouncing Muhammad and the Qur'an. Jesus had subjected himself to the authorities even when he was condemned to be crucified. By exemplifying subjection the brothers were, in Francis's opinion, making Muslims aware of who Jesus really was and of the meaning of his Gospel.

Why did Francis insert these instructions into the *Rule* of 1221? The obvious explanation is that he wanted to share with the brothers his experiences before the sultan. He had first exhibited subjection and humility and then, when he was in the presence of the sultan, had urged the latter to convert and be baptised. Francis had not denounced Muhammad or the Qur'an. He had not engaged in a formal disputation. Undoubtedly, Francis knew that Giles had behaved in a similar manner.

J. Hoeberichts argued that Francis had in mind Innocent III's bull summoning Christians to the fifth Crusade. Innocent had insisted that all Christians, male and female, young and old, ought to 'deny themselves and take up their crosses' on behalf of Christ either by enlisting in or supporting the Crusade. Like feudal vassals, all Christians were bound to come to the aid of their Lord. Then Innocent denounced Muhammad as a false prophet and the Muslims as perfidious. After

Innocent's death, Honorius III and then Gregory IX perpetuated Innocent's policies.[7] Francis, according to Hoeberichts, set forth a policy that advocated approaching the Muslims peacefully and demonstrating to them Christ-like bahaviour and love rather than coming against them with swords drawn and shouts of denunciation.[8]

At the chapter held at the Porziuncula in 1219, during which Francis decided to go to Egypt, he also sent six brothers to the Almohad ruler in Morocco. These brothers were Vitalis, Beraldus, Peter, Adiutum, Accursius and Otho. In the kingdom of Aragon Vitalis became ill and ordered the other five to go ahead without him. Going first to Portugal, the brothers went on to Seville where, after staying with a Christian host for a week, they decided to go to the mosque. The Muslims refused to allow them to enter, so they went to the palace, where they told the prince: 'We are Christians and we come from the Roman districts. We are sent to you from the king of kings, the Lord our God, for the salvation of your souls.'[9]

From Seville the friars were taken to Morocco, where they were executed, on 16 January 1220.[10] According to the *Passio*, when Francis heard about the execution of the brothers he exclaimed: 'Now I can truly say that I have five brothers.'[11] However, Jordan of Giano says:

> When the life and history of these aforementioned martyrs were
> brought to Blessed Francis, hearing that he himself was praised
> in them and seeing that the other brothers were taking pride in
> the sufferings of these brothers, inasmuch as he held himself
> in the greatest contempt and despised praise and glory, he spurned
> the accounts and forbade them to be read, and said: 'Everyone
> should glory in his own suffering and not in that of another.'[12]

Did Francis have these five brothers in mind when he drafted chapter 16 of the *Rule* of 1221? We can never know with any certainty, but it is certainly a possibility. In the rule which Honorius III confirmed on 29 November 1223 chapter 16 was reduced to these words:

> Let those brothers who wish by divine inspiration to go among the
> Saracens or other non-believers ask permission to go from their
> ministers provincial. These ministers, however, may not grant
> permission except to those whom they see fit to be sent.[13]

Although Francis's instructions about submission and the conduct of missionaries were dropped from the approved *Rule*, the Franciscans retained the notion that missionaries should first set an example by their works before they preached.[14]

## FRIARS AS PAPAL AND ROYAL ENVOYS
## TO THE MONGOLS

Europeans were shocked when news reached them that an unknown army had struck the Russian principalities, Poland and Hungary between 1237 and 1240. Then, in 1241, another army swept through Poland and defeated the Germans before halting on the shores of Dalmatia, facing the Adriatic Sea. Temujin (Temuchin), the Mongol leader, had been born in the 1160s. By the time he died, in 1227, he was called 'Supreme Ruler', or Chinggis Khan (Jenghiz Khan). His armies had swept over northern China, central Asia and northern Persia. Batu, who led the Mongols to the Adriatic in 1241, was Temujin's grandson. He established a principality in southern Russia that he called the Golden Horde. Its capital was Sarai on the Volga.

In 1258, another grandson of Temujin, Hulagu, captured Baghdad, abolished the Caliphate and advanced towards Egypt. However, the Mamluk Baybars won a victory over the Mongols at Ain Jalut in 1260. Nevertheless, Syria, Mesopotamia and Persia became part of another Mongol principality, based in Persia. In China, Kublai, yet another of Temujin's grandsons, was elected khan in 1260. He ruled until his death in 1294. The Mongols also conquered southern China and plundered Hanoi in 1258. Hence, the authority of the Mongol khans extended from eastern Europe to south-east Asia from the middle of the thirteenth into the second half of the fourteenth centuries.[15]

Since 1237 Gregory IX and Emperor Frederick II (d. 1250) had been locked in a war that on both sides rapidly became an apocalyptic struggle to the death. Innocent IV badly needed to blunt the threat of the Mongols. He decided to send two papal bulls to the great Khan and entrusted them to two Franciscans, John of Plano Carpini and Lawrence of Portugal. Benedict the Pole joined them because he had contacts with the princes of eastern Europe and also spoke some of the languages of the area. The trio of friars left at the beginning of Lent 1246. By midsummer they had reached the camp of Orda, the oldest brother of Batu. On 22 July they arrived at the camp of Güyüg, who had just been elected the great khan. They gave the papal bulls to Güyüg. They refused to take Mongol envoys back with them but did take the khan's letter to the pope. In 1247, they were back at Batu's camp on the Volga and were given permission to go to Kiev, from where they could return to the papal court.[16]

John of Plano Carpini's *History of the Mongols* was written shortly after he returned to Italy. The work is remarkable for the relatively objective perspective from which he was able to view the Mongols and the care with which he made his observations and recorded them.

> The [Mongols] are quite different from all other men, for they are broader than other people between the eyes and across the cheek-bones. Their cheeks are also rather prominent above their jaws; they have a flat and small nose, their eyes are little and their eyelids raised up to the eyebrows. For the most part, but with a few exceptions, they are slender about the waist; almost all are of medium height.[17]

They practised polygamy and married their relatives, except for their mother, their daughter or their sister by the same mother (they could marry sisters born to other mothers). They lived in tents made of twigs and slender poles, covered with felt. A hole was left in the centre for the smoke from the fire to escape. All of these dwellings were portable. The Mongols were exceedingly rich in animals, camels, oxen, sheep, goats and especially horses and mares. However, they had no pigs or cattle.[18]

> They believe in one God, and they believe that he is the maker of all things visible, and invisible; and that it is he who is the giver of the good things of this world as well as the hardships; they do not, however, worship him with prayers or praises or any kind of ceremony.[19] They did have idols, representing men and also representing udders, and they made offerings of milk.[20]

John was struck by the loyalty of the Mongols to their leaders and also by the peaceful relationships between them. Fights and murder never occurred, and thefts were rare. The Mongols were patient and disdained luxury, and there was no litigation between them. Their diet consisted of meat and milk. Children were taught to ride from the time that they were 2 or 3 years old and from childhood were taught to handle and shoot arrows from bows. One of the reasons for their military success was that they were able to ride all day, every day without becoming fatigued on their fast horses. Hence, European leaders believed that the Mongol armies must have been much larger than they were, because reliable witnesses reported them in places so distant from each other that no European army, with their large horses and heavily armoured knights, could have covered the same ground:

> Young girls and women ride and gallop on horseback with agility like the men. We even saw them carrying bows and arrows. Both the men and the women are able to endure long stretches of riding...Their women make everything, leather garments, tunics, shoes, leggings

and everything made of leather; they also drive the carts and repair them, they load the camels, and in all their tasks they are very swift and energetic. All the women wear breeches and some of them shoot like the men.[21]

Next, John inserted a brief history of the Mongols that began with the rise of Temujin and outlined their conquests. Then he described the organisation, equipment and tactics of the Mongol armies and the policies they practised towards peoples that they conquered. John offered advice on how European rulers could resist and defeat the Mongols in the light of the threat by the Great Khan Güyüg to conquer 'the Roman Empire and all Christian kingdoms and the nations of the west, unless they obey the instructions he is sending to the Lord Pope, the rulers and the peoples of the west'.[22]

Finally, John recounted the journey itself. His book made an immediate sensation. The chronicler Salimbene wrote:

> Behold, Brother John of Piano Carpini returned from the king, to whom he had been sent by the pope, and he had with him the book that he had written on the Tartars. The brothers then read the book in his presence, and he himself interpreted it and explained passages that seemed difficult or hard to believe. And I ate with Brother John, both at the convent of the Friars Minor and in abbeys and other important places not once nor twice. For he was gladly invited to lunch and to dinner, for a number of reasons – because he was a papal legate, because he was ambassador to a king, because he had gone among the Tartars, but also because he was a friar minor.[23]

John of Piano Carpini had gone to the Mongols as an envoy of Pope Innocent IV. His was a diplomatic mission, the purpose of which was to assess the threat posed by the Mongols and if possible to open negotiations between the Great Khan and the pope. In 1252/3, William of Rubruck was sent by Louis IX of France to Sartaq, a son of Batu, Khan of the Golden Horde. The king had heard that Sartaq was a Christian. Thus William's goal was religious. He was to find out whether Sartaq was a Christian and, if he was, to enlist his support for the Crusade against the Muslims. Bartholomew of Cremona accompanied William. A clerk named Gosset had charge of the presents that Louis IX had sent to Sartaq. The fourth member of the group was named Homo dei or Abdullah, who was to act as interpreter.[24]

On 7 May 1253, William and his party set sail from Constantinople on the Black Sea, and by 21 May they were at Sudak on the Crimean peninsula, where merchants equipped them for their journey to the ordas of Sartaq and Batu. Orda is the Mongol name for the encampments in which the Mongol khans had their courts. Before continuing to trace his journey, William described the Mongols briefly. Most of his description is similar to that given earlier by John of Piano Carpini. However, William did insert a section on the making of *cosmos*, the milk from mares that served as the chief food of the Mongols. The group reached the River Don on 22 July 1253 and arrived at Sartaq's orda on 31 July.[25]

On 1 August, William presented the letter from King Louis IX to Sartaq and showed him the Psalter and the Bible that he had brought, as well as sacred vestments. Sartaq kept the letter, which William had had translated into Arabic and Syriac, but sent the other gifts back with William and his group. Because of diplomatic issues raised in the letter, Sartaq said that William had to travel to Batu. Leaving the Psalter behind, William then travelled eastwards to the orda of Batu. The Franciscan was warned, however, by the servants of Sartaq:

> 'Do not say that our master is a Christian, for he is not a Christian but a Mongol'[26]...This is because the word Christianity appears to them to be the name of a race, and they are proud to such a degree that although perhaps they believe something of Christ, nevertheless they are unwilling to be called Christians, wanting their own name, that is Mongol, to be exalted above every other name...[27]
>
> As for Sartaq, whether he believes in Christ or not, I do not know. But I do know that he does not wish to be called a Christian, rather indeed he seems to me to hold Christians in derision.[28]

William found Batu's orda on the bank of the River Volga. His first sensation was fear:

> For [Batu's] own houses seemed like a great city stretching out a long way and crowded round on every side by people to a distance of 3 or 4 leagues. Just as the people of Israel knew, each one of them, where they should pitch their tents in relation to the tabernacle, so these know on what side of the orda they are to place themselves when they unload their dwellings. In their tongue the court is called 'orda', which means the middle, because it is always in the middle of his people, with the exception that no one places himself due south, for the doors of the court open in that direction. But to the right and to the left they stretch out as far as they wish according to the number of sites required, so long as they do not set themselves down right in front of or opposite the court.[29]

Batu asked William to tell him who the enemy was against which King Louis IX was waging war. William answered that Louis IX was fighting the Saracens, 'who are violating the house of God in Jerusalem'. Batu also asked if Louis had ever sent envoys to him, and William answered that Louis had never sent envoys to Batu himself. This meeting between Batu and William of Rubruck took place nearly five years before Hulagu's army took Baghdad, destroyed the Caliphate, moved westwards into Syria and threatened Egypt (1258). Such an attack was undoubtedly already in the minds of the Mongol leaders. Batu thus decided that William had to be sent to the court of Mangu, the great khan.[30]

During his journey to Mangu, William encountered Buddhists:

[They] build their temples from east to west, and on the north side they make an alcove, projecting as a choir, or sometimes, if the building is square, it is in the middle of the building. On the north side they shut off an alcove in place of a choir. And there they put a chest, long and wide like a table, and behind that chest they place their chief idol facing south: the one I myself saw at Caracorum was as big as St Christopher is depicted.[31]

All their priests shave their heads all over, and their beards, and they wear saffron garments and observe chastity from the time they shave their heads; they live together, one or two hundred in one community...As long as they are in the temple they keep their heads uncovered, and they read to themselves and keep silence.[32]

Another religion that William encountered was Manichaeanism. Mani, who lived in the Persian empire in the second half of the third century AD, was a dualist who believed that there were two gods, one representing good, the other evil. Earthly life was dominated by the struggle between those two principles. Augustine of Hippo was for some years an adherent of Manichaeanism because it seemed to explain satisfactorily the problem of how evil could exist in a good world. Dualism survived the efforts of the Church to repress it and appeared in thirteenth-century Europe as Catharism.[33] William calls the Manichaeans *tuins*.[34]

The Nestorians were William's principle concern, however, because they were Christians. Nestorius was consecrated patriarch of Constantinople in 428, having been chosen by the Roman Emperor Theodosius II. In 429, he preached against the notion that Mary, the mother of Jesus, was *theotokos*, 'God-bearing'. He was deposed and condemned in 430; he died c.451. Nestorius defended the notion that Jesus Christ possessed two complete natures, the one divine and the other human. His opponents attacked him on the ground that his theology did not put sufficient emphasis on the unity of these two natures in the one person. Nestorius's disciples were driven out of the Roman empire by their opponents, the Monophysites and the Chalcedonians. They then fled into the Persian empire and from there eastwards through central Asia to China. They were sometimes called Chaldeans.[35]

Muslims were of course numerous among the peoples ruled by the Mongols. The Mongol khans held to their own shamanist religion, and their policy towards the varied religious groups was tolerant. William, whose ostensible purpose was religious, found himself in a situation that must have been both exciting and scary. He could learn about and try to convert these people, but he also could create trouble for himself if he took a wrong step.

William and his party reached the orda of Mangu in December 1253. Mangu almost immediately summoned them to appear before him and asked why they had come. William replied: 'We heard that Sartaq was a Christian; we went to him; the French king sent him a private letter by us; Sartaq sent us to his father; his father sent us here. He must have written the reason why.'

The Mongol officials asked: 'Does the king wish to make peace with us?'

> William answered: He sent a letter to Sartaq as a Christian, and if he had known that he was not a Christian, he would never have sent him a letter. As for making peace, all I can say is he has never done you any injury; if he had done anything to give you grounds for making war on him and his people he would gladly wish, as a just man, to make amends and seek peace. If you, without cause, desire to make war on him and his people, we trust that God, who is just, will come to their aid.

William adds that the Mongols' pride convinced them that the whole world wanted to make peace with them, but that he, if he had been 'given leave' would have preached war 'throughout the whole world with all my strength' against them.[36] Pressed by the Mongols on why he had come to the orda of Mangu, William answered simply that he had come because Batu had ordered him to come.[37]

William stayed at the orda of Mangu until June 1254. During this period he repeatedly met Mangu and representatives of the other religious communities that lived in the vicinity of the orda. Near the end of this period, Mangu ordered that a kind of disputation be held over which three of his scribes would preside. William held his own during the discussion. At the end 'they all listened without a word of contradiction, yet not one of them said, "I believe, I wish to become a Christian."'[38] At his final audience with Mangu, the khan told William that the Mongols believed that there was but one God. Then he criticised the Christians because they have the Scriptures but do not obey them. The Mongols, Mangu said, have soothsayers, and they follow their advice strictly and live in peace.[39]

Mangu had a letter composed that William was to take back to Louis IX that stated that there was one god and one lord on earth, the khan of khans (Mangu). Mangu had wished to send envoys, but William refused to take them, citing the dangers of the journey. Therefore, Mangu was sending this letter to Louis, urging him to read it and, if he wished, to obey Mangu and be at peace with him to send envoys to Mangu.[40]

John of Piano Carpini and William of Rubruck had been sent as envoys of Innocent IV and Louis IX, even if William insisted that his only mission was to meet Sartaq and find out whether he was a Christian. Odoric of Pordenone seems to have undertaken his far-reaching journey with no more incentive than the possibility of making conversions on the way. As his name suggests, Odoric was born in Pordenone, located in the Friulian plain north of Venice, sometime after 1265 and not later than 1286. He became a Franciscan in either his late teens or early 20s and showed a definite preference for the eremitical life. He began his journey to the Orient in 1318 at the latest but perhaps as many as four years earlier. He returned from it in 1330 and died on 13 January 1331. He probably dictated his *Relatio*, the manuscripts of which show that the work has had a complicated and tangled history.[41]

Odoric set out from Venice and went first to Constantinople, from which city he travelled to Trebizond on the Black Sea and thence overland to Iest (modern-day Yazd), some 300 miles south-east of Tehran. At some point during this journey, Odoric went into the area of modern-day Iraq, where he observed a wedding that he later recounted:

> I saw a young man who was taking to wife a beautiful young woman, and she was accompanied by other beautiful maidens, who were weeping and wailing, whilst the young bridegroom stood by in very gay clothes, with his head hanging down. And by and by the young man mounted his ass, and the bride followed him barefoot and wretchedly dressed, and holding by the ass, and her father went behind blessing them until they reached the husband's house.

Clearly, the bride's father had had a prominent role in arranging the marriage, a marriage about which the bride was not happy.[42] Arranged marriages were also common in Christian Europe, but during the later twelfth and thirteenth centuries the Church required both parties to a marriage to give their personal consent to the union, a requirement that gave women some relief from conditions like those that Odoric described.

Friar Thomas of Tolentino had been one of the friars from the March of Ancona who, like Angelo Clareno, had been imprisoned by their provincial chapter at the time of the second Council of Lyons in 1274. Later, Thomas and three other Franciscans, James of Padua, Peter of Siena and Demetrius, arrived in Tana in southern India. The four brothers were staying clandestinely with a married Christian couple, but one day the couple quarrelled and the wife in anger revealed the presence of the friars to the kadi. The friars refused to convert to Islam, denounced Muhammad and the Qur'an, and were condemned to death. They survived attempts to burn them but were finally executed in April 1321. Odoric arrived in Tana after the martyrs had been killed and collected their bones, which he then took to the Franciscan friaries at Zaytun (Zhangzhou) in southern China.[43]

Odoric visited Malabar on the south-west coast of India from where pepper came, and the growing of which he describes in some detail. The rivers in that area also contained crocodiles.[44]

From India Odoric went to Sumatra and Java and then to a kingdom that he called Zampa (Da Nang?) located on the coast of Vietnam.[45] From Vietnam Odoric travelled up the coast of southern China, which he called Upper India. Then he visited Canton, where he was amazed that one could buy 300 pounds of fresh ginger for less than a groat, and that the geese were much bigger and finer and cheaper than anywhere else.[46]

Finally, Odoric reached Beijing:

> I, friar Odoric, was full three years in that city...and often present at [the Mongol khan's] festivals...for we friars minor have a place assigned to us at the emperor's court and we are always duty-bound to go and give him our benison ...[47] The great khan has set up a system of hostelries, called *yams*, throughout the Mongols' khanates where any traveller can have two free meals. The great khan has also established a system by which important news can be sent to the khans by means of mounted messengers or messengers who travel on foot.[48]

After his three-year stay in Beijing Odoric travelled back to Italy, where his minister provincial, Friar Guidotto, ordered him to record in writing what he had seen and done on his journey. Odoric dictated this *Relation* (*Relatio*) to Friar William of Solagna in May 1330, a year before he died.[49]

## JOHN OF MONTECORVINO AND RAMON LLULL

In 1286, Argun, khan in Persia, sent Rabban Sauna as his envoy to the west. Sauna arrived in Rome in 1287. He was a Nestorian, whose disciple, Mark, had become head of the Nestorian Church in 1281, bearing the title of Mar Jabalaha III. Rabban Sauna was cordially received at the papal court. Sauna's request for missionaries motivated Nicholas IV, a Franciscan, to send a missionary to China.[50] Argun was sufficiently pleased by the friars' zeal to build a chapel for Sauna that communicated with the royal tent, and Argun may also have promised to receive baptism when an alliance of Mongols and western Christians had conquered Jerusalem. Unfortunately, the papacy was preoccupied with the struggle between the Angevins and the Aragonese for Sicily, and only Edward I of England grasped the possibilities of the alliance, but his efforts were fruitless. Acre fell in 1291 to the Muslims and by that time Argun had already died.[51]

John of Montecorvino was the friar chosen to go to the Mongols. Nicholas IV gave John letters to Kublai in Beijing and to Kaidu in central Asia. John set out from Rome in 1289, visited Argun in Tabriz and then, in 1291, went to visit Kublai in Beijing. Because of wars, John had to go by way of India, where he spent a year at Mylapur in Madras. When he reached Beijing Kublai had just died, but his successor, Timor, welcomed John, who remained in Beijing until his death in 1327. After the friar overcame initial opposition from the Nestorians, the khan permitted him to build a church and a convent near the royal residence that included a tower with six bells. This was finished by 1299. By 1305 John had baptised some 6,000 people. He had also purchased in the market forty boys who were the sons of pagans. John baptised them and taught them Latin and the Latin rite. He also wrote for them some thirty Psalters and hymnals, as well as two breviaries. He taught them to sing and clearly hoped that they would form the basis of a native priesthood. By 1305, John was building another church. In that year he wrote back to the west reporting what he had done and strongly requesting that more friars be sent. In 1306, he sent another letter to the leaders of the order because he had heard nothing as a result of the first. An expeditionary force of seven bishops was sent out as a result of the second letter. Three arrived in Beijing and consecrated John archbishop of Beijing.[52]

John died in Beijing in 1327 and was probably archbishop when Odoric was there. Letters also survive from Brother Peregrinus, bishop of Zaytun, and from another bishop, Brother Andrew of Perugia, who was also in Zaytun. Friar John of Marignollo was sent from Avignon in 1338 and arrived in Beijing in 1342. He stayed until 1347, when he started back to Avignon. James of Florence, the last bishop of Zaytun, was martyred by the Chinese in 1362, and in 1369 the friars were expelled from Beijing. The friars had come with the Mongols and so were associated in Chinese eyes with them – hence they were expelled with them.[53]

While John of Montecorvino was intent on building up a Latin Christian church among the Mongols and their allies in China, Ramon Llull (1232?–1316?) was a married courtier of Jaime I of Aragon when he experienced a conversion that led him to make provision for his wife and children, sell his possessions and dedicate himself to three goals: 'to be martyred as a missionary; to write a book against the errors of the infidels; and to urge the establishment of missionary colleges'.[54] He studied Arabic until he could speak, read and write it. Jaime I funded a missionary college that Llull founded at Miramar on Majorca which flourished briefly (1276–92). He went to Tunis in 1292–3 and to Algeria in 1307, from both of which he was deported after trying to engage learned Muslims in debates. He wrote his *Ars Magna* in 1270 and lectured tirelessly on it at royal courts and also at the papal court, as well as at universities. He also propagandised for the widespread establishment of missionary colleges that would teach Arabic. Llull was responsible for the decree of the Council of Vienne in 1311 that ordered the establishment of such colleges at the universities of Rome, Salamanca, Bologna, Paris and Oxford. In 1294 or 1295 Lull became a Franciscan tertiary. Late tradition has it that he was stoned to death at Bugia, Algeria, in 1315 or 1316.[55]

## CONCLUSION

From the initial journeys of Giles and Francis on, a stream of friars dedicated themselves to missions, especially among the Muslims and the Mongols. Francis's advice to set an example first before preaching was excluded from the *Rule* but seems nonetheless to have been fairly widely heeded. The Mongol conquests and the establishment of khanates from the Volga to China created an opportunity that the friars John of Piano Carpini, William of Rubruck and, most especially, John of Montecorvino grasped. They enjoyed some success in Beijing and Zaytun, but their numbers were too few, the size of the task was too huge and their fortunes were too closely linked to the political survival of the Mongol khans. By the middle of the fourteenth century, the tide had turned and missionary efforts were wound down, not to be revived until Columbus opened the way to the New World at the end of the fifteenth century.

## Notes

1  1 Cel., 25.
2  1 Cel., 30. Two lives of Giles survive. The shorter version, attributed to Brother Leo, has been edited and translated by Rosalind Brooke in an appendix to her *Scripta Leonis, Rufini et Angeli Sociorum S. Francisci. The Writings of Leo, Rufino and Angelo, Companions of St Francis*, OMT (Oxford, 1970, corrected reprint, 1990), pp. 305–9. For the journey to Santiago, see *The Life of Blessed Brother Giles*, c. 3, ibid., pp. 322–5 (hereafter *Shorter Life of Giles*). The longer version (hereafter *Longer Life of Giles*) is now part of the *Chronica XXIV Generalium Ordinis Minorum*, in *Analecta Franciscana* (Quaracchi, 1928), vol. III, pp. 74–115; on the journey to Santiago, see pp. 76–7. The authorship of the longer life is uncertain.
3  *Shorter Life of Giles*, c. 4, in R. B. Brooke (ed.), *Scripta Leonis*, pp. 324–5; see also the *Longer Life of Giles*, pp. 77–8.
4  *Longer Life of Giles*, p. 77. J. R. H. Moorman, *A History of the Franciscan Order: From Its Origins to the Year 1517* (Oxford, 1968), p. 227, dates Giles's pilgrimage to Palestine to 1215.
5  1 Cel., 55–7. J. Hoeberichts, *Francis and Islam* (Quincy, Ill., 1997) pp. 43–59, argues that Francis went on a peace mission, not a quest for martyrdom. Jordan of Giano, no. 10, pp. 25–6:

> [Francis], burning with love for the passion of Christ, he himself the same year that he sent his brothers out [1219], faced the certain dangers of the sea and, crossing over to the infidels, betook himself to the sultan. But before he came to him, he was beset with many outrages and insults and, being ignorant of the language of his tormentors, he cried out amidst the blows: 'Sultan! Sultan!' And thus he was led before the sultan, was honourably received by him and was treated kindly in his infirmity. But since he could not harvest any fruit among them and was disposed to return home, he was led at the order of the sultan by an armed guard to the Christian army that was at the time besieging Damietta.

6  Jordan of Giano, nos. 11–17, pp. 26–34; Moorman, *History*, pp. 48–52.
7  L. and J. Riley-Smith, *The Crusades: Idea and Reality 1095–1274*, Documents of Medieval History, 4 (London, 1981), pp. 118–24.
8  Hoeberichts, *Francis*, pp. 7–134.
9  *Passio sanctorum martyrum fratrum, Beraldi, Petri, Adiuti, Accursii, Othonis in Marochio martyrizatorum*, in *Analecta Franciscana*

(Quaracchi, 1928), vol. III, p. 584. My translation. The complete *Passio* is found on pp. 579–96.

10   Ibid., p. 590.

11   Ibid., p. 593.

12   Jordan of Giano, no. 8, p. 24.

13   The *Rule* of 1223, c. 12, in *FAED*, vol. I, p. 106.

14   E. Randolph Daniel, *The Franciscan Concept of Mission in the High Middle Ages* (Lexington, 1975 and St Bonaventure, 1992), pp. 37–54.

15   C. Dawson, *Mission to Asia* (New York, 1966), originally published as *The Mongol Mission* (London, 1955), pp. xi–xv.

16   Ibid., pp. xv–xviii.

17   Ibid., p. 6.

18   Ibid., pp. 6–8.

19   Ibid., p. 9.

20   Ibid., p. 9.

21   Ibid., p. 18.

22   Ibid., p. 44. Güyüg Khan's letter to Pope Innocent IV is translated on pp. 85–6.

23   Salimbene, p. 203.

24   Dawson, *Mission*, pp. xx–xxi.

25   Ibid., pp. 89–116.

26   Ibid., pp. 117–21.

27   Ibid., p. 121.

28   Ibid., p. 123.

29   Ibid., p. 126.

30   Ibid., p. 128.

31   Ibid., p. 138.

32   Ibid., p. 139.

33   S. Runciman, *The Medieval Manichee* (New York, 1961), pp. 12–17, 116–80.

34   Dawson, *Mission*, pp. 191–4.

35   J. Chapman, 'Nestorius', *The Catholic Encyclopedia*, 15 vols. (New York, 1908), vol. X, pp. 755–9; J. Pelikan, *The Christian Tradition*, vol. I: *The Emergence of the Catholic Tradition (100–600)* (Chicago, 1971), pp. 231–56.

36   Dawson, *Mission*, pp. 149–50.

37   Ibid., p. 150.

38   Ibid., p. 194.

39   Ibid., p. 195.

40   Ibid., pp. 202–4.

41   Moorman, *History*, pp. 430–1; Odoric of Pordenone, *The Travels of Friar Odoric*, trans. Sir Henry Yule, intro. P. Chiesa (Grand Rapids, 2002), pp. 1–9, 160–4.

42   Odoric, *Travels*, pp. 74–5.

43   Ibid., pp. 79–95, 122–3; Daniel, *Franciscan Concept*, pp. 117–18; the *Passio* has been edited as an appendix to the *Chronica XXIV Generalium Ordinis Minorum*, pp. 597–613.

44   Odoric, *Travels*, pp. 96–8.

45  Ibid., pp. 104–12.
46  Ibid., pp. 121–2.
47  Ibid., p. 139.
48  Ibid., pp. 142–4.
49  Ibid., pp.160–1.
50  Dawson, *Mission*, pp. xxviii–xxx; Moorman, *History*, p. 236.
51  Ibid., p. xxx.
52  Moorman, *History*, pp. 236–8; Dawson, *Mission*, pp. xxxi–xxxiii. Dawson includes a translation of the two letters on pp. 224–31.
53  Dawson, *Mission*, pp. xxxiii–xxxiv; Moorman, *History*, pp. 237–8, 430–2. Dawson includes translations of the letters of Brothers Peregrinus and Andrew on pp. 232–7.
54  Daniel, *Franciscan Concept*, pp. 66–7.
55  Ibid., pp. 68–72; Moorman, *History*, pp. 230–2.

# 16 Pope John XXII, the Franciscan order and its *Rule*

## PATRICK NOLD

> The *Rule* and life of the Friars Minor is this: to observe the Holy Gospel
> of Our Lord Jesus Christ by living in obedience, without anything of
> one's own, and in chastity.
>
> (RB, 1)

Roughly a century after the approval of the Franciscan *Rule* by Honorius
III, members of the order claimed that a pope was trying to destroy it.
For an order previously so dependent on the papacy for protection,
patronage and privileges, this was a remarkable *volte-face*. Blame for
the alienation of affection is invariably directed at Pope John XXII
(1316–34): several medieval Franciscan sources portray John as a heretic,
and historians have followed suit in casting the pope as an enemy of the
order, like William of Saint-Amour, a Parisian master of theology very
critical of the theological basis for the pastoral role played by the
mendicants. But to style John as the architect of an attack against
Franciscans obscures the fact that the pope's actions were fundamentally reactions – responses to legal appeals and supplications from the
friars themselves, who, as ever, looked to the papacy to solve their
problems. John's reform of the Franciscan order was fitful, piecemeal
and unplanned.

John XXII began his pontificate by honouring the order in canonis-
ing a friar, Louis of Toulouse (d. 1297). The canonisation bull, *Sol
oriens* (April 1317), reveals the pope's benign disposition towards the
Franciscans. John praised Louis's poverty: his moderate use of goods
necessary for the exercise of the episcopal office, his love for the poor
and his wearing a 'shabby' (*vilis*) habit in observance of the *Rule*.
Poverty was praiseworthy and unproblematic: in no way was it a source
of conflict or controversy. Before becoming pope, John had been associated with Louis's family, the Angevin rulers of Naples. He was elected
on 7 August 1316, two years after the death of Clement V (1305–14).
Clement, at the Council of Vienne (1311–22), hosted debates over

Franciscan poverty. Ubertino da Casale spoke for friars unified by the desire for a stricter observance and inspired by the writings of Peter of John Olivi (1248–98): a group usually called 'the Spirituals'. This group was opposed by the order's leadership, speaking for 'the Community'; these conventuals provided an *apologia* for the *status quo* defined in papal *Rule* commentaries like Nicholas III's *Exiit qui seminat* (1279). Clement imposed a compromise in *Exivi de Paradiso*. He decreed that the *Rule* did require poor use (*usus pauper*) of goods, but the leadership could decide on the degree. Clement asked that new superiors sympathetic to the Spirituals be appointed, and this happened in the southern French convents of Narbonne, Béziers and Carcassonne. When Clement died in 1314, his compromise came undone. Old guardians were restored to office. Shortly thereafter, the Spirituals drove these guardians out of Narbonne and Béziers. The friars argued that they were preserving Clement's compromise, and they appealed to the next pope to hear their case. This was all made possible by local ecclesiastical support and a strong lay following known as the Beguines. Different were events in Tuscany where, at the end of Clement's pontificate, rigorist friars also evicted guardians; but, without the support of ecclesiastical and lay authorities, their rebellion proved short-lived. They fled to Sicily, where a more receptive audience awaited them.

Upon becoming pope, John XXII inherited a schism in the Franciscan order. There are numerous sources for his reaction, but the two most important are narratives: *The History of the Seven Tribulations of the Franciscan Order* by Angelo Clareno, which deals with the early part of the pontificate (1316–22), and the *Chronicle of Nicholas the Minorite*, which deals with the later (1322–34). Both sources seem ingenuous; both are biased. Angelo's *History* recounts how St Francis's poverty was betrayed by lax leaders from Brother Elias to Bonagrazia of Bergamo who persecuted the 'Spiritual' upholders of the founder's intentions. Long an advocate of strict poverty, Angelo obtained permission from Celestine V (1294) to observe the *Rule* outside the order: his group, the Poor Hermits of Pope Celestine, came to be called *fraticelli*. When Boniface VIII (1294–1303) succeeded Celestine, he voided his predecessor's legislation, and Angelo's company fled east. Angelo returned west to witness the Vienne debates. Encouraged by Clement's compromise, he remained in Avignon to gain recognition for his group as a religious order. Angelo's *History* is thus the account of a plaintiff, not simply a witness.

Angelo's account can be cross-checked against an annotated inventory of Spiritual–Conventual polemics compiled by Raymond of

Fronsac, procurator general of the order. Raymond and Angelo attest that, shortly after his election, John was approached by the new minister general, Michael of Cesena. Michael designated Bonagrazia of Bergamo, an enemy of the Spirituals, banned from the papal court by Clement, to present five requests to the pope: first, that the state of the *fraticelli* be repudiated; secondly, that the Tuscan friars who fled to Sicily be restored to discipline; thirdly, that the appeals from Narbonne and Béziers be quashed; fourthly, that Ubertino da Casale be censured; and fifthly, that the Beguines not be considered members of the Third Order of St Francis. These supplications anticipate John's actions.

Raymond suggests that the pope was hesitant to intervene in writing: instead, he gave his opinion orally in consistories, or public meetings of the cardinals, and worked through intermediaries. For instance, he annulled the state of the *fraticelli* only verbally, probably in spring 1317. Regarding the Tuscan fugitives, he asked the cardinals 'whether schismatics should be supported, and whether the friars in Sicily were to be considered schismatics'. After discussion, several cardinals wrote to Sicilian bishops, describing the friars as members of a 'sect' of 'pseudo-friars', and warned against aiding them. Likewise, when asked about Narbonne and Béziers, the pope directed the minister to instruct the friars to surrender the convents. He also held a consistory where he instructed certain cardinals to put his will in writing about the habit. Their letter evokes the principle of religious uniformity: 'it has been soundly established by the sacred canons that there should be no difference in habit or observance among those who preach one Gospel and are of the same profession, but all should conform to the same rule and habit, because otherwise much scandal is generated and unity is impossible.'

Nevertheless, the friars from Narbonne and Béziers wished to continue their appeal by personally putting their case to the pope. Accordingly, John summoned the friars in a letter in which he, exasperated, refers to 'certain appeals and protests that not only detract from the state of the order but are reasonably supposed to have encouraged scandal and derogated from the honour of the apostolic see'. Raymond attests that, when some sixty friars arrived in Avignon, 'the pope spoke to induce them to the good of obedience and charity' and encouraged them to drop their appeal. But the friars pressed on and were granted a hearing in consistory. Raymond and Angelo confirm that objections were raised by the leadership against the friars' spokesmen: Bernard Délicieux, for leading a revolt against the Inquisition many years previously, and William of Saint-Amans, for improperly disposing of Franciscan goods belonging to the Holy See.

Angelo suggests that the pope did not allow the friars to present their case: he forbade Ubertino to speak on their behalf, and other defenders were disqualified. While Angelo mentions written materials submitted by the leadership, nothing is said about a 'Spiritual' dossier. Angelo thus implies that the pope was not well-informed. Raymond, however, does mention their submission of a large file of complaints. Certainly, in *Quorundam exigit* (October 1317) John showed a good grasp of the friars' case. In fact, he carefully underscored how extensively he had listened: 'From either side, things have been proposed before us and the cardinals in writing ... About all this we have seriously listened to the aforesaid arguments. We have fully understood them and wish to put the aforementioned debate to a definitive end.'

*Quorundam* begins with sharp words about 'the blind scrupulosity of certain [friars ... for whom] it is preferable to reverence their own ideas under the guise of conscience than to follow prudently the decisions of the prelates of their order by virtue of obedience'. The bull was a restatement of *Exivi* on two grey areas in the *Rule*: first, what constituted shabbiness (*vilitas*) with regard to the habit, and, secondly, whether stores of grain and wine for communal use were permitted. Clement endorsed a 'Spiritual' reading of the *Rule* in saying that the habit should be shabby and that friars ought not to have stores of consumables. But Clement granted superiors the discretionary power to make exceptions based on local conditions. The Spirituals disputed their superiors' decisions. In *Quorundam*, John restated Clement's judgement and added that friars who disagreed with their superiors' decisions must not accuse them of violating the *Rule*. Although not mentioning Narbonne and Béziers, John here denied the appeal to the Holy See and to conscience.

*Quorundam* had conciliatory qualities. The pope included a personal homage to the order, saying, 'already when we were young, the fervour of our love and devotion glowed for this holy order of Friars Minor'. Nor did the pope denigrate the appellants as 'pseudo-friars' – perhaps in acknowledgement of their punctilious following of legal procedure. Moreover, John sought to reassure the appellants that they would not suffer reprisals: he urged superiors to be 'sweet and soft, kind and mild' to the 'prodigal sons'. Of paramount importance, however, was that the disciplinary structure of the order, based on a hierarchy of vows, be maintained: 'The Franciscan order will be ruined if its members withdraw themselves from holy obedience ... for poverty is indeed great, but greater still is purity, and obedience is the greatest, if kept unharmed.'

The implementation of John's constitution rested with the leadership. Almost immediately, Michael and Bonagrazia gathered friars from Narbonne and Béziers to ask whether they would obey their superiors on the habit and stores of consumables, and, if not, whether the pope had the power to command the things he did in *Quorundam*. The second question was a well-designed trap, for it made obedience a doctrinal issue, so that rebels might be made heretics. A majority accepted the constitution and were reassigned to new convents where many, in violation of *Quorundam*, suffered imprisonment on Michael's instruction. However, twenty-five responded negatively, and their responses were presented to the pope with a request for inquisitorial proceedings. In November 1317, John provided a Franciscan inquisitor with a written mandate to move against the 'pseudo-friars' and 'false professors' of the *Rule* who were 'splattered with the stain of heresy'.

What was the heresy? The Marseilles inquisitor was not certain, and he asked academics in Avignon, including four Franciscans, to judge three propositions. The first was whether it was heretical to assert that one may disobey a superior requesting that shabby habits be put aside because it would be against the *Rule*, and consequently the Gospel – and that anyone who demands this is a heretic. The second repeated the loaded question of Michael and Bonagrazia: whether it was heretical to say that the pope did not have the power to issue *Quorundam*. The third asked whether it was heretical to say that obedience was not due to the pope or superiors over *Quorundam* since it was against counsels of Christ in the *Rule*, against which the pope might do nothing. All experts judged the propositions heretical for their denial of papal power. In the end, four friars were condemned and burned in May 1318. The inquisitor's final sentence corrects the friars' identification of *Rule* and Gospel:

> The Roman pontiff would not go against the Gospel and Christian faith if he were to legislate against, change or suppress the Rule of St Francis; that *Rule* is not the same as the Gospel but is rather a particular, praiseworthy form of religious life approved and confirmed by the Roman pontiffs and subject absolutely to their interpretation, alteration or any other arrangement.

In the interval between *Quorundam* and the burning of the Marseilles four, the pope began to take action against other dissidents – doubtless convinced of the need by *Quorundam*'s reception. His next bull, *Sancta romana* (December 1317), may be seen as a written response to the order's fivefold supplication: having fulfilled two *desiderata* (Ubertino had been transferred to the Benedictines in October 1317, and the Narbonne and Béziers appeals were rejected with *Quorundam*), John XXII now acceded to requests concerning the *fraticelli* and Beguines. The pope notes that these groups behave as new religious orders. Some 'profess to observe the *Rule* of St Francis to the letter, although they do not devote attention to obeying the minister provincial of the same order' – an ironic allusion to the *Rule*'s emphasis on obedience. The *fraticelli* 'pretend that they have a privilege for their state or life from our predecessor Celestine' to observe the *Rule*, but this is impossible, since Boniface VIII annulled all such things. The bull also follows the order's talking-points in identifying the Beguines as wolves in sheep's clothing who, 'asserting themselves to be of the Third Order of St Francis, called "of Penance", attempt to disguise themselves under the veil of such a name, since such a mode of living is in no way conceded in the rule'. Vague allusion is made to their deviance from the Catholic faith and contempt for its sacraments.

A month later *Gloriosam ecclesiam* (January 1318) took aim at the last target of the order's supplication: the rebels in Sicily. But *Gloriosam* is actually about much more. The pope mentions events in France in recounting the disagreements over poverty – of the appearance of factions which 'put forth various questions and grievances against the whole order concerning the *Rule*, as if they and their accomplices alone understood and observed [it]'. John emphasises Clement's consultation of experts before summarising *Exivi*, once again underscoring its passages on ministerial discretion and obedience. John describes the Tuscan friars in terms reminiscent of *Sancta romana* and *Quorundam*: they attempted to set up a 'new religious order' in electing their own superiors; they have also assumed 'short, tight, strange and squalid habits with small hoods, different from those of the community of the order'.

*Sancta romana* alluded to the doctrinal deviance of the Beguines; *Gloriosam* condemned specific beliefs, described as 'in part heretical, in part insane, and in part fantastical'. The most important error is that:

> [They] imagine two churches: one carnal, overwhelmed with riches,
> overflowing in ornament, stained by evil deeds, to which, they
> assert, the Roman protectors and other inferior prelates are
> subjected. The other church, a 'spiritual' one, pure with frugality,
> decorated with virtue, girdled with poverty, of which they
> themselves and their accomplices alone are a part.

The pope restates the traditional teaching that there is one Church, of perfect and imperfect, led by the Roman pontiff – and whatever riches it has are for charity. John also corrects several ecclesiological corollaries: for instance, that the sacramental ministry of the Church is compromised by its corruption. The last error concerns the theology of history: the rebels reckon 'that the Gospel is completed in them alone in our time, and that up to this point, it was hidden, or rather extinguished ... and that the promise of Our Lord concerning the Holy Spirit was not fulfilled in the apostles but in them'. *Gloriosam* condemned fundamental beliefs that underlay rebellion in and around the Franciscan order, not only of the friars in Sicily, but of Spirituals and Beguines in Languedoc as well. Significantly, the first and last errors echo themes present in Olivi's *Apocalypse Commentary*.

This echoing is surely one reason why, shortly after the Marseilles four's condemnation, John appointed an academic panel to look into Olivi's *Apocalypse Commentary* for heresy. The impetus for the investigation came from the leadership of the order, which had long vilified Olivi as the guru of Franciscan dissidents and agitated for his condemnation. Bonagrazia had impugned the orthodoxy of Olivi in his debates with Ubertino at Vienne, and such accusations were repeated to John XXII. Likewise, the condemnation of the Marseilles four mentioned the poisonous influence of Olivi's teaching. Moreover, the general chapter of 1319 condemned Olivi – a move probably intended to encourage the commission and the pope.

The commission on Olivi's *Apocalypse Commentary* reported sometime after the chapter, and the report followed the lead of *Gloriosam* and the inquisitor's sentence. Condemned was the identification of the Roman Church with Babylon, the city of the devil, and the great whore. Also censured was the idea that previous ages of history were superseded by a new 'age of the Spirit' in the revelation of St Francis of Assisi, just as the age of the Son of the New Testament had superseded the age of the Father of the Old Testament. The commission – which included the Franciscan Bertrand de la Tour – also condemned Olivi's identification of the *Rule* and the Gospel.

More pressing than the commission's report was the march of events. Persecution sparked a fire of resistance outside the order: Beguines began to fall victim to Dominican inquisitors in southern France from 1319 onwards. But questions remained about this 'new' heresy: John XXII received at least one query from a bishop asking for clarification, and he delegated the Dominican inquisitor Jean of Beaune to respond. Much inquisitorial testimony has survived, and a recurring statement is that John XXII's *Quorundam* forced the Franciscans to accept common property in the form of stores of grain and wine. This was held to be against the *Rule*'s vow of poverty and against the Gospel, because 'Christ and the apostles had nothing individually or in common'. Thus, the pope had become a heretic. The identification of the *Rule* and Gospel here repeats itself in a more precise form. And precisely this theological statement prompted another Franciscan legal appeal to Avignon. In 1321, Jean of Beaune was about to condemn publicly a Beguine for heresy when a Franciscan lector, Berengar Talon, defended the statement that Christ and the apostles had nothing individually or in common, and he mentioned *Exiit* as supporting his position. When asked to recant, the Franciscan appealed to the pope.

The story is told in the *Chronicle of Nicholas the Minorite*. The work is not so much a chronicle as a collection of documents with contextual introductions, probably first assembled in dossier form by the lawyer Bonagrazia. He and Michael of Cesena fled Avignon in 1328, allegedly because of their fidelity to a doctrine of poverty condemned by a 'heretical' pope. The *Chronicle* serves as both a justification for their actions and an indictment of John: it is a 'case for the prosecution' which, like all such cases, tells a story of 'crime' that is partial and one-sided. The *Chronicle* indicts John as an isolated, uncompromising heretic who must to be tried by a council because he intentionally contradicted a Church doctrine defined in *Exiit*, and because he resisted correction from a united Franciscan order led by Michael and Bonagrazia. Excluded from this account are details inconvenient to the case, and this (along with its occasional evidence-tampering in misquoting the pope) makes the *Chronicle* a source best used with caution.

The *Chronicle*'s narrative starts abruptly in 1321, supplying no context or motive for the pope's acceptance of Talon's appeal other than 'to contradict those things defined in *Exiit*'. It implies that this 'theoretical' poverty controversy was something completely new. Yet John probably accepted the appeal for a straightforward reason: to have a recurrent Beguine statement (generated as a consequence of *Quorundam*) distinguished from orthodox belief and condemned. And the process began in spring 1322 by introducing that statement to a consistory for consultation on 'whether it is heretical to assert that Christ and the apostles had nothing individually or in common'.

'To have nothing individually or in common' was a distinctly Franciscan way of defining poverty. Other orders required their members to renounce personal possessions, but communally its members owned things – just as the Church itself corporately owned property. The Franciscans were the exception: the *Rule* stated that 'the friars should appropriate nothing to themselves: neither house nor place nor anything else' (RB, VI). From Gregory IX's *Quo elongati* (1230) onwards, this physical destitution was abstracted into a renunciation of property rights. The Franciscans would appropriate nothing to themselves in legal terms: they would not own houses or places or anything else but only 'use' them. The owner would be the papacy: this arrangement began in 1245 with Innocent IV's *Ordinem vestrum* and reached its apotheosis in Nicholas III's *Exiit*, which specified that the Franciscans enjoyed only a 'simple use of fact' over goods whose property rights were reserved to the Holy See. Naturally, secular clergy and other orders were unconvinced by the legal fiction, and Nicholas had to respond to criticism that the *Rule* was 'illicit, unobservable and invidious'. He did so by saying that the 'individual and common renunciation of property (*proprietas*) over all things was meritorious and holy', and that 'Christ taught this doctrine by word and deed'. A more heavy-handed response was Nicholas's sentence of excommunication prohibiting discussion of *Exiit*'s contents.

In 1322, this excommunication sentence needed to be lifted for consultation on Talon's appeal. A *viva voce* suspension inaugurated a consistory debate in Avignon. Franciscan prelates put forward qualified defences of the position that apostolic and Franciscan poverty were related, if not identical. One is reported to have said:

> It is a hard thing for me to affirm that the profession of blessed
> Francis, whose rule proposes not to possess anything individually or
> in common, is heretical. And the Roman Church says in the decretal
> *Exiit*: 'This is the rule and life which Christ taught in His words and
> affirmed in His example.'

Prelates from other orders and the secular clergy, in contrast, tended to restate the traditional teaching of the Church on apostolic property based on Acts 4: 32: 'They [the apostles] had everything in common.' Since oral debates proved inconclusive, John XXII solicited written opinions on the same day that he issued *Quia nonnumquam*, which formally suspended *Exiit*'s excommunication sentence. The pope justified this act by saying: 'We wish to open the way of truth and to remove the dangers posed to literate, particularly scholarly, men by the aforesaid prohibitions, especially since doubts have arisen anew, which could open the way to error and endanger the truth.' The 'new doubts' seem to refer to the consequences of *Quorundam* and to early theological disagreements in John's consultation.

John stressed that *Quia nonnumquam* was not a *carte blanche* to impugn the *Rule*. Still, the order's leadership feared the new freedom of speech and viewed the curial discussion as an eruption of criticism stifled since 1279. It reacted defensively, issuing two letters from the general chapter of 1322: the first begged the pope to reinstate *Exiit's* excommunication; a second, more audacious letter, to all Christendom, attempted to answer definitively the pope's question in affirming that Christ and the apostles had nothing individually or in common by the rights of *proprietas* (property) and *dominium* (ownership), or indeed any right (*ius*) at all – and *Exiit* was cited in support. In writing the letter, the leadership hoped to cut off debate.

Meanwhile, in Avignon position-papers from legal and theological experts were trickling in. Those by non-Franciscans were almost uniformly critical of the Beguines' statement, and of communal poverty generally. Even Franciscans disagreed among themselves about how to define apostolic poverty by property rights: how a Franciscan idea of poverty could be modified to allow for the apostles' status as bishops in charge of Church goods.

In November 1322, the pope issued a constitution, *Ad conditorem*, which begins: 'There is no doubt it suits the legislator of canons that when he learns of certain statutes, published by himself or his predecessors, which harm rather than help, that he should prevent them from doing more harm.' The bull focused on the arrangement between the papacy and the order that allowed the Franciscans to claim to have nothing in common. John XXII notes that experience has revealed the unintended, harmful consequences of this agreement: rather than liberating Franciscans from worldly cares, the renunciation of common *dominium* has made them more anxious about material things. It has caused them to boast that they are more perfect than other orders based on a 'poverty' that was more nominal than real – as in claiming not to have the *dominium* of their food. Was this *Exiit's* intention? Another harm was providing occasion for dangerous schismatics to arise within the order – a danger that would continue as long as the *status quo* remained. And the Franciscans were not the only ones injured: the papacy drew no benefit from owning things like Franciscan food, and it had been drawn into unedifying litigation with bishops and clergy over Franciscan property. Thus, to prevent more harm, John XXII decreed that henceforth the Roman Church would no longer accept the *dominium* of Franciscan goods. *Ad conditorem* did theoretically what John had already been accused of doing in practice: making the Franciscans accept common property, especially of consumables.

*Ad conditorem* was not well received by the order's leadership, which, in reaction to the *usus pauper* of the Spirituals, had defined

Franciscan poverty in legalistic terms. Bonagrazia formally appealed against *Ad conditorem* on the grounds that the pope had been misinformed. His appeal contained legal arguments about the legitimacy of separating *dominium* from use, even in the consumables: Bonagrazia argued Nicholas intended to reserve the *dominium* of all such things, and that this was consistent with civil, canon and natural law. Also included was a theological argument: St Francis in the *Rule* intended poverty to be the abdication of common *dominium*, and this could not be harmful because Christ and the apostles practised it. In effect, Bonagrazia denied the *modus operandi* of *Ad conditorem* with theological and legal verities.

John responded to Bonagrazia with a more detailed, argumentative version of *Ad conditorem*. The pope objected to the idea of a 'simple use of fact': one cannot separate use from ownership in consumables and, even in things not consumed in use, some 'right' must always accompany the use of a thing for it to be just. While John XXII engaged Bonagrazia's legal arguments, he left the theological objection unanswered. The consequence of *Ad conditorem* did not change in its second redaction: the Franciscans lost their uniquely privileged status as the poorest of all religious orders and began to own things in common. The pope concluded: 'We now think it just and appropriate that the professors of the said [Franciscan] order should make their claim of being a more perfect state and having a "higher poverty" than other mendicant orders based on clear works aided by the truth and not just on mere words and feigned acts.'

Only later did John move into the realm of theology. Almost a year after *Ad conditorem*, a second bull, *Cum inter*, appeared. The beginning reads:

> Since among scholarly men it has frequently been called into doubt, with various and contrary opinions being advanced, whether to affirm obstinately that our Lord and Redeemer Jesus Christ and his apostles did not have anything, individually or in common, should be condemned as heretical, we wish to put an end to this argument. Since Sacred Scripture asserts in many places that Christ and the apostles had some things, obstinate assertion of this sort expressly contradicts Sacred Scripture through which the articles of orthodox faith are proven. In openly supposing that Scripture contains the seeds of falsehood, the foregoing assertion consequently renders the Catholic faith doubtful and uncertain by depriving it of all proof on this matter. Therefore, on the counsel of our brothers,

we declare by perpetual edict that this proposition is to be
condemned as erroneous and heretical.

Here the pope condemns the bald statement of the Beguines that Christ
and the apostles had absolutely nothing as heretical because it explicitly contradicts Scripture. Academically speaking, the first paragraph
of *Cum inter* was uncontroversial: even Franciscans acknowledged that
Christ and the apostles, literally, had some things – what mattered was
the definition of 'having'.

Real difficulty hung on rights of possession – a vexing issue anticipated in *Ad conditorem*'s discussion of 'simple use of fact'. The remainder of *Cum inter* reads:

> In turn, one may obstinately affirm from the above that, regarding
> those things which, according to Sacred Scripture, Our Redeemer
> and his apostles did have, a right of using or of consuming did not
> apply to them, nor did they have the right to sell or give away these
> things and acquire others. Sacred Scripture, however, attests that
> they did do these things, or clearly supposes that they could have
> done them. Such an assertion obviously constrains use and conduct
> in such a way as to make them unjust. It is wicked to say this about
> the use, conduct or deeds of Our Redeemer. Therefore, We, on the
> counsel of Our brothers declare this assertion, as contrary to Sacred
> Scripture and inimical to the Catholic faith, to be henceforth
> condemned as erroneous and heretical.

Drafts – on which John was advised by Bertrand de la Tour – reveal that in
the end the pope adopted a minimalist position to reflect the expert
consensus. The pope sought to avoid a direct contradiction of a doctrinal
statement of *Exiit*: whereas Nicholas had said that Christ and the
apostles renounced all *proprietas*, John XXII stated that Christ and the
apostles must have enjoyed some rights over things. Here the notion of
an apostolic 'simple use of fact', defined as a use without rights, is
implicitly repudiated. But the omission of the actual term provided a
path to reconciliation through a redefinition of 'simple use of fact' to
encompass the rights specified in the bull. And, indeed, Bonagrazia took
this path in a tract harmonising *Exiit* and *Cum inter*: the latter constitution being interpreted as another condemnation of the Spirituals.

The debate might have ended with such harmonisations, but it was
given an unexpected fillip when supporters of the pope's political
enemy, Ludwig of Bavaria, drafted the cause of the poverty into their
dispute with John for his refusal to recognise Ludwig as 'king of the

Romans', or emperor-elect. In the *Sachsenhausen Appeal* (1324), the imperialists turned the tables on the pope to raise doubts about his legitimacy by adding to their list of grievances a 'Minorite Excursus' which accused John of heresy. The *Appeal* recalled how previous opponents of poverty like William of Saint-Amour had been condemned: it equated the denial of poverty with the error of Jews, Saracens and the Antichrist in a passage taken from Olivi. Crucially, the *Appeal* claimed: 'What in faith and morals the Roman Pontiffs have once defined through the key of knowledge should remain immutable so that it is not permitted for their successors to call it into doubt or to affirm the contrary.' John was accused of contradicting the teachings of several pontiffs, most especially Nicholas III in *Exiit*. To suggest a hermeneutic of contradiction, the *Appeal* relied heavily on the text of *Ad conditorem*, and for the carefully worded *Cum inter* it supplied a historical context of alleged papal hostility towards *Exiit* – a stratagem later used by the *Chronicle of Nicholas the Minorite*.

John XXII defended himself in *Quia quorundam* (1324). His immediate response to the accusation of heresy was to note that his constitutions had been issued only after expert consultation. The pope then argued that *Cum inter* did not doctrinally contradict *Exiit* on the poverty of Christ, and that any contradiction between *Exiit* and *Ad conditorem* did not matter, since it dealt with Church discipline. Still, the politicisation of poverty reduced room for equivocation in Avignon. The pope hardened his position in *Quia quorundam* to condemn explicitly the idea that Christ and the apostles had only a 'simple use of fact'. The order's leadership, Michael and Bonagrazia, were content to use John's constitutions as new weapons in old fights; they concentrated their energies on a renewed push for a condemnation of Olivi's *Apocalypse Commentary* (something made desirable by the imperialist use of his writings) and for the punishment of the Benedictine Ubertino. Meanwhile, John came to suspect them of tepidly enforcing adherence to his bulls within the order and of sympathising with Ludwig. Events came to a head in 1328, when Ludwig invaded Italy, was crowned emperor, symbolically deposed John XXII in Rome and installed a Franciscan as anti-pope. Soon after these events, Michael and Bonagrazia, together with William of Ockham and Francis of Ascoli, defected from the papal curia to Pisa, a pro-imperial city. Michael and Bonagrazia followed the *Sachsenhausen Appeal* in using the writings of Olivi, their old whipping-boy, to accuse the pope of heresy. The pope replied *in extenso* to one of their tracts, the *Appellatio in Forma Minori*, in *Quia vir reprobus* (1329) – directed against Michael and refuting his interpretation of *Ad conditorem*, *Cum inter* and *Quia quorundam*. The most original mind in the Michaelist group was Ockham, who gave the group's case against the pope a degree of philosophical sophistication in works such as the *Opus nonaginta dierum* and the *Dialogus*.

In their polemic, the Michaelists maintained that they represented the beliefs of the whole Franciscan order as embodied in *Exiit*, just as they had in their polemics against the Spirituals. The order did not, however, follow these leaders into schism and soon fell into line under a new leadership. After fleeing Avignon, Michael was deposed as minister general by John XXII, and Bertrand de la Tour was installed as vicar until the 1329 general chapter could elect a replacement. They elected Bertrand's relative, Guiral Ot, who sought to issue new constitutions for the order. Guiral's abortive reform over the handling of money at the general chapter of 1331 provoked the last, and most revealing, intervention of John XXII. St Francis had said in the *Rule*:

> I strictly command all my brothers not to receive coins or money in any form, either personally or through intermediaries ...
> nevertheless, ministers and custodians alone may take special care through their spiritual friends to provide for the needs of the infirm and the clothing of the brothers according to places, seasons and cold climates, as they judge necessary, saving always that, as stated above, they do not receive coins or money.
>
> (RB, IV)

This prohibition proved difficult to observe, and its neglect caused scandal. Guiral proposed to reinterpret the *Rule* so that the order could receive money through intermediaries for the needs of any infirmity, whether bodily or spiritual. His proposal emphasised the leadership's discretion in the *Rule*'s observance, as popes had done in *Exivi* and *Quorundam*. Yet John's response in consistory surprised Guiral and impressed the Franciscan Alvarus Pelagius:

> 'This interpretation... is twisted and against the rule, and We do not believe that one in a thousand friars would agree with you in this interpretation' ... And a certain cardinal said to me [Alvarus] afterwards: 'Truly, when we were with the pope, St Francis himself was with us – that is to say, to defend his rule.'

Was this reaction consistent with John XXII's earlier reforms? Initially, the pope followed the leadership, and previous papal bulls, in emphasising ministerial authority and discretion in interpreting contentious grey areas of the *Rule*. In the middle years of his pontificate (1322–4),

John parted company with the leadership: he did not find the renunciation of property rights supported by the *Rule* or the Gospel but considered it a disposable arrangement of his predecessors. Near his
pontificate's end, he rejected a new leadership's proposal to release friars
from an explicit prohibition in the *Rule*. The pope's refusal indicates
that he took the *Rule* of St Francis rather seriously. Indeed, John XXII's
reactions to the legal appeals and supplications from the order suggest
that the pope tried to be a faithful, if literal, interpreter of the Franciscan
*Rule* rather than an antagonist who sought to destroy it.

# 17 The ecumenical appeal of Francis

PETÀ DUNSTAN

St Francis was for centuries a saint widely revered, yet only by Roman Catholics. After the East–West split of 1054 within the Church, the Eastern Orthodox churches rarely engaged with those declared holy by Rome in the following centuries. After the fracture of the Church in the west at the time of the Reformation in the sixteenth century, Protestants included in their theological outlook a rejection of what they saw as the false claims for saints and their cults, along with the monastic system itself. A founder of a medieval religious order such as Francis therefore had little appeal for them. Even Anglicans, whose ecclesiastical position became eventually a mix of Catholic structures and reformist views, found a saint like Francis too associated with what they regarded as mawkish superstition and misdirected fervour. In any case, political events in the sixteenth and seventeenth centuries stoked fears of 'papism', meaning there could be little attraction in any saint closely associated with loyalty to Rome.

All the more remarkable therefore was the marked change in the nineteenth century, a period that ended with St Francis being the medieval saint most admired by Anglicans and Protestants. Adopted in various guises as one of the most inspiring religious figures in Christian history, his emergence as an ecumenical icon was astonishing.

## THE ROMANTIC MOVEMENT

The origin of this change can be found in the Romantic Movement. From the final years of the eighteenth century, the social and political pressures wrought by revolutionary ideology and the chaos of the Napoleonic wars, and also by the beginnings of the Industrial Revolution, saw a reaction that involved looking back in history for inspiration. The result was that the defence against the fallout of the 'Age of Reason' became the imagination and faith of the medieval period. Writers and thinkers in Protestant countries as well as Catholic began a reassessment of the Middle Ages. For so long dismissed by Protestants as a time of superstition and backwardness – the necessary backcloth to justifying the upheaval of the Reformation – they became admired instead as a period of order and chivalry, when faith flourished, even if religious institutions were judged degraded. Gothic art and architecture were now lauded as representing a high point of culture. Their lines and decoration became fashionable again, and the 'neo-Gothic' came to dominate much of nineteenth-century design. Even in Britain, whose intellectual tradition could prove more sceptical of continental ideas, the shift was fuelled by young members of the richer classes travelling through Europe – for some, the extensive 'Grand Tour' – a trend intensified by the collecting of art and artefacts on these travels. Italy was one of their main destinations. The influence of the Romantic Movement then spread and became popular as the mode of a new era.

This opened the way for looking again at St Francis. First Catholic writers and then Protestant scholars began to take on the spirit of the age, and various historians began to 'romanticise' the story of Francis's life. Johann Joseph von Görres (1776–1848) in Germany and Frederick Ozanam (1813–53) in France were two of the prime examples of this trend among Catholics. In Britain, Sir James Stephen (1789–1859), a lawyer and distinguished civil servant, who in 1849 became Regius Professor of Modern History at Cambridge, made a plea for a British scholar to review the saint's life and contribution. Stephen was an Evangelical Anglican, married to a daughter of the founder of the Church Missionary Society, Revd John Venn. This religious background, however, did not deter him from championing St Francis. When reviewing two (French) biographies of Francis for the *Edinburgh Review* in 1845, he praised the saint as the greatest reformer and preacher prior to Luther, saying he had produced 'enthusiasm' greater than Wesley or Whitfield had done in the eighteenth century.[1] Of the Franciscans he concluded:

> In an age of oligarchic tyranny they were the protectors of the weak; in an age of ignorance the instructors of mankind; and in an age of profligacy the stern vindicators of the holiness of the sacerdotal character, and the virtues of domestic life.

Stephen was implying that St Francis was not just a historical figure, but someone whose values were relevant to the contemporary issues of the nineteenth century, and they could be claimed even by Christians outside the Roman Catholic fold. He ended his article with a plea to 'revive the memory of a once famous Father of the Church, now fallen into unmerited neglect and indiscriminate opprobrium among us', and for a scholar to write the 'complete story of St Francis, and estimate impartially his acts, his opinions, his character, and his labours'.

A fresh biography in English, however, had to wait nearly two decades – and when it did appear, it was not by a university scholar but a writer primarily known as a novelist: Margaret Oliphant (1828–97). The widowed Mrs Oliphant, saddled with impecunious dependants for much of her life, wrote prolifically to earn money. Her enormous output of novels and articles included also some 'popular' non-fiction and biography. Having travelled in Italy in the previous decade, she did not let her (Calvinist) Free Church of Scotland background deter her from an interest in St Francis. She read all she could and in 1868 produced an accessible biography in which she praised the saint as an ideal. In her previous (1862) biography of the Protestant preacher Edward Irving she praised Irving for 'a higher style of Christianity, something more magnanimous, more heroical than this age affects'. The same could be said of her view of Francis – he was someone to inspire eternal Christian values in an era of uncertainty and change. Such religious leaders rise above denomination and controversy. This became a significant component in St Francis's appeal.

Published by Macmillan in their series The Sunday Library for Household Reading, a series title that eloquently expressed the target audience of families reading for both pleasure and edification after Sunday church, Oliphant's *Saint Francis of Assisi* was an immediate success. A second edition followed in 1871, and reprints and reissues followed at regular intervals well into the twentieth century. This proved an influential book, creating the 'image' of St Francis for British readers for generations to come. It was based mainly on Mrs Oliphant's reading of French and German writers, particularly Ozanam's 1852 book on Franciscan poets and the work of Karl August von Hase (1800–90), a Protestant professor of theology at Jena, who published a substantial study of St Francis in 1856. These sources were drenched in the Romantic spirit, and Mrs Oliphant reproduced its approach in a popular genre. In the introduction, she characterised the thirteenth century as a period of transition when crises were changing the foundations of society and settling 'all the nations anew upon an altered basis', mirroring the upheavals of the current age. So, she implied, St Francis was relevant to her contemporaries. In chapter 8, St Francis is idealised as 'a man overflowing with sympathy for man and beast', and it is claimed that 'The magnetism of the heart, that power which nobody can define, but which it is impossible to ignore, surrounded him like a special atmosphere.' So Francis is shown to have universal and not sectarian appeal, a saint for Christians, not specifically Catholics.

The more concerning aspects of the saint's life for an Anglican or Protestant audience were downplayed. The stigmata, for example, were dealt with in chapter 16 (towards the book's conclusion) but as not central to the story: 'the stigmata, if they existed, would seem to have been ignored by their possessor'. If they were a 'miracle', 'the evidence is not so complete or satisfactory as to warrant us in thus acknowledging and classifying the event'. St Francis was therefore 'safe' for non-Roman Catholics to revere. You could admire the man without having to accept what Mrs Oliphant perceived to be an unnecessary array of fables.

## THE POWER OF NATURE

St Francis was also attractive to the nineteenth-century reader because of his links with nature. The century was not only one of economic and political change, but also one of scientific advance. The study of the natural world was seen as a godly pursuit, for understanding the creation would surely lead to understanding the Creator. The 'natural theology' of William Paley (1743–1805) was still influential, especially among those of an Evangelical persuasion in the Church of England. Many Anglican clergy pursued botany and the like as serious pursuits. However, developments such as those in geology, and then the publication of the theory of evolution (1859), brought science into more conflict with some religious ideas, especially biblical literalism. Scientific discoveries and theories appeared to portray the physical world and its laws as harsh, random and amoral – so where was God? But St Francis could be employed as a powerful antidote. He was valued as being 'in tune' with nature and animals, demonstrating harmony in a universe created by God and spoiled only by human sin. Mrs Oliphant expressed this as

> the noble concept of a redeemed world, a universe all pervaded by the sense of the Creator's presence and the Saviour's love. Men then, as now, were sadly unsatisfactory beings to have had so much love and care lavished upon them ... Francis ... turned, sick at heart, from the perpetual strife and contention of his time, from fighting cities, rapacious nobles, a whole world of blood and oppression, and, with an unspeakable relief, heard the gentle birds singing in the woods, the harmless creatures rustling among the trees.

This sentimental view of nature and its healing properties was immensely popular, because it was so comforting. Everyone could enjoy nature and the attraction of animals and plants. For the Reformed Churches, as they grappled with contemporary scientific challenges, Francis was too valuable to be ignored. They interpreted him as having an 'ethic' of nature that firmly rooted scientific observation in theism rather than agnosticism and doubt. It could be judged that, in this area, he was more relevant to Protestants than to Rome, because the former had less emphasis on tradition and were therefore more vulnerable to the agnostic world-view if the Bible was assumed not to be literal, historical truth. As late as 1933, Charles Raven (1885–1964), Regius Professor of Divinity at Cambridge 1932–50, reiterated this point in a foreword to a book on Franciscanism:

> Moreover, as has lately been noted by a prominent French Catholic, St Francis among all the saints of the Roman Church is the one, almost the only one, known, revered, and loved by the Reformed Churches. Whether or not it be true, as the same writer maintains, that the broad difference between Protestant and Catholic Christendom is best illustrated by the fact that love of nature and animal life is characteristic of the former and almost wholly lacking in the latter, at least the Saint of Assisi is a shining exception; and it is probably his enthusiasm for the brotherhood of birds and beasts, more than the stigmata, that for us sets the seal upon his saintliness.[2]

## NON-CONFORMITY

However, non-Roman Catholics could not push St Francis as an ideal and simply ignore his relationship to Rome. The saint's writings and other sources made clear his acceptance of papal authority and traditional doctrine. Reformist writers countered this by emphasising Francis's criticisms of his contemporaries' religious attitudes and the call he received to 'save the Church'. He may have been obedient to ecclesiastical authority, but he was also challenging it and was therefore a 'non-conformist', a reformer aspiring to change the Catholic Church three centuries before Luther made the attempt. An example of this interpretation would be found in a letter to *The Times* in December 1870. Arthur Stanley (1815–91), who was Dean of Westminster 1864–91 and a widely read and influential 'Broad Church' Anglican, referred to Francis in these terms:

I ventured to call him a 'Non-Conformist' as a short mode of
expressing that the Non-Conformists bear the same relation to the
Church of England as the religious orders did to the Church of Rome.

Stanley implied that Francis was closely related to, yet 'outside', the
Church of Rome, just as he regarded Methodists being near, yet not of,
the Church of England. This is an odd judgement to make – as it was
plainly not true – but shows how important claiming the influence of St
Francis had become to a member of the Anglican establishment.

Elsewhere in Europe, the French writer Ernest Renan (1823–92)
produced a controversial study of Jesus in 1863 in which the supernatural was expunged and dogmatic definition discarded. He then took a
similar view of Francis, placing him beyond doctrinal creeds or traditions. It was to be his pupil, Paul Sabatier (1858–1928), a Calvinist
pastor who later taught at the University of Strasbourg, who would write
an *academic* biography that made St Francis acceptable to a Protestant
audience. *The Life of St Francis of Assisi* was first published in French
in 1893, but translations quickly appeared elsewhere. In its use of
original sources Sabatier's book is more scholarly than most other
nineteenth-century biographies of the saint, but it remains imbued
with the Romantic spirit that seeps through them all. Yet it also has a
more distinct political motive.

Sabatier's view implied that although Franciscanism might be
undeniably Roman Catholic, in contrast Francis himself belonged to
Protestantism every bit as much as Luther or Calvin. In the introduction to the book, his subject is positioned as part of a movement that
was popular and of the laity, 'wresting then sacred things from the
hands of the clergy'. The priest is 'almost always the enemy'. Francis
'divined the superiority of the spiritual priesthood'. He was loyal to the
Church in the same way that the first French revolutionaries of 1789
believed themselves 'good and loyal subjects of Louis XVI'. He 'surely
believed that the Church had become unfaithful to her mission ... He
longed for a true awakening of the Church in the name of the evangelical ideal which he had regained.' For Sabatier, then, Francis was a
reforming 'protestant'. He was also a modernist, ditching dogma and
orthodoxy for a radical freedom based on poverty and unity with nature.
Like the other writers mentioned, it may be judged that Sabatier was
projecting on to St Francis the values and beliefs that he held himself.
Nevertheless, his book stimulated a rash of further studies by Protestants, both popular and scholarly, and not only on Francis, but on
Franciscan art, history and spirituality too.

## THE CHALLENGE OF POVERTY

As the nineteenth century moved on, the ecumenical appeal of St Francis was boosted by a further factor: the issue of poverty. The Industrial Revolution had changed the landscape, especially as modest towns grew to large cities; and both a steep rise in population as well as the advent of factories and cheap slum dwellings to house their workers produced a new range of urban social problems. They arose very quickly and were impossible to ignore. As Britain had been the first site of the Industrial Revolution, the Church of England was faced early on with responding to it. In particular, the construction of churches in newly built areas and the challenge of evangelising the increasing numbers of poor people crowded into urban slums pressed on its leaders urgently. Many recognised that the parish system alone could not deal with all these problems. Some turned to political campaigns, and followers of 'Christian Socialism' emerged in the 1840s, but they did not coalesce into a distinct movement, some being more politically involved while others concentrated on workers' education. All ended up campaigning therefore as individuals and not as part of a defined organisation, which limited their impact. For others, the answer lay not in political activity but in founding religious communities dedicated to social outreach, an aspiration that dovetailed with theological developments in the Church.

The Tractarians in the 1830s had reawakened among Anglicans the prospect of reclaiming their Catholic heritage, one aspect of which was the revival of religious life. Despite arguments among bishops and others about the validity and status of vows in such communities, foundations for women began to be made from the mid 1840s. These grew rapidly, and eventually foundations for men followed from the 1860s. By the end of the nineteenth century, the revival of religious life had spread to Anglicans throughout the world. Numerically small by Roman Catholic or Orthodox standards, these communities were nevertheless influential. By the time of the 1897 Lambeth Conference, they were accepted as a permanent element in Anglicanism.

The Anglo-Catholic movement also encouraged the study of saints. St Francis, being one of the most attractive for the reasons given above, soon became the focus of attention also because of his love of poverty. Faced with overwhelming social problems, a saint who embraced poverty with joy was a role model both for the poor them- selves and also for those who longed to alleviate the sufferings and deprivations of the 'lower classes'. St Francis offered a charism of living with the poor and sharing their poverty rather than ministering from a place of security and relative comfort. It was not a matter only of service, then, but also of identification. Religious communities looked like a way of achieving this.

## FOUNDING FRANCISCAN RELIGIOUS COMMUNITIES

From the perspective of specifically Franciscan foundations, the first impulse was to follow the notions of Francis put forward by the Romantic Protestant biographers, that is, separating the saint from the institutional Church. The Church of England was very much seen as the 'establishment', tied to the political structures and channels of power. So, one of the early pioneers, James Adderley (1861–1942), was determined to be 'outside' this 'institution'. From a privileged background, with a family prominent in Parliament and the Church, after his own ordination he nevertheless turned against preferment and material comfort. Instead, he went on road missions and tramped with wayfarers. His ideas were not at first Franciscan in name, but his developed vision, expressed in a novel, *Stephen Remarx*, outlined a community of people vowed to a *Rule* but working individually in humble employment. Community life would be intermittent, centred at a rural friary that would serve as a place of prayer and retreat for the members whenever they needed rest periods. The idea bore a similarity to a group of Franciscan Third Order Regulars. This arrangement, Adderley believed, would allow the members to escape from the trap of serving the institutional Church directly, which he believed blunted their potential witness and made them liable to collude with the social and economic systems that created poverty in the first place. They would be prophets *outside* the structures of the Church, able to serve the poor while freed from association with power and control. In St Francis and his *Rule*, Adderley came to see a blueprint from within the Christian tradition for his own ideas. Yet Adderley's own personal poverty could only be a 'Romantic' notion, as he could never leave behind his background, especially his education and the security it bestowed.

In order to found the Society of the Divine Compassion (SDC) in 1894 James Adderley was forced at the outset to compromise on implementing his full vision. He and his companions, Henry Chappell (1867–1913) and Andrew Hardy (1869–1946), took charge of a mission district in Plaistow, in the East End of London, to provide a physical home and a small income for the new religious community. The following year,

Andrew became the first man in nearly 480 years to be ordained a priest in the Church of England clad in a Franciscan habit.[3] Henry and Andrew had a more parochial vision than James, believing that Franciscans needed to work with the Church and show from *within* the structures how to witness to the Gospel among the poor. In this sense, they were much truer to the saint's charism and more connected to what they saw as the original vision. The compromise proved too much for Adderley, who resigned as superior in 1897 and in frustration left the SDC. He tried to found another community, which did not thrive, and ironically then spent the rest of his life as a parish priest.

The brothers he left behind in Plaistow grew in numbers, implementing two practical expressions of their policy: they eschewed any material amenities denied to their parishioners; and their lay brothers worked in local industries, such as clock-mending and printing, sharing therefore the anxieties and pressures of their neighbours. Rather than witnessing to the Church as rebels on the outside, they instead witnessed on behalf of the Church from within its structures. It was a crucial difference.

The idea of itinerant friars was not entirely forgotten, however. One of the SDC novices, Giles, asked to be allowed to roam the casual wards, the government-funded shelters for wayfarers. These offered just two nights' lodging with food in return for a day's work, after which the wayfarer had to tramp to the next casual ward, meaning a life of perpetual 'moving on' that especially in winter was harsh. Sleeping 'rough' in streets or fields was illegal until 1935, and so the alternative to tramping was arrest and a prison sentence. Solidarity with those coping with this pattern of life was Giles's call, but the SDC chapter believed that while St Francis 'embraced poverty literally', nevertheless if living in the early twentieth century he would have been concerned with the dignity of labour, 'not to beg with the beggar, but to work with the worker ... Love for the poor – or rather the oppressed and starving – is best expressed in helping them to work.'[4]

Giles felt compelled to withdraw from the community and so became a solitary friar of the roads, but his hope of a religious house where wayfarers he met on his journeys could be invited, and where, through work on the land, they could regain their confidence and self-esteem, remained unfulfilled. After service in the armed forces in the First World War, he resumed this life, but with so many former soldiers on the roads as wayfarers, the public mood had changed. Instead of being dismissed as unemployed 'dossers', they were now war heroes shockingly neglected by an ungrateful government. Giles was offered support by significant patrons. Initially, he considered founding a friary on the outskirts of Oxford, but in 1921 he moved to Flowers Farm, near Hilfield in Dorset, to a property owned by the earl of Sandwich. Others joined him to found the Brotherhood of St Francis of Assisi (BSFA), with the full backing of the Church. However, he was unable to sustain his commitment and left the community; the venture had to be rescued by someone else in 1922.[5]

That person was, unexpectedly, an Evangelical Anglican priest, raised a Methodist, a man suspicious of Anglo-Catholic practices and the customs of the religious life, such as wearing habits. Douglas Downes (1878–1957) was no stranger to ministry to the poor, however. In his curacy, he had lived at the top of a working-class tenement with orange boxes for furniture. Then, as a teacher in India, he lived with his Indian students in a hostel, avoiding all the privileges of the British Raj. After being a chaplain in the First World War, he ministered in Oxford, where he met Giles and encouraged his work. Unable to see the Dorset project fail, he took on the wardenship of the BSFA, despite not seeing himself as a friar in the Catholic tradition and being content to have volunteers from other traditions such as Quakers and Congregationalists involved. Through the 1920s, Douglas would learn the value of the traditions of religious life, but the dominant concern under his leadership was social work. Homes for wayfarers, and later for refugees, were set up in different counties, and Douglas helped pioneer a campaign for reform of the casual ward system, finally realised under the 1929–31 Labour government. Much was achieved. Yet the community as a religious order did not grow.

Nevertheless, the involvement of Douglas and other evangelically minded Christians showed the wide sympathy that the previous fifty years had generated for St Francis. Brother Douglas had not studied the saint's life, nor was he well read in Franciscan studies, as he had not been raised as an Anglo-Catholic or educated in that strand of the Anglican tradition. Yet St Francis was his saint. The man from Assisi standing arms outstretched surrounded by birds and animals was an icon for those who ministered to the poor, even when they knew little of his story or his beliefs. However, to more Catholic-minded Anglicans, the BSFA was an example of the 'pop' Franciscanism that they believed undermined opportunities for developing what they saw as a more rigorous and authentic Franciscan order in their Church.

Some interest was generated from the universities too, especially with the 700th anniversary of St Francis's death approaching in 1926. At Cambridge, a University Franciscan Society was founded, with

F. C. Burkitt (1864–1935), the Norris-Hulse Professor of Divinity, as its president. Its student secretary, John Moorman (1905–89), would go on to be a bishop and a noted Franciscan scholar. In Oxford, a group of undergraduates held a meeting and a retreat early in 1924, eager to encourage one another to consider a future as Anglican friars, but the Anglo-Catholic clergy discouraged their initial enthusiasm for building a community based around the BSFA. Elsewhere, other Franciscan communities were also founded.[6] The most crucial influence came from Anglicans adopting a *Rule* for tertiaries. In one case, a confraternity evolved in 1913 into the Order of St Elizabeth of Hungary, another non-cloistered sisterhood active in missions, teaching and retreat work, in the UK and Australasia. In India, the Christa Seva Sangha (CSS) in Pune witnessed to the need for equality among different nationalities in the face of the racism inherent in the colonial system. The founder, Jack Winslow (1884–1974), pioneered a multi-racial ashram, including both married and single members. It had a Franciscan ethos from its beginning in 1922, and St Francis became formally the co-patron with St Barnabas in 1928. One member, Algy Robertson (1894–1955), set up a branch house in St Ives, Cambridgeshire, when, unable to cope with the Indian climate, he had to return to Britain. Algy was one of the CSS members who wished the community to evolve a First Order instead of simply a Third Order.

During the 1930s, it was the various groups of tertiaries of all these communities who became the catalyst for uniting many of the disparate Anglican Franciscan experiments into the one Society of St Francis (SSF). This united community then grew considerably after the Second World War and established provinces in Australia and the Pacific. The Order of St Francis or OSF in the USA amalgamated with the SSF to become its province of the Americas. There were also houses for some decades in Zambia and Tanzania. All provinces founded enclosed contemplative communities of Second Order Clares, although not all these have survived.[7]

Communities were also founded among Lutherans. An SSF friar helped with the beginnings of the Heliga Korsets Brodraskap in Sweden in 1960, but, after founding a community house in 1965, the brothers adopted a Benedictine *Rule* rather than a Franciscan one. Inaugurated in 1971 at Rättvik, the Franciskus Tredje Orden in the Swedish Church is part of the European province of the Third Order of the Anglican SSF. A second attempt (with the help of the Anglican SSF) at creating a Franciscan Lutheran friary in the 1970s was also unsuccessful. However, before the members left the Church of Sweden they had helped to create a sisterhood, which is still in existence: the Helige Franciskus Systraskap, located at Klaradal convent in Sjövik. Among German Lutherans, while the Evangelical Sisterhood of Mary founded in 1947 by Mother Basilea Schlink in Darmstadt is not Franciscan, the parallel men's community affiliated to it is: the Evangelische Kanaan Franziskus-Bruderschaft. Tertiaries are represented by the Evangelische Franziskanerbruderschaft der Nachfolge Christi, founded in 1927 within the Hochkirchliche Vereinigung. In Denmark, the Assisi-Kredsen is an ecumenical society, founded in 1974, which arranges journeys to Assisi and other Franciscan sites. In North America there are also Lutheran Franciscan communities. The ecumenical inspiration of St Francis is therefore not restricted only to Anglicans.

The end of the twentieth century saw fewer vocations to Anglican First Order Franciscan communities in Europe and North America, a trend seen in almost all religious communities, except in some areas of the developing world, such as Melanesia. The Solomon Islands and Papua New Guinea are now distinct provinces of the SSF, and there are also vocations in South Korea. However, the continuing inspiration found in St Francis is shown most significantly by the growth in the Third Order SSF, in 2009 numbering over 3,000 world-wide, including a substantial novitiate, which suggests further expansion.

## CONTEMPORARY RELEVANCE

This poses a question: if the ecumenical appeal of St Francis originated in Romanticism, the study of nature and the struggle against poverty, why has that appeal continued in an age of different pressures and challenges?

The challenge of poverty remains the major constant: the area of concern has widened, however. Although there are still pockets of deprivation, particularly in cities, in the developed world, state social support is more available than in the past. So, many in the Church in the richer nations are now focusing their sense of solidarity on those in parts of the developing world whose deprivation is revealed graphically by modern media. Whether it results from unjust social structures or the consequences of war or natural disasters, the plight of the poor throughout the world cannot be hidden in the age of television and the internet. The Anglican, Lutheran and other Protestant denominations are world-wide, and therefore the channels for aid and support are already established. The compassion for the poor and the embrace of poverty in solidarity with them that marked Francis's witness can therefore speak to a modern generation as much as to those of the past.

The issue of 'nature' is also still relevant, but with a different emphasis. The ecological damage wrought by human activity, especially industry and transport, has prompted a new movement of those concerned to safeguard the delicate balances of the Earth's bio-systems. In particular the issue of climate change has become a significant anxiety for many. Under these threats, St Francis with his sympathy for the natural world in its entirety has been adopted as an obvious 'patron saint' for those praying about and campaigning on environmental issues. It is not nature in its richness but now in its fragility that makes an appeal via Francis still relevant.

The decline of religious practice in parts of the world increases the push for evangelism among all churches. St Francis as a saint is not alone in being an advocate of evangelising the lapsed and the indifferent with the Gospel message, but his approach has an immediate appeal in contemporary contexts. For example, advocating freedom from power, particularly institutional power, is especially important to those from Christian traditions where there has been a historical suspicion of hierarchy. It also appeals to the individualism of modern western society, where approaches by institutional representatives can appear to be more like recruitment to an organisation than an invitation to share values. St Francis can be interpreted more easily than many saints as advocating personal contact and winning hearts by example rather than explaining rules or beliefs.

In other parts of the world, where religious practice remains more widespread, and where rivalry with other faith groups can be intense, St Francis's example of dialogue with other faiths has a contemporary application. His desire to make friendships across divisions, illustrated by his journey to engage with Muslims, and thereby witness to the need for peace, resonates with a twenty-first century dilemma. How can one show respect for the traditions and beliefs of other faiths (a necessary demand of liberal democracy), while still witnessing to one's own religious beliefs, which in turn require an evangelistic outreach? This is a question for all Christians of whatever denomination, and St Francis provides a way to answer it.

Finally, the flexibility of the Franciscan *Rule*, allowing for a Third Order witness, is something that has appeal in contemporary western society. A Third Order commitment allows identification with a set of values without the perceived inflexibility of being part of an institution. Just as joining campaigns on issues is preferred to the commitment of being a member of a political party, similarly tertiary vocations to the religious life are more likely than to a First Order in an individualistic society. Many too interpret the approach of St Francis as 'laicising' religious life, bringing it out into society instead of taking people away to a more intense and separate way of life. A Franciscan Third Order can be readily adapted to be quite distinct – and if necessary separate and independent in its governance – from a First Order, for example, among the Swedish Lutherans.

For all these reasons, the ecumenical appeal of St Francis therefore remains strong a century and a half after his rediscovery by those outside the Roman Catholic Church.

## CONCLUSION

The roots of the ecumenical appeal of St Francis are found in the political, economic and social conditions of the late eighteenth and early nineteenth centuries, out of which the Romantic Movement emerged. Christians outside the Roman Catholic Church were able to embrace Francis partly because of his love of 'Nature' in an age when science was becoming stronger and threatening traditional religious positions. Also, by emphasising his criticisms of his own Church rather than his deep loyalty to it, Anglicans and Protestants were able to see Francis as a forerunner of their own rebellion against Rome. Finally, the saint's identification with the poor was significant for those dealing with the social deprivations stemming from the Industrial Revolution. Consequently, St Francis has become arguably the most revered of medieval saints among non-Roman Catholic Christians.

### Notes

1   Review published in no. 73 of the journal; reprinted as chapter 2 of J. Stephen, *Essays in Ecclesiastical Biography*, 5th edn (London, 1867), republished regularly over subsequent decades.

2   P. Cowley, *Franciscan Rise and Fall* (London, 1933), p. vii.

3   I am grateful to Dr Michael Robson for the following reference to the previous such ordination: 28 March 1517: (Quat. temp.), priestly orders conferred by Nicholas (West), bishop of Ely, in the chapel of Ely Palace on 28 March 1517 on Walter Leger: Ordinis Minorum jurisdictione Cant. (CU.EDR.G/1/7, fol. 84r, West, in J. R. H. Moorman, *The Grey Friars in Cambridge 1225–1538* (Cambridge, 1952), p.191).

4   A. Clifton Kelway, *A Franciscan Revival* (Plaistow, 1908), p. 10.

5   For detailed accounts of these events and those that follow in the rest of this section, see the relevant chapters of Petà Dunstan, *This Poor Sort* (London, 1997).

6   The Brotherhood of the Holy Cross (founded in 1923) ran a boys' home in Peckham. In the USA, the first Franciscan brothers, the Society of the Atonement or SA (1898), became Roman Catholics in 1909, but another community, the Order of St Francis or OSF (1919), became established in the 1920s on New York's Long Island. Both the SA and OSF had parallel foundations for women. Among women in the Church of England, the branch of the Society of the Most Holy Trinity at Ascot Priory took on aspects of a Franciscan ethos in the late nineteenth century. The Society of the Incarnation of the Eternal Son (SIES) was founded in Plaistow in the 1890s, a sisterhood working alongside the brethren of the SDC. However, the SIES sisters followed James Adderley, and they settled in Birmingham when he moved there. The Community of St Francis was founded in 1905; by the 1920s the sisters were nursing poor women in Dalston in London. The Community of St Giles (1914) cared for lepers under the guidance of the SDC, and the Franciscan Servants of Jesus and Mary (1930) did parish work.

7   These included the Poor Clares of Reparation and Adoration, Long Island (now extinct); and the Community of St Clare at Freeland, near Oxford, and at one time also at Stroud, New South Wales, Australia. Some brothers in Australia founded a separate contemplative men's community, the Little Brothers of Francis, in 1987, inspired by St Francis's *Rule for Hermitages*.

# A guide to further reading

## GENERAL STUDIES ON THE ORDER AND ITS HISTORY

Brooke, R. B., *Early Franciscan Government: Elias to Bonaventure*, Cambridge Studies in Medieval Life and Thought, 2nd Series, 7 (Cambridge, 1959).

Brooke, R. B. and Brooke, C. N. L., *Popular Religion in the Middle Ages: Western Europe 1000–1300* (London, 1984).

Carmody, M., *The Franciscan Story: St Francis of Assisi and His Influence since the Thirteenth Century* (London, 2008).

Esser, K., *Origins of the Franciscan Order* (Chicago, 1970).

Fleming, J. V., *An Introduction to the Franciscan Literature of the Middle Ages* (Chicago, 1977).

Fortini, A., *Francis of Assisi*, trans. from the Italian, *Nova Vita di San Francesco*, by H. Moak (New York, 1981).

Gratien de Paris, *Histoire de la fondation et de l'évolution de l'ordre des frères mineurs au xiiie siècle* (Rome, 1926), reprinted with an updated bibliography by M. D'Alatri and S. Gieben, Bibliotheca Seraphico-Capuccina cura instituti historici ord. Fr. Min. Capuccinorum, 29 (Rome, 1982).

Grundmann, H., *Religious Movements in the Middle Ages: The Historical Links between Heresy, the Mendicant Orders, and the Women's Religious Movement in the Twelfth and Thirteenth Century, with the Historical Foundations of German Mysticism*, trans. from the German, *Religiöse Bewegungen im Mittelalter: Untersuchungen über die geschichtlichen Zusammenhänge zwischen der Ketzerei, den Bettelorden und der religiösen Frauenbewegung im 12. und 13. Jahrhundert und über die geschichtlichen Grundlagen der deutschen Mystik*, by S. Rowan (Notre Dame, Ind., 1995).

House, A., *Francis of Assisi* (London, 2001).

Iriarte, L. de A., *Franciscan History: The Three Orders of St Francis of Assisi*, trans. from the Spanish, *Historia Franciscana*, by P. Ross (Chicago, 1982).

Jeffrey, D. L., *The Early English Lyric and Franciscan Spirituality* (Lincoln, Nebr., 1975).

Knowles, D., *From Pachomius to Ignatius: A Study in the Constitutional History of the Religious Orders* (Oxford, 1966).

*The Religious Orders in England* (Cambridge, 1948).

Lawrence, C. H., *Medieval Monasticism: Forms of Religious Life in Western Europe in the Middle Ages*, 3rd edn (London, 2001).

*St Edmund of Abingdon: A Study of Hagiography and History* (Oxford, 1960).

*The Friars: The Impact of the Early Mendicant Movement on Western Society* (London, 1994).

Le Goff, J., *Saint Francis of Assisi*, trans. from the French, *Saint François d'Assise*, by C. Horne (London, 2004).

Manselli, R., *Saint Francis of Assisi*, trans. from the Italian, *San Francesco d'Assisi*, 2nd edn by P. Duggan (Chicago, 1988).

Merlo, Grado G., *In the Name of Saint Francis: History of the Friars Minor and Franciscanism until the Sixteenth Century*, trans. from the Italian, *Nel nome di san Francesco: Storia dei Frati Minori e del francescanesimo sino agli inizi del secolo XVI*, by R. Bonnano and R. J. Karris (New York, 2009).

Monti, D. V., *Francis and His Brothers: A Popular History of the Franciscan Friars* (Cincinnati, Ohio, 2009).

Moorman, J. R. H., *A History of the Franciscan Order: From Its Origins to the Year 1517* (Oxford, 1968).

*Saint Francis of Assisi* (London, 1950, 1979).

Nimmo, D., *Reform and Division in the Medieval Franciscan Order: From Saint Francis to the Foundation of the Capuchins*, Bibliotheca Seraphico-Capuccina cura instituti historici ord. Fr. Min. Capuccinorum, 33 (Rome, 1987).

Robson, M. J. P., *The Franciscans in the Middle Ages* (Woodbridge, 2006).

Short, W. J., *Poverty and Joy: The Franciscan Tradition*, Traditions of Christian Spirituality (London, 1999).

Vauchez, A., *The Laity in the Middle Ages: Religious Beliefs and Devotional Practices*, ed. D. Bornstein, trans. from the French, *Les Laïcs au Moyen Âge: pratiques et expériences religieuses*, by M. J. Schneider (Notre Dame, Ind., 1993).

## PART I: STUDIES ON FRANCIS OF ASSISI

### Primary sources

Consult the notes and edition of the writings and biographies of Francis of Assisi already cited along with the abbreviations for the particular biographies.

Andrews, F., *The Early Humiliati*, Cambridge Studies in Medieval Life and Thought, 4th Series, 43 (Cambridge, 1999).

Armstrong, R. J. (ed. and trans.), *Clare of Assisi: Early Documents*, Revised and Expanded (New York, 2006).

Bartoli L. A., *Gli autografi di frate Francesco e di frate Leone*, Corpus Christianorum Autographa Medii Aevi, 4 (Turnhout, 2000).

Brooke, R. B. (ed.), *Scripta Leonis, Rufini et Angeli Sociorum S. Francisci. The Writings of Leo, Rufino and Angelo, Companions of St Francis*, OMT (Oxford, 1970, corrected reprint, 1990).

*The Coming of the Friars*, Historical Problems, Studies and Documents, 24 (London, 1975).

Cusato, M. F., 'An Unexplored Influence on the *Epistola ad fideles* of Francis of Assisi: The *Epistola universis Christi fidelibus* of Joachim of Fiore', *FS*, 61 (2003), 253–78.

'Francis of Assisi, the Crusades and Malek al-Kamil', in Cusato, *Early Franciscan Movement*, pp. 103–28 (slightly different version orig. publ. in *Daring to Embrace the Other: Franciscans and Muslims in Dialogue*, Spirit and Life, 12 (St Bonaventure, 2008), pp. 3–37, esp. 8–37).

'Guardians and the Use of Power in the Early Franciscan Movement', in Cusato, *Early Franciscan Movement*, pp. 249–81.

'Of Snakes and Angels: The Mystical Experience behind the Stigmatization Narrative of 1 Celano', in Cusato, *Early Franciscan Movement*, pp. 209–48 (orig. publ. in *The Stigmata of Francis of Assisi: New Studies, New Perspectives* (St Bonaventure, 2006), pp. 29–74).

*The Early Franciscan Movement (1205–1239): History, Sources and Hermeneutics*, Saggi, 14 (Spoleto, 2009).

'The Early Franciscans and the Use of Money', in D. Mitchell (ed.), *Poverty and Prosperity: Franciscans and the Use of Money*, Spirit and Life, 14 (St Bonaventure, forthcoming).

'The Letters to the Faithful', in Cusato, *Early Franciscan Movement*, pp. 153–207 (to be published in *Essays on the Early Franciscan Sources*, vol. 1, ed. M. Blastic, J. Hammond and W. Hellmann (St Bonaventure, forthcoming)].

'The Tau', in Cusato, *Early Franciscan Movement*, pp. 69–80 (orig. publ. in *The Cord*, 57.3 (2007), 287–301).

'The *Umbrian Legend* of Jacques Dalarun: Toward a Resolution of the Franciscan Question', *FS*, 66 (2008), 479–510.

'To Do Penance/*Facere penitentiam*' in Cusato, *Early Franciscan Movement*, pp. 49–67 (orig. publ. in *The Cord*, 57.1 (2007), 3–24).

Flood, D., 'Assisi's Rules and People's Needs: The Initial Determination of the Franciscan Mission', *Franzikanische Studien*, 66 (1984), 91–104.

*Francis of Assisi and the Franciscan Movement* (Quezon City, The Philippines, 1989).

'Peace in Assisi in the Early Thirteenth Century', *Franziskanische Studien*, 64 (1982), 67–80.

and Matura, T., *The Birth of a Movement: A Study of the First Rule of St Francis*, trans. Paul Lachance and Paul Schwartz (Chicago, 1975).

Johnson, T. J., 'Lost in Sacred Space: Textual Hermeneutics, Liturgical Worship and Celano's *Legenda ad Usum Chori*', *FS*, 59 (2001), 109–32.

Paolazzi, C., 'La "Regula non bullata" dei Frati Minori (1221), dallo "stemma codicum" al testo critico', *AFH*, 100 (2007), 5–148.

'Le *Admonitiones* di frate Francesco, testo critico', *AFH*, 102 (2009), 3–88.

'Le *Epistole* maggiori di frate Francesco, edizione critica ed emendamenti ai testi minori', *AFH*, 101 (2008), 3–154.

'Nascita degli "Scritti" e costituzione del canone', in A. Cacciotti (ed.), *Verba Domini Mei: Gli Opuscula di Francesco d'Assisi a 25 anni dalla edizione di Kajetan Esser, OFM*, Medioevo, 6 (Rome 2003), pp. 55–87.

'Per gli autografi di frate Francesco: dubbi, verifiche, riconferme', *AFH*, 93 (2000), 3–28.

Zutshi, P. and Robson, M. J. P., 'An Early Manuscript of the *Admonitions* of St Francis of Assisi', *Journal of Ecclesiastical History*, 62 (2011).


SECONDARY SOURCES

### Chapters 1–4

Armstrong, R. J., *St Francis of Assisi: Writings for a Gospel Life* (New York, 1994).

Brooke, R. B., *The Image of St Francis: Responses to Sainthood in the Thirteenth Century* (Cambridge, 2006).

    'The "Legenda antiqua S. Francisci", Perugia Ms.1046', *Analecta Bollandiana*, 99 (1981), 165–8.

    'The Lives of Saint Francis of Assisi', in T. A. Dorey (ed.), *Latin Biography*, Studies in Latin Literature and Its Influence (London, 1967), pp. 177–98.

    'Recent Work on St Francis of Assisi', *Analecta Bollandiana*, 100 (1982), 653–76.

Brown, R., *The Roots of St Francis: A Popular History of the Church in Assisi and Umbria before St Francis as Related to His Life and Spirituality* (Chicago, 1982).

Chesterton, G. K., *St Francis of Assisi* (London, 1923, 1996).

Cunningham, L. S., 'Francis Naked and Clothed: A Theological Meditation', in J. M. Hammond (ed.), *Francis of Assisi: History, Hagiography and Hermeneutics in the Early Documents* (New York, 2002), pp. 164–78.

Cusato, M. F., *Francis of Assisi: Performing the Gospel Life* (Grand Rapids, Mich., 2004).

    'Francis of Assisi, Deacon? An Examination of the Claims of the Earliest Franciscan Sources 1229–1235', in Cusato and G. Geltner (eds.), *Defenders and Critics of Franciscan Life: Essays in Honor of John V. Fleming*, The Medieval Franciscans, 6 (Leiden, 2009), pp. 9–39.

    'Francis of Assisi, the Crusades and Malek al-Kamil', in Cusato, *Early Franciscan Movement*, pp. 103–28 (slightly different version orig. publ. in *Daring to Embrace the Other: Franciscans and Muslims in Dialogue*, Spirit and Life, 12 (St Bonaventure, 2008), pp. 3–37).

    *The Early Franciscan Movement (1205–1239): History, Sources and Hermeneutics*, Saggi, 14 (Spoleto, 2009).

Frugoni, C., *Francis of Assisi: A Life*, translated from the Italian, *Vita di un uomo: Francesco d'Assisi*, by J. Bowden (London, 1998).

Moorman, J. R. H., *Richest of Poor Men: The Spirituality of St Francis of Assisi* (London, 1977).

Robson, M. J. P., *St Francis of Assisi: The Legend and the Life* (London, 1997).

Short, W. J., 'Francis, the "New" Saint in the Tradition of Christian Hagiography: Thomas of Celano's Life of Saint Francis', in Jay M. Hammond (ed.), *Francis of Assisi: History, Hagiography and Hermeneutics in the Early Documents* (New York, 2004), pp. 153–63.

Thomson, W. R., 'The Earliest Cardinal-Protectors of the Franciscan Order: A Study in Administrative History, 1210–1261', *Studies in Medieval and Renaissance History*, 9 (1972), 21–80.

Vauchez, André, *François d'Assise* (Paris, 2009).

## Chapters 5–9

Alberzoni, M. P., *Clare between Memory and Silence* (Cincinnati, Ohio, 2010).
*Clare of Assisi and the Poor Sisters in the Thirteenth Century* (St Bonaventure, 2004).
Bartoli, M., *Clare of Assisi* (Quincy, Ill., 1993).
Brooke, R. B. (with Brooke, C.N.L.), 'St Clare', in D. Baker (ed.), *Medieval Women, Dedicated and Presented to Professor Rosalind M. T. Hill on the Occasion of Her Seventieth Birthday*, Studies in Church History, Subsidia, 1 (Oxford, 1978), pp. 275–87.
Carney, M., *The First Franciscan Woman: Clare of Assisi and Her Form of Life* (Quincy, Ill., 1993).
Cotter, F. J., *The Friars Minor in Ireland from Their Arrival to 1400*, ed. R. A. McKelvie, Franciscan Institute Publications, History Series, 7 (St Bonaventure, 1994).
Delio, I., Warner, K. D., Wood, P., and Edwards, D., *Care for Creation: A Franciscan Spirituality of the Earth* (Cincinnati, Ohio, 2008).
Emery, R. W., *The Friars in Medieval France* (New York, 1962).
Frances, T., *The Living Mirror: Reflections on Clare of Assisi* (London, 1995).
Freed, J. B., *The Friars and German Society in the Thirteenth Century* (Cambridge, Mass., 1977).
Godet-Calogeras, J. F., 'A New Look at Clare's Gospel Plan of Life', *Greyfriars Review*, 5: Supplement (1991).
Johnson, T., 'Reading between the Lines: Apophatic Knowledge and Naming the Divine in Bonaventure's *Book of Creation*', *Franciscan Studies*, 60 (2002), 139–58.
Kehnel, A., 'The Narrative Tradition of the Medieval Franciscan Friars on the British Isles: Introduction to the Sources', *FS*, 63 (2005), 461–530.
Knox, L. S., *Creating Clare of Assisi: Female Franciscan Identities in Later Medieval Italy*, The Medieval Franciscans, 5 (Leiden, 2008).
McMichael, S. J. and Myers, S. E. (eds.), *Friars and Jews in the Middle Ages and Renaissance*, The Medieval Franciscans, 2 (Leiden, 2004).
Millett, B., 'The Friars Minor in County Wicklow, Ireland, 1260–1982', *AFH*, 77 (1984), 110–36.
Moorman, J. R. H., *The Franciscans in England* (London, 1974).
Nothwehr, D. M. (ed.), *Franciscan Theology of the Environment: An Introductory Reader* (Quincy: Franciscan Press, 2002).
Peterson, I., *Clare of Assisi: A Biographical Study* (Quincy, Ill., 1993).
Saggau, E. (ed.), *Franciscans and Creation: What is Our Responsibility?* (Saint Bonaventure, 2003).
Sorrell, R., *St Francis of Assisi and Nature: Tradition and Innovation in Western Christian Attitudes toward the Environment* (New York and Oxford, 1988).
*The Life of Saint Douceline Beguine of Provence*, Library of Medieval Women, trans. from the Occitan by K. Garay and M. Jeay (Woodbridge, 2001).
Tolan, J., *Saint Francis and the Sultan: The Curious History of a Christian–Muslim Encounter* (Oxford, 2009).
Tugwell, S., 'The Original Text of the Regula Hugolini (1219)', *AFH*, 93 (2000), 511–13.

## PART II: THE HERITAGE OF FRANCIS OF ASSISI

### Primary sources

Angela of Foligno, *Complete Works*, trans. and intro. Paul Lachance, pref. Romana Guarnieri, Classics of Western Spirituality (New York, 1993).

Angelo Clareno, *A Chronicle or History of the Seven Tribulations of the Order of Friars Minor*, trans. from the Latin by David Burr and E. Randolph Daniel (New York, 2005).

Bonner, A., *Coming of the Friars Minor to England and Germany, being the chronicles of Brother Thomas of Eccleston and Brother Jordan of Giano*, trans. from the critical editions of A. G. Little, MA, FBA, and H. Boehmer by E. G. Salter (London, 1926).

*Doctor Illuminatus: A Ramon Llull Reader* (Princeton, 1993).

Cousins, E. trans. and intro., *Bonaventure: The Soul's Journey into God, The Tree of Life, The Life of St Francis*, Classics of Western Spirituality (New York, 1978).

Field, S. L., 'Marie of Saint-Pol and Her Books', *English Historical Review*, 125 (2010), 255–78.

*The Writings of Agnes of Harcourt: The Life of Isabelle of France and the Letter on Louis IX* (Notre Dame, Ind., 2003).

*Fratris Thomae vulgo dicti de Eccleston Tractatus de adventu Fratrum Minorum in Angliam*, A. G. Little (ed.) (Manchester, 1951).

*The Seventh Crusade, 1244–1254: Sources and Documents*, Crusade Texts in Translation, 16 (Farnham, 2007).

Jackson, J. (ed.), *William of Rubruck Itinerarium: His Journey to the Court of the Great Khan Möngke*, trans. Jackson and D. Morgan, Hakluyt Society, 2nd Series, 173 (London, 1990).

Jacopone da Todi, *The Lauds*, trans. S. and E. Hughes, Classics of Western Spirituality (London, 1982).

Maier, C. T., *Crusade Propaganda and Ideology: Model Sermons for the Preaching of the Cross* (Cambridge, 2000).

Marston, T. E., and Painter, G. D. *The Mongol Mission: Narratives and Letters of the Franciscan Missionaries in Mongolia and China in the Thirteenth and Fourteenth Centuries*, trans. from the Latin by C. Dawson (London, 1955).

Mazzoni, C., *Angela of Foligno, Memorial*, trans. J. Cirignano (Woodbridge, 2000).

Mokry, R. J., 'The *Summa de sacramentis* of Henry Wodestone, O.Min., A Critical Edition', *AFH*, 94 (2001), 3–84.

Pieper, L., 'A New Life of St Elizabeth of Hungary: The Anonymous Franciscan', *AFH*, 93 (2000), 29–78.

Skelton, R. A., Marston, T. E., and Painter, G. D. (eds.), *The Vinland Map and the Tartar Relation*, 2nd edn (New Haven and London, 1995).

Vauchez, A., *Sainthood in the Later Middle Ages*, translated from the French, *La sainteté en Occident aux derniers siècles du Moyen Âge*, by J. Birrell (Cambridge, 1997).

SECONDARY SOURCES

### Chapters 10–13

Callus, D. A., *Robert Grosseteste Scholar and Bishop: Essays in Commemoration of the Seventh Centenary of his Death* (Oxford, 1955).

Cannon, J. and Vauchez, A., *Margherita of Cortona and the Lorenzetti: Sienese Art and the Cult of a Holy Woman in Medieval Tuscany* (Pennsylvania, 1999).

Carney, M., Godet-Calogeras, J. F. and Kush, S. (eds.), *The History of the Third Order Rule: A Source Book* (St Bonaventure, 2008).

Courtenay, W. J., *Adam Wodeham: An Introduction to his Life and Writings*, Studies in Medieval and Reformation Thought, 21 (Leiden, 1978).

*Schools and Scholars in Fourteenth-Century England* (Princeton, 1987).

'The Instructional Programme of the Mendicant Convents at Paris in the Early Fourteenth Century', in P. Biller and R. B. Dobson (eds.), *The Medieval Church: Universities, Heresy and the Religious Life. Essays in Honour of Gordon Leff*, Studies in Church History, Subsidia, XI (Woodbridge, 1999), pp.77–92.

'The Parisian Franciscan Community in 1303', *FS*, 53 (1993), 155–73.

Cross, R., *Duns Scotus*, Great Medieval Thinkers (Oxford, 1999).

*Metaphysic of the Incarnation from Thomas Aquinas to Duns Scotus* (Oxford, 2002).

Cullen, C. M., *Bonaventure*, Great Medieval Thinkers (Oxford, 2006).

Davis, A. J., *The Holy Bureaucrat: Eudes Rigaud and Religious Reform in Thirteenth-Century Normandy* (Ithaca, 2006).

Field, S. L., *Isabelle of France: Capetian Sanctity and Franciscan Identity in the Thirteenth Century* (Notre Dame, Ind., 2006).

Flood, D., 'The Franciscan and Spiritual Writings of Peter Olivi', *AFH*, 91 (1998), 469–73.

Gaposchkin, M. C., *The Making of Saint Louis: Kingship, Sanctity, and Crusade in the Later Middle Ages* (Ithaca and London, 2008).

Gecser, O., 'The Lives of St Elizabeth: Their Rewritings and Diffusion in the Thirteenth Century', *Analecta Bollandiana*, 127 (2009), 49–107.

Havely, N., *Dante and the Franciscans: Poverty and the Papacy in the Commedia*, Cambridge Studies in Medieval Literature, 52 (Cambridge, 2004).

*The Lyf of Oure Lady: The ME translation of Thomas of Hales' Vita Sancte Marie*, Middle English Texts, 17 (Heidelberg, 1985).

Horrall, SC., M., *Thomas of Hales, OFM: His Life and Works, Traditio*, 42 (1986), 287–98.

Labage, M. W., *Saint Louis: The Life of Louis IX of France* (London, 1968).

Lawrence, C. H. (ed.), *The Letters of Adam Marsh*, 2 vols., OMT (Oxford, 2006 and 2010).

'The Letters of Adam Marsh and the Franciscan School at Oxford', *Journal of Ecclesiastical History*, 42 (1991), 218–38.

Levy, B. J., (ed.), *Nine Verse Sermons by Nicholas Bozon: The Art of the Anglo-Norman Poet and Preacher*, Medium Aevum Monographs, New Series, 11 (Oxford, 1981).

Little, L. K., 'Saint Louis' Involvement with the Friars', *Church History*, 33 (1964), 125–48.

McElrath, D. (ed.), *Franciscan Christology*, Franciscan Institute Publications, Franciscan Sources, no. I (New York, 1980).

McEvoy, J., *Robert Grosseteste*, Great Medieval Thinkers (Oxford, 2000).

'Robert Grosseteste and the Reunion of the Church', *Collectanea Franciscana*, 45 (1975), 39–84.

'Robert Grosseteste's Greek Scholarship: A Survey of Present Knowledge', *FS*, 56 (1998), 255–64.

*The Philosophy of Robert Grosseteste* (Oxford, 1982).

McKelvie, R. A., *Retrieving a Living Tradition: Angelina of Montegiove, Franciscan, Tertiary, Beguine* (St Bonaventure, 1997).

Moorman, J. R. H., *The Grey Friars in Cambridge 1225–1538* (Cambridge, 1952).

Musto, R. G., 'Franciscan Joachism at the Court of Naples 1309–1345: A New Appraisal', *AFH*, 90 (1997), 419–86.

O'Carroll, M., (ed.), *Robert Grosseteste and the Beginnings of a British Theological Tradition*, Bibliotheca Seraphico-Capuccina cura instituti historici ord.Fr.Min. Capuccinorum, 69 (Rome, 2003).

Osborne, K. B. (ed.), *The History of Franciscan Theology* (St Bonaventure, 1994).

Raedts, P., *Richard Rufus of Cornwall and the Tradition of Oxford Theology*, Oxford Historical Monographs (Oxford, 1987).

Robson, M. J. P., 'Queen Isabella (*c.*1295–1358) and the Greyfriars: An Example of Royal Patronage Based on Her Accounts for 1357–1358', *FS*, 65 (2007), 325–48.

'The Franciscan Custody of York in the Thirteenth Century', in N. Rogers (ed.), *The Friars in Medieval Britain: Proceedings of the 2007 Harlaxton Conference*, Harlaxton Medieval Studies, xix (Donington, 2010), pp. 1–24.

Roest, B., *A History of Franciscan Education (c.1210–1517)*, Education and Society in the Middle Ages and Renaissance, 11 (Leiden, 2000).

'Franciscan Educational Perspectives: Reworking Monastic Traditions', in G. Ferzoco and C. Muessig (eds.), *Medieval Monastic Education* (Leicester, 2000), pp. 168–81.

*Franciscan Literature of Religious Instruction before the Council of Trent*, Medieval and Early Modern Studies, 117 (Leiden, 2004).

'The Role of Lectors in the Religious Formation of Franciscan Friars, Nuns and Tertiaries', *Studio e studia: le scuole degli mendicanti tra XIII e XIV secolo*, Società internazionale di studi francescani, Atti del XXIX convegno internazionale, 2001 (Spoleto, 2002), pp. 83–115.

Röhrkasten, J., 'Early Fourteenth-Century Franciscan Library Catalogues: The Case of the Gubbio Catalogue (*c.*1300)', *Scriptorium*, 59 (2005), 29–50.

'Friars and the Laity in the Franciscan Custody of Cambridge', in N. Rogers (ed), *The Friars in Medieval Britain: Proceedings of the 2007 Harlaxton Conference*, pp. 107–24.

'Local Ties and International Connections of the London Mendicants', in J. Sarnowsky (ed.), *Mendicants, Military Orders, and Regionalism in Medieval Europe* (Aldershot, 1999), pp. 145–83.

'Londoners and London Mendicants in the Late Middle Ages', *The Journal of Ecclesiastical History*, 47 (1996), 446–77.

'Mendicants in the Metropolis: The Londoners and the Development of the London Friaries', in M. Prestwich, R. H. Britnell and R. Frame (eds.), *Thirteenth-Century England*, vol. vi (Woodbridge, 1997), pp. 61–75.

'Reality and Symbolic Meaning among the Early Franciscans', in A. Müller and K. Stöber (eds.), *Self-Representation of Medieval Religious Communities: The British Isles in Context*, Vita Regularis, 40, (Münster, 2009), pp. 21–41.

'The Creation and Early History of the Franciscan Custody of Cambridge', in M. Robson and J. Röhrkasten (eds.), *Canterbury Studies in Franciscan History*, (Canterbury, 2008), vol. I, pp. 51–81.

*The Mendicant Houses of Medieval London 1221–1539*, Vita Regulars, 21 (Münster, 2004).

'The Origin and Early Development of the London Mendicant Houses', in T. R. Slater and G. Rosser (eds.), *The Church in the Medieval Town* (Aldershot, 1998), pp. 76–99.

Şenocak, N., 'The Earliest Library Catalogue of the Franciscan Convent of St Fortunato of Todi c.1300)', *AFH*, 99 (2006), 467–505.

Sheehan, M. W., 'The Religious Orders 1220–1370', in J. I. Catto (ed.), *The History of the University of Oxford, The Early Oxford Schols* (Oxford, 1984), vol. I, pp. 193–223.

Southern, R. W., *Robert Grosseteste: The Growth of an English Mind in Medieval Europe* (Oxford, 1986).

Stewart R. M., *'De illis qui faciunt Penitentiam', The Rule of the Secular Franciscan Order: Origins, Development, Interpretation*, Bibliotheca Seraphico-Capuccina cura instituti historici ord. Fr. Min. Capuccinorum, 39 (Rome, 1991).

Swanson, J., *John of Wales: A Study of the Works and Ideas of a Thirteenth-Century Friar*, Cambridge Studies in Medieval Life and Thought, 4th Series (Cambridge, 1989).

Williams, T. (ed.), *The Cambridge Companion to Duns Scotus* (Cambridge, 2003).

## SECONDARY SOURCES

### Chapters 14–17

Bordua, L., *The Franciscans and Art Patronage in Late Medieval Italy* (Cambridge, 2004).

Brooke, R. B., 'St Bonaventure as Minister General', in *S. Bonaventura francescano*, vol. XIV, Convegni del Centro di Studi sulla Spiritualità Medievale, (Todi, 1974), pp. 75–105.

Burnham, L., *So Great a Light, so Great a Smoke: The Beguin Heretics of Languedoc* (Ithaca, 2008).

Burr, D., 'History as Prophecy: Angelo of Clareno's Chronicle as a Spiritual Franciscan Apocalypse', in M. F. Cusato and G. Geltner (eds.), *Defenders and Critics of Franciscan Life: Essays in Honor of John V. Fleming* (Leiden, 2009), pp. 119–38.

*Olivi and Franciscan Poverty: The Origins of the Usus Pauper Controversy* (Philadelphia, 1989).

*The Spiritual Franciscans: From Protest to Persecution in the Century after Saint Francis* (University Park, PA, 2001).

Coleman, J. 'Using, Not Owning – Duties, Not Rights: The Consequences of Some Franciscan Perspectives on Politics', in M. F. Cusato and Geltner (eds.), *Defenders and Critics of Franciscan Life: Essays in Honor of John V. Fleming* (Leiden, 2009), 65–85.

Cusato, M. F., 'Whence *The Community*?' *FS*, 60 (2002), 39–92.

Denis, Fr., *Father Algy* (London, 1964).

Dunstan, P., 'The Twentieth-Century Anglican Franciscans', in G. R. Vans (ed.), *A History of Pastoral Care* (London, 2000), pp. 328–44.

*This Poor Sort: A History of the European Province of the Society of St Francis* (London, 1997).

Etzkorn, G. J., 'Ockham at Avignon: His Response to Critics', *FS*, 59 (2001), 9–19.

Fisher, M., *For the Time Being* (Leominster, 1993).

Francis, Fr, *Brother Douglas: Apostle of the Outcast* (London, 1959).

Geltner, G., 'William of St Amour's *De periculis novissimorum temporum*', in M. F. Cusato and G. Geltner (eds.), *Defenders and Critics of Franciscan Life: Essays in Honor of John V. Fleming*, (Leiden, 2009), pp. 105–18.

*William of St Amour's De Periculis Novissimorum Temporum: A Critical Edition, Translation and Introduction* (Paris, 2008).

Jackson, P., *The Mongols and the West, 1221–1410* (Harlow, 2005).

Kelly, S., *The New Solomon: Robert of Naples (1309–1343) and Fourteenth-Century Kingship* (Leiden, 2003).

Lambert, M. D., *Franciscan Poverty: The Doctrine of the Absolute Primacy of Christ and the Apostles in the Franciscan Order 1210–1323* (New York, 1998).

Lambertini, R., 'Poverty and Power: Franciscans in Later Medieval Political Thought', in J. Kraye and R. Saariren (eds.), *Moral Philosophy on the Threshold of Modernity* (Dordrecht, 2005), pp. 141–63.

Maier, C. T, *Preaching the Crusades: Mendicant Friars and the Cross in the Thirteenth Century*, Cambridge Studies in Medieval Life and Thought (Cambridge, 1994).

Mäkinen, V., *Property Rights in the Late Medieval Discussion on Franciscan Poverty* (Leuven, 2001).

Nold, P., 'Bertrand de la Tour OMin.: life and works', *AFH*, 94 (2001), 275–323.

*Pope John XXII and His Franciscan Cardinal: Bertrand de la Tour and the Apostolic Poverty Controversy* (Oxford, 2003).

'Pope John XXII's Annotations on the Franciscan Rule: Content and Contexts', *FS*, 65 (2007), 295–324.

'Two Views of John XXII as a Heretical Pope', in M. F. Cusato and G. Geltner (eds.), *Defenders and Critics of Franciscan Life: Essays in Honor of John V. Fleming*, (Leiden, 2009), pp. 139–58.

Piron, S., 'Censures et condamnation de Pierre de Jean Olivi: enquête dans les marges du Vatican', in *Mélanges de l'Ecole française de Rome: Moyen Âge*, 118/2 (2006), 313–73.

Shogimon, T., *Ockham and Political Discourse in the Late Middle Ages* (Cambridge, 2007).

Szittya, P. R., *The Antifraternal Tradition in Medieval Literature* (Princeton, 1986).

Thomson, W. R., *Friars in the Cathedral: The First Franciscan Bishops 1226–1261*, The Pontifical Institute of Mediaeval Studies, Studies and Texts, 33 (Toronto, 1975).

'The Image of the Mendicants in the Chronicles of Matthew Paris', *AFH*, 70 (1977), 3–34.

Vauchez, A., *The Laity in the Middle Ages: Religious Beliefs and Devotional Practices*, ed. and intro. Daniel Bornstein and trans. from the French, *Läics au Moyen Âge*, by M. J. Schneider (Notre Dame, c.1993).

Walsh, K., *A Fourteenth-Century Scholar and Primate: Richard FitzRalph in Oxford, Avignon and Armagh* (Oxford, 1981).

Williams, B., *The Franciscan Revival in the Anglican Communion* (London, 1982).

# Index

For EU product safety concerns, contact us at Calle de José Abascal, 56–1°,
28003 Madrid, Spain or eugpsr@cambridge.org.

www.ingramcontent.com/pod-product-compliance
Ingram Content Group UK Ltd.
Pitfield, Milton Keynes, MK11 3LW, UK
UKHW020339140625
459647UK00018B/2222